Young Milton

Young Milton

The Emerging Author, 1620–1642

EDITED BY

Edward Jones

OXFORD

UNIVERSITY PRESS

Great Clarendon Street, Oxford, OX2 6DP,
United Kingdom

Oxford University Press is a department of the University of Oxford.
It furthers the University's objective of excellence in research, scholarship,
and education by publishing worldwide. Oxford is a registered trade mark of
Oxford University Press in the UK and in certain other countries

British Library Cataloguing in Publication Data
Data available

ISBN 978-0-19-969870-7

Printed in Great Britain by
MPG Books Group, Bodmin and King's Lynn

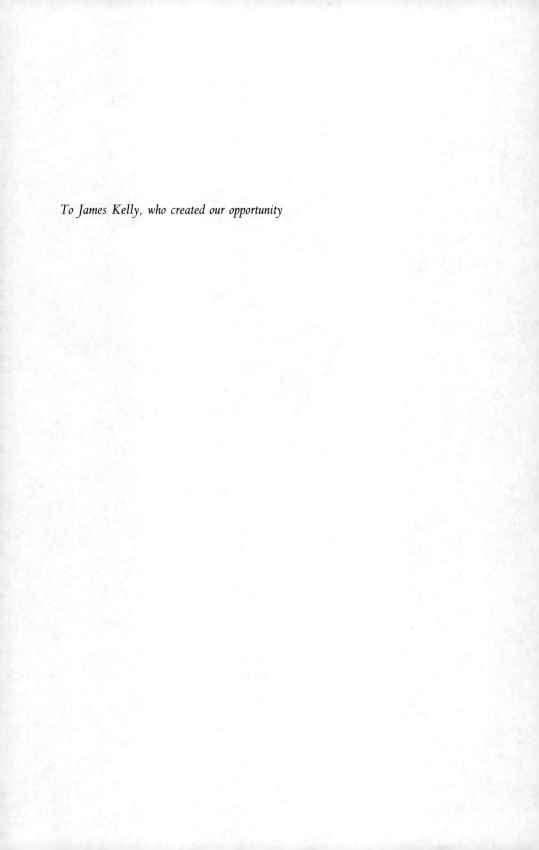

To James Kelly, who created our opportunity

PREFACE

The experimental and diverse writings of John Milton's early career offer tantalizing evidence of a precocious and steadily ripening author. Traditionally scholars have looked to *Poems 1645* for evidence of his poetic development and its bearing upon his career as a prose writer for over two decades, but such an approach has sometimes obscured and more often ignored the unique accomplishment of Milton's early career by characterizing his juvenilia as self-conscious writing designed to chronicle artistic progression.

The essays in this book for the most part reject the idea of a linear development in favour of achievement of various kinds, unequal in merit, and not predicated upon maturation over time. Such maturity may occur, but the early writing of Milton unquestionably resulted from a wide variety of occasions—religious holidays; family celebrations; grammar school exercises and university requirements; the deaths of family members, ministers, university officials, and personal friends; aristocratic celebrations and commissions. This occasionality challenges the argument for the young author's uniform progress. After all, the writing includes 'Lycidas', one of the most celebrated elegies ever written in English, and 'The Passion', an unfinished poem declared by its author to involve a subject beyond his grasp.

That a considerable part of this work is in Latin also offers the chance to fill a long time void in the formidable body of Milton criticism that has been produced in the last six decades (this will be the first essay collection focused exclusively on his writing from the 1620s, 1630s, and the first years of the 1640s). While discussions of Milton's Latin verse have appeared from time to time in miscellaneous studies of the Latin poetry of his contemporaries, not until the recent work of John Hale, Estelle Haan, and Stella Revard has Milton's Latin poetry become a subject in its own right. Several contributors to this volume continue their efforts to accord Milton's non-English verse a full hearing. It is diverse and accomplished poetry often equal to that the young Milton chose to write in the vernacular. Understanding the success (and occasional failure) of the early writing requires rigorous attention to the historical, religious, linguistic, educational, and political contexts informing and inspiring its creation. As a reading of the essays will disclose, their authors share this view.

Milton scholars recognize the quadricentennial year of his birth produced much—three new biographies, the first volume of the Oxford *Complete Works*, international conferences, poetry readings, and radio interviews, some of these aided by technology to reach across the globe. The birthday year also gave occasion to hear yet once more the not so new ideas about Milton the blind poet, the republican, the freedom advocate, the Christian prophet. This volume, whose origin dates from a conference held at Worcester College, Oxford in March 2009, takes issue with the corollary of another: that Milton's early career is best gauged and understood by reference to the three long poems of his mature years. Such a retrospective view overlooks the particular features and nature of Milton's creative experimentation by evaluating the early poetry as evidence of burgeoning potential found later in the figures of Satan and Samson. Even if it is true that Milton started his life work early and finished it late, and that his was, as he writes in his first published poem on Shakespeare, a 'slow-endeavoring art', such formulas do not fully capture the special achievements of his twin poems or the Nativity Ode.

Binary thinking has marked the long history of Milton criticism, and Milton's shorter poems have not fared well as a result. Nor has his early life. The young Milton has been typecast as either a radical in waiting or, more recently, a conservative who turns radical once the policies of the Laudian church become personal. Such approaches to the early life and career have singled out notable achievements (the excellence of the Nativity Ode, *A Maske*, 'Lycidas', and the praise Milton receives from Sir Henry Wotton), but they have effectively misgauged or ignored in the process several subjects examined in this collection: letters as gift expressions of nuanced friendships; memorial poetry's part in seventeenth-century views of untimely and early death; the impact of seventeenth-century clergymen on Milton's postgraduate vocational concerns; his multifaceted participation in university life as a Latin poet whose writing was delivered not just by him but by others; and the role of tragedy and self-study in the making of the early and later writer. Most of these subjects find little place in a paradigm designed to see the child/ adolescent prodigy in the later man. The studious, even arrogant 'Lady' of Christ's College may confirm the view of those who believe great artists live in many ways apart, but is such a view warranted by what we know about Milton's formative years in London, his university experience in Cambridge, and his postgraduate years in Hammersmith, Horton, and abroad? Such a question and others posed by authors in this collection speak to this book's overarching aim: to approach the early life and career of John Milton free from the constraints of dichotomy and buoyed by a flexibility and tolerance capable of articulating the complex ways life and art converge.

E.J.

New College, Oxford
December 2010

ACKNOWLEDGEMENTS

The efforts of many have allowed this book to emerge, and I must start and end with thanks to Dr James Kelly who in the wake of the quadricentennial year of Milton's birth, convened a conference on the Young Milton at Worcester College, Oxford in March 2009. For that venue the essays comprising this collection took their earliest form, and I want to thank all of the contributors for their efforts in transforming work prepared for oral delivery into published form in a timely fashion. The support of Oxford University Press has been present from the start in the person of Jacqueline Baker who not only attended the conference but has offered solutions to both small and not so small matters that have come up during book production. Her colleagues Ariane Petit and Jenny Townshend helped me organize and prepare the volume for production with generosity and good will. Jo North, Albert Stewart, my production editor Brendan Mac Evilly, and production manager Veeralakshmy Sadayappan have made valuable suggestions and raised necessary questions that I would other-wise have overlooked. To all I am grateful. At my home university, I have been fortunate to have consistent support for my research from Professor Carol Moder, head of English, and Professor Peter Sherwood, Dean of the College of Arts and Sciences. No small thanks must go to Professor Paul Klemp for his careful reading of the entire manuscript (it is appreciably better as a result of his efforts) and Dr Joel Halcomb for astute decision making in compiling the index.

The four images appearing on the dust jacket and the ten illustrations found throughout the volume would not have been possible without the generous efforts of individuals located throughout the UK. At the University of Cambridge, I would like to thank Mr Sandy Paul, Sub-Librarian at the Wren Library at Trinity College; Dr Gavin Alexander and Naomi Herbert at Christ's College; Dr Frances Wilmoth, Librarian of the Old Library at Jesus College, Cambridge, and Louise Clarke, Deputy Superintendent of the Manuscript Reading Room at University Library. At Lambeth Palace Library, I wish to thank Ruth Benny; at the British Library, Auste Mickunaite; at the City of Westminster Archives Centre, Alison Kenny; and at the

Hammersmith and Fulham Archives and Local History Centre, Anne Wheeldon. I am especially grateful for Dr Davide Messina's generous efforts to help me secure the reproduction of the 1638 Malatesti dedication housed in the National Library of Scotland for the dust jacket. For years of cooperation for manuscript material of various kinds, I wish to thank the staff of the Large Map Room at the National Archives in Kew Gardens and Sue Baxter and Sara Charlton at the Centre for Buckinghamshire Studies in Aylesbury.

Special thanks must go out to John Creaser for early wise advice on this project, to Will Poole for a memorable term at New College, and to James Kelly for generous accommodations at Queens College, Cambridge when time was short and tasks were many. Extended family support from a distance has always been there from Lorraine and Patricia Jones, who must know I am grateful. Closer to home for debts and patience immeasurable, I wholeheartedly thank Elizabeth Lohrman, Kalin Jones, and the charming new spirit, Tsegan.

CONTENTS

ILLUSTRATIONS

NOTE ON THE TEXT AND
LIST OF ABBREVIATIONS

Unless otherwise indicated, the place of publication for all books is London, and all biblical references are to the Authorized Version (AV).

BL	British Library
Campbell, *Chronology*	Gordon Campbell, *A Milton Chronology* (Harlow, 1997)
Campbell and Corns	Gordon Campbell and Thomas N. Corns, *John Milton: Life, Work, and Thought* (Oxford, 2008)
CPB	Milton's Commonplace Book
CPW	*Complete Prose Works of John Milton*, ed. D. M. Wolfe et al., 8 vols. (New Haven, Conn., 1953–82)
CW	*The Works of John Milton*, ed. Frank Allen Patterson et al., 18 vols. (New York, 1931–8)
Darbishire	*The Early Lives of Milton*, ed. Helen Darbishire (1932)
French, *LR*	*Life Records of John Milton*, ed. J. M. French, 5 vols. (New Brunswick, N.J., 1949–58)
Lewalski, *Life*	Barbara Lewalski, *The Life of John Milton: A Critical Biography* (Oxford, 2000)
ODNB	*Oxford Dictionary of National Biography*
Parker	William R. Parker, *Milton: A Biography*, 2nd edn., rev. Gordon Campbell, 2 vols. (Oxford, 1996)
TNA	The National Archives

NOTES ON CONTRIBUTORS

Cedric C. Brown, Emeritus Professor at the University of Reading, is founding editor and now co-editor of the long-running series *Early Modern Literature in History*, and author of *John Milton: A Literary Life* (1995) and *John Milton's Aristocratic Entertainments* (1985) which has recently been reissued by Cambridge University Press. His essay in this volume on Milton and Diodati is but a part of a larger set of materials for a book about the discourses of friendship exchange.

Blaine Greteman, Assistant Professor of English at the University of Iowa, has published articles in *Renaissance Quarterly*, *ELH*, and *College Literature*, as well as for popular magazines such as *Time* and *Ode*. He is completing a book on the politics and poetics of youth in Milton's England.

Edward Jones, Professor of English at Oklahoma State University, is the author of *Milton's Sonnets: An Annotated Bibliography, 1900–1992* (1994), editor of the *Milton Quarterly*, and a past President of the Milton Society of America. As editor of volume 11 of the Clarendon Milton, he is preparing a new edition of Milton's letters of state. His most recent essays on Milton appear in the *Oxford Handbook of Milton* (Oxford University Press, 2009) and *Milton in Context* (2010).

Sarah Knight, Senior Lecturer in Shakespeare and Renaissance Literature in the School of English, University of Leicester, works on early modern English and Latin literature, particularly student writing and academic drama. She has edited and translated Leon Battista Alberti's *Momus* (I Tatti Renaissance Library, 2003); the accounts of Elizabeth I's progress visits to Oxford for the new critical edition of John Nichols's *Progresses* (Oxford University Press); and John Milton's *Prolusions* (Oxford University Press). She has co-edited two essay collections, *The Intellectual and Cultural World of the Early Modern Inns of Court* (Manchester) and *A Companion to Ramism: An Intellectual Phenomenon* (Brill).

John Leonard, Professor of English, University of Western Ontario, has published widely on Milton, and he has twice won the Milton Society's

James Holly Hanford Award as well as the University of Western Ontario's Edward G. Pleva Award for excellence in teaching. He is the editor of *Milton's Complete Poems* (1999) for Penguin and a past President of the Milton Society of America. His reception history of *Paradise Lost* will be forthcoming from Oxford University Press.

Jeffrey Alan Miller received his D.Phil from Magdalen College, Oxford in 2011. His 'Reconstructing Milton's Lost *Index theologicus*: The Genesis and Usage of an Anti-Bellarmine Theological Commonplace Book' (2011) has recently been published in *Milton Studies*. With Thomas Roebuck, he is co-editing a volume of essays on John Selden.

William Poole, Galsworthy Fellow and Tutor in English at New College, Oxford, has interests in early modern literary and intellectual history and bibliography. His publications include *Milton and the Idea of the Fall* (2005), *The World Makers: Scientists of the Restoration and the Search for the Origins of the Earth* (2010), and *John Aubrey and the Advancement of Learning* (Oxford University Press, 2010). He is editing the correspondences of John Aubrey and of Robert Hooke, and researching for a new book on early European sinology.

Noam Reisner, lecturer in the Department of English and American Studies at Tel Aviv University, is the author of *Milton and the Ineffable* (Oxford University Press, 2009) and *John Milton's 'Paradise Lost': A Reader's Guide* (2011). His writing on Milton has also appeared in the *Milton Quarterly*.

Stella P. Revard is Professor Emerita, Southern Illinois University, Edwardsville, Honored Scholar of Milton Society of America, and past President of the International Association for Neo-Latin Studies. She is the author of *The War in Heaven* (1980), *Milton and the Tangles of Neaera's Hair* (1997), *Pindar and the Renaissance Hymn-Ode: 1450–1700* (2001), and *Politics, Poetics, and the Pindaric Ode: 1450–1700* (2009). She is also the editor of *Milton's Shorter Poems* (2009) in original spelling and punctuation.

Thomas Roebuck recently completed his D.Phil. in early-modern British Antiquarianism at Magdalen College, Oxford and has been awarded a Mellon-funded Postdoctoral Fellowship in early-modern manuscripts from the English Faculty at Oxford University. In addition to particular interests in learned correspondence and early-modern scholarship on the near east, he is preparing an edition of the classical scholar Richard Bentley's unpublished correspondence, an edition of the correspondence of the ecclesiastical historian Henry Spelman, and articles on the intellectual world of the late seventeenth-century scholar, antiquary, biographer, correspondent, and non-juror, Thomas Smith (1638–1710).

Christopher Tilmouth is a University Senior Lecturer at the Faculty of English, Cambridge, and a Fellow of Peterhouse. His publications include articles on Shakespeare, Milton, Burton's *Anatomy of Melancholy*, and the English reception of Descartes's thought in the later seventeenth century. He is the author of *Passion's Triumph over Reason: A History of the Moral Imagination from Spenser to Rochester* (Oxford University Press, 2009).

Andrew Zurcher, a Fellow in English at Queens' College, Cambridge, has published a number of books and articles on law and literature in the early modern period, including *Spenser's Legal Language* (2007) and *Shakespeare and Law* (2010). He is collaborating on a new Oxford University Press edition of the *Collected Works of Edmund Spenser*.

Part I

Archival, Educational, and Religious Contexts

1

The Archival Landscape of Milton's Youth, University Years, and Pre-London Residencies

Edward Jones

Ever so slowly have documents created during Milton's youth, his time at the University of Cambridge, and his postgraduate years in Hammersmith and Horton surfaced, their discovery more often resulting from accident than design. In the wake of the pioneering work of David Masson in the nineteenth century and the compiling of life records by J. Milton French in the twentieth, concerted searches of archives have been infrequent. The scholarship of Masson and French has largely withstood scrutiny, and when it has proved otherwise, the assiduous work of William Riley Parker, Maurice Kelley, Leo Miller, John Shawcross, and Gordon Campbell has not just corrected error but expanded knowledge in doing so.[1] Even though important particulars about Milton's life remain unknown (the date and location of his first marriage, the contents of his father's will, and the birth and death years of his sister, to name a few), the inclination to conduct further investigation has been slight, no doubt because of the small yield that has resulted from such activity over the last half century.

Indeed recent discoveries support this view. In 1996 Jeremy Maule noticed on display in the Hammersmith and Fulham Record Office an assessment document listing Milton's father as one of the parishioners of St Paul's, a chapel-of-ease consecrated by William Laud in 1631 (Fig. 1). While chancery records found in the Public Record Office in 1949 had alerted scholars to the Milton family residency in Hammersmith, evidently no one in the ensuing half century had followed up and examined the local records.[2] Similarly, archivists at Cambridge alerted Gordon Campbell and Thomas Corns to new material as they were preparing their account of Milton's university years for *John Milton: Life, Work, and Thought*: Milton's name appears in the Cambridge Grace Books (Fig. 2).[3] The records and the procedure that created them were unknown to Milton scholars prior to 2007. In 2009 Sarah Knight discovered that during a visit from the Cambridge University Chancellor, Henry Rich, the first Earl of Holland, two of Milton's Latin poems, *Naturam Non Pati Senium* and *De Idea Platonica*, were delivered as part of the academic activities. Notations on MS 770 in the Lambeth Palace Library allow their composition dates to be assigned to September 1629 (see Fig. 9).[4] Finally, in 2010 Davide Messina found the manuscript of Antonio Malatesti's *La Tina*, a collection of fifty erotic sonnets with his dedication to Milton, in the National Library of Scotland in Edinburgh.[5] On all four occasions, unexpected information emerged while other subjects were being canvassed, a pattern likely to mark future discoveries. While systematic search remains valuable (it accounts for some of the records discussed in this essay), chance and accident have proved equally valuable in the recovery of extant records, and only the naïve will ignore them. The four examples provide good news—documents await discovery. This review of the surviving archival evidence from the first three decades of Milton's life will proceed mindful of how encounters between concerted effort and the unexpected assist those who continue to search.

With three more biographies of John Milton appearing in 2008 (there are now over a hundred), his life has obviously continued to be a subject of interest about which many have something to say (Anna Beer and Campbell and Corns write accounts approaching five hundred pages).[6] Concentrating upon an extended period of that life about which Miltonists oftentimes know very little and virtually all the time less than they should, this essay will consider both the known and little known, acknowledge the information gap marking his early years, and offer suggestions as to how it might be improved. Based upon the assumption that an understanding of historical contexts must precede an assessment of Milton's early compositions, it

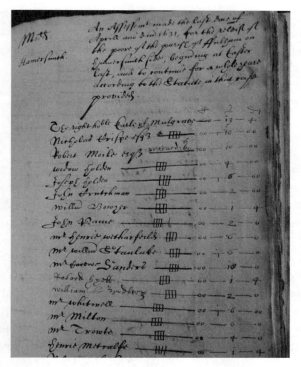

Fig. 1. Hammersmith and Fulham Record Office, Parish Rate Book (1631)

accordingly assigns significance to setting (whether Milton composed in his rooms in Cambridge or in homes in London, Hammersmith, or Horton); resources (whether that writing involved access to his own books, those in libraries, or neither); and occasions (a death in the family, an observance of a religious holiday, a commission ensuing from a family connection, a visit to the university by a dignitary). Since several essays in this volume address such

Fig. 2. Cambridge University Archives, Grace Book Z (1625)

matters, the following overview has been conceived as preliminary and supplementary to those efforts. Out of necessity discussion will focus on the 1620s and 1630s because it is highly unlikely that many records pertaining to Milton's childhood (1608–19) were ever created.

I.

As I have noted elsewhere, one should not expect to find much evidence for Milton's youth besides his birth notice and school records.[7] As the son of a well-connected and financially successful scrivener whose education at St Paul's was supplemented by private tutors, Milton was set upon the path leading to the university at an early age. Such a plan thus eliminated one of the few sources of materials available for early modern youth, those of indentures relating to apprenticeship. Unfortunately, whatever school records may have been created during his time at St Paul's (and we do not know what they may have been) were destroyed by the Great Fire of London in 1666. Indeed documentary evidence for his attendance consists of a brief notation in the Christ's College Admissions Book that he had studied at St Paul's under Alexander Gil (Fig. 3).[8] This shred of evidence serves as a reminder (which has not always been heeded) that the knowledge of Milton's early education rests upon a porous foundation comprised of his own comments, those of his brother and nephew, and the well-intended speculation of scholars.[9] In fact, the one surviving manuscript that has been brought forth to fill the evidentiary chasm that marks Milton's pre-university education—a single sheet of paper found with Milton's Commonplace Book in the nineteenth century—is itself problematic. The three Latin compositions on the sheet—a prose theme on one side and two poems on the other—have been correctly identified as grammar school exercises, but are they Milton's? That

Fig. 3. Cambridge University Archives, Christ's College Admissions Register (1624/5)

he never published them introduces scepticism that is increased by palaeo-graphic evidence in the manuscript often at odds with the surviving auto-graphs of Milton's hand from 1623, 1625, 1627, and 1629. Even though the three works have been accepted as Milton's since the nineteenth century, the case for attribution remains less than secure.[10]

For the period of Milton's life prior to 1625 when he begins his university study at Cambridge, the archival landscape is essentially barren. However, two sources, one long known, the other recently uncovered, supply viable collateral evidence. The first involves the business affairs of Milton's father initially documented by French and supplemented by Parker and Camp-bell.[11] They establish an important context for understanding Milton's early exposure to the world of money brokering and land transfers, two activities that mark his adult life. In an informative study of the origins of English deposit banking, Frank Melton describes Milton's father as a money-scrivener in whose shop 'all manner of conveyances were drawn up', but whose income 'came largely from putting out other men's money at interest'.[12] The extant records support such conclusions, but the larger subject of how this world and its activities found expression in Milton's writing has only just begun to be explored and assessed.[13] The extensive records of the Chancery court as well as those of the Common Pleas, Equity, High Commission, and Requests have not been thoroughly searched. In some instances, they have not been searched at all. The formidable nature of such tasks will likely dissuade most, but the absence of a full account of Milton senior's four decades of conducting business out of the family home disallows a confident assessment of his elder son's knowledge of and participation in such a world as a young man. If there is any doubt about the quantity of documentation produced by such activity, the Clayton papers, which are dispersed in no fewer than 34 public record offices and libraries, make clear that scrivener records were not just detailed and complex but encompassed a wide array of transactions.[14]

The other source that can enrich the archival record for Milton's pre-university life derives from his sister Anne's marriage to Edward Phillips in 1623.[15] For the next decade approximately fifty hitherto unreported records from the parish chest of St Martin-in-the-Fields furnish a way to monitor the activities of Milton's extended and immediate family. Many are financial—assessments for poor relief and contributions to help plague victims—but others are more personal, concerned with the births and deaths of Milton's nephews and nieces, as well as the death of his brother-in-law in 1631 and the remarriage of his sister in 1632 to Phillips's close friend Thomas Agar.[16] Records from the parish registers have long been known, but their potential as sources of knowledge about Milton's life has remained largely unexplored. While the financial documents from the parish chest allow us to identify the increasing prosperity of the Phillips family and monitor their location and relocation within the parish, the value of the records from the parish registers has been essentially confined to a single incident. In January 1628, the death of Milton's niece Anne has been identified as the likely source for her uncle's 'Elegy on the Death of a Fair Infant'. A subsequent entry in the registers for 9 April 1628 reporting the baptism of another niece Elizabeth Phillips has sometimes been cited (but also overlooked) as support that the expectant mother addressed in the poem is the fictional equivalent of its author's historical sister.[17] While source hunting of this kind has been accorded its appropriate place in Milton studies, its emphasis upon finding parallels and one-to-one equivalencies has effectively stopped further enquiry into the affairs of the Phillips family for over half a century.

For this situation to change, scholars need to recognize how records created within and outside of a parish can fill in long-standing gaps in Milton's early life. For instance, because they include a burial register within them, the St Martin churchwarden accounts corroborate information in the registers (the death of Milton's niece) and add details that are sometimes telling (burial expenses). The high costs of Edward Phillips's funeral in 1631 suggest an elaborate affair that increases the likelihood that both the immediate and extended family were present.[18] Such information may appear slight within the context of Milton's entire life, but for a time period for which we currently have very little, it brings into focus possible ways Milton participated in family events, whether by attending his brother-in-law's funeral or writing a poetic tribute to his sister on the occasion of her daughter's death. Moreover, the juxtaposition of parish records with others ostensibly created for different reasons can occasionally furnish unexpected insight into Milton's life in the 1620s, as a set of events from 1627 illustrates.

On 25 May 1627, Milton's father purchased property from Anthony and Johan Rudd in his daughter Anne's parish of residence, St Martin-in-the-Fields. The purchase involved her brother John who signed an indenture and is described in the documents created by the transaction as 'John Milton the younger of the University of Cambridge' (Fig. 4).[19] This record, created for the Close Rolls, can be linked to parish records that suggest Milton senior's motivation for acquiring the property arose in part from outbreaks of the plague and the desire to have a second home outside of the city of London.[20] This plan developed in two stages: an initial alternate residence in Westminster followed by a further remove to Hammersmith by April 1631. If the parish register records are viewed as more than birth and death notices, their link to and coherence with the chancery document can be glimpsed. By 1629, the St Martin burial registers confirm that the first three children of Edward and Anne Phillips have died. While no cause of death is provided in any of the three instances, several other parish documents attest to the need for dealing with the hardships created by plague outbreaks in 1625, 1626, and 1630.[21] When one considers that the births of the two sons who survive, Edward and John, do not appear in the St Martin registers, it is hard to resist the conclusion that the Milton family's relocation to Hammersmith was motivated by their past experience with such events. Even though the exact location of the Rudd property purchased by Milton senior remains unidentified, the parish poor relief assessments establish an approximate location and keep track of the Phillips family when it relocated from the water side to the land side of the parish.[22] In essence, then, a chancery record's intersection with a number of parish records has created an entry way into the world of the Milton family affairs.

Of course, what must not be forgotten in all of this is the clear evidence of Milton in London during a time when the university was in session. His presence extends the scope of the chancery record. The Rudd transaction

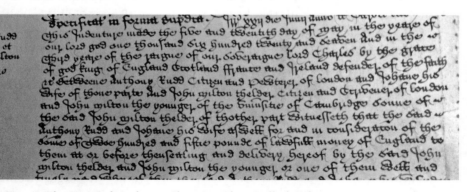

Fig. 4. The National Archives, Chancery Close Rolls (1627)

took place approximately two weeks before another, the loan Milton senior arranged with Richard Powell in June 1627.[23] His son's participation in this matter as well gives plausible support to arguments that it was during this term that he fell out with his tutor William Chappell.[24] Milton's appearance in London would otherwise not be known but for his signatures on the two documents. Thus the intermingling of chancery and parish records creates a vantage point from which to gauge events taking place in his life and at the same time serves the greater purposes of biography.[25] In the end, the archival landscape for Milton's life in the 1620s benefits from the family's expansion through marriage. The records created in the wake of such alliances establish his whereabouts on several occasions and illuminate his activities and conduct.

II.

Unfortunately, for the 1630s, some of the very advantages just discussed disappear. For the period encompassing Milton's last years at Cambridge and his return to London following his tour of the Continent, information is hard to come by. For a brief period in the middle of the last century, expectations were raised by a breakthrough almost three hundred years in the making—that the Milton family split its time between two rural settings in Hammersmith and Horton. As discussed earlier, the evidence for the Hammersmith residency appeared in Chancery court depositions spanning a four-year period from the later part of 1632 to the middle of 1635.[26] In each deposition, Milton's father declared under oath that he was a resident of Hammersmith. French dutifully added these documents to his already long list of transcriptions to be included in the five volumes of life records he published in the middle of the twentieth century, but having been alerted to a new place for possible evidence regarding Milton and his family, scholars have been unable to come up with much. The parish chest records for Hammersmith and Horton pale by comparison to those found in St Martin-in-the-Fields. Having looked himself with little success, William Riley Parker, in a gesture of possible encouragement, composed a set of questions for future scholars to answer regarding both residencies.[27] If we gauge progress simply by numbers, it has been negligible. Of Parker's approximately fifty questions, John Shawcross settled one in 1963 and I answered a second in 2007.

The extant evidence concerning Milton in the 1630s can be arranged into three groups of years and described as adequate but less than robust (1630–3); scarce and potentially misleading (1634–6); and good (1637–9). New records for the first four and final three years have been found while the middle years (1634–6) remain much as they have always been, elusive, obscure, and frustrating. We still do not have a clear date of when the family relocated from Hammersmith to Horton, but it most likely occurred during the middle of the decade; nor do we know why they did so or why Milton senior and Christopher relocated again to Reading some time in the final months of 1640 or the first months of 1641.

Fortunately, the value of what the late Jeremy Maule found in 1996—poor rate assessment records for the Hammersmith side of the All Saints parish in Fulham—is unambiguous. The rate books cover 1631 and 1632, and Milton senior signs the parish audit books for 1633.[28] While Maule's discoveries do not firmly establish the date the family took up residence in Hammersmith, they do locate the Miltons in the area by April 1631, a full year earlier than the date of the first Chancery deposition. Of greater importance, they alert scholars to a series of records (poor relief and tax assessments) that have unaccountably been overlooked or understudied. Truly a beneficiary of Maule's efforts, I have been able to recover the Phillips family parish records for the 1620s and similar documents concerning the Webber family (Christopher Milton's in-laws) in the parish of St Clement Danes, and Milton's nine years in Petty France in the 1650s. An additional set of records for 1631, 1632, and 1633 requires a closer look.

As was the case in the 1620s, attention to Milton's extended family can ultimately inform us about him. Anne Milton Phillips's marriage to Thomas Agar in 1632 is corroborated by two documents in the parish chest of St Martin-in-the-Fields. The first, entitled 'A Collection for the Repair of Knightsbridge and Chelsea Bridge and for the Building of the Brentford Bridge', is dated 19 April 1632; the second is the parish rate book for the period from Easter 1632 through Lady Day 1633.[29] Both records derive significance from an event that predates them: the death of Edward Phillips in August 1631.

The death of Anne Milton's husband deserves a fuller hearing because decisions made before and after it involve her family as well as her father and brothers in Hammersmith. John Milton senior, for one, witnessed Edward Phillips's will composed a little more than three weeks before his demise, and therefore was prepared for the possibility that his newly widowed and seven-month pregnant daughter might relocate to her parents' home in Hammersmith with her one-year-old son Edward for the remainder of her pregnancy.[30] At the end of Easter term in mid-July, Anne's brothers, John and Christopher, may or may not have returned to the Hammersmith home; but it is more likely that in late August both returned to Westminster for Phillips's burial. Following the burial, the immediate family—Milton senior, his wife Sara, their three children, and their year-old grandson Edward Phillips—returned to Hammersmith. Presumably in early October John and Christopher Milton departed for Cambridge to begin Michaelmas term on 10 October. Milton's entry in his Bible, written years later, dated the birth of John Phillips 'about October', a phrasing that would reflect his approximate recall of the time of year in light of the university term to which he was mindful of returning.[31] Anne Milton Phillips would not remain in Hammersmith for long; the parish records from St Martin's speak to the presence of her new family by 1632, her marriage to Thomas Agar taking place in the parish of St Dunstan in the East on 5 January 1632 as discovered by Clavering and Shawcross in 1960.[32] The missing link in this series of events is the Hammersmith registers which do not survive; if they had, the probability is high that they would establish the birthplaces and christenings of John and Edward Phillips; for Edward to be born in Hammersmith his grandparents would have had to take up residence by August 1630, a date certainly within the realm of possibility, even though evidence at present is lacking. Admittedly, juxtaposing records from different locations cannot furnish definitive answers in this case, but the process does allow plausible solutions to emerge, and it points out how evidence from various quarters enlightens an otherwise obscure set of events.

A closer look at the two documents from St Martin's permits more certainty. The collection record reveals that Edward Phillips's name has initially appeared but has been subsequently replaced by that of Mr Agar (Fig. 5). The parish official created a ledger by copying the list of parishioners from the poor relief account books from the previous year. He then determined the rates those individuals would pay to furnish aid to repair projects taking place within the confines of the parish. The replacement of Phillips by Agar indicates that Anne Agar, a widow for only four months, elected to return to her former parish for all of 1632 and the first quarter of 1633 after her marriage in January 1632, a decision confirmed by the second record, the parish rate book for 1632–3: Agar's poor relief assessment and payments are recorded

Fig. 5. City of Westminster Archive Centre, Parish assessment (1632)

through Lady Day 1633.[33] Combining these two documents with the Hammersmith records, we have more documentary evidence for the first four years of the 1630s about the Milton family, if not Milton himself, than ever before.

The next three years, unfortunately, turn out to be more like what we have become accustomed to—an occasional piece of evidence that proves more elusive than conclusive. We lose sight of Thomas and Anne Agar after 1632 for a few years, and the records supporting the Miltons' residency in Hammersmith decrease dramatically. There are two legal records from Chancery for all of 1634 and a final deposition on 8 January 1635.[34] After that date it is anyone's guess as to how long they stay in the parish.

III.

For Milton's Horton period archival remains are not abundant but better now than they have ever been. The only evidence indicating the family relocation in May 1636—notation in a record book of the company of Scriveners—disappeared in the twentieth century.[35] Thus uncertainty marks the transition from Hammersmith to Horton, and the reason for relocating is also a matter of speculation: did Milton senior move a greater distance from London in order to facilitate his retirement and disengage from activities common to his profession, i.e., court appearances, law suits, and land transfers? If such was the aim, it does not appear to have worked. During 1635, 1636, and 1637 legal documents indicate that the scrivener's difficulties continued, although they do not disclose where Milton's father was residing at the time of the law proceedings.[36] For the most part, Horton remains in Miltonic lore as the place where his mother died and he wrote 'Lycidas', both dating from 1637, a year of change from an evidentiary standpoint.

Three documents created in early April 1637 firmly establish the Milton family's presence in Horton. On 1 April Christopher Milton submitted an affidavit claiming his father to be too infirm to attend court in Westminster. Since Milton's father lived for another decade, the real reason for the non-appearance was likely the illness of his wife. Indeed, two days later Sara Milton died, and three days after that she was buried. Edward Goodall, the rector of the parish, entered both dates into the parish register, and Milton's mother was buried in the chancel with her name engraved on a blue marble slab that is still legible almost four centuries later.[37] Commentators have attributed various degrees of significance to this event in Milton's life, but the cause of death was apparently old age, a view warranted by the absence of a designation of the plague next to her entry in the parish burial register that was given to others who appear for the years 1636 and 1637. While these facts have been long known, they have not been considered in connection to a writ issued for Milton's father and witnessed by Thomas Agar on 10 March concerning the former's ongoing court case with Sir Thomas Cotton.[38] Agar's involvement with his father-in-law's legal affairs links the extended family residing in either London or Westminster to the immediate family in Horton and suggests that the Milton family may have already started to gather in anticipation of Sara Milton's death. With Agar would be his wife, Milton's sister Anne, the surviving children from her first marriage, Edward and John Phillips, and two daughters from her second marriage, Mary and Anne Agar. By the beginning of April, the affidavit attests to the presence of Christopher Milton, and a week after Sara Milton was buried, John Agar, Thomas's brother, witnessed the scrivener's answer to the writ of 10 March.[39] The family assembly thus appears still in place by mid-April. The presence of Agar and his two stepsons may also account for how the Horton residency was uncovered. Edward Phillips was the first biographer to note his uncle's time in 'Horton, near Colebrook in Berkshire'.[40] Was it the family gathering that the seven-year-old recalled? It has remained the lone piece of evidence linking Phillips to the village.

Undoubtedly the most often cited event from the Horton years has been the composition of 'Lycidas'. Among its heralded passages, those expressing its author's denunciation of English church practices in the 1630s have been singled out as evidence of an incipient religious radicalism.[41] The discovery of an inspection of the Horton church dated 8 August 1637 has provided an additional possibility for Miltonic dissent. Created as a result of a jurisdictional dispute between Archbishop Laud and Bishop John Williams of Lincoln, the report cited John Milton senior for having an elevated church seat, and it also indicated a problem with the burial of Sara Milton, though she is not mentioned specifically. This document and another created in its wake are to date the only two instances of any member of the Milton family appearing in the records of the English church courts.[42]

An additional document produced during 1637 offers a final perspective on events in Horton and a transition to the remaining records for 1638 and 1639. On 23 November 1637 Milton wrote a letter to Charles Diodati while in London. Why was he there rather than in Horton? The burial register of the family's former parish of All Hallows, Bread Street, offers an answer.[43] On this day, Milton's brother-in-law's father, Thomas Agar, was buried in the chancel, and Milton, along with other members of his family, likely attended the funeral. The content of the letter implies as much insofar as it brings together Thomas Agar, Christopher Milton, and John Milton and prompts the last to speak to Diodati of plans to relocate to the Inns of Court:

there is a pleasant and shady walk; for that dwelling will be more satisfactory, both for companionship, if I wish to remain at home, and as a more suitable headquarters, if I choose to venture forth. Where I am now, as you know, I live in obscurity and cramped quarters.[44]

Two details attract notice: Milton's apparent familiarity with the setting of the Inns (perhaps through visits to his brother?) and his unfavourable description of his situation in Horton (which does not resemble published accounts of the family's rented home, Berkin Manor).[45] A preference for urban life marked by freedom and companionship comes through here. The implication to Diodati is that neither was available in Horton, although whether such sentiments truly speak to Milton's state of mind in late 1637 or have resulted from spending time with his brother and brother-in-law earlier in the day remain irresolvable matters. More clarity becomes available if one construes Milton's comments as indicative of an increasing restlessness that leads to his decision to leave England for the Continent in May 1638. In such a view, the Inns of Court represent to the 29-year-old Milton, who had never lived away from his family except during university terms, an opportunity to be on his own experiencing the freedom his brother Christopher has had since entering the Inner Temple in 1632.[46] In any event, the need for change—the seed for the continental tour—is present in the letter.

Milton's remarks in his letter to Diodati are worthy of additional notice because they obliquely address a long-held assumption that Milton would never leave England without arranging for the care of his father.[47] That assumption has been based on the idea that Christopher Milton had married Thomasine Webber before Milton's departure and that she and her husband were residing in Horton with Milton senior by the spring of 1638. The recent discovery that the marriage took place months after Milton had left England (13 September 1638) indicates that some other arrangement was in place. The location of the marriage in the parish of St Andrew Holborn is also telling— it is where Thomas Agar and his family have relocated to by 1638. Agar is listed as a resident of Shoe Lane in the parish return appearing in the 1638 Settlement of Tithes for the City of London.[48]

While it may have been handled with extreme delicacy, it does appear that on the basis of the death notice in the Horton registers of 26 March 1639 an infant son of Christopher and Thomasine Milton had been conceived prior to their marriage in September 1638.[49] Presumably, Thomasine remained with her mother, the widow Isabel Webber with whom Mary Powell would live for a short period in 1645. In 1636, the widow and her two daughters Thomasine and Isabel had relocated from Westminster to Kingsbury.[50] Her relocation to Horton would be calculated so as to allay any suspicions from Milton senior.[51] This matter, never considered before, becomes something worthy of thought now that the marriage date has been established.

The search for records concerned with Milton's life will no doubt go on, notwithstanding Gordon Campbell's estimate of 'about 2000 references in some 600 documents housed in more than fifty archives'.[52] If one were to focus solely on the 1630s, the areas that remain largely unexplored are the Court of Requests, the church courts, including the Commissary and Consistory records for Hammersmith and the Consistory Court records for Horton which came under the jurisdiction of the Bishop of Lincoln. Certainly estate records related to Hammersmith and Horton might contain some documentation regarding the leasing of the residences occupied by Milton's father and family. A now deceased churchwarden for Horton who had a keen interest in Milton residing in his parish believed the Miltons did not live at Berkin Manor but in a smaller house in a less prominent part of the village. Would this account for Milton's description of cramped quarters? Hearsay of this kind has sometimes led to results. Indeed if the attempt to locate records created centuries earlier can teach anything, it may be to distrust predictability and logic. In archival research, where something should be is often not where it is. For future investigators fond of Miltonic puzzles, there remain many to solve.

Notes

1. David Masson, *The Life of John Milton: Narrated in Connexion with the Political, Ecclesiastical, and Literary History of His Time* (1859–94; repr. New York, 1946), 6 vols. plus Index (1894); rev. edn. of vol. i (1881); vol. ii (1894); French, *LR*; Parker; Maurice Kelley, 'Additional Texts of Milton's State Papers', *Modern Language Notes*, 67 (1952), 18–19, and 'Milton's Dante—Della Casa—Varchi Volume', *Bulletin of the New York Public Library*, 66 (1962), 499–504; Leo Miller, *John Milton and The Oldenburg Safeguard* (New York, 1985) and *John Milton's Writings in the Anglo-Dutch Negotiations* (Pittsburgh, Pa., 1992); John T. Shawcross, *John Milton: The Self and the World* (Lexington, Ky., 1993) and *'The Arms of the Family': The Significance of John Milton's Relatives and Associates* (Lexington, Ky., 2004); Campbell, *Chronology*.

2. The dates and document numbers of the four chancery records, all housed in the National Archives, are 14 September 1632 (C24/587/46), 17 April 1634 (C24/591/2), 5 August 1634 (C24/596/33), and 8 January 1635 (C24/600/37). Unfortunately, Maule died before providing an account of the Hammersmith records. They are identified in Campbell, *Chronology*, 43–9 and discussed later in this essay.

3. The entries for Milton's BA and MA degrees appear respectively in Cambridge University Archives, Grace Book Z, 158 and 224.

4. For a full account see Sarah Knight, 'Royal Milton', *Times Literary Supplement*, 5 February 2010, 15, and 'Milton's Student Verses of 1629', *Notes and Queries*, 255 (2010), 37–9.

5. For a full account see Davide Messina, 'La Tina Regained', *Milton Quarterly*, 45 (2011), 118–22.

6. The three are Campbell and Corns; Anna Beer, *Milton: Poet, Pamphleteer, and Patriot* (2008); and Neil Forsyth, *John Milton: A Biography* (2008).

7. Edward Jones, '"Ere Half My Days": Milton's Life, 1608–1640', in Nicholas McDowell and Nigel Smith (eds.), *The Oxford Handbook of Milton* (Oxford, 2009), 3–25.

8. Cambridge University Archives, Christ's College Admissions Book, 12 February 1624/5.

9. For the seventeenth-century sources, see Milton's autobiographical digression in the *Second Defence* (1654); John Aubrey's 'Minutes of the Life of John Milton' (*c.* 1681-2) for information provided by Christopher Milton; and Edward Phillips's *The Life of John Milton* in *Letters of State. Written by Mr. John Milton. To most of the Sovereign Princes and Republicks of Europe. From the Year 1649, Till the year 1659* (1694). Two long-standing accounts of his early education are David Lemen Clark, *John Milton at St Paul's School* (New York, 1948) and Harris Francis Fletcher, *The Intellectual Development of John Milton* (2 vols., Urbana, Ill., 1956–61).

10. The autographs include his signatures on his sister's marriage settlement (Pierpont Morgan Library, New York, MS MA 953); two Chancery documents (National Archives, C54/2715/20 and C152/61); and his matriculation, supplication, and subscription records at Cambridge (Cambridge University Archives, University Matriculation Book for 9 April 1625; Supplicats *1627, 1628, 1629*, fol. 331; and Subs *1*, 286). The manuscript of the school exercises (HRC MS 127) is housed at the Ransom Center in Austin, Texas. The classical foundations for all three works have been discussed by Maurice Kelley in 'Grammar School Latin and John Milton', *The Classical World*, 52 (1959), 133–8.

11. See French, *LR* and *Milton in Chancery: New Chapters in the Lives of The Poet and His Father* (New York, 1939); Parker, vol. ii; and Campbell, *Chronology*.

12. Frank Melton, *Sir Robert Clayton and the Origins of English Deposit Banking, 1658–1685* (Cambridge, 1986), 25.

13. A recent discussion of Milton's use of the term 'convey' appears in John T. Shawcross, *The Development of Milton's Thought: Law, Government, and Religion* (Pittsburgh, Pa., 2008). See also Nicholas von Maltzahn's observations on usury in the Milton family, 'Making Use of the Jews: Milton and Philo-Semitism', in Douglas A. Brooks (ed.), *Milton and the Jews* (Cambridge, 2008), 57–82; and most recently, David Hawkes, 'Milton and Usury', *English Literary Renaissance*, 41 (2011), 502–28.

14. See Appendix 4 in Melton, *Sir Robert Clayton*, 243–51, where locations are conveniently recorded.

15. They were married on 22 November in the London city parish of St Stephen, Walbrook.

16. The birth and death notices from the St Martin registers have been recorded in French, *LR* and Campbell, *Chronology*. Some of the parish chest records were reported for the first time in Edward Jones, 'Select Chronology: "Speak of things at hand/ Useful"', in Angelica Duran (ed.), *A Concise Companion to Milton* (Oxford, 2006), 217–34.

17. The St Martin churchwarden (F3) and overseer accounts (F350–9) document the presence of the family annually from 1623 through 1632. The linking of burial record to poem dates as far back as Masson, though later commentators (Parker, Campbell, *Chronology*) have noted the discrepancy between the death notice and Milton's Latin formula for dating it in 1673 (*'anno aetatis* 17'). If Milton has not erred (though many believe he did), then the composition of the elegy must be assigned to either late 1625 or some time in 1626.

18. Even though it was conducted at night (which may or may not have been a cost-cutting move), the Phillips burial cost £10, 6 shillings, and 8 pence.

19. The indenture recording the property purchase is C54/2715/20 housed in the National Archives.

20. For a plausible account of the second home theory, see Rose Clavering and John T. Shawcross, 'Anne Milton and the Milton Residencies', *Journal of English and Germanic Philology*, 59 (1960), 680–90.

21. In addition to its overseer accounts, during these years the parish created additional ledgers for the relief of plague victims (F3355) and the parish poor (F1011).

22. See note 17.

23. The transaction (C152/61) takes place in London on 11 June, and Milton signs the statute staple (LC 4/56) which mentions him.

24. An account of the fallout between Milton and his tutor can be found in Leo Miller, 'Milton's Clash with Chappell: A Suggested Reconstruction', *Milton Quarterly*, 14 (1980), 77–87.

25. The link between the chancery records and Milton's rustication has been made, but that between the parish register records and the property purchase has not.

26. See note 2.

27. The questions for Hammersmith appear in Parker, ii. 780–1; those for Horton in ii. 799–800.

28. The Hammersmith documents include assessments for 1631 (PAF/1/21/fo. 68) and 1632 (PAF 1/21/fo. 85). The scrivener signed the audit of the parish overseer accounts on 12 May 1633 (PAF 1/21/fo. 92v.).

29. The collection book is designated as F3346, the 1632–3 overseer accounts F359.

30. The will, created on 1 August 1631, is PROB 11/160/99.

31. The entry is on the flyleaf of the Bible now British Library Add MS 32,310.

32. See Clavering and Shawcross, 'Anne Milton and the Milton Residencies', 685n20.

33. Agar's name inserted over Phillips's appears on fo. 25r in the collection book; his poor relief assessments are recorded on fo. 3v.

34. See note 2.

35. The last person to have seen this record was Hyde Clarke who discusses it in *Athenaeum*, 2746 (12 June 1880), 760–1.

36. See the entries in Campbell, *Chronology* for 4 May, 8 May, and 13 June 1635; 28 May 1636; and 23 and 27 January, 13, 16, and 18 February, and 10, 16, and 22 March 1637.

37. The affidavit can be found in the Court of Requests (Req 1/141/fo. 218). The death and burial dates for Sara Milton appear in the parish registers of St Michael's Horton (PR 107/1/1) housed in the Centre for Buckinghamshire Studies in Aylesbury.

38. The writ can be found in the Court of Requests (Req. 2/360).

39. Milton's father answers Cotton's bill on 13 April 1637 (Req. 2/630).

40. Horton and Colnbrook are now in Buckinghamshire according to county boundaries established in the nineteenth century. Thus Phillips's designation is accurate.

Both Horton and Colnbrook were considered in Berkshire in the seventeenth century.

41. Scores of articles on 'Lycidas' are conveniently recorded in P. J. Klemp, *The Essential Milton* (Boston, Mass., 1989), 156–71 and C. A. Patrides (ed.), *Milton's 'Lycidas': The Tradition and the Poem*, 2nd edn. (1961; Columbia, Mo., 1983). Both can now be supplemented by Calvin Huckabay and David Urban, *John Milton: An Annotated Bibliography, 1989–1999* (Pittsburgh, Pa., 2011).

42. The inspection report (D/A/V/15) and follow up (D/A/V/4, 149r) are housed in the Centre for Buckinghamshire Studies.

43. GLMS 5031, 188.

44. Letter 8 in *CPW*, i. 327. The 1674 *Epistolarum Familiarum* and *CW* (xii. 23–9) designate this text as Letter 7.

45. See D. Masson, 'Local Memories of Milton', *Good Words*, 34 (1893), 41–4, and G. W. J. Gyll, *History of the Parish of Wraysbury, Ankerwycke Priory, and Magna Carta Island; with the History of Horton, and the Town of Colnbrook, Bucks* (1862).

46. His date of admission was 22 September. See the Inner Temple Archive Admissions Book 1571–1640, 593.

47. Masson and Parker as well as Shawcross in his opening chapter on Christopher in *Arms* discuss this matter (see note 1).

48. The marriage entry appears in GLMS 6668/1, the register for St Andrew Holborn, 1559–1698. The tithe return has been published as *The Inhabitants of London in 1638*, ed. T. C. Dale (1931). The burial record of Mary Agar indicates that Agar continued to live in St Andrew Holborn at least through May 1641. See Burial Register 1623–42, St Andrew Holborn (GLMS 6673/2).

49. Horton Parish Registers, PR 107/1/1. There remains, of course, the possibility of a premature birth of an undeveloped infant.

50. Their residency in Kingsbury has been established through the October 1636 marriage allegation between Isabel Webber (the daughter) and Henry Jackson. The widow approved the marriage by a proxy, but she is listed as a resident of Kingsbury.

51. See David Cressy, *Birth, Marriage, and Death: Ritual, Religion, and the Life-Cycle in Tudor and Stuart England* (Oxford, 1997) for the seventeenth-century concern with illegitimacy.

52. Gordon Campbell, 'The Life Records', in Thomas N. Corns (ed.), *A Companion to Milton* (Oxford, 2001), 483.

2

'The Armes of Studious Retirement'? Milton's Scholarship, 1632–1641

William Poole

a Gentleman, whose proper calling is the service of His Countrey...is most properly concerned in Moral, and Political knowledge; and thus the studies which more immediately belong to His calling, are those which treat of virtues and vices, of Civil Society, and the Arts of Government, and so wil take in also Law and History.[1]

I. Introduction

John Milton graduated as *magister artium* from Cambridge in July 1632 and promptly abandoned the academy. Almost a decade later, in May 1641, he published his first prose tract, *Of Reformation*. The interim years were spent in study, in travel, in teaching, and in writing many of the poems that he was to collect in the *Poems* of 1645, and in preparing himself for the prose onslaught of the dozen separate tracts he published in the five years following the collapse of Charles I's Personal Rule. The 1630s saw men with university degrees

comparable to Milton's own MA publicly tortured for their political interventions, and yet for Milton the decade was largely a time of disengagement,
of intense personal study, and it is his reading in this period that this chapter
addresses. In retrospect we may justly say that Milton was arming himself;
and indeed it would seem that he had a glimmer of what was to come when
he set to his books in a still-peaceful nation. Yet the precise path he took was
not a straight one, and we cannot simply see the man in the youth.[2]

The resources for such an investigation are various. At the most obvious
level, a few of Milton's own book purchases from the 1630s survive; and his
Commonplace Book Manuscript (hereafter CPB), rediscovered in 1874, provides us with some seemingly thick description of Milton's post-academic
study—although, as we shall see, its domain is rather restricted. (Milton's
chiefly poetic papers, now gathered as the Trinity College Manuscript, are in
this respect far less informative.[3]) At the level of inference, the 1640s publications provide evidence of further aspects of Milton's reading not witnessed in the CPB. His continental tour certainly involved some book
purchasing and reading, although we know less about this than we would
like. We can also make some inferences about Milton's reading and indeed
rereading by collation of his ideal syllabus as detailed in *Of Education* (1644)
with the account of the curriculum implemented by Milton in his own
teaching, as later recalled by his nephew Edward Phillips. Finally, at the level
of informed conjecture we have the resources of the various libraries
potentially open to Milton throughout the 1630s, and it is here that I shall
offer a few new ideas. I shall proceed roughly chronologically: first there is
Milton in his 'Hammersmith and Horton' periods, time traditionally associated in part with the reading recorded in the CPB. Then there is Milton's
own book-buying and his proximity in Horton to the libraries of Kedermister
and Eton. Next there is his continental tour. Finally, there is his return to
England, his setting up as a private teacher, and his preparations for the
writings of his left hand.

II. Commonplace learning

After Milton left Cambridge, he returned to London to live with his family.
His intention was to study. Whereas his brother Christopher, who left

Cambridge with Milton but after only five terms of study, went immediately into the law, Milton suspended his formal education, but not for the moment his priestly vocation. At least, this was what he was telling some of his acquaintance, for around 1633 his application to private scholarship provoked complaint from an unidentified but avuncular, probably clerical figure, who had criticized Milton for avoiding his preaching vocation: 'you said', Milton recalled, 'that too much love of learning is in fault, & that I have given up my selfe to dreame away my yeares in the armes of studious retirement.' Milton's fascinating letter to the unknown correspondent, drafted twice immediately following his meeting with the unidentified friend, betrays Milton's own awareness of 'a certaine belatednesse in me'. For all his anxiety, however, he did not back down: he would persist in his study, and that for 'honour & repute & immortall fame'.[4]

The Horton reading is mainly visible to us through the sole surviving example of one of Milton's commonplace books. This manuscript consists of three 'indices', labelled *ethicus*, *economicus*, and *politicus*. It has been blocked out so that the ethical index is apportioned two quires of the available paper stock, while the remaining two divisions are apportioned one-and-a-half quires apiece.[5] In contemporary terms, Milton's CPB is therefore restricted to the domain of Aristotelian moral philosophy, divided up in the textbook tradition into 'general' and 'special' components, the former labelled 'ethics', and the latter subdivided into 'politics' and 'economics'. 'Ethics' covered basic moral principles, and the special components of economics and politics then applied these principles to the household and to the state.[6] Milton's headings within his three sections likewise correspond to conventional moral topics. This extremely precise domain explains why we do not find theological, legal, medical, literary, or scientific topics discussed in the CPB, or only insofar as they pertain to ethical heads. Milton may therefore have maintained other commonplace books, although the CPB, in moral philosophy was undoubtedly his major focus. It also existed, at least in its later phase, in special relationship to a lost manuscript in polemical divinity, the *Index theologicus*. From the surviving cross-references, we can tell that the lost index contained the headings *de Religione non cogenda*, *Papa*, *de bonis ecclesiasticis, de Idololatria*, and *Ecclesia*, and was at least forty-two pages long, and potentially much longer. As Milton cross-referenced the heading *de bonis ecclesiasticis* five times (in four entries) we can conjecture that this topic was of particular importance to him. This lost manuscript is emphatically not an early version of Milton's treatise in systematic divinity, which he commenced as part of his teaching strategy in the early 1640s, but is rather a collection of Reformed versus Roman Catholic positions, partially articulated in terms of the topics of Robertus Bellarminus's benchmark *Disputationes de Controversiis Christianæ Fidei Adversus huius Temporis Hæreticos*, which appeared from 1586.[7] Many such anti-Bellarmine manuscripts survive today, and although it is unlikely that Milton ever intended to work up his notes into a published text, if he had done so it would probably have resembled the *Bellarminus enervatus* (1625–9, many editions to 1658) of William Ames, the celebrated Christ's College Nonconformist.

The surviving CPB, therefore, demonstrates that although Milton had left the academy, he still thought in largely academic categories, and structured his note-taking accordingly. So as Milton worked his way through a formidable diet of private reading, he marked passages fit for inclusion, probably— to judge by Milton's surviving books and the palaeography of the CPB itself—by underlining or marginal sigla. Then, when he had finished a book, he reviewed his annotated prompts and entered extracts under given heads, often writing the heading and the first extract under it in one scribal visit. There his moral commonplaces lay refrigerated in their stacks, frozen until reanimated in the prose publications of the 1640s. (We can tell that Milton did not necessarily enter his moral commonplaces at the same time as his basic reading because he often scribes in one visit a series of extracts that are disparate in his source text. This means that, strictly speaking, we can only reconstruct the order of Milton's *review* of his reading, and not the order of his reading itself.)

If the form of Milton's major reading record, then, follows that of contemporary Aristotelian moral philosophy, we may well expect the content to behave likewise. Consulting the popular Aristotelian general textbook of Franco Burgersdijck, for instance, the *Idea Philosophiae tum Naturalis, tum Moralis* (five Oxford editions 1631 to 1667), we encounter as the touchstone texts in moral philosophy the Aristotelian ethical corpus, with side-roles played by Seneca, Cicero, Boethius, the odd Stoic and Epicurean from Diogenes Laertius, and the occasional illustration from the New Testament. But this is not at all what we get when we turn to Milton's manuscript. Partly this is because Milton had long since absorbed the foundational texts of moral philosophy, and plodding through Cicero's *Tusculanae Disputationes*, for instance, was a task for schoolboys. Nor was Milton the kind to cite textbooks, and so there is no mention in the Commonplace Book of Keckermann or Burgersdijck, the standard Christ's College cribs in moral philosophy. Rather, Milton turned to a genre more befitting the weaned scholar, the discipline that was commonly described as 'moral philosophy teaching by examples': history.[8] Overwhelmingly, Milton's chosen reading tracked Western ecclesiastical and political history from the patristic period right up to fairly recent British and Irish history.

We might ask, therefore, whether Milton followed any curricular path here too. Moral philosophy, after all, pointed to historiography, but stopped short of recommending an exact cursus of texts. For that, we must turn to a late English flowering of the *artes historicæ*, in the person of the first Camden Professor of History, Degory Wheare (1573–1647). Wheare's famous textbook was his *De Ratione et Methodo Legendi Historias Dissertatio* (1623, first extended text 1625, many subsequent editions). Wheare divided his subject into *political/civil*, and *ecclesiastical* histories. He also distinguished between the *modes* or what we would call genres of history: *chronicles*, *lives*, and *relations/narratives* (*relationes*).[9] The reading of history itself required *order*, *judgement*, and for the materials thus gathered to be 'regularly disposed as it were in a Granary'.[10] With respect to the first of these requirements, the reader of history was therefore instructed to treat authors in an unbroken chronological chain, and one practical use of Wheare's manual is to stipulate how to thread together the surviving fragments of historical authors. We recall here Milton's claim that he conducted his reading 'in the method of time'.[11] Later, Wheare repeated the advice of the Spanish educationalist Juan Luìs Vives, and here the dictates of chronology ('the method of time') and moral philosophy coincide:

In Reading Histories (saith he [Vives]), *the first thing to be observed is the Order of times, and in the next place all Words and Actions which will afford any example for the imitating of what is good, or the avoiding what is evil.*[12]

These readings will fall into either *philological* or *philosophical* categories, i.e., for the improving of language, or the improving of morals. These are to be collected into a commonplace book, and Milton's CPB is obviously of the *philosophical* kind. Wheare specifies 'philosophical' abstraction as covering 'all the *Moral*, *Politick*, *Oeconomick* and *Military* Examples', in essence Milton's division (Milton both abstracted and later taught from 'military' works too). Wheare's gloss '*Moral* [*Ethica* in the Latin text], *Politick*, *Oeconomick*' is also a signal that by 'philosophy' Wheare strictly means 'moral philosophy', as opposed to the other two philosophies, viz. natural and metaphysical.[13] I shall not go so far as to claim that Milton was reading with Wheare's syllabus copied out and tacked onto the wall—the fullest form of Wheare's textbook, the *Relectiones Hyemales*, appeared only in 1637—but Wheare himself sits at the end of a tradition into which Milton too fits, and we need only browse the relevant chapters of Wheare to confirm that Milton followed an extremely similar course through Western history to that advocated by Wheare, albeit restricting himself largely to ecclesiastical history.

The dating of Milton's entering of notes from his reading into his CPB is a tentative affair, and depends largely on palaeographical evidence and the order suggested by format. It would seem, perhaps surprisingly, that the CPB was only commenced in perhaps late 1637, shortly before the continental trip.[14] If we follow the usual consensus based on Milton's distinctive shift from an epsilon-ε into an italic-e, we can say that Milton concentrated his first studies in four major areas: the church history of the patristic era (Eusebius, Socrates Scholasticus, Evagrius Scholasticus, Sulpicius Severus); slotting into Byzantine history (Procopius, the *Historia Miscella* [i.e., the *Historia Romana* of Paulus Diaconus, continued by Landolphus Sagax], Nicephorus Gregoras, Cantacuzenus); with some Italian vernacular literature (Dante, Boccaccio, Ariosto); and finally some general patristic study, such as with which he might have commenced his BD had he remained in Cambridge (Clement of Alexandria, Cyprian, Prudentius, Ignatius, Tertullian, and Justin Martyr).

Nevertheless there is a slight dislocation here: Milton was certainly entering new territory, as he implies in his correspondence of the time. But the historical reading of this period was still essentially a piece of advanced arts reading, following an arts curriculum, distilled into arts headings. Although Milton had turned his back on the academy, the content and rationale of his reading were still controlled by that world. Gordon Campbell has suggested that Milton's personal study functioned as a private continuation of the academic *cursus*, in accordance with his MA oath to spend the next seven years in study. If this is so, then the ecclesiastical dimension of Milton's reading is particularly pertinent: for he was, in his own way, studying as if for the Baccalaureate in Divinity, and as if he had never left Christ's College. This gives us an important insight into Milton's mentality, one which harmonizes with his polemic rhetoric too: Milton writes as a scholar for scholars, deriding the intellectual shortcomings of his opponents. His preferred insult is to call someone 'stupid'.[15]

III. Book purchasing

We can be sure that Milton purchased many of the books he read over these years. Granted, a disappointingly small number of books survive which can be shown to have been Milton's copies, but it is interesting to note that they were all purchased in this early period, a factor that may point to Milton ceasing to sign his own copies after a certain date, as we know from his correspondence that he remained keen on purchasing often deluxe books even after the loss of his sight.[16] In December 1629 Milton bought and annotated Della Casa's *Rime e Prose* (Venice, 1563); in 1631 he acquired and annotated Aratus's *Phænomena* (Paris, 1559); in 1634 he purchased Lycophron's *Alexandra* (Geneva, 1601) and annotated a two-volume quarto Euripides (Geneva, 1602); in 1636 he acquired and lightly emended the parallel Greek–Latin folio edition of Dio Chrysostom's *Orationes LXXX* (Paris, 1604); and finally in 1637 he purchased Heraclides (or Heraclitus) of Pontus's *Allegoriæ in Homeri Fabulas de Diis* (Basel, 1544).[17]

Doubtless Milton made dozens of other book purchases in this period, but this limited group of six texts does furnish occasion for some reflections. First, none is cited in the CPB, and this last consideration underlines just how partial a record of Milton's reading that manuscript provides, especially as only the Aratus falls clearly outside the ambit of a commonplace book in moral philosophy, and Milton's annotations to that volume are solely philological (as indeed are most of his surviving annotations). Secondly, it is notable that all these texts are old continental imprints, acquired therefore on the English second-hand market, probably in London. Yet these are far from second-class imprints, representing rather the finest of Geneva, Paris, and Basel typography and scholarship. His Aratus, for instance, is a fine Morelius quarto with folding-out star-map, typeset throughout in Greek. His Lycophron is a Stephanus quarto, with stacked Greek/Latin main text, surrounded by twin-columned commentary entirely in Greek by Isaac Tzetzes. And his Heraclides is an elegant octavo from the workshop of Oporinus, surely the most eclectic scholar-printer of his day. Milton also prized his books and annotated them with care: his Aratus, for instance, has Milton's Ovidian pentameter *cum sole, et lunâ semper Aratus erit* written astride the printer's ornament on the title page, broken across the caesura; and his annotations throughout are exceptionally neat, consisting entirely of philo-logical/textual suggestions, cross-referenced to two other editions of the text[18] (Fig. 6). Where Milton's purchase prices survive they too are suggestive: 2s 6d for his Aratus, a comparatively common text, is reasonable; but 5s for his rarer Heraclides, 13s for his finely printed Lycophron, and finally 18s for the grand Paris Chrysostom, the work of the printer to Henri IV, are hefty prices for second-hand texts. (To put this in some Miltonic context, we may recall that in 1645 the Bodleian Library paid 10d first-hand for Milton's *Areopagitica* and 2s for *The Doctrine and Discipline of Divorce*.[19]) What this points to is that wealthy young Milton, regularly collecting his £12 p.a. interest from Richard Powell on the latter's unfortunate bond, was not just a scholar but a bibliophile, something corroborated by the general quality of editions con-sulted for the CPB. (Some of these are still bibliographic treasures: John Guillim's *Display of Heraldry*, for instance, which I suspect Milton owned in its revised 1632 edition, was—despite its manifold typographical blunders—designed to be hand-coloured throughout, and I imagine that Milton's copy, like many other surviving copies, was so completed.) Milton, ever the manipulator of his own image, portrayed himself in this period as secluded in study. True, to a degree; but this was not monastic text-crunching: Milton clearly engaged in some pleasant bibliophily in the metropolis. This, after all, is the Milton who wrote cheerfully from Hammersmith to the younger Gil in late 1634 that Gil should soon expect to meet Milton in London 'among the Booksellers'.[20]

IV. Reading away from home

If we know a good deal about what Milton read in his Hammersmith and Horton period, it is reasonable to ask where he did his reading. Doubtless most of his reading took place at home. But did Milton punctuate his home study with library visits? Milton's letters are full of comments on the value of scholarly company, and as he notes in the *Second Defence* ('exchanging... sometimes the country for the town'), he intermitted his rural solitude with

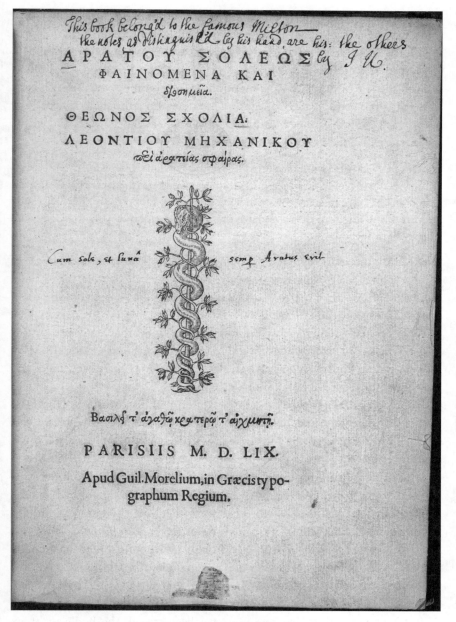

Fig. 6. British Library, C.60.1.7, title page of Aratus's *Phenomena*

trips to learned centres. There is a window of about four years in which Milton lived in semi-rural retirement, but still close enough to London to invite the question of what kind of book provision was available to him to exploit in the capital. One library comes into focus, based on a comment Milton made to Gil in late 1634, mentioning 'our business with that Doctor, this year's President of the College'.[21] That detail on annual elections allows us to identify 'the College' as Sion College, chartered in 1626 and, as its president explained in 1648:

much enlarged by the munificent addition of a Publique *Library*, for the use of all Ministers and ingenious men resorting thither, together with divers chambers to be letten at low rates to Yong men, students in Divinity, and expecting a call to the Ministry, who might in the *interim* have the accommodation of a good Lodging and Library both together.[22]

Was Milton therefore envisaging residing in Sion College for his next phase of study? Sion College library's benefactors book, modelled on that of the Bodleian, shows that many of the earliest gifts were collected editions of patristics, exactly the kind of book Milton was reading in this decade. The earliest printed catalogue was published in 1650, by that date already 162 pages long.[23] But, frustratingly, the library's *album admissorum* skips the years 1633–9, throughout which a separate, lost register may have been used, and Milton is not recorded as a donor to the library.[24]

There were other possibilities outside London. Milton must still have been in good intellectual and literary standing in Cambridge, but Oxford was much nearer, and according to Anthony Wood, who had it 'from [Milton's] own mouth to my friend' (sc. John Aubrey), Milton incorporated his MA at Oxford some time in the academic year 1635–6. Wood believed Aubrey, as he himself knew that John French, the University Registrar, appointed in 1629, had throughout his term of office habitually neglected to enter Cambridge incorporations, and Milton was only one of many so omitted. I think it is therefore reasonable to believe Wood, who had no reason to be friendly towards Milton. More precisely, we may conclude that Milton incorporated in order to use the Bodleian, as he later donated books to the Bodleian, and addressed Latin verse to its librarian. Although no record of Milton's presence there in these years has been traced, the Bodleian, then, is a plausible site for Milton's consultation of rarer or just less portable works.[25]

But the library only two miles or so away from Milton in Horton was the Kedermister Library of Langley or Langley Marish, a few miles out of modern Slough. Milton's period of residence in Horton was first made known to commentators by Edward Phillips in his 1694 Life of his uncle and noted again by Toland in 1698. Writing his account of the poet in 1734, Richardson the Elder also mentions the village.[26] Yet while Milton's connection to Horton was established, his use of the Kedermister Library was not. The first instance I know is Mark Pattison's comment in his *Milton* (1879) that for 'Milton's style of reading, select rather than copious, a large collection is superfluous...Milton can never have possessed a large library. At Horton he may have used Kederminster's [*sic*] bequest to Langley Church.'[27] The Kedermister Library, almost all of which survives in period painted Jacobean furniture, was set up by Sir John Kedermister, who in 1613 was granted a faculty (that is, an ecclesiastical dispensation) to build a room adjoining Langley Church to house a collection of books for the benefit of ministers, local or regional. Although under lay control, the library was therefore clerical in character, 'a miniature college library'. It is still entered today through the Kedermister family's private raised pew, boxed off and with split-cane meshwork windows, adorned within with biblical texts and painted eyes forbiddingly inscribed *deus vidit*. A 1638 manuscript catalogue survives for the collection, allowing reconstruction of the original size and layout of the library annexe, which boasted 307 books on eighteen shelves, for the most part arranged alphabetically. It is one of the oldest non-private libraries in England, alongside the parish library of Bury St Edmonds (1595), the Francis Trigge Library in Grantham (1598), the Ipswich Public Library (1612), and Chetham's Library in Manchester (1653).[28]

The possibility of Milton's use of the library has been exhaustively and judiciously analysed by Edward Jones.[29] Jones's collateral evidence is strong. The terms of Kedermister's will and the subsequent library trust foundation permitted Milton access: the library was open to both county clergy and 'such other in the county of Berks' as were interested. At the Miltons' temporary home, John Milton senior was legally harassed and apparently too ill to travel to London, and his wife was dying; perhaps Milton junior sought some secluded study away from that environment. He certainly described himself to Diodati in 1637 as living 'in obscurity and cramped quarters', and announced his intention to return to London and reside in one of the Inns of Court. The Miltons' local rector was Edward Goodall, like Milton a recent Cambridge graduate, and moreover one with connections to

Milton's childhood tutor Thomas Young. As Jones discovered, the inspection of Bishop Williams resulted in both Goodall and Milton Senior being required to lower their pews, presumably something both men could have interpreted as an insult. Goodall, Jones argues, must surely have recommended to the younger Milton this rarity: a purpose-built research library in the adjoining parish. At any rate, Milton can scarcely have lived in the vicinity for years without learning of its existence.

But what of the evidence from within the library itself? Jones calculated that of the 307 available volumes, twenty-seven titles from sixteen authors could have functioned as sources for eighty-three entries in the CPB. Unfortunately, the rules governing use of the library are not conducive to provenance research: readers were monitored by liveried incumbents of the almshouses built by Kedermister himself nearby for the purpose; no book was to be alienated from the library; and no reader to be left unattended. It is not surprising, therefore, that no Kedermister volume bears marks of Miltonic use.[30] (A few of the texts known to have been present in Milton's time and excerpted by Milton in the CPB—Lactantius, Gower, Holinshed, Purchas—are no longer in the library, so we cannot check these copies.) A more significant problem with the Kedermister thesis is that very few of the Kedermister editions correspond to the ones from which Milton signalled he was taking notes. Jones therefore argued that Milton did not always read one author in one edition at one stretch. This may be so, but it entails that the Kedermister editions, if used, were typically ancillary to the editions to which Milton then referred.[31] But the law of parsimony then applies. If Milton sought out Kedermister for its peace and quiet, we would expect this environment to be especially conducive to note-taking, and not to function as a secondary resource. So while the collateral persuasions are strong, the lack of consistent or even predominant fit between the Kedermister imprints and those referred to by Milton is a serious hurdle for the Kedermister hypothesis. If Milton read in the Kedermister Library we have no record of it. It seems improbable that Milton did not visit this remarkable new institution; but the mismatch of editions supports my earlier hunch: that Milton was a bibliophile who acquired his own editions.

There is a further possibility, however, and as this avenue has never really been investigated fully, I wish to spend some time opening it up. This is nearby Eton College, the one book-rich institution in the vicinity of Horton that we can be sure Milton visited. Eton College possessed a well-stocked library for the fellows, of probably well over a thousand titles by the time of Milton's stay in the vicinity, although there is no reason why Milton would have been given access to this essentially private collection.[32] Milton met the Provost Sir Henry Wotton there in early 1638, and sent him a follow-up letter in April with a copy of A Maske; Wotton's reply so flattered Milton that he exhibited it before A Maske in the 1645 Poems. Only Wotton's reply survives, but in it he identifies the broker of the Eton meeting as the 'learned' 'Mr H.' Now 'Mr H.' may be John Harrison, the Head Master until 1636, who owned a fine private library, rich in both scientific and humanistic texts, to which the very young Robert Boyle, at Eton with his brother from 1635 to 1638, had some access over these years.[33] But 'learned' suggests rather the celebrated John Hales (1584–1656), sometime Regius Professor of Greek at Oxford, and now the 'walking library' of Eton, 'a compendium of colleges and libraries' as Wotton called him.[34] Hales was certainly a man whose acquaintance the young Milton would have been eager to make. He was a famous intellect, a link back to the great scholarly generation of Sir Henry Savile and Sir Thomas Bodley, as the young Hales was employed as a scribe by Bodley's first librarian Thomas James, and when Hales moved to Eton he had worked closely with Savile, Wotton's predecessor, on his celebrated Greek Chrysostom, printed at Eton in eight volumes between 1610 and 1612.[35] Hales himself usually shunned publication, but was already developing in the years before he attended the Synod of Dort his distinctively irenic philosophy, opposed to Calvinist dogmatism, and espousing theological tolerance. He had known poetic and artistic tastes; and Samuel Hartlib also heard that Hales had constructed elaborate anatomical atlases. John Beale, who entered Eton in 1622 and who would become a keen observer of the older Milton, remembered discussing zoological subjects with his tutor Hales. In short, Hales was a celebrated philologist, theologian, casuist, connoisseur, and dabbler in natural philosophy. This was a man to whom Milton must have taken every opportunity to address himself while living nearby.[36]

What follows is pure speculation, but it at least allows me to introduce a new document to literary historians. If Milton's 'Mr H.' was Hales, then Milton may have had some form of access to Hales's private library, the most famous of its time; as Clarendon said of Hales, 'he had made a greater and better collection of books, than were to be found in any other private library that I have seen.'[37] Alas Hales was later forced to disperse the library upon ejection from Eton, and it was bought by the scholarly entrepreneur

Cornelius Bee in 1649 for the huge but apparently still cut-price sum of £700, and I have not been able to establish its subsequent fate.[38] But there exists in the Eton College archives a manuscript shelf-list of a library dating from no earlier than 1624 of around 750 books of exceptional interest, and clearly not the fellows' collection, to which it bears little resemblance. The shelf-list is scribed into the back of the bursarial accounts for 1621, a year in which Hales was himself one of the two bursars. The list is written chiefly in a fine italic hand befitting its largely Latin-language content. But headings, English titles, and the odd telling annotation ('giuen to Mr Bagley'; 'giuen to my brother Francis') are in a secretary hand identifiable as that of Hales himself who used three or even four hands with notable fluency, and there is a probability that this is a shelf-list of Hales's own library as it existed in the mid-1620s in his chambers at Eton. I will proceed on this assumption.[39] Did Milton have access to this library a little over a decade later? By 1623 Hales certainly owned many of the authors Milton was reading in the 1630s.[40]

Hales's own library was already two-and-a-half times the size of the Kedermister collection by the mid-1620s, and presumably grew significantly over the next few decades. His folios covered all the major classical, patristic, and scholastic authors, and he also had interests in medicine, law, mathematics, astronomy, optics, history, geography, numismatics, zoology, and even some contemporary literature, including quite a few French books. Some of his folios were very recent publications, too, for instance Francis Bacon's *The Historie of the Raigne of King Henry the Seventh* (1622), John Selden's edition of Eadmer (1623), and Philip Clüver's *Italia Antiqua* (1624). Hales's quartos and lesser formats are even more interesting. Apart from scores of titles in Reformed-Roman Catholic and Remonstrant-Contraremonstrant polemical divinity, Hales also owned a striking quantity of astronomical and mathematical works, including a stunning nine Kepler texts at a date when Kepler was still alive. Perhaps Hales's most impressive set of books, however, were Socinian imprints, which always tended to smaller formats for ease of concealment. Hales surely boasted the most extensive collection of such books in the British Isles at this date: the Rakov imprints of Smalcius, Völkel, Moscorovius, and Socinus himself, as well as the rebuttals they provoked, bulk large in the lists. Unsurprisingly, these books were accompanied by many Hugo Grotius texts, as the Dutch jurist and theologian attempted to define his position against Contraremonstrants on one side and Socinians on the other. All in all, Hales's library, if it is his, proves to be every bit as exciting as his contemporaries claimed. Perhaps Milton did not work there; perhaps he did not borrow books from Hales; perhaps he only knew of Hales's library by reputation. But if he was granted even only a brief tour of this Eton collection, housed as fifteen very long 'rows' running presumably right across the length of a chamber, he will have had his enthusiasm fired by the connoisseurship and eclecticism of the great Hales of Eton College. Milton, alas, failed to mention in the *Second Defence* this aspect of his rural retreat; but, as Jones has commented, the *otium-negotium* dynamic controlling Milton's apologetic self-presentation of himself in that work perhaps precludes any detailed discussion of intellectual gregariousness; and by the mid-1650s, there was a political gulf separating the two scholars.

V. Reading abroad

In May 1638 Milton departed for the Continent, armed with an introduction to the English ambassador Lord Scudamore at Paris from Wotton himself. There, Milton briefly met the great Grotius, and then headed south for Italy, where, as he assures us, he achieved a certain amount of literary fame. But Milton's continental tour will have provided opportunity for reading, too, as this is how educated travellers passed the time when on the road. We should not see Milton hefting huge folios over the Alps; it seems more likely that he busied himself with smaller format vernacular books, bought en route for the purpose. We certainly know that in Venice Milton shipped home chests—plural—of the books he had accumulated while abroad, just as we know that he toured the Vatican library and inspected some manuscripts in the company of Lucas Holste.[41] His book-chests may have contained titles such as Bernardo Davanzati's very recent *Scisma D'Inghilterra* (in the Florence, 1638, edition; originally Rome, 1602, based on the Englishman Nicholas Sanders's famous *De Origine ac Progressu Schismatis Anglicani* [1585, expanded edition 1586]);[42] the Scots Franciscan George Conn's *De Duplici Statu Religionis apud Scotos Libri Duo* (Rome, 1628), dedicated to Cardinal Barberini as *Magnæ Britanniæ Protector*; and very possibly Galileo's banned *Dialogo Sopra i due Massimi Sistemi del Mondo* (Florence, 1632), because Milton adapted or alluded to their imprimaturs when mocking that practice in *Areopagitica* six years later.[43] Although Milton could easily have used the London booksellers specializing in imports, it is likely that a good proportion of the recent continental imprints cited in the CPB were also purchased abroad, such as the Florence imprints of Villani and Guicciardini, or the Venetian imprints of Boccalini, Dante, Savonarola, Tassoni, and Tasso. One chest also contained musical scores, including the recent works of Monteverdi, Lucca Marenzio, Orazio Vecchi, Antonio Cifra, the wife-murdering prince of Venosa Carlo Gesualdo, 'and several others'. These are part-books rather than scores, and must reflect Milton's continued interest in performing domestic music, and suggest too that the Hammersmith and Horton years were not all silence— Milton surely played and sang with his father and friends, just as he was to teach his nephews to sing upon his return to England. And this was complicated stuff: assuming Milton was purchasing the madrigal-style music for which all these composers were famed, his Marenzio was one or several of Marenzio's books of madrigals in four to six parts, or his *villanelle* for three voices; Monteverdi's various books of madrigals in print by this date employed typically between five and eight parts, the later books with notated continuo too; and Vecchi's various *canzonette* and *madrigali* ranged from three to ten parts, sometimes accompanied.

One enduring question about the continental tour is whether Milton took his CPB with him. There is perhaps a codicological hint here. The manuscript once consisted of 126 folios, numbered in pages from 1 to 250 with an additional folio for the index. The lower halves of pp. 1–14 have been cut away, and the leaves that were once presumably paginated 33–6, 83–98, 207–8, 225–8, 231–4 have been entirely excised. In other words, just over one quarter of the pages has been tampered with in some way *after* pagination had been added. The pagination itself is in Milton's hand, and his index shows that no entries have been lost through these cuts. Given the care not to excise any of the entries, it is plausible that Milton himself made these excisions. And at what better time than while he was travelling, when immediate supplies of paper may have been lacking?[44] This manuscript, therefore, has performed the functionally opposed roles of repository for text and paper stock, possibly at the same time, a bi-functionality necessarily obscured by modern editions. But this must remain the mildest of conjectures, because some careful member of Milton's household may just as easily have made these excisions at a later date, and if Milton did take the manuscript with him abroad, I do not think it received heavy use.

VI. Reading and teaching at home

Milton returned to England in July 1639. Where he initially domiciled is not clear, but he must have found cases of books awaiting him. Soon afterwards, in 1640, he set up as a private schoolteacher in London, lodging first in a tailor's house, and then subsequently moving to a larger property in Aldersgate. His pupils were initially his nephews John and Edward Phillips, but he appears to have taken on some further, unnamed charges too. If we trust the palaeographical consensus on the CPB, then it is to this and to the following few years that we should ascribe Milton's continued reading for the purpose of harvesting moral exempla. Again, this reading can be divided into some subgroups. First, there is a small continuation of patristics and early ecclesiastical history (Lactantius, Cyprian, Sozomen). Secondly, Milton unsurprisingly now spread into later European history: the northern reformation (Sleidan), Italy (Paolo Giovio, Paolo Sarpi); France (de Thou, Girard, de Commines, Gilles); and Britain (Bede, William of Malmesbury, Stow, Holinshed, Speed, du Chesne [writing in French, but on Britain], Camden, Hayward). Milton also read in this period a number of books which are harder to classify, but which have obvious relevance to his intellectual predicament: a sermon of Savonarola, Machiavelli on war, Smith's *De Republica Anglorum*, Lambarde's *Archeion*, Ascham's *Toxophilus*, and, rather interestingly, the *Geneanthropeia*, a brand-new (1642) scholarly sex manual by the Roman physician Giovanni Sinibaldi. Milton excerpted from this book a comment about sex without affection, under the heading 'divorce'. Surely this reference was made after July 1642, when Milton appears to have spent an extremely awkward first night in bed with his bride, Mary Powell.

No doubt this last item was not for teaching to the young Phillips brothers. But what is significant for Milton's reading here is that Edward Phillips much later (1694) recalled in detail the curriculum to which he had been subjected as a mere ten-year-old, and it overlaps significantly with the ideal curriculum detailed in *Of Education* (1644). This suggests that Milton had already practised the punishing curriculum he later preached in *Of Education*. We would be ill-advised to neglect this confluence just because Milton was acting as a teacher and not a pupil; as Edward Phillips himself said, 'Thus by teaching he in some measure increased his own knowledge.'[45] And again the 'Phillips' curriculum reaffirms Milton's basically humanistic outlook. Milton's charges learned the three sacred languages, starting with Latin, and adding some Aramaic and Syriac to their Hebrew. These were supplemented with modern Italian and French. The Latin authors often duplicate those named in *Of Education*, and included Cato, Varro, Columella, Palladius, Celsus, Pliny the Elder, Vitruvius, Frontinus, Lucretius, and Manilius. Greek was studied through the poetic texts of Hesiod, Aratus, Dionysius Periegetes, Oppianus, Smyrnaeus, Apollonius Rhodius; and Greek prose included Plutarch, Geminus, Xenophon, Aelianus Tacticus, and Polyaenus. No doubt from the boys' point of view much of this reading was grammatical and philological in emphasis, but Milton himself was presumably topping up on his knowledge of many less mainstream disciplines, including complex works on medicine (Celsus), strategy (Frontinus, Polyaenus, Aelianus), astronomy/astrology (Manilius, Aratus, Geminus), as well as works on architecture (Vitruvius), farming (Cato, Varro, Columella, Palladius), and fishing and hunting ('Oppianus', each poem now thought to be by a different writer). Teaching modern languages also offered Milton the opportunity to review medieval Florentine history through Giovanni Villani's chronicle, and the set French text Phillips recalled was Pierre d'Avity's geography. To this we should add the quadrivial subjects, covered by the textbooks of Urstitius (a Ramist arithmetician who taught at Basel), Ryff (a Ramist geometrician, also of Basel), Pitiscus (trigonometer, coiner of the term 'trigonometry'), and Sacrobosco (thirteenth-century Aristotelian astronomer), respectable but slightly dated works. Sundays were occupied not only by the Greek New Testament, but also by the taking down from dictation a systematic treatise in theology—the first draft of the *De Doctrina*.[46] Perhaps also to this period we should assign the commencement of Milton's lost Latin dictionary, which he compiled by working through eighteen Latin standard authors, including several he taught to the Phillips boys.[47]

Milton's own reading in the early years of teaching is again represented in the CPB and demonstrates his continuing interest in patristics and in ecclesiastical and political history. But again these entries do not exhaust his reading, and we can pick up from references in the early prose tracts a slightly broader spread of texts: Edwin Sandys's *Relation of a Journey* (first edition, 1621), and Franciscus a Sancta Clara's *Apologia Episcoporum seu Sacri Magistratus* (1640), for instance.[48] Sandys demonstrates that Milton kept abreast of contemporary vernacular travel writing, and we know that Milton began to abstract from Samuel Purchas at some point in the 1640s too.[49] The *Apologia* of Franciscus a Sancta Clara (the name in God of the Franciscan

Christopher Davenport) defended the order of bishops, and was written by a Roman Catholic residing in London, protected by Charles I, and describing himself as *à Sacris* or 'chaplain' to Henrietta Maria.[50] Franciscus was better known for his *Deus, Natura, Gratia* (1634) which attempted a harmonization of the Thirty Nine Articles with Roman Catholic teachings.

VII. Reading at least one clandestine manuscript?

I would like to conclude with one final conjecture regarding Milton's reading in this period. It is right at the upper chronological boundary of this essay, but it may help to complement the perhaps rather conservative image of Milton's reading I have been assembling. The conjecture concerns the most controversial clandestine manuscript of the age, Jean Bodin's *Colloquium Heptaplomeres* (*c*.1593), the 'Colloquium of the Seven', in which seven sages discuss religion, the most powerful voices being assigned not to the Christian speakers, but to a speaker usually described as a 'Deist', and to a Jew. Now it has long been known that Milton possessed certain works in manuscript, including this most explosive text, which Milton subsequently sent to an unnamed friend in Germany in 1662. This friend has plausibly been identified as John Dury.[51] But how and when did Milton get his hands on such a manuscript? Two initial paths suggest themselves. First, it has long been known that Hugo Grotius held a copy of the treatise in 1634–5, at the end of which period he was in Paris, three years before Milton met him there. The second path runs through Henry Oldenburg, with whom Milton later corresponded. Oldenburg encountered a copy of the work in Paris in the summer of 1659, and in a letter to Samuel Hartlib Oldenburg wrote he would attempt to commission a scribal copy. But he confessed that such a job would take a scribe well over a week and would be extremely costly, and it seems unlikely that Oldenburg's copy was ever made.[52] Although Grotius and Oldenburg have biographical connections to Milton, I doubt Milton obtained his manuscript via either of these routes: the early meeting between the great humanist and the aspiring poet was scarcely the right forum for discussing let alone lending or selling clandestine manuscripts; and Oldenburg's manuscript may never even have existed. But there is a third route. Hartlib told John Worthington of Cambridge in 1660 that he himself had once owned a copy of the *Heptaplomeres*. Now, in the course of a strong rebuttal of the recent querying of Bodin's authorship of this work, Noel Malcolm has noted a 1641 London letter of Theodore Haak and Joachim Hübner to Marin Mersenne, in which it is acknowledged that Mersenne has just sent from Paris a copy of the *Heptaplomeres*. As Malcolm comments, 'this episode . . . may perhaps account for the copy later owned by Samuel Hartlib.'[53] Now it may also account for the copy owned by Milton, and suggest a date for its acquisition (or, more likely, composition, as Milton presumably commissioned a copy). Hübner, Haak, Dury, and Hartlib were at this very time confirming their pansophist mission with Jan Amos Comenius in London. Haak and Milton were certainly acquainted, although our earliest reference dates from 1648.[54] But Hartlib and Milton were soon to become close enough, at least for a short time, for the former to commission Milton's *Of Education* (1644). Of these three routes for Milton to acquire the *Heptaplomeres*, this new possibility seems most persuasive. Hartlib was presumably rather disappointed by Milton's *Of Education*, an intellectually unstable amalgam of a modernizing French academy for aristocratic youths, nourished on a reactionary textual diet of solely classical, traditional authors.[55] But it is a pleasing irony of Milton's early reading that the commissioning and writing of *Of Education* may be embroiled in Milton's acquisition of a copy of Bodin's most notorious work.

VIII. Conclusions

There are several different types of conclusion we can draw from all of this. First, Milton was of course a heavy reader, but it must be confessed too that he was a somewhat conventional historian in both method and scope. In an age of antiquarian innovation, sticking to a curriculum of big printed editions of established texts, Milton displayed no interest at all in documentary sources. In this he was slightly reactionary, keener on ploughing the accepted corpus of historians in the manner of Wheare and the older *ars historica* than in the new historical school which took its cue from the chorographical tradition of William Camden, and which was turning away from print, and towards the manuscript, the monument, and the coin.[56] Perhaps it is a little unkind to assess Milton on the evidence of the CPB alone, which is rather tied to curricular practice, but his eventual performance in *The History of Britain* tends to confirm that Milton was content to appear in print in 1671 as a rather old-school historian. In 1691 Anthony Wood waspishly complained as much in the *Fasti*: in an age of documentary compendia, Milton's work was a patchwork of previous printed publications, and was largely greeted as such.[57] In 1657, I grant, Milton could arrange access to manuscripts in private hands, as well as in the semi-public resources of the Cotton Library and the Tower.[58] But he does not appear to have had much interest in such resources himself, even before his blindness. Another way of putting this is that Milton did not really possess what we might call the 'common law' mentality underpinning much of the new antiquarianism, preferring instead the older humanist philological and philosophical approaches.

Next, we might ask if a close study of Milton's reading in this period suggests any new avenues for research. One direction is that if Milton read all of the books from which he excerpted in the CPB from cover to cover, then we might look for ideas in Milton's authors that appear to have influenced his thought but which were not themselves relevant to the CPB in moral philosophy, and hence not noted there by Milton. This is necessarily a huge and hazy area, but one example may suffice to show the kind of results I envisage. We know from the CPB that Milton read Lactantius's *De Ira Dei*. He was probably reading this text carefully at about the time he commenced the *De Doctrina* with the Phillips boys. Now the general thesis of Lactantius's work—not discernible through the quotations Milton recorded in the CPB—is that God does indeed feel anger. Lactantius's argument is that God must be capable of feeling anger if he is to be said to love: either God feels many emotions, or he feels none, and as we know God is a God of love, then he must of necessity be a fully emotionalized being. Now this argument, which to seventeenth-century theologians was a clear example of the mistake of anthropopathy, or the ascribing of human emotions to God, obviously influenced Milton in the *De Doctrina*, where he boldly endorses a God who gets angry, who hates, and who even fears. Milton is (therefore) at pains to classify these emotions as void in God of their human negativity, and so not strictly an example of anthropopathy, but the basic principle is clear: God feels emotions of a kind.[59] Lactantius argued as a philosopher against the philosophers, whereas Milton wrote as a biblical exegete against the biblical exegetes, to be sure; but I find it hard to believe that Milton was not digesting his reading of Lactantius at this point of the *De Doctrina*. This offers us one interesting example, therefore, of Milton's real engagement with heterodox patristic writing, even as he was declaring in the anti-prelatical pamphlets how tedious and unprofitable patristic scholarship was.[60]

The final type of conclusion is a comment on Milton's own intellectual development. A reappraisal of his research in the decisive 1630s offers us a perhaps unwittingly conflicted Milton. It is important to recognize that Milton, gradually cooling towards a clerical future, was a comparatively rich young man, with a tolerant, moneyed father, a lucrative investment port-folio, freedom from professional work, expensive tastes in books, fluent Latin and Italian, good Greek, competent reading French, Spanish, and Hebrew, with a bit of Syriac and Aramaic, a talented polyglot with foreign friends, at home with some Oxford and Eton and even slight aristocratic connections, great intellectual ambition, and a strongly cosmopolitan mentality. He thought of himself more as a late (but not a belated) humanist rather than an inchoate revolutionary. The Milton of the 1630s is therefore not a knowingly subversive figure. His reading was not a corrective to but a continuation of his university study, and the notion that Milton was forging his own innovative intellectual trajectory in this period must be resisted.

Nevertheless, we should not go too far down that route. Milton had an exceptionally strong sense of his own intellectual power and independence, even at this point, and it is uncanny just how well his 1630s research fed into his 1640s writing. So many of his CPB entries were deployed in his later prose that we must declare the CPB 'weaponized'; and in consequence we must conclude too that Milton, as an intelligent observer of 1630s politics, intuited a great deal of what was coming. In the 1645 headnote to 'Lycidas', Milton famously says that his 1637 composition 'foretells' the ruin of the clergy, granting the reader present-tense access to an earlier moment of prophecy, sealed as such by its fulfilment. Now either we allow Milton his wonted prophetic status; or, more realistically, we acknowledge that he perceived to some extent where the now eight-year-old Personal Rule was tending. But I doubt that when he turned himself to 'moral philosophy teaching by examples' Milton really knew that it would soon come to captain and colonel and knight-at-arms. All the same, Milton in his late twenties worried about tyrants and about liberty; and it is vain to deny that these were merely scholarly concerns to him until, say, 1637, and the Prynne,

Bastwick, and Burton mutilations. Indeed, if we must seek an earlier pressure-point for Milton, should it not be the incarceration and near-mutilation of Gil in 1628, an admired older friend and teacher of Milton, and a formidable neo-Latin poet?[61] If Milton became radicalized, I do not think it can have been so sudden. My own feeling is that Milton was an intellectual radical before he was a practical radical, and when he was reviled as the latter without respect to the former he was horrified. For he did not think of himself as straying away from a political centre; ever the moralizing scholar, he rather envisaged crown policy as having done so, and therefore being in need of just correction. The fact that this genuine, bookish radicalism could arise out of an (almost) impeccably conservative reading programme is surely the point of lasting interest.

We need to reconnect to this bookish Milton, the almost accidental radical. Milton himself, I think, tried to reconnect too: his somewhat naïve trajectory from 'solidarity' anti-prelate to solitary divorcer was met with public scorn; and, alienated by those for whom he had first placed his pen in his left hand, Milton tried to reaffirm his freedom to be various with the 1645 *Poems*, a curious cacophony of radical and conservative voices, anxious to promote both his precocity and prophecy. Milton certainly never backed off: his reaction to the reception of the first edition of *The Doctrine and Discipline of Divorce*—expanded republication—is an odd mixture of courageous defiance and career suicide. Likewise in the 1645 *Poems*, Milton wanted to have it both ways: 'Lycidas' hunts the clergy in a manner that cannot be tamed as mere pastoral convention, and the austerity of the Nativity Ode is that of a 'precise' young man; yet his masquery for aristocrats, his elegizing of Laudian bishops, his rather hearty Cambridge student poetry, his parading of the courtly Wotton and the learned Mr *H.* as fans of Promising Young Milton, cannot be disregarded either. Milton became a radical, but he did so by mutating his own views incrementally from a broadly orthodox reading programme—a body which perhaps contained all the 'radicalism' Milton would ever need.

Notes

I am grateful to Gordon Campbell, Thomas Fulton, Edward Jones, and Nicholas McDowell for their comments on a draft of this chapter. Some of the material I present here will appear in the forthcoming edition of the CPB and the Outlines for Tragedies for the Clarendon Milton (in vols. ix, xi); and I draw too on my 'The Genres of Milton's Commonplace Book', in Nicholas McDowell and Nigel Smith (eds.), *The Oxford Handbook of Milton* (Oxford, 2009), 367–81. The Eton College angle

explored below was first rehearsed as a paper delivered to the Young Milton conference held at Worcester College, Oxford, 2009. This chapter has been written with
Gordon Campbell's *Chronology* at my side.

1. 'Mr Locke's Extemporè Advice &c.' in John Locke, *Some Thoughts Concerning Education*, ed. John W. Yolton and Jean S. Yolton (Oxford, 1989), 319.
2. Campbell and Corns, 67–102.
3. The reading referenced in that manuscript consists of the chronicles of William of Malmesbury, Raphael Holinshed, John Speed, Eusebius's *De Præparatione Evangelii* (probably from the collected *Historiae Ecclesiasticae Scriptores Graeci* [Geneva, 1612]), and Ludovicus Lavaterus's *In Libros Paralipomenon sive Chronicorum Commentarius* (Zurich, 1573; 2nd edn. Heidelberg, 1600). See *CPW*, viii. 555, 556, 569f.
4. 'Letter to a Friend' in John Milton, *Poems, Reproduced in Facsimile from the Manuscript in Trinity College, Cambridge, with a Transcript* (Menston, 1970), 6–7. The recipient is usually con-jectured to be Thomas Young, but Milton otherwise wrote to his old tutor in Latin.
5. John T. Shawcross, 'A Survey of Milton's Prose Works', in Michael Lieb and John T. Shawcross (eds.), *Achievements of the Left Hand: Essays on the Prose of John Milton* (Amherst, Mass., 1974), 291–391 at 371.
6. Mordechai Feingold, 'The Humanities', in Nicholas Tyacke (ed.), *The History of the University of Oxford IV: The Seventeenth Century* (Oxford, 1997), 306–27; Poole, 'Genres of Milton's Commonplace Book' *passim*.
7. Gordon Campbell, 'Milton's *Index Theologicus* and Bellarmine's *Disputationes de Contro-versiis Christianae Fidei Adversus Huius Temporis Haereticos*', *Milton Quarterly*, 11 (1977), 12–16.
8. Feingold, 'The Humanities', 327–57 and also 317 for the use of history in moral philosophy.
9. Degory Wheare, *The Method and Order of Reading Both Civil and Ecclesiastical Histories*, trans. Edmund Bohum (1685), 16–18. This is based on Wheare's expanded *Relectiones Hyemales* of 1637.
10. Wheare, *Method*, 20.
11. *CPW*, i. 889–93.
12. Wheare, *Method*, 320, quoting from Juan Luìs Vives, *De Disciplinis* (1612), 352. These sentiments were of course conventional: compare Thomas Blundeville, *The True Order and Methode of Wryting and Reading Hystories* (1574), sigs. Fiv–iir, and cp. sigs. [Hiii] r–[Hivr] on commonplacing.
13. Wheare, *Method*, 322–4, 341.
14. See the corroborative evidence provided by Milton's correspondence in *CPW*, i. 319, 323, 327.
15. See *CPW*, iii. 198.
16. *CPW*, vii. 497–8.
17. Although 1544 might strike us as a rather old imprint, it was in fact the second of only three texts available to Milton (1505, 1544, 1586), of which the third was only published as an appendix to an edition of Homer (*Héraclite: Allégories d'Homère*, ed. and trans. Félix Buffière (Paris, 1962), xliii). There is a cross-connection to Dio Chrysostom here, as Milton's Heraclides also contained in translation Dio's oration on Homer.

18. British Library, C 60. l. 7. This book is in its Miltonic binding, elegant without being luxurious, with gold-tooling on the spine, but simple blind-tooling on the panels. The style of four frames of fillets on the panels is a recognizable Cambridge style of the early seventeenth century; Milton presumably therefore had it rebound there.

19. Bodleian Library, MS Lib. recs. b 36.

20. *CPW*, i. 322; cf. the remarks on 324 to Diodati on booksellers Milton obviously knows personally.

21. *CPW*, i. 322.

22. Cornelius Burges, *Sion College, What It Is, and Doeth* (1648), 4.

23. John Spencer, *Catalogus Universalis . . . Collegii Sionii* (1650). It lists editions of all the 'early' Commonplace Book authors (on these authors see note 40), bar Holinshed.

24. Lambeth Palace Library, Sion College Manuscripts, Arc L 40.2/E 29, covering the years 1632, 1640–66, 1671–93. Another library just possibly open to Milton was the Royal Library, significantly augmented by Prince Henry's collection after the young prince's death in 1612. Its librarian from that year was Patrick Young (1584–1652), who may have been one of Milton's teachers, and was certainly his acquaintance (see Campbell and Corns, 389n42). At some point after 1645 Milton presented Young with a bound collection of ten of his tracts (now Trinity College, Dublin, R.dd.39). That Young taught Milton rests on Francis Junius's comment to Isaac Vossius that Milton was 'discipulum *Patricii Junii*', an odd mistake, if it be so, for '*Thomæ*' coming from one whose own Latinized surname was Junius (*Sylloges Epistolarum*, ed. Peter Burmannus [Leiden, 1727]), iii. 168). But it is unlikely Milton was allowed to use this library for any intense or extended work.

25. Anthony Wood, *Athenæ Oxonienses/Fasti Oxonienses*, ed. Phillip W. Bliss, 2 vols. (Oxford, 1691–2), i. cols. 480–6 (biography from Aubrey), 452 (French's carelessness). Unfortunately Aubrey's own manuscript life does not mention the Oxford incorporation. I argue *pace* William R. Parker, 'Wood's Life of Milton: Its Sources and Significance', *Papers of the Bibliographical Society of America*, 52 (1958), 1–22.

26. Darbishire, 55, 88, and 256.

27. Mark Pattison, *Milton* (1909 [1879]), 44.

28. Jane Francis, 'The Kedermister Library: An Account of Its Origins and a Reconstruction of Its Contents and Arrangement', *Records of Buckinghamshire*, 36 (1994), 62–85, with a transcript of the 1638 catalogue; for a summary with illustrations of the library and its church environs, see *Sir John Kederminster's Library* (Langley, 1999).

29. Edward Jones, '"Filling in a Blank in the Canvas": Milton, Horton, and the Kedermister Library', *Review of English Studies*, 53 (2002), 31–60. The documentary claims made below are referenced by Jones.

30. A couple of the books Jones proposed as potentially handled by Milton do contain marks of ownership or readership (the 1589 Antwerp Cyprian and the 1617 Cologne Tertullian), but these are pre-Kedermister markings, and certainly not Miltonic. A few other books in the library bear interesting annotations, e.g., a 1542 Paris Theophylact, but these are again typically pre-Kedermister markings; there is very little evidence of book marking or even use *in situ*.

31. At Kedermister, the 1611 Basel *Historia Ecclesiastica*, the 1616 Leiden Clement, the 1589 Antwerp Cyprian, the 1617 Cologne Tertullian, the undated and missing Lactantius, the 1612 Bede in three volumes, the undated and missing Holinshed, Brent's English translation of Sarpi, the (presumably 1625) missing Purchas, and the missing 1532 Gower might all have furnished Milton with the texts we know he read of these authors; but barring the missing books, no edition present today unproblematically matches those from which Milton took his notes. A point of comparison is perhaps offered by the Town Library of Ipswich, which held *opera omnia* of all these authors, bar the unecclesiastical Holinshed, Sarpi, and Gower; see John Blatchly (ed.), *The Town Library of Ipswich* (Woodbridge, 1989).

32. Sir Robert Birley, *The History of Eton College Library* (Eton, 1970), esp. 26–31. I base the estimate on Eton's earliest surviving catalogue, an interleaved copy of the Bodleian 1674 Hyde, maintained for the next two decades, and into which were entered over 1,600 titles.

33. Sir Wasey Sterry, *The Eton College Register, 1441–1698* (Eton, 1943), 45; Robert Birley, 'Robert Boyle's Head Master at Eton', *Notes and Records of the Royal Society of London*, 13 (1958), 104–14.

34. Parker, i. 147, ii. 808; Campbell and Corns, 104.

35. Milton cited Chrysostom in Latin, probably from a parallel edition, but it is tempting to speculate that he acquired the famous, but solely Greek, edition of Eton, not least because after Savile's death Eton College was selling off copies for only a third of the initial asking-price, down from £9 to £3.

36. The standard study of Hales is still James Elson, *John Hales of Eton* (New York, 1948), but see most recently the judicious Jean-Louis Quantin, *The Church of England and Christian Antiquity: The Construction of a Confessional Identity in the Seventeenth Century* (Oxford, 2009), 209–13.

37. Cited in John Hales, *Works*, 3 vols. (Glasgow, 1765), i. xi.

38. Hartlib Papers, 28/1/32A.

39. Eton College Records 62/55. The secretary portions may be compared to Hales's various autographs, e.g., Bodleian MS Savile 47, fo. 39r; Bodleian MS Ballard 1, fos. 36r–37v. Scott Mandelbrote and I are preparing an edition and study of this important booklist. Although the list is certainly in Hales's hand, it should be stressed that it is as yet probable rather than certain that it represents his own collection; we might note, for instance, that the Provost of Eton, Thomas Murray, died in 1623, and Hales's list contains three gifts to a 'Charles Murray', although Hales's list does not otherwise look like a chattels inventory at all. See Elson, *John Hales*, 18.

40. If, for instance, we take the eleven authors (I lump all the ecclesiastical historians together) employed by Jones to test the Kedermister hypothesis, then Hales lists over half the relevant authors: *Eusebij &c. Ecclesiastica Historia. GræcoLat.*; *Clemens Alexandrinus Gr. Lat.*; *Cypriani Opera.*; *Tertullianus Junij.*; *Bedæ Opera. vol: 3bus.*; *Cypriani Opera.* (Alas Hales does not specify editions.) Hales does not list Lactantius, Gower, Holinshed, Sarpi, or Purchas; but Sarpi had only just been published, in 1619; and Purchas was as yet unprinted when this shelf-list was made.

41. *CPW*, v. pt. 1, 619; Darbishire, 21, 38, 59, 95; *CPW*, i. 798–805. Book-collecting on one's grand tour was a well-established habit: see the examples in John Stoye, *English Travellers Abroad, 1604–1667*, rev. edn. (New Haven, Conn., 1989), 42, 105, 298–301, 317.

42. See William Shullenberger, '"Imprimatur": The Fate of Davanzati', in Mario Di Cesare (ed.), *Milton in Italy: Contexts, Images, Contradictions* (Binghampton, N.Y., 1991), 175–96.

43. Leo Miller, 'The Italian Imprimaturs in Milton's *Areopagitica*', *Papers of the Bibliographical Society of America*, 65 (1971), 345–55. It is striking that Milton cites real imprimaturs affixed to studies of specifically Scottish and English history: he obviously set out to locate and presumably purchase (hostile) continental works on the British situation.

44. Thomas Fulton, *Historical Milton: Manuscript, Print, and Political Culture in Revolutionary England* (Amherst, Mass., 2010), 64n74.

45. Darbishire, 60.

46. *CPW*, iv. 614.

47. Anon, revising Adam Littleton *et al.*, *Linguæ Romanæ Dictionarium Luculentum Novum: A New Dictionary in Five Alphabets* (Cambridge, 1693), sig. A2r, where the use and content of Milton's three-volume manuscript dictionary are detailed. It is impossible now to extract from the dictionary its Miltonic ingredient.

48. *CPW*, i. 527, 553.

49. Hartlib Papers, 32/21/21A.

50. On the work, see John Berchmans Dockery, *Christopher Davenport: Friar and Diplomat* (1960), 96–7.

51. Louis I. Bredvold, 'Milton and Bodin's *Heptaplomeres*', *Studies in Philology*, 21 (1924), 399–402. We may recall, too, that Milton also owned the pseudo-Ralegh 'Cabinet Council' Manuscript, which he published in 1658.

52. R. H. Popkin, 'The Dispersion of Bodin's *Dialogues* in England, Holland, and Germany', *Journal of the History of Ideas*, 49 (1988), 157–60.

53. Noel Malcolm, 'Jean Bodin and the Authorship of the *Colloquium Heptaplomeres*', *Journal of the Warburg and Courtauld Institutes*, 69 (2006), 95–150 at 102n34, reference to Marin Mersenne, *Correspondance*, gen. ed. Cornelis de Waard, 17 vols. (Paris, 1932–88). See x. 727 (letter of 29 August 1641).

54. Hartlib Papers, 32/21/21A.

55. Timothy Raylor, 'Milton, the Hartlib Circle, and the Education of the Aristocracy', in Nicholas McDowell and Nigel Smith (eds.), *The Oxford Handbook of Milton* (Oxford, 2009), 382–406.

56. Graham Parry, *The Trophies of Time: English Antiquarians of the Seventeenth Century* (Oxford, 1995), and classically Arnaldo D. Momigliano, 'Ancient History and the Antiquarian' (1950), in *Studies in Historiography*, 13 (1966/69), 1–39.

57. Wood, *Athenæ Oxonienses/Fasti Oxonienses*, i. col. 883.

58. *CPW*, vii. 497–8.

59. *CPW*, vi. 134–6.

60. *CPW*, i. 568, 626.

61. A point also made by Nicholas McDowell, 'The Caroline Court', in Stephen B. Dobranski (ed.), *Milton in Context* (Cambridge, 2010), 237–47 at 240–1.

3

Milton and the Confessionalization of Antiquarianism

Thomas Roebuck

In *Of Reformation*, Milton famously distinguished between '*Antiquaries*, whose labours are useful and laudable' and '*Antiquitarians*' who are the 'hinderers of Reformation'. By 'antiquaries' Milton probably meant the figures associated with the recovery and renewal of national histories, through an analysis of documents, physical artefacts, monuments, coins, and so on.[1] This massively complex and diverse European movement was intimately related to the development of humanist philology: as humanists (like Lorenzo Valla) developed means of analysing language as a historically situated phenomenon, so too antiquaries developed means of extracting historical context from their objects of study.[2] Humanist antiquarianism is a phenomenon that was central to the culture in which the young Milton was educated. The evidence from Cambridge probate inventories shows how popular antiquarian books were in the university in the late sixteenth and seventeenth centuries.[3] Milton's interest in history has, however, been surprisingly little studied, outside a preoccupation among some critics with millenarian and apocalyptic modes of thought.[4] This is where a book on the young Milton is particularly helpful: Milton's historical reading may not be the key to understanding *Paradise Lost* or *Samson Agonistes*, but antiquarian, historical modes of thought are characteristic of the young Milton. In particular,

I want to frame a detailed treatment of Milton's early historical reading and writing with two speculative questions: why does Milton say he wants to write an epic about King Arthur? And why does he abandon this project? This essay will offer some context in which these questions might be answered. It will contend that young Milton, the Milton up until around 1642, was preoccupied with history and antiquarianism, interests made evident by surveying Milton's reading in these fields, particularly focusing on his Commonplace Book (hereafter CPB). Moreover, a fresh account of the role of historical methodologies in the debates on episcopacy in the early 1640s can reveal how Milton began to distinguish his role in this controversy from that of the Smectymnuans: he did so because of the ways his modes of historical thought were developing throughout the controversy.

I. Milton and the Arthurian epic

In his two longest and most substantial Latin poems, *Epitaphium Damonis* and *Mansus*, Milton outlines his plan to write an epic poem on King Arthur, his defence of the British, and his conquest of the Saxons. In *Mansus*, Milton's neo-Latin poem in imitation of Tasso, written in 1638 for the Italian neo-Latinist Giovanni Battista Manso, he plans to *indigenas revocabo in carmina reges* ('to recall my native kings in songs', 80).[5] Particularly he would tell of King Arthur, and Milton imagines himself in this poem *[f]rangam Saxonicas Britonum sub Marte phalanges* ('smashing the Saxon phalanxes under a British Mars', 84).[6] *Epitaphium Damonis* (1639), Milton's pastoral elegy for his friend Charles Diodati, reveals the projected Arthurian epic in more detail (162–8). It would feature the crossing of the Trojan Brutus into Britain, the rules of the ancient British kings (drawn from Geoffrey of Monmouth), the assimilation of the 'Armoricos' (inhabitants of Brittany) to the Trojan-British rule, and finally the birth of Arthur. Both of these long poems appear as the concluding works in the *Poemata*, Milton's Latin counterpoint to the first book of vernacular poems published with them in 1645. The Latin poems revisit matters from the first book: *Epitaphium Damonis*, for instance, forms a pair with 'Lycidas', the pastoral elegy which concludes the vernacular poems.

In both poems, historical modes of description are prevalent, particularly the tradition of neo-Latin chorographic poetry: verse which describes history as it is embedded in the landscape. This tradition, in England, reaches back to the first Englishman to be described as an 'antiquary', John Leland, whose *Cygnea Cantio* describes English history in the context of a swan's river journey.[7] *Epitaphium Damonis*'s debt to chorographic writing can be seen in the transition between the description of Milton's projected British epic (162–8) to the contextualization of his own life and writings within the many rivers and waters of Britain (175–8). He imagines his reputation echoing across the rivers that designate important boundary points in ancient Britain: the *Orcades*, the most northerly point of Britain as described in Tacitus's *Agricola*; the *Abra*, or Humber, a key battle-line between the British and invaders from northern Europe; the *Tamara*, a point beyond which the British retreated after Saxon invasions; and, most of all, the *Thamesis*, the centre of the Roman military occupation of Britain.[8] In *Mansus*, Milton describes an ancient British land, where druids are imagined reciting poems about *Corinëida Loxo*, the daughter of Corineus, king of Cornwall in Geoffrey of Monmouth (42–8). Druids are themselves here seen as poet-historians, the preservers of oral history.[9] So these poems not only describe a British epic, but also borrow modes from historical writing and substantive matter from ancient British history. They themselves constitute mini-epics on British-historical subject matter.

But in early-modern historiography, confessional issues are always to the fore: what kind of primitive church existed in Britain? how far is that church a model for present practice? The best way into understanding the relevance of this question to Milton's Latin poetry is through Giovanni Battista Manso's short epigram for Milton that was reprinted as part of the *Testimonia* at the opening of the *Poemata* (1645):

Ut mens, forma, decor, facies, mos, si pietas sic,
Non Anglus, verum hercle Angelus ipse fores.

In Lawrence Revard's recent translation this reads: 'If your piety were such as your mind, figure, grace, appearance, manners, then not an Angle but, by Hercules, an angel you would be.'[10] This little epigram can be read in a complex dialogue with Milton's *Mansus*. Manso's pun (*Anglus* into *Angelus*) is drawn from an episode in Bede's *Historia Ecclesiastica Gentis Anglorum*. Bede tells of Pope Gregory I seeing boys at a slave-market, and on discovering that they were English, he quipped that were they Christians they would be *Non Angli, sed angeli* ('Not Angles, but angels'). This was the moment, according to Bede, which inspired Gregory to send Augustine's mission to convert the English, and Augustine later became the first Archbishop of Canterbury.[11] So Manso's epigram figures Milton as one of the beautiful heathen slaves Gregory sees: capable of being converted from his Protestantism to Catholicism and so becoming an *Angelus*, but currently merely an *Anglus*. This witty and erudite joke with a serious purpose adumbrates the confessional conflicts which are at stake in differing treatments of British history. Manso's epigram privileges Bede's account of history in which the Pope sends an (obviously Catholic) bishop to convert the heathen Saxons. This is the key moment of transformation of the British Isles into a land whose people follow the Christian faith. It is therefore understandable that Counter-Reformation polemicists in the sixteenth century privileged Bede's account as the definitive document for the history of the British church. The clearest example here is the Catholic Thomas Stapleton's 1565 Antwerp translation of Bede as *The History of the Church of Englande*, which features a polemical preface describing the 'Differences betweene the Primitiue Faithe of England Continewed Almost these thousand yeares, and the late pretensed [sic] faith of protestants: gathered out of the History of the churche of England compiled by Venerable Bede an English man, aboue DCCC. yeares paste' (sig. 3v).[12] Manso's epigram invokes Bede's role as a polemical weapon in Counter-Reformation debates.

Milton's invocation of Arthur and British history more broadly has, therefore, a subtly inflected polemical edge—especially in the context of Manso's epigram. Milton plunges more deeply into British history, travelling back to a primitive time before Augustine's conversion of the Saxons.[13] The first chapter of Matthew Parker's *De Antiquitate Britannicae Ecclesiae* (1572), *De Vetustate Britannicae Ecclesiae Testimonia*, argues that after the conversion of the ancient British (pre-Saxon) inhabitants to Christianity, the *British nunquam postea desciuisse ad veteres gentium errores* ('never afterwards withdrew to the old errors of the people').[14] Moreover, this was an especially pure kind of Christianity because it derived most closely from Christ himself: the Apostles had directly converted the British to Christianity. So in conflicts between Protestants in England and Catholics abroad this sort of ancient British history (or perhaps, better, pseudo-history) was immensely useful. It allowed the British to claim a priority for their church, and hence a doctrinal superiority, which the European Catholic church could not claim. So any British epic Milton wrote would always be a religiously polemical epic. In some respects, this is fine: Milton was, of course, one of the most famous polemicists of his day. But Milton was writing in very fast-changing circumstances. In the 1630s polemic might mainly have been anti-Catholic polemic. But in the 1640s, polemic was definitively targeted against the dominant wing of the English church itself. Milton's polemic turned inwards. And in that period, too, Milton embarked on a huge programme of historical study. To contextualize why Milton might have abandoned his British epic—why circumstances had rendered it inappropriate or irrelevant—we need to follow Milton's reading in history very carefully. It is this reading to which we now turn.

II. Young Milton's encounters with history

Milton would have been no stranger to antiquarian, historical writing from the time he was at school onwards. Various figures in his milieu had connections to the world of history writing. Milton was taught at St Paul's by Alexander Gil the Elder. Gil contributed a commendatory poem to John Speed's *Theatre for the Empire of Great Britaine* (1611), one of the most important works of chorographic history published in the early seventeenth century. Gil was himself interested in history: in the preface to his celebrated *Logonomia Anglica*, he attempted to provide a historical account of language change, which took into account the pressure of war and violent rupture on language.[15] At Oxford, Milton's great friend Charles Diodati contributed to the University's volume of elegies for William Camden.[16]

Milton's CPB is a record of his reading in the late 1630s and 1640s. However, it is not an unproblematic, transparent record, and we need to sketch briefly what kind of book this is. First of all, this book does not seem to constitute Milton's 'notes on reading' from the 1630s: it seems much more likely to constitute 'notes on notes on reading'. The guides to commonplace-book keeping available in the seventeenth century (brilliantly analysed by Ann Blair) recommended the keeping of not only rough notes from reading, but also at least one distilled collection of that reading, under subject headings. The analogy was often made to the financial ledgers of accountants, one which might record income and expenditure on a transaction-by-transaction basis, the other which would synthesize the totals (at the end of the day, for instance).[17] Secondly, this is a work of moral philosophy, as its three subject headings of 'Ethics', 'Politics', and 'Economics' would have immediately signalled to any good Cambridge-educated boy from the period.[18] In particular, the CPB reflects Milton's reading in history. Two kinds of history are represented: civil and ecclesiastical. It is important to note first of all that, although modern historians of historiography frequently either work on antiquarianism (broadly meaning British history) or on church history, few scholars are familiar with both fields. This was not a division of labour which would have been appreciated in the seventeenth century. Degory Wheare's *De Ratione et Methodo Legendi utrasque Historias, Civiles et Eccelsiasticas* (Oxford, 1637) was one of the most popular and influential guides in the seventeenth century to the order in which historians should be read.[19] The work initially guides the reader through primary and secondary materials relating to British history, advising that the reader should begin by looking at some of the key secondary studies, especially Camden's *Britannia*, and move on to the primary materials afterwards. In Section 32 of the work, Wheare then introduces the *Ad Historiam Ecclesiasticam Transitio*, and recommends beginning by studying the early church through reading the major sixteenth-century church historians, such as Baronius, before moving on to Eusebius and others.[20] So it is important to separate Milton's reading into two groups, civil and ecclesiastical, while remembering that both are parts of a larger programme of historical reading.

In civil history, we have works on British history, especially Holinshed's *Chronicles* (1589), Speed's *Theatre for the Empire of Great Britain* (1611), and Camden's *Annales . . . Regnante Elizabetha* (1615). It is useful to distinguish such contemporary secondary literature on British history from Milton's reading in the sources of British history, which includes works such as Bede's *Historia Ecclesiastica* and William of Malmesbury's *De Gestis Regum Anglorum*.[21] Milton was also filling in his knowledge of contemporary European history, particularly with Jacques de Thou's *Historia sui Temporis* (Geneva, 1620), the second most frequently cited work. The majority of his reading, however, was in church history, and we can group that reading into several clusters. The first is works concerned with the ancient Christian church. In this area, he read both primary source documents (the early fathers themselves) and early ecclesiastical historians. In the primary source documents, we have several of the important early fathers represented: Ignatius, Basil, Tertullian, Justin Martyr, and Cyprian.[22] He also read all the significant early church historians, who continued one another's works: Eusebius, the first ecclesiastical historian, was followed by Socrates, Theodoret, Sozomen, and Evagrius. Milton probably encountered all these historians in Greek in a single volume: *Ecclesiasticae Historiae Autores* (Paris, 1544). Later Byzantine church historians, such as Procopius, reflect another cluster, and one which begins to overlap with political and civil history. Finally, many of the major works relating to the history of the Reformation are represented, including Johannes Sleidan's *Ioan. Sleidani Commentarii de Statu Religionis et Reipublicae* (Strasburg, 1555) and Paolo Sarpi's history of the Council of Trent.[23]

There has been much excellent work which attempts to ascertain the order in which Milton read these works, and on which libraries he might have used to read them.[24] But to make an assessment of the kinds of historicism which interested the young Milton, and which he was preparing to practise in his poetry and prose, we need to think briefly about how he read the works in his CPB. The structuring of notes under headings mitigates against detailed engagement with historical context or even historical narrative. The entries in the CPB frequently read like historical exempla, fragmented from their original context. So although we can see from the book that Milton was attempting a systematic reading of civil and ecclesiastical history in this period, it does not really prepare us for the kind of engagement with the processes of historical transmission, and the corruption of that tradition, which we find in a work like *Of Prelatical Episcopacy.*[25]

This sort of engagement with historical process and context is further mitigated against by the fact that it seems very likely that Milton was using the technologies of information storage and retrieval provided by the editions he was using. This has not really been stressed sufficiently before by Miltonists: while Milton *may* have read the whole of the church fathers, say, all the way through, the CPB alone does not suggest this. There are two clear examples from the CPB of this sort of use of finding aids within books which should be mentioned here briefly: one is Milton's use of Fronton du Duc's edition of Basil in parallel Greek and Latin; the second is Milton's use of Nicholas Rigault's edition of Tertullian.[26] Milton cites Basil's distinction between a king and a tyrant: 'the one considers at every point his own advantage, the other provides what is helpful to his subjects.'[27] If we look up this reference in Basil, we can see that the editors have already marked this little *sententia* in the margin: *Tyrannus a Rege quid Differt* (I.456). It is not significant here that Basil is an early Greek father, that he invented monasticism, or anything else much about the historical context of his writing. This is a memorable phrase, already invited to be extracted from Basil's corpus by the editors of the Paris edition. The second instance of Milton's possible use of such finding technologies can be seen in his engagement with Tertullian. There are four references to Tertullian. Two are to the same work, *De Spectaculis*, a book which Milton clearly has read all the way through and thought about because he paraphrases it.[28] However, the other two notes are rather more opportunistic. One is on 'gluttony' (*gula*), which Tertullian describes as a 'man-slayer' (*homicida*). Milton gives the specific page reference to Rigault's edition for this (703). There is no necessary connection between Tertullian and writing about gluttony: this is once again a historically decontextualized *sententia*. It is very likely to have been retrieved by Milton using Rigault's index, in which we find several entries under *gula*, one of which is specifically *gula homicida* (sig. Oir). This is reinforced by the fourth entry on Tertullian, which comes under the very long heading *Rex*, which fills two pages of the CPB. Milton picks out a *sententia* from Rigault's edition on the role of the king as father of the country: *qui pater patriae est, quomodo dominus est*? This passage could easily be accessed again using Rigault's index, with the heading *paterfamilias, non dominus*, which takes the reader straight to the passage Milton quotes. What is still not clear is whether Milton might have been brought to these references by a secondary work which cited Tertullian on gluttony, say, and then looked up these references in the index to find an accurate quotation; or whether he might have entered the heading *gula* in his CPB, and then looked into Rigault's index to Tertullian to find what he had to say on the subject. However, for our present purposes this distinction is immaterial: Milton's historical engagement with these two sources of the early church is slight and context-free.

Attention to the CPB entries which may very well have relied on such finding aids throws light on references to books where no such finding aids were available. Milton's use of church historians such as Eusebius was of a quite different order to his use of Basil and Tertullian. The 1544 Paris edition is simply blank, unadorned, unindexed Greek prose.[29] This encourages an engagement with the historical progression recounted by Eusebius, from the earliest apostolic times until his own day. This is clearest in Milton's long entry on 'Marriage'. He begins by considering Eusebius's account of the early church, and says that 'The Apostles are shown to have contracted marriage by Eusebius.' He then cites Eusebius's earliest continuator, Socrates, paying specific attention to the textual state of Socrates's works: 'either he wrote this himself or someone afterwards, as could easily happen, inserted these words as his own opinion.'[30] Milton follows up these citations from the early historians by citing one of the earliest church fathers, Ignatius, before giving a round-up of Clement of Alexandria and Cyprian's accounts of marriage. What is at stake here is that Milton is using these accounts for their historical, factual content: What can they tell us about what the early church was like? This sort of detailed antiquarian engagement with sources must be distinguished from the more opportunistic, decontextualized treatment of Basil. The CPB is a witness not only to Milton's reading in historians, but also to different forms of historicism within his historical reading. Such fine distinctions allow us to understand the multiple forms of historicism which feed into the anti-prelatical tracts.

III. History in the anti-prelatical tracts: the early church

In the early 1640s, Milton had his first opportunity to put his historical reading into use, in the religious polemics which arose over episcopacy.[31] Joseph Hall had been urged by Laud (who had suspected Hall of sympathizing with Puritans and anti-episcopalians) to write a defence of episcopacy. This work, *Episcopacie by Divine Right Asserted*, was followed by Hall's *An Humble Remonstrance to the High Court of Parliament*. A group of ministers, including Thomas Young, Milton's former tutor and correspondent, formed a grouping called Smectymnuus to write a response to Hall.[32] The Smectymnuans issued their *An Answer to a Book Entitled an Humble Remonstrance*. Appended to this work is a postscript, almost certainly by Milton, in which the antipathy between bishops and monarchs in British history from Augustine's embassy to the Anglo-Saxons onwards is recounted in detail.[33] This is Milton's first entry into the anti-prelatical debates, in support of the group led by his former tutor. Hall responded to the Smectymnuans with *A Defence of the Humble Remonstrance*. This spurred Milton into his first full anti-prelatical tract, published anonymously in 1641: *Of Reformation*. This book attempts to show that not only is episcopacy not justified by scripture or by the practice of the early church, in practice episcopacy has always historically been a great hindrance to other kinds of ecclesiastical reformation.

At a slight angle to the debate between Hall and the Smectymnuans were the interventions of the great Irish scholar and Archbishop of Armagh, James Ussher.[34] Hall had been urging Ussher to intervene in the episcopacy debate: he was still a hugely respected figure in the 1640s, and moreover had stood out against the Laudian church and the Earl of Strafford's reforms in Ireland.[35] He thus maintained credibility with ministers across the spectrum of views on episcopacy. Ussher ultimately would try to seek a more moderate way through the controversy by producing a programme for reduced episcopacy.[36] However, at this stage, Ussher's position is not dissimilar to Hall's, and he publishes a tract which attempts to give a detailed historical reconstruction of the early church: *The Judgement of Doctor Rainoldes* (1641). He would expand this tract (in a collection of treatises on episcopacy, which he himself probably edited, called *Certain Brief Treatises* [Oxford, 1641]), into 'Of the Original of Metropolitans and Bishops'. Milton responded to the first version of this tract in *Of Prelatical Episcopacy*: this short work, as we will see, is young Milton's most thoroughgoing exercise in historical, factual reconstruction. In the meantime, Hall stepped back into the debate in response to Smectymnuus, with *A Defence of the Humble Remonstrance*, which provoked Milton's *Animadversions*. After the publication of *Certain Brief Treatises*, Milton publishes a response which is a watershed in his own career, the first tract to which he gives his name: *The Reason of Church-Government*. This work is also a watershed because in it we see Milton shifting the terms of the debate away from the historical reconstruction of the practices of the early church, towards a systematic theological analysis of the scriptural grounds for episcopacy. In this tract we witness the end of the young Milton's uses of non-scriptural history (fathers, British history); he would never approach theological debate in the same way.[37] The seeds for that shift away from history are already contained in the debates over episcopacy in the early 1640s, and to understand them we need to step back from the mêlée of pamphlet publication to put the religious politics of ecclesiastical history writing into context.

Hall's *Episcopacie by Divine Right Asserted* established the terms and methodologies on which this debate was going to be conducted: what was the structure of authority like in the early church? To find out, disputants needed mastery not just of scripture, but of the church fathers. The first question raised here concerns the relationship between the fathers and scripture.[38] Across the religious divides of the Reformation, almost everyone referred at some level to the authority of the fathers of the church.[39] Thomas Young might have been no friend of episcopacy, but his work on the Sabbath, *Dies Dominica*, cited Ignatius's epistle to the Magnesians on its title page, and book 1, chapters 2–3 are a tissue of citations from (especially the Latin) fathers on the early church.[40] Richard Baxter, himself no mean authority on the fathers, in his translation of *Dies Dominica* in the 1670s describes Young as 'eminent in his time . . . especially for his acquaintance with the writings and teachings of former ages'.[41] But Protestant *sola scriptura* principles tended to diminish the authority of the fathers, at least to beneath the level of scripture: according to one line of thought, fathers could be used to help interpret knotty passages of scripture, but they did not count as authorities on doctrine in their own right.[42] This encouraged a search for scriptural authority for episcopacy, which both Ussher and Hall felt they had found in the seven Angels of the Church of Asia in Revelation, which they glossed as a reference to the church's seven bishops.[43] However, another line of thinking on the relationship between scripture and the fathers suggested that the fathers could count as authorities on matters that were not mentioned in the scriptures, or mentioned in some way which was unclear. The most authoritative statement of this principle to be found in the seventeenth century is Henry Hammond's very brief treatise, 'Of the way of Resolving Controversies, which are not clearly stated and resolved in the Scriptures'.[44] He points out that scriptures were written for their original audience, who did not need certain matters of day-to-day reality and practice explained to them: 'Because in those *times* wherein . . . the *Scriptures* of the *New Testament* were written, these things were already so exactly known in their *Originals*, and in all other *circumstances* of them, that any larger *description* of them was perfectly *superfluous*' (sig. B6v). To supply these points missing from the scriptures, God 'hath *graciously* provided a competent *supply* by those *Records* of *Primitive* and *pure Antiquity*' (sig. B7r), which survive among the fathers. The history of the early church could reveal things that were not worth mentioning in scripture, and thus were of parallel authority to the scripture.

The larger distinction here is between treating the fathers as authorities on doctrine or as witnesses to the practices of the ancient church.[45] Hall stresses (crucially) that as well as being witnesses to the practice of the church, the early fathers, in particular, are sources of doctrine, because they establish what practices were passed directly from Christ to the Apostles, to the Apostolic fathers (Ignatius, Clement of Rome, etc.). This is why the early church (and the closer to Christ's time the better) is so important in these debates: it is, logically, likely to be purer, less corrupt, than the later church.[46] Theologians, historians, and polemicists disagreed on whether or not it was necessary to trace the practices of the church all the way back to Christ, or if only tracing them back to the Apostles was sufficient. Hall is clear that, in his eyes, proof of Apostolic practice is sufficient: 'That not onely the government, which was directly commanded, and enacted; but that which was practised and recommended by the Apostles to the Church, is justly to be held for an Apostolicall Institution' (sig. E3v). The Apostles, Hall points out, would not break the process of historical transmission and arbitrarily abandon the rulings of Christ. He is bolstered here by a passage from Tertullian, who points out 'That shall clearly appeare to be delivered by the Apostles, which shall have been religiously observed in the Churches of the Apostles' (sig. F4v). He goes on to say that we clearly must trust the Apostles, if not as authorities on doctrine, at least as recorders of the simple facts of the early church. It would be absurd, he points out, if no father 'ever saw, or spake the truth, not of doctrine onely, but not of fact' (sig. I3r). A further means to eke out these facts about the early church from the historical record is provided by a principle taken from Augustine, 'That which is held by the universall Church, and not ordained by any Councell, but hath beene alwayes retained in the Church, is most truly believed to be delivered by no other than Apostolicall authority.' This not only helps to discover early church practices (i.e., something is universal if there is evidence for it and it is not ordained specifically in any council), but also provides a means of safely distinguishing between early church practices which are essential, and those which are local or non-essential. In all these arguments, fact necessarily entails doctrine. Historical reconstruction of the early church is therefore of direct relevance to contemporary clerical authority. Although earlier it was necessary to emphasize the similarity between civil and ecclesiastical history (both come under the broad heading of Milton's historical reading), here it is important to disaggregate the two: civil history does not have the same universalist implications that ecclesiastical history does.[47] Ecclesiastical history, for Hall and others who follow the kinds of logical treatment of the fathers he pursues, has a direct, immediate impact on present policy.

Essential to any kind of reconstruction of the early church were not just historical principles on how to extrapolate from the limited sources available in the fathers, but also how to establish proper texts of the fathers themselves. In Europe in the seventeenth century, a new emphasis was being placed on the process of removing textual errors from the fathers. Thomas James, Bodley's first librarian, had provided in his *A Treatise of the Corruption of Scripture, Councels, and Fathers* (1611) a programme for editorial work on the fathers which would seek to purge them of interpolations he believed had been inserted for polemical popish ends.[48] The greatest such philological and editorial project in England in the seventeenth century was Henry Savile's edition of Chrysostom in Greek.[49] The 1610s and 1620s also saw in a renaissance in Jesuit patristic scholarship, partly in response to the work of Savile, led by Fronton du Duc and Jacques Sirmond.[50] In the 1630s, Patrick Young, the Royal Librarian in England, published the next European masterpiece of patristic scholarship, his edition of the first epistle of Clement.[51] A new awareness of such textual corruption had particularly focussed on editorial research into the Ignatian epistles. Ignatius had made a very clear distinction between *episcopos* and *presbuteros*, but scholars and polemicists alike were aware that the present collection of Ignatian epistles both contained entire epistles which were spurious and interpolations within genuine epistles.[52] Such textual confusion encouraged the Protestant sceptic and darling of the Great Tew Circle, Jean Daillé to publish his *Traicté de l'employ des Saincts Peres* (Geneva, 1632), which argued that the fathers were far too textually corrupt to constitute any kind of authority at all.[53]

It must be emphasized that in the debate between Hall and the Smectymnuans, Hall was far more knowledgeable about contemporary scholarship on the fathers. Hall was directly in touch with the two greatest patristic editors in Britain, James Ussher and Patrick Young, and was clearly familiar with Young's edition and its importance long before Milton.[54] Hall was far more familiar with the Greek fathers than the Smectymnuans seem to have been. Most of the Smectymnuans' citations are from the Latin fathers Jerome and Augustine and from Cyprian's writings in Latin.[55] Moreover, the Smectymnuans do not even engage with the textual debates on the interpolations into Ignatius, which would have enormously supported their arguments. The Greek writings of the apostolic fathers were of far greater value as contemporary witnesses to the practice of the early church. Hall's greater familiarity with contemporary scholarship gave him a huge polemical advantage.

Milton's awareness of philological debates in patristic scholarship was patchy. He was fairly ecumenical in the editions of the fathers he used. He made use of the Jesuit Fronton du Duc's edition of Basil, which was itself an extraordinary ecumenical project, and he carefully studied Vedelius's Ignatius. But interestingly he does not quote from the Eton Chrysostom.[56] And only *The Reason of Church-Government* mentions the Epistle of Clement, and then in a second-hand way.

Smectymnuus did offer a challenge to this historical methodology. They point out that just because an institution has endured for a long time, it should not therefore continue to endure. As they put it, 'It is a good observation of *Cyprian*, that Christ said, *Ego sum via, veritas & vita*, not *Ego sum consuetudo*; and that *Consuetudo sine veritate est vetustas erroris*, Christ is Truth, and not Custom. and Custome without Truth, is a mouldy errour: and as Sr *Francis Bacon* saith, *Antiquity without Truth, is a Cypher without a Figure*' (sig. C3r). However, they all broadly accept the way Hall has presented the debate: they engage with him on historical grounds. Their central point is that there is no scriptural warrant to show that a bishop was of greater authority over a presbyter: they do not accept Bishop Hall's analogy between the superiority of Apostles over disciples and bishops over presbyters. They are also clear that the Bible offers no historical warrant for thinking the bishop is superior to the presbyter: this is the Bible treated as a historical document to the practice of the early church. They also argue that the witnesses of the early fathers are not necessary, because the Bible is perfectly clear and authoritative on this matter.[57] However, crucially, they do not attack the authority of the fathers wholesale—for instance, by dismissing them as textually corrupt—because they also need to rely on the later fathers to bolster their argument. They cite Jerome to the effect that '*Bishops* and *Presbyters* are originally the same ... that Imparitie that was in his [Jerome's] time betweene Bishops and Elders, was grounded upon Ecclesiastical Custome, and not upon divine Institution; ... that this was not his private judgement, but the judgement of Scripture' (sigs. D3v–D4r). However, they do not engage much with the contemporary source documents relating to the early church (beyond scripture): this is the consequence of their unfamiliarity with the Greek sources. The tradition of the church still edges forwards from the times of Christ to the Apostles and to the apostolic fathers. The Smectymnuans also accept that the laws of the Apostles are divine laws, but are much less happy to extrapolate from the early sources (e.g., fathers alive at the same time as the Apostles, but not themselves apostles) to find out what the Apostles practised. The apostolic law needed to be laid down absolutely explicitly, not inferred by historical deduction. There might be some polemical advantage here: although they insist that episcopacy is not divinely ordained, their arguments do not entail the opposite claim that episcopacy is divinely prohibited. Emphasizing the *lack* of detail about the early church leaves open the possibility that some sort of reduced episcopacy might turn out to be sufficiently in line with early church practice as to be warrantable. Wiggle-room within the fast-moving episcopal debate in the early 1640s was thus preserved.[58]

So how does this debate shape the historicism of Milton's pamphlets? It is useful to treat the first three anti-prelatical tracts (*Of Reformation* to *Animadversions*) as a group that employ similar historical methodologies. Milton presents church history as a developing tradition from the time of Christ onwards. We can see this most clearly in *Of Prelatical Episcopacy*, where he begins by dealing with scripture, then moves on to the Ignatian epistles, then Irenaeus, Tertullian, and so on through the early church. We need to distinguish this approach to history from the far more opportunistic engagement with *exempla* that we have found earlier in the CPB. The entry under 'marriage', discussed briefly above, is more similar to the tracing of historical continuities (and discontinuities) which Milton engages with in the anti-prelatical tracts.[59]

It is important, however, to differentiate Milton's historical methodologies from those of the Smectymnuans, even if he was broadly supportive at this stage of their conclusions. Milton's is a heavily primary source-based account of history. We have seen that the Smectymnuans made little use of the writings of Ignatius and relied heavily on the later Latin fathers. But Milton's works are steeped in primary source documents, including some of the Greek apostolic fathers. He dismisses Theodoret, for instance, as an inadequate witness to the early antiquity of the church because he is one of the 'authorities of later times, and therefore not to be receiv'd for their Antiquities sake to give in evidence'.[60] But Milton also goes much further than the Smectymnuans in critiquing those primary source documents. It has been pointed out since the nineteenth century that Milton used Nicholas Vedelius's textual commentary on Ignatius to fuel his own polemic against the mangled and interpolated textual state of that apostolic father. However, his critique of the early church is much broader than this. He argues that the councils, too, were subject to interpolation around the year AD 1000.[61] This is a point he makes in both *Of Prelatical Episcopacy* and in *Animadversions* with slightly different emphases.[62] But as well as arguing that the ancient church is irrecoverable because of textual corruption, he more radically counters the prevailing nostalgia for the early church which can be found across early-modern denominations. Milton argues that corruption had set in to the early church, even in apostolic times. In *Of Reformation*, for instance, he points out that: '*Ignatius* in his early dayes testifies to the Churches of *Asia*, that even then Heresies were sprung up'.[63] This is to go much further than the Smectymnuans, who preferred instead to make the crucially different argument that past practice was not a necessary guide to present church policy, especially if that practice cannot be shown to be *de Iure Apostolica*. For Milton, the established church is nearly constantly corrupt. This might be one of the reasons he pays far more attention to pre-Reformation heretics than the other Smectymnuans. He emphasizes throughout the anti-prelatical tracts that Wycliffe was a forebear of the sixteenth-century reformers: God 'knockt once and twice and came againe, opening our drousie eye-lids leasurely by that glimmering light which *Wicklef*, and his followers dispers't.'[64] Martyrs such as Wycliffe, but also the Hussites or the Waldensians, constitute the only visible remnant of the true church of God. This revaluation of Protestant martyrs as witnesses to the continuity of the visible church throughout the centuries is continuous with the thinking of figures such as Foxe and George Abbot.[65] But Milton is unusual in not combining that sense of the continuity of the invisible church with any sense that the visible church preserved itself from corruption, even in apostolic times.[66] His historical critique is far more radical, reckless even, than that of the Smectymnuans, because it threatens to eliminate the entirety of church history as a worthwhile body of precedent for modern doctrine.

From *The Postscript* to the anti-prelatical tracts, through *Of Reformation*, and to *Of Prelatical Episcopacy*, Milton is moving backwards in time. He begins the controversy in post-Augustinian British history, after the Archbishopric of Canterbury has been established. His aim is to show, not that episcopacy was not historically practised (of course it was), but that it inevitably led to conflict with the monarchy. The institution of episcopacy could be shown to be, historically, a corrupting force within the state. In *Of Reformation*, Milton is keen to show something of the same thing: episcopacy has been a hindrance to the progress of the Reformation, and this can be demonstrated historically from the more recent sixteenth-century past.[67] But it is at this point Milton already begins to render such historical arguments irrelevant. In launching such a wholesale, thoroughgoing attack on the early church and its records, Milton placed himself on a trajectory which would lead to biblical history being the only kind of history with any validity: either as ascertainable fact, or as divine authority for current practice. We see this process culminating in the very different kinds of arguments Milton uses to respond to Lancelot Andrewes in *The Reason of Church-Government*. In that work, we also witness a corresponding diminishment of interest in engaging with primary historical sources. Although he cites Clement and the Shepherd of Hermas, he does so explicitly from a secondary source: he is arguing that the early church was already rent by schism, which 'wee finde in *Clements* Epistle of venerable authority written to the yet factious *Corinthians*, that they were still govern'd by Presbyters. And the same of other Churches out of *Hermas*, and divers other the scholers of the Apostles by the late industry of the learned *Salmatius* appeares.'[68] The kind of sustained engagement with the historical accretion of every kind of corruption (textual, spiritual) is abandoned. The historical arguments found in *The Postscript* would no longer be relevant to ecclesiastical or theological debate for Milton, although he would continue to use such arguments in the political tracts, such as *The Tenure of Kings and Magistrates*.

IV. Conclusion: the turn away from a British epic

Let us return, by way of conclusion, to the second speculative question with which I began this essay. Why did Milton abandon his Arthur epic? This survey of Milton's developing historical methodologies may have offered some ways of approaching this question. I showed at the outset that Arthur was bound up with beliefs about the early British church, the pre-Augustinian church which was believed to have been founded in apostolic times. By the time the anti-prelatical tracts were being written, such an Arthurian epic might start to look rather unattractive. First of all, it was fairly clear that the early British church was an episcopal church.[69] In fact, Hall issues a challenge on precisely this point in his *Defence of the Humble Remonstrance*:

I challenge you before that awfull Bar, to which you have appealed, name but one yeare ever since Christianity had footing in England, (which was under the British

Roman Government) wherein there were no Bishops in this Land; If you can name neither yeare nor Author, be ashamed to say this truth hath had any contradiction, or else I hope the Readers will be ashamed of you. (sig. f4v)

This is a challenge Milton never answers, partly because his developing historical methodologies were rendering it irrelevant: the ancient British church could not be any authority for the present church government. But of course, if this sort of argument were being rendered irrelevant, then an epic which would partly revolve around defending this sort of national church would also be increasingly irrelevant. When polemic was waged against Catholics, the ancient British church was a helpful answer to the perennial 'Where was your Church before Luther?' question. But in polemic between episcopacy and presbytery, the ancient British church was far more useful for the bishops than it was for Milton and the Smectymnuans. And not only irrelevant, but actively undesirable to defend, if that church was likely to be episcopal—and possibly, according to Milton's emphasis on the almost immediate spread of heresy after Christ's lifetime, likely to be schismatic too. Speed's *History of Great Britaine* (a work cited many times in the CPB) specifically praises Arthur as a great founder of the abbey of Glastonbury:

Also in the same Charter amongst many other Kings, there is mention made of King Arthur, to be a great Benefactor vnto that Abbey [of Glastonbury]; whose Armes vpon the stone walles, both in the Chapell (called S. Ioseph) and in diuers other places of the Abbey, are cut: which is an Eschucheon, whereon a Crosse with the Virgin Mary in the first quarter is set, and is yet to this day remaining ouer the Gate of entrance, and is held to be also the Armes of that Abbey.[70]

So the sort of historical reading Milton was undertaking in the late 1630s and 1640s would have revealed a doctrinally suspect Arthur, the defender of an ancient British church that might well not have been worth defending.

Finally, there is Milton's gathering scepticism about historical sources. It seems very unlikely to me that he initially accepted the Arthur legend as historical fact, and then was persuaded of its untruth. By the 1630s a century of English antiquarianism had already done massive damage to the credibility of the Arthur story. But there is, perhaps, another religious dimension here. It is easy to laugh at Renaissance beliefs that Joseph of Arimathea or St Paul founded Christianity in Britain in apostolic times. But these stories were responding, after a fashion, to the authority of the fathers. Both Origen and Tertullian had stated there were Christians in Britain in their own times, and even earlier. This put Christians in Britain at least around the year 100. These two fathers were constantly cited in any treatment of the British church: Archbishop Matthew Parker's *De Antiquitate Britannicae Ecclesiae*, which we encountered at the start of this essay, cites both of them on its first page.[71] Parker goes on to use these fathers as evidence that the church in Britain *primum per Apostolos propagato . . . non a Roma sede* (sig. Air). As I have been trying to show throughout this chapter, the history of the early church is not siphoned off from other national histories. Any attack on the authority of the fathers threatened to undermine faith in the ancient British church altogether. Milton's reading in civil and ecclesiastical history was unlikely to have had much of an effect on his views on the historicity of Arthur, but it was likely to have subjected the religious society of which he was the leader to a vigorous and withering critique.

Notes

1. *CPW*, i. 544. The study of antiquarianism over the last fifty years has created a vast bibliography. Two classic starting points are the opening chapter, 'Ancient History and the Antiquarian', in Arnaldo Momigliano's *Studies in Historiography* (1966/69), 1–39 and Roberto Weiss, *The Renaissance Discovery of Classical Antiquity* (Oxford, 1969).

2. The best introduction to scholarly methodologies in the Renaissance is G. J. Toomer, *John Selden: A Life in Scholarship*, 2 vols. (Oxford, 2009), especially i. 28–68. On antiquaries' uses of physical remains in particular, see William Stenhouse, *Reading Inscriptions and Writing Ancient History: Historical Scholarship in the Late Renaissance* (2005) and Michael H. Crawford (ed.), *Antonio Augustin Between Renaissance and Counter-Reform* (1993).

3. Elisabeth S. Leedham-Green, *Books in Cambridge Inventories: Book Lists from Vice-Chancellor's Court Probate Inventories in the Tudor and Stuart Periods* (Cambridge, 1986).

4. David Loewenstein, *Milton and the Drama of History: Historical Vision, Iconoclasm and the Literary Imagination* (Cambridge, 1990).

5. References to Milton's Latin poems are to *John Milton: Complete Shorter Poems*, ed. Stella P. Revard (Oxford, 2009).

6. On Milton's neo-Latin poetry generally see Stella P. Revard, *Milton and the Tangles of Neaera's Hair: The Making of the 1645 'Poems'* (Columbia, Mo, 1997); on the specific impact of his trip to Italy on his Latin writing see Estelle Haan, *From Academia to Amicitia: Milton's Latin Writings and the Italian Academies* (Philadelphia, Pa., 1998).

7. See 'antiquary', *a.* and *n.*, sense B.2., which cites Richard Grafton's description of Leland as 'the excellent antiquary' in 1563 (*OED Online* 2nd edn. [Oxford, 1989]). For the poem itself see John Leland, *Cygnea Cantio* (1645). Recently on John Leland see the definitive edition of his *De Viris Illustribus*, ed. James P. Carley (Toronto, 2010).

8. The *locus classicus* here is Tacitus's description of Britain in his *Agricola* I.x.

9. For a recent survey of classical references to the druids see Ronald Hutton, *Blood and Mistletoe: The History of the Druids in Britain* (New Haven, Conn., 2009).

10. Revard, *Complete Shorter Poems*, 132–3.

11. See Bede *Ecclesiastical History*, ed. J. E. King 2 vols. (Cambridge, Mass., 1930), vol. i. II.1.

12. These disputes have been explored well by Donna Hamilton, 'Catholic Use of Anglo-Saxon Precedents, 1565–1625', *Recusant History*, 26 (2003), 537–55.

13. For more generally on British history and polemic see Felicity Heal, 'What Can King Lucius Do for You? The Reformation and the Early British Church', *English Historical Review*, 120 (2005), 593–614.

14. Matthew Parker, *De Antiquitate Britannicae Ecclesiae* (1572), 8.

15. Alexander Gil, *Alexander Gil's Logonomia Anglica* (1619), ed. and trans. B. Danielsson and A. Gabrielson (Stockholm, 1972).

16. On Diodati, see David C. Dorian, *The English Diodatis* (New Brunswick, N. J., 1950). Interestingly, it seems very likely to have been William Chillingworth through whom Diodati got the opportunity to contribute to the Camden volume. Diodati is clearly the odd member out in the volume, both because he is the youngest contributor, and because most of the poets who contributed to the volume edited by Degory Wheare, *Camdeni Insignia* (Oxford, 1624), had some connection with one of the institutions with which Camden was connected (Westminster School, Broadgates Hall, or Christ Church). Only two, Chillingworth and Diodati, were from Trinity. Chillingworth was an older member of Trinity at the same time as Diodati, and so seems more likely to have been able to find his way into the Camden volume. Chillingworth is also connected with Milton through Diodati in the late 1620s, when we find Chillingworth reporting Alexander Gil the younger's indiscrete comments about Laud to the Bishop.

17. See Ann Blair, 'Note Taking as an Art of Transmission', *Critical Inquiry*, 31 (2004), 85–107, especially 90–7. On the massive literature on commonplace books, see in particular Peter Beal 'Notions in Garrison: The Seventeenth-Century Commonplace Book', in W. S. Hill (ed.), *New Ways of Looking at Old Texts* (Binghamton, N.Y. 1993), 131–47.

18. Jill Kraye, 'Moral Philosophy', in Charles B. Schmitt, Quentin Skinner, Eckhard Kessler, and Jill Kraye, *The Cambridge History of Renaissance Philosophy* (Cambridge, 1988), 171–97.

19. It is translated as *The Method and Order of Reading Both Civil and Ecclesiastical Histories* (1685) and reprinted several times. It is possible that Milton may have used a combination of the first edition of Wheare's work, *De Ratione et Methodo Legendi Historias Dissertatio* (1625) to guide his reading in British history, followed by the expanded edition in 1637 for his reading in ecclesiastical history. The comparison between the works recommended for study in the latter volume and the works of ecclesiastical history Milton was reading is very close.

20. It is interesting that Milton never cites Baronius in his CPB; he is, however, an ecclesiastical historian he must have consulted. The best account of Baronius can be found in Jean-Louis Quantin, *Le Catholicisme Classique et Les Pères de l'Eglise: Un Retour aux Sources (1669–1713)* (Paris, 1999), 200ff.

21. Milton would have read Bede in Jerome Commelin, *Rerum Britannicarum* (Heidelberg, 1587), a collection of early British historians. Bede was the British historian with whom continental European readers were most likely to be familiar, both because of his importance to counter-Reformation polemic and because he provided material for editions of the church councils. On the former, see Felicity Heal, 'Appropriating History: Catholic and Protestant Polemics and the National Past', *Huntington Library Quarterly*, 68 (2005), 109–32. He read William of Malmesbury in the most important source-book of medieval English historians so far published, *Rerum Anglicarum Scriptores* (1596). He also cites Henry of Huntington from the same volume.

22. The starting point for any study of the fathers in the Anglican church is now Jean-Louis Quantin, *The Church of England and Christian Antiquity: The Construction of a Confessional Identity in the 17th Century* (Oxford, 2009).

23. On Sleidan as a historian see Alexandra Kess, *Johann Sleidan and the Protestant Vision of History* (Aldershot, 2008). The best available account of Paolo Sarpi in English can be found in J. G. A. Pocock, *Barbarism and Religion: Volume 2: Narratives of Civil Government* (Cambridge, 1999).

24. On the chronology of Milton's CPB see the classic article, James Holly Hanford, 'The Chronology of Milton's Private Studies', *PMLA*, 36 (1921), 251–314. On where Milton did his reading see Edward Jones, '"Filling in a Blank in the Canvas": Milton, Horton, and the Kedermister Library', *Review of English Studies*, 53 (2002), 31–60. On Milton's lost *index theologicus*, see Gordon Campbell, 'Milton's *Index Theologicus* and Bellarmine's *Disputationes De Controversiis Christianae Fidei Adversus Huius Temporis Haereticos*', *Milton Quarterly*, 11 (1977), 12–16.

25. For more on the impact of the culture of commonplacing on thought see Ann Moss, *Printed Commonplace-Books and the Structuring of Renaissance Thought* (Oxford, 1996).

26. The best available study of editions of Basil in the Renaissance is Irena Backus, *Lectures Humanistes de Basile de Césarée: Traductions Latines, 1439–1618* (Paris, 1990). Nicolas Rigault deserves a full study, but for a very valuable short overview see Ingrid de Smet, 'Nicolas Rigault', *Centuriae Latinae II: Cent une Figures Humanistes de la Renaissance aux Lumières* (Geneva, 2006), 727–33.

27. *CPW*, i. 453.

28. *CPW*, i. 489–90.

29. Although Milton may have used the parallel text edition, *Historiae Ecclesiasticae Scriptores Graeci*. See Constance Nicholas, 'The Edition of the Early Church Historians used by Milton', *Journal of English and Germanic Philology*, 51 (1952), 60–2.

30. *CPW*, i. 394.

31. The excellent recent survey of this topic, David Weil Baker, '"Dealt with at his Owne Weapon": Anti-Antiquarianism in Milton's Prelacy Tracts', *Studies in Philology*, 106 (2009), 207–34, does not treat some of the finer nuances in debates on church history.

32. On the Smectymnuans see Tom Webster, *Godly Clergy in Early Stuart England: The Caroline Puritan Movement, c.1620–1643* (Cambridge, 1997), 319–26.

33. A strong case for Milton's authorship is made in David L. Hoover and Thomas N. Corns, 'The Authorship of the Postscript to *An Answer to a Booke Entituled, An Humble Remonstrance*', *Milton Quarterly*, 38 (2004), 59–75.

34. On Ussher's involvement in the episcopacy controversy, see Alan Ford, *James Ussher: Theology, History and Politics in Early-Modern Ireland and England* (Oxford, 2007), Hugh Trevor-Roper, 'James Ussher', in *Catholics, Anglicans, and Puritans: Seventeenth Century Essays* (Chicago, Ill., 1987).

35. On Ussher's antipathetic relationship with Laud and Strafford see Amanda L. Capern, 'The Caroline Church: James Ussher and the Irish Dimension', *Historical Journal*, 39 (1996), 57–85.

36. Circulated in manuscript and then published by Nicholas Bernard posthumously, as James Ussher, *The Reduction of Episcopacy unto the Form of Synodical Government Received in the Ancient Church* (1656).

37. Ultimately, this would lead to the production of *De Doctrina Christiana*. On that work's systematic theology, see Gordon Campbell, *et al.*, *Milton and the Manuscript of 'De Doctrina Christiana'* (Oxford, 2007).

38. John Downe's treatise, *Not the Consent of Fathers but Scripture the Ground of Faith*, published as part of a collection of tracts, *A Treatise of the True Nature and Definition of Justifying Faith* (Oxford, 1635), is a good example of the moderate Calvinist position in the Laudian church. He argues that if the scriptures are deemed to be difficult to interpret, then the Fathers are even worse, and so do not provide an unambiguous guide to scripture: 'To proceed, the Scriptures you say are obscure and ambiguous, and therefore you may not rest vpon them saue onely as they are Fathers. If so, then if the Fathers also bee obscure and ambiguous, neither may you rest your Faith vpon them. Now certainly the Fathers are as darke and doubtfull as the Scripture' (235).

39. See the two chapters by Jean-Louis Quantin, 'The Fathers in Seventeenth-Century Catholic Theology' and 'The Fathers in Seventeenth-Century Anglican Theology', in Irena Backus (ed.), *The Reception of the Church Fathers in the West: From the Carolingians to the Maurists*, 2 vols. (Leiden, 1997), ii. 842–65.

40. Thomas Young, *Dies Dominica* (1639), 5–18.

41. Thomas Young, *Dies Dominica, or The Lords Day*, trans. Richard Baxter (Oxford, 1672), sig. A6r-v.

42. John E. Booty, *John Jewel as Apologist of the Church of England* (1963), 126–49, remains a very valuable account.

43. For more on reading the book of Revelation in the Renaissance, see Irena Backus, *Reformation Readings of the Apocalypse: Geneva, Zurich and Wittenberg* (Oxford, 2000).

44. Henry Hammond, *A Letter of Resolution to Six Quaeres of Present Use in the Church of England* (1653), 1–33. For more on Hammond see John W. Packer, *The Transformation of Anglicanism, 1643–1660, with Special Reference to Henry Hammond* (Manchester, 1969).

45. On the related development of positive theology in France see Quantin, *Le Catholicisme Classique*, 105ff.

46. On nostalgia for the early church see Bruno Neveu, 'L'érudition Ecclésiastique du XVIIe Siècle et la Nostalgie de l'antiquité Chrétienne', in Keith Robbins (ed.), *Religion and Humanism* (Oxford, 1981), 195–223. More broadly on views of the early church in the Reformation and Counter-Reformation, see Irena Backus, *Historical Method and Confessional Identity in the Era of the Reformation (1378–1615)* (Leiden, 2003), esp. 326–91.

47. On the importance of this distinction, see the classic, Arnaldo Momigliano, 'The Origins of Ecclesiastical Historiography', in *The Classical Foundations of Modern Historiography* (Oxford, 1992), 132–52.

48. See the superb recent essay, Paul Nelles, 'The Uses of Orthodoxy and Jacobean Erudition: Thomas James and the Bodleian Library', *History of Universities*, 22 (2007), 21–70.

49. Essential reading on this edition is: Jean-Louis Quantin, 'Du Chrysostome Latin au Chrysostome Grec. Une Histoire Européenne (1588–1613)', in Martin Wallraff and Rudolf Brändle (eds.), *Chrysostomosbilder in 1600 Jahren: Facetten der Wirkungsgeschichte eines Kirchenvaters* (Berlin, 2008), 267–346.

50. An excellent account can be found in Jean-Louis Quantin, 'L'Orthodoxie, La Censure et La Gloire: La Difficle Édition Princeps de L'Épître de Barnabé, de Rome à Amsterdam (1549–1646)', in Mariarosa Cortesi, *'Editiones Principes' delle Opere dei Padri Greci e Latini* (Firenze, 2006), 103–62, esp. 115–20.

51. Young deserves a full modern treatment. In the absence of one, there is the nineteenth-century biography and edition of his correspondence, Patrick Young, *Patricius Junius (Patrick Young) Bibliothekar der Könige Jacob I und Carl I von England. Mitteilungen aus Seinem Briefwechsel*, ed. Johannes Kemke (Leipzig, 1898).

52. The best survey of this issue can be found in a masterpiece of nineteenth-century polyglot erudition, J. B. Lightfoot, *The Apostolic Fathers*, 5 vols. (1889–90), ii. 1. Hugh de Quehen, 'Politics and Scholarship in the Ignatian Controversy', *The Seventeenth Century*, 13 (1998), 69–84 is largely derivative of Lightfoot's work.

53. Hugh Trevor-Roper's account of Great Tew remains useful, 'The Great Tew Circle', in *Catholics, Anglicans, Puritans,* 166–230. On their interest in Daillé see Quantin, *The Church of England,* 209–51.

54. Hall points out that Young's edition of Clement (*Clementis Ad Corinthios Epistola Prior* [Oxford, 1633]) was based on a manuscript sent to Charles by the patriarch of the Greek church, Cyril Lukaris (see Hall, *Episcopacie*, sig. T4r–v). For more on the contacts between the Greek and Laudian churches see Hugh Trevor-Roper, 'The Church of England and the Greek Church in the Time of Charles I', in *From Counter-Reformation to Glorious Revolution* (Chicago, Ill., 1992), 83–111.

55. Hall rather tartly refers to '*Cyprian*, whom you frequently cite' in his *Defence of the Humble Remonstrance*, sig. B4r.

56. Given evidence elsewhere in this volume that Milton may have used the Eton College library, it seems even more surprising that he does not cite this edition in the CPB.

57. See e.g., sig. C4r.

58. James Ussher's desire to maintain flexibility within ecclesiastical polemics is emphasized in Ford, *James Ussher*, 241.

59. I doubt the CPB was a targeted preparation for writing the early tracts, despite the overlap in the materials cited.

60. *CPW*, i. 634.

61. The best book-length survey of the European editing of the councils is Henri Quentin, *Jean-Dominique Mansi et les Grandes Collections Conciliaires* (Paris, 1900). A new study of this topic would be of enormous value.

62. See *CPW*, i. 629, 684–5.

63. *CPW*, i. 549.

64. *CPW*, i. 704.

65. George Abbot, *A Treatise of the Perpetuall Visbilitie and Succession of the True Church in All Ages* (1624). On this subject see Anthony Milton, *Catholic and Reformed: The Roman and Protestant Churches in English Protestant Thought, 1600–1640* (Cambridge, 1995), ch. 6 and the excellent essay by Euan Cameron, 'Medieval Heretics as Protestant Martyrs', in Diane Wood (ed.), *Martyrs and Martyrologies* (Oxford, 1997), 185–207.

66. Compare Abbot, *A Treatise of the Perpetuall Visibilitie*.

67. See *CPW*, i. 528ff.

68. *De Episcopus et Presbyteris, contra D. Petavium Loiolitam Dissertatio Prima* (Leiden, 1641), 250–3. A full study of Milton's reading of Salmasius would be desirable.

69. Henry Spelman gives evidence that British bishops attended the Council of Arles (which he dates to AD 314) in 'Concilia, Decreta, Leges, Constitutiones', in *Re Ecclesiarum Orbis Britannici* (1639), 39–43.

70. John Speed, *The History of Great Britaine* (1611), 207.

71. Matthew Parker, *De Antiquitate Britannicae Ecclesiae* (1572), 1. For modern editions of Tertullian and Origen's references to Britain see Tertullian, *Aduersos Iudaeos*, VII.4., in *Corpus Christianorum. Series Latina* (Turnhout, 1953–), II. 1354; Origen, *Homilia IV in Ezechielem*, in *Patrologiae Cursus Completus. Series Graeca* (Paris, 1857–1912), XIII.698A.

4

Milton and the Conformable Puritanism of Richard Stock and Thomas Young

Jeffrey Alan Miller

I. Introduction

Studies of Milton have long considered his early associations with puritan clergymen a subject worthy of notice, often with the status of those clergymen as 'puritans' having been stressed by scholars to an exclusive degree ('Young John Milton had a Puritan pastor at All Hallows, Richard Stock, and a Puritan tutor at home, Thomas Young').[1] Even John Aubrey thought it pertinent to note that Milton's hair had been cut short by an early schoolmaster who 'was a puritan in Essex', presumably Young, thereby insinuating what many scholars have subsequently taken as a given: from the very beginning, Milton was being shaped, literally, by the puritans whose ranks he would ultimately join.[2] When to such observations are added Milton's own statements in *Of Reformation* declaring his allegiance with so-called '*Puritans*' and 'precise *Puritanisme*', it is hard not to conclude that this was the puritan reformer he was born, or at least bred up, to be.[3]

Assessing the actual significance of Milton's early exposure to those puritan clergymen, however, has long been a problematic affair. There are doubtless many reasons why, but one of the main is that, throughout the history of Milton studies, identifying someone in early seventeenth-century England as a 'puritan' has remained effectively synonymous with identifying him or her as a 'radical'. Most commonly, this has led to the reflex assumption that since Milton's boyhood pastor and most esteemed boyhood tutor were themselves puritans, they must have served to nurture in Milton 'a commitment to reformist, militant Protestantism', as if that were the very definition of puritanism, rather than but a species of it.[4] More recently, on the other hand, it has been argued that since the young Milton would appear not to have been a radical militant, those early puritan connections must have 'failed to turn the young Milton into a puritan' whatsoever.[5] In either case, while the young Milton himself has thus been variously placed along the early modern spectrum of English religious and political opinion, the puritan clergymen who populated the young Milton's life have rarely been permitted to inhabit any position but the radical pole.

The ensuing essay seeks to demonstrate that the two puritan clergymen most closely associated with Milton's early life—Richard Stock (1568/9–1626) and Thomas Young (c. 1587–1655)—both appear to have been 'moderate' or 'conformable' puritans, a kind of puritan that Milton scholarship has tended either to overlook or to misconstrue.[6] In arguing as much, however, this essay does not mean to contend that Stock and Young must have served to turn the young Milton himself into such a puritan. Rather, this essay restricts itself to pursuing the claim that the young John Milton was regularly connected, both by his own choice and by the choices of his family, to conformable puritan clergymen over the course of the first three decades of his life. What those connections may tell us abut the young Milton and his family, and the extent to which those connections may have influenced the ultimate trajectory of Milton's later life, must be left to future studies. The hope is that this essay, in refining our understanding of Milton's early puritan associations, will help to pave the way.

Before we proceed, the terms 'puritan', 'moderate puritan', and 'conformable puritan' require some preliminary comment. Generally speaking, puritans represented the more zealous wing of early modern English Calvinism.[7] No single doctrinal or disciplinary position marked one out as a puritan.[8] However, as Richard Stock himself observed across a number of sermons, many were 'mocked, & accompted superstitious & precyse'—that is, accounted *puritans* or *precisians*—for being 'more carefull then others' when it came to 'observing the sabboth', having 'a strickt care of their cariage', 'striving to liue well' ('well' meaning 'godly'), and 'making a conscience of small sinns'. To those characteristic traits might also be added a more strident commitment to the belief that 'Gods word is the sure rule & touche stone, & that which agrees therwith is true, & the contrarie false', as Stock also put it to his parishioners.[9] Such an insistence on the sole supremacy and sufficiency of scripture was by no means the preserve (or always the practice) of puritans, but it did mean that puritans tended to be warier of those facets of the English Church believed to be less firmly rooted in the demands of scripture, as in the case of the church's ascendant ceremonialism.

Moderate puritan clergymen subscribed to the episcopal church settlement and worked to conform to the doctrine and discipline insisted upon by the church's acknowledged, ecclesiastical authorities. By and large, this distinguished moderates from more radical puritans 'whose scruples about conformity or episcopacy' variously led to obdurate nonconformity, ministerial deprivation, self-imposed exile, or, in the extreme, an outright advocacy of separatism.[10] Even if moderate puritans harboured a desire for further reform, even if they advocated for it in a calculated way, in the meanwhile they accommodated themselves to the church's rule. In their eyes, and in their self-presentation, they were integrated and loyal members of the Church of England, not opponents of it, even if that church was to be a ceremonial or episcopal one. For some, this may have been little more than an unprincipled dodge, but the majority of moderate puritans considered conformity rather to be a spiritual obligation—to God, to their national church, and to their parishioners. As a result, more often than not, these moderates 'remained continuously in their ministerial posts and pulpits', even in the face of the church's growing intolerance to puritans of any kind.[11]

Like 'puritan', the term 'conformable puritan' began as a hostile epithet. Coined by Archbishop Samuel Harsnett (1561–1631), it was meant to describe those puritans who were willing to subscribe to the church's (shifting) doctrinal and disciplinary demands, and even to practice the mandated ceremonies, but who did so with at least a modicum of misgiving, or who regarded any aspect of their conformity as less than theologically essential. A 'conformable puritan', in other words, was a moderate one, and moderate puritans came to embrace the designation and to instil it with positive connotations, just as puritans in general had done with the epithet 'puritan'.[12] Over the decades of Milton's youth, however, conformability became increasingly fraught, as radical bishops and their radical opponents pushed to polarize the religious and political landscape. Ecclesiastical authorities from Harsnett to Laud would no longer settle for conformity. They wanted only *conformists*, who conformed for the proper reasons. As Richard Montagu famously railed, conformable puritans were merely 'pretending *conformity*'. They were a 'Faction' that needed to be discovered and expelled in a fashion no different from their nonconforming brethren.[13] This notorious 'moving of the goal posts', as Peter Lake has phrased it, changed what it meant to be a conforming member of the English Church, and what it meant to be a conformable puritan changed in turn.[14] Such was the environment in which John Milton was raised, and in which his early association with conformable puritan clergymen took place.

II. Richard Stock

Richard Stock was Milton's boyhood minister at All Hallows, Bread Street, baptizing him on 20 December 1608.[15] Throughout Milton's youth, Stock preached two different sermons every Sunday, one in the morning and one in the afternoon, and he was known to be a devoted instructor of the young during 'the *weeke days*' also. His lifelong friend, Thomas Gataker (1574–1654), would indeed make special mention of this at Stock's funeral on 24 April 1626, recalling his '*pious care* and *diligence* in the *religious instruction* and *education* of those that were vnder his *priuate charge, children* and others'.[16] Milton's father did not seek out Stock's parish. Stock began working at All Hallows in 1604 as an assistant for the church's infirm rector Thomas Edmonds (d. 1611). By that point, the Miltons had been parishioners for several years, the earliest evidence of their presence dating from an entry in the burial register recording the burial on 12 May 1601 of 'A crysome childe of Mr John Myltons of this parishe, scrivener.'[17] Nevertheless, while the Miltons did not choose to *become* Stock's parishioners, they chose to remain under his pastoral care for twenty-two years, and thereby, aside from the young Milton's immediate family, Stock became the most consistent presence in the boy's pre-Cambridge life.

Just two days prior to Milton's birth, Stock's *A Sermon Preached at Paules Crosse* was entered into the Stationer's Register (7 December 1608). It is a good place to begin a consideration of his moderate, or conformable, puritanism, not least because that sermon has been frequently cited as proof of his militant puritanism.[18] Stock originally preached the sermon at Paul's Cross, arguably the most famous pulpit in the land, on 2 November 1606—essentially the one-year anniversary of the Gunpowder Plot. The sermon is virulently anti-papist, as one would expect. Stock called Roman Catholics 'the greatest enemies of the kingdome of Christ; the grossest idolaters of all the king-domes of the world, and the most pestilent enemies of this kingdome and state', and he stressed to the nation's magistrates that no method was too severe when it came to eradicating the papist threat within England, from 'confiscation of goods, to imprisonment, banishment, or death it selfe, according to the qualitie of their offences'.[19] This is strong stuff, even for the occasion. Throughout, Stock urged an unrelenting course of action that James I would never prove willing to pursue. Yet the occasion nonetheless must be kept in mind, as should the king's own belief that the Pope was antichrist. James, in fact, was the first English monarch to profess that belief in writing, and by 1608, the mutual hostilities exacerbated by the Gun-powder Plot and by the ensuing Oath of Allegiance (1606) had erupted into a protracted conflict in print that saw the king himself pitted against the arch-nemesis of early modern Protestantism, the Jesuit Cardinal Robert Bellarmine.[20] All of which is to say that Stock's sermon, itself repeatedly lashing out at Bellarmine, was not so very out of line with the anti-Catholi-cism of the church's highest-ranking ecclesiastical authorities (none, of course, being higher than James) when Stock preached it in the fall of 1606. And by the winter of 1608, when it was registered for publication, Stock's sermon had become even more in line with official positions.

If anything about Stock's *Sermon Preached at Paules Crosse* most reveals the true nature of his puritanism, it may well be his dedication of the work to the recently minted bishop James Montagu (1568–1618), who had been conse-crated Bishop of Bath and Wells in April of 1608. As part of Montagu's consecration ceremony at Lambeth Palace, a sermon 'defending the honour-able function of BISHOPS' had been preached by George Downame (d. 1634), who in 1616 would himself be consecrated as the Bishop of Derry.[21] Down-ame's sermon, published only about a month after it was delivered, provoked an immediate uproar, especially among radical puritans. Together with the exhaustive *Defence of the Sermon* which Downame subsequently wrote in response to some of his early attackers, it would stand for a generation as the most notorious profession of *iure divino* episcopacy made by an English divine prior to Joseph Hall's *Episcopacie by Divine Right* in 1640. Indefatigables such as William Ames, Paul Baynes, and Andrew Melville all went on to contribute furious rejoinders. Melville composed his 'A Schort Confutation of D. Downames apologetick Sermon maid for the dignitie of the episcopall office' while imprisoned in the Tower.[22]

In his dedication to Montagu, Stock extolled the fact that Montagu, 'beeing called to be a reuerend Bishop, a gouernor of the Church', was 'now aduanced to a speciall place of gouernment in the Church, and haue that authoritie in your hands' (sigs. *4r, *5r).[23] He never even alluded to the controversy that Montagu's consecration had aroused. Moreover, while it is impossible to imagine that Stock would have agreed with Downame's contention that episcopal church government had been instituted by divine right, his dedication made clear that the institution by no means contravened divine right. Stock opened by addressing Montagu as one who had been called 'by Gods prouidence' to be 'Lord Bishop of *Bathe*, and *Welles*' (sig. *3r), and he concluded by praying that 'the Lord of glorie' would aid Montague in his duties both to the international Protestant church 'in generall' and to the Protestant Church of England in particular, 'whereof you are made ouerseer' (sigs. *6v–7r). At the very moment in history when Montagu's ascension to the bishop's seat had become a lightning-rod of anti-episcopal dissidence, even if not for anything Montagu himself had done, Stock chose to dedicate to the bishop one of the only four works he would ever publish during his lifetime. And in the process of doing so, he unequivocally maintained the right and salutary possibilities of the office that Montagu now held.

To be sure, Stock's dedication to Montagu came explicitly freighted with certain personal and political motivations. As the first master of the newly founded Sidney Sussex College in Cambridge, Montagu had offered Stock a fellowship upon the latter's receipt of his MA from the neighbouring St John's College in 1594. Stock declined the offer, but he remembered in the dedication the 'auncient fauour which you bore towards mee in the Vniuersitie; and that good respect, though vndeserued, which you had of mee, for my good and preferment there: as also since . . . even now when you are aduanced to honour and place of dignitie' (sig. *6v). Stock also, more puritanically, encouraged Montagu to use his influence 'to incite' the king to take harsher measures against the papists residing in England and to inspire 'others in authoritie, both in Church and common wealth', to 'take some round and constant courses in reforming of abuses both in manners and doctrine'. The 'sinnes of the time' that Stock appears to have had in mind, however, were those of the multitude—the profaners, and 'malefactors', and 'specially Romish Idolaters'—and not those of the church authorities stationed above them (sigs. *5r, *3r–4r).

Stock's attitude to ecclesiastical authority in his *Sermon Preached at Paules Crosse* has been read in modern times as oppositional, even as 'potentially schismatic', but there is no evidence that it was ever so viewed by any of his contemporaries, least of all by the sermon's dedicatee.[24] While James I was still living, Montagu, who has been called 'the epitome of mainstream Jacobean conformist Calvinism', was entrusted with editing the king's *Workes* (1616).[25] The edition, which Montagu dedicated to Prince Charles, began with a preface by Montagu wherein he made special note of the king's work concerning '*this point of* Antichrist' and implicitly critiqued the king's policy of '*extending his Mercy to all* [English Roman Catholics], *that were not personall workers in that* Powder-Plot'. 'Catholicks', Montagu wrote, should be thankful for '*his* Maiesties *long* Patience', instead of complaining of their '*Miseries*' under James I, for '*the Church and Comonwealth both, doe trauail and groane vnder the burthen of your* [the Catholics'] *disobedience*'.[26] Stock's dedication, it would seem, had not fallen deaf upon the bishop's ears. Or rather, more likely, Stock had risked the posture of sternly advising Montagu and James I not as a kind of threat but precisely because he knew (or believed there to be) a common bond and shared objective among them, or at the very least between himself and Montagu.

Anti-papist polemic, the most consistent feature of Stock's extant writings, functioned as both the key ingredient and the key indication of his conformable puritanism. In this, as in many respects, Stock was powerfully indebted to his mentor, William Whitaker (1547/8–1595), the master of St John's College, Cambridge while Stock was a student there. Perhaps the most famous moderate puritan of his day, Whitaker earned international renown as one of Protestantism's greatest confuters of Bellarmine. Yet Whitaker took care to ensure that his attacks on the Church of Rome did not become, as they did for many more radical puritans, an opportunity for simultaneous critique of the Church of England. Whitaker's ardent anti-popery, in fact, underwrote a dedicated allegiance to the English Church and a vocal commitment to its defence. This accounts for why Archbishop Whitgift, while notoriously impeding the publication of other puritan anti-papal treatises, nonetheless remained an enthusiastic patron of Whitaker's works. When Whitaker died, Whitgift wrote to Thomas Neville that 'Mr Whitaker's death doth affect me exceedingly in many respects; he being a man whom I love very well and had purposed to have employed him in matters of great importance'.[27] Indeed, along the 'spectrum of puritan opinion', Peter Lake locates Whitaker at the far, moderate right, 'with the relatively quiescent acceptance of the demands of the national Church that seems to have characterised [Whitaker's] career'.[28]

Stock's contemporary biographer recalled that Whitaker had 'favoured Master *Stock* very much for his ingenuity, industry and proficiency in his Studies' during Stock's time as a student at St John's, and Stock repaid that favour by imbibing and then emulating Whitaker's particular brand of puritanism throughout his career.[29] In all of Stock's publications and other extant sermons, one finds the same scrupulous intertwining of an unwavering opposition to the Church of Rome with an unwavering commitment to the Church of England, even if not to an uncritical endorsement of all the latter's policies and habits. The first of Stock's published works, in fact, was an English translation of the very piece of anti-papal polemic through which Whitaker had himself first 'gained the pseudo-official position as champion of the English church against Rome that remained the backbone of his career for the rest of his life': Whitaker's famous *Ad Rationes Decem Edmundi Campiani Responsio* (1581), translated by Stock as *An Answere to the Ten Reasons of Edmund Campian* (1606).[30]

Among many possible examples of the characteristically conformable bent of Stock's anti-papist polemic is a sermon he preached to the congregation of All Hallows (with Milton's father potentially present) on 14 June 1607. Having declared that 'Gods word is the sure rule, & touche stone, & that which agrees therwith is true, & the contrarie false', Stock expounded the implications of that conviction as follows:

The 1 use of this doctrine teacheth that the Churche of Rome is in an errour, which besides the word would haue vs to receyue from the aucthoritie of the Church & from the Popes bosome. Whatsoever the Churche delivers out of the word of God it is to be receyved, otherwise not, although it haue the aucthoritie of a hundred Bishopps, for that which one poore single person doth deliver & teache out of Gods word & wares, from scripture, is better & of more force then all the former. (BL MS Egerton 2877, 120r)

Stock's proclaimed willingness to privilege the teaching of one single preacher over and against 'the aucthoritie of a hundred Bishopps' might seem to imply a concomitant opposition to the Church of England and its authorities—or, at least, it might appear to trend in that radical direction. Other puritans certainly followed this same anti-papal argument to precisely that anti-episcopal conclusion. Stock, however, drew it to a *defence* of the Church of England. This 'serveth to prooue *our* Churche to be *the* true churche', he told his congregation, 'because we haue *the* word trulie, & sincearlie taught & preached. And further this doctrine overthrowes all Bellarmynes 15 notes of *the* true churche' (119v).

Nor did Stock stop there, but instead immediately pivoted into a rebuke of the Church of England's other determined opponents, radical English Protestants:

The Brownists saie we haue not *the* true churche, because we haue manie ceremonies. Indeed we can not be free from errour, because we are but men, but we saie, That if we err not in *the* fundamentall pointes, albeit manie things are not pure, yet is it a true church. (119v)

Moments like this, where Stock can be found referring openly to an ongoing *intra*-Church of England controversy, are rare. (The same, not coincidentally, holds true of Whitaker's extant works.)[31] Here, however, Stock not only cast his lot with the church in opposition to the radical Brownists, puritans whose congregational and anti-ceremonial beliefs had led them into separatism. He even defended the church's ceremonialism specifically. His defence of those ceremonies should not be (and would not have been) mistaken as conformist, not with Stock's insinuation that some unspecified portion of that ceremonialism might indeed constitute an error on the church's part. Rather, his defence was thoroughly conformable: it made conforming to the (ceremonial and episcopal) Church of England not just acceptable but right— for the English Church was '*the* true churche'. Failing to conform amounted to a sinful failure of perspective. It is hard to know exactly how ceremonial Stock kept his own service at All Hallows, but he maintained his ministry there until his death in 1626 with no citations or accusations of nonconformity.[32]

In the last years of his life, Stock helped found the Feoffees for Impropriations, a group of ministers, lawyers, and merchants who sought to procure tithes impropriated by the laity and to use them to install puritan lectureships throughout the country. Stock was one of the four founding ministers, together with Richard Sibbes, John Davenport, and Charles Offspring. The likes of Laud and Peter Heylyn would come to view the Feoffees as radical puritan subversives, and in 1633 the Feoffees were summoned before the high commission and disbanded.[33] Stock, of course, died prior to these later developments, but his brief involvement with the Feoffees has nonetheless been given a very Laudian reading by some Milton scholars, who have cited this activity as further proof of his 'nonconformist', radical puritanism.[34] Yet as Tom Webster has made clear in his study of the 'godly clergy' in early Stuart England, the Feoffees conceived their mission in altogether different terms. In their founding document, drawn up and adopted in February 1625, Stock and the other founding members stipulated that they would 'not present any Minister [to] be admitted and placed in any of their Church livings, but such as are *conformable* to the discipline and doctrine and government of the Church of England' (emphasis added). The founding Feoffees composed this document in private and for private purposes, never intending it for public view, and its recorded imperatives, therefore, cannot simply be dismissed as shrewdly duplicitous. William Gouge, who replaced Stock as a Feoffee upon his death, in fact 'protested himself wholly in favour of conformity to Bishop Laud'. Gouge had even 'been used by the authorities as a consultant to persuade recalcitrant nonconformists to compromise'. By the 1630s, again, the goal posts had moved: Laud increasingly refused to distinguish between conformable and radical puritans. But even at their trial, the Feoffees maintained that there was indeed a difference between the two. They reaffirmed, however futilely, that to the best of their knowledge they had only appointed lecturers who were 'conformable to the doctrine and discipline of the Church of England'.[35]

Scholars need to recognize the view of puritanism to which they are subscribing if they fail to acknowledge the very category of conformable puritanism that Church of England clergymen like Richard Stock expressly sought to foster. Stock was neither a conformist nor a radical, and if one insists on construing him as either one or the other, his conformability simply unravels into a fray of contradictions. At the same time that he was founding the Feoffees with the idea of establishing parish lectureships for young puritan clergymen like Edward Goodall (who would become the Miltons' rector in Horton in the later 1630s), Stock was also employing Brian Walton (1600–61) as his curate at All Hallows.[36] The future Bishop of Chester, as well as the future editor of the London polyglot Bible, Walton soon became a committed supporter of the Laudian and Royalist causes during the 1630s and 1640s. In 1641, he was attacked in print by his own parishioners for (among other reasons) his alleged unwillingness to emulate Stock's long-time practice of delivering a second sermon on Sunday afternoons. Parliament would ultimately deprive Walton of his benefices, and he would not have them reinstated till after the Restoration.[37] This is not to suggest that Stock might have countenanced or predicted the trajectory of Walton's career, but it is to show that Stock was conformable enough to hire a clergyman whose career would quickly move in that direction, and that such a clergyman was willing to begin his London ministry in Stock's parish. In his will, Stock remembered Walton (to the tune of five pounds) as his 'minister and helper'.[38]

Stock's congregation at All Hallows included avowed puritans such as Sir Henry Yelverton (1566–1630), who was known to be a dedicated patron of godly preaching, and who sent his eldest son to Cambridge to study under the famous puritan John Preston (1587–1628).[39] But it also included men like Milton's father, who, upon the family's relocation to Hammersmith, would become a member and possibly a churchwarden of a Laudian chapel-of-ease. He sent his own elder son, the young John Milton, to Cambridge to study under the lapsed puritan and future Laudian William Chappell (1582–1649).[40] A proper Calvinist, Stock's catechism belabours God's decree of irresistible election (for some) and irresistible reprobation (for many), and it refers to Arminianism as 'the Arminian heresie'.[41] Yet Stock himself continued to conform to a church increasingly in that heresy's grip, and that church never found cause to censure him. He unequivocally opposed its antagonists, both papists *and* radical Protestants. Like Whitaker, Stock refused for the Church of England to be ruled by 'a high Priest or chiefe Bishop', i.e., by the Pope, but he unequivocally supported its being governed by bishops.[42] He was no presbyterian, but he helped bring the young Milton under the tutelage of the future Smectymnuan Thomas Young, which proved to be one of the more important experiences of Milton's youth.

III. Thomas Young and the Gataker circle

Thomas Young's puritanism requires less teasing-out than Stock's primarily because, unlike Stock, Young lived through the 1630s, the events of which ultimately served to make it plain. The son of 'a vocal presbyterian' minister from Luncarty, Perthshire, and a graduate of St Leonard's College, St Andrews (MA, 1606), a university whose curriculum had been reformed along Ramist lines by Andrew Melville, Young's precise whereabouts in the years immediately following his graduation from St Andrews remain unknown. Some time after 1611 and before 1617 or 1618, however, he became an assistant to Thomas Gataker, rector since 1611 of St Mary's, Rotherhithe, in Surrey.[43] Outside of Gataker's having delivered Stock's funeral sermon at the Milton family's church, a service which the family likely would have attended, no surviving evidence connects Gataker with the Miltons directly. Yet over the course of Milton's youth, the Miltons would be directly connected with no fewer than three different ministers who were themselves directly connected with Gataker: Richard Stock, Thomas Young, and Edward Goodall. Indeed, those three together formed part of a circle of puritan clergymen of which Gataker was the hub. It was almost certainly through Gataker, for example, that Young became known to Stock, and thence to the Miltons. As such, the nature of Gataker's own puritanism bears noting.

Gataker entered Whitaker's St John's College, Cambridge as an undergraduate three years behind Stock, but their time there as students nonetheless overlapped enough for the two to become enduringly close. As he had done for Stock, James Montagu also procured a fellowship at Sidney Sussex for Gataker upon his graduation from St John's. Unlike Stock, however, Gataker accepted the position. He would resign the fellowship before long, but while at Sidney Sussex he shared a room with another of the college's young fellows, William Bradshaw (1570–1618), who grew to be both a notorious nonconformist and Gataker's other closest friend. Gataker, indeed, would ultimately preach Stock's and Bradshaw's funeral sermons, as well as contributing their biographies to Samuel Clarke's puritan *Lives*.[44] Along the spectrum of English puritanism, Gataker fell somewhere in between the two, yet by and large he appears to have shared Stock's commitment to conformability. It is telling that some twenty years after Bradshaw's death, Gataker prepared a revised edition not of Bradshaw's anti-conformable *Triall of Subscription* (1599) nor of his radical manifesto *English Puritanisme* (1605) but rather of Bradshaw's anti-separatist *Unreasonablenesse of the Separation* (1614).[45] Similarly, as Peter Lake has noted, Gataker's biography of Bradshaw in Clarke's *Lives* worked to portray Bradshaw as more moderate than he had been, with Gataker going 'out of his way to quote the admiring opinion of Bradshaw held by Bishop Joseph Hall'.[46] Gataker himself was only ever suspended from his ministry once, and even then only for a brief period of time in the 1620s and not for a failure to conform. He sent his son to Sidney

Sussex to be educated under the auspices of the exceedingly moderate puritan Samuel Ward (1572–1643), a former British delegate to the Synod of Dort and a man with whom Gataker corresponded for years. The rising tide of Arminianism in the English church troubled Gataker deeply, yet not even Laudianism drove Gataker into nonconformity or outright opposition to episcopacy. Modern historians have confidently identified him as a 'quintessential moderate puritan minister'.[47]

Through the associations between Gataker and Stock, Young began working as a tutor to the young Milton in either 1617 or 1618. It is not known whether Young was Milton's first private tutor or merely one of his first. Milton's statement that he was taught from his 'first yeeres ... by sundry masters and teachers both at home and at the schools' suggests Milton may have had several tutors.[48] Whatever the case, the arrangement with Young in particular lasted for no longer than three years, and most likely nearer to two. By April 1620, Young had accepted the post as chaplain to the English Merchant Adventurers in Hamburg. The relationship that Milton and he had formed by the time of his departure, however, proved to be a remarkably enduring one. While Young was abroad, they exchanged letters, and Milton even composed for Young a Latin elegy (Elegy IV), which he enclosed in the correspondence and later published in the 1645 *Poems*. When in 1628 Young returned to England and accepted a living in the Suffolk parish of Stowmarket, he and Milton continued to stay in touch, though it is difficult to know exactly to what extent. A letter sent to Young from Milton while still at Cambridge signals an intention to visit Young's new home, but more evident contact would come in the early 1640s with Milton's contribution to the first Smectymnuan tract, whose primary author was said to have been Young himself.[49]

Young's presbyterian origins in Scotland, and his presbyterian terminus as a Smectymnuan, should not lead us to conclude that Young had arrived in England as a presbyterian opponent of the country's episcopal church. Indeed, quite the opposite seems to have been the case. His clerical office in Hamburg was not that of a puritan exile, but was rather a position officially within the church.[50] So, too, of course, was Young's living in Suffolk, which he maintained unmolested throughout the Laudian ascendancy. Like Gataker, he would eventually be appointed to the Westminster Assembly, and there he would sit as an English clergyman, not as one of the Assembly's Scottish commissioners.[51]

As with Stock, and many a conformable puritan, the linchpin of Young's conformability seems to have been a zealous opposition to popery and, thereby, an equally zealous commitment to Protestant unity. About a year after arriving in Hamburg, Young had the opportunity to preach before the exiled Elector Palatine, Frederick V, who had recently been overthrown as the king of Bohemia by the imperial Catholic forces as part of the Thirty Years' War. Support of the Protestant Frederick, who was James I's son-in-law, became an increasingly polarizing issue within the English Church during the war. Many in England, especially the staunch Calvinists, believed that the Thirty Years' War was nothing less than a fight for the soul of Europe and the future of international Protestantism. James, however, was determined to stay free of the conflict, and he actively looked to suppress anything which might arouse calls for him to do otherwise. He even went so far as to forbid public prayer for Frederick. This had an exacerbating effect upon divides within the English Church, but James's policy did not just provoke alarm and unrest among the church's more radical clergymen: conformable puritans such as Gataker and various Calvinist authorities, from then bishops John Davenant and James Ussher to the future bishop Joseph Hall, all considered the Protestant struggle in Germany to be their own.[52]

Young's preaching before Frederick—with Young 'in his prayer beseeching God very affectionately for him', reported Joseph Mede shortly thereafter— evidently moved the Elector greatly:

the king [Frederick], when sermon was done, came and took him [Young] by the hand, thanked him, and desired him and others to do the like, as he trusted in God shortly to do well; that if our king, his father-in-law [James I], would undertake the protection of the Palatinate, for Bohemia, and the rest, he should, with God's assistance, do well enough, though things at the present were not as might be wished.

Whatever Young had said, it inspired Frederick to view him as a natural proponent of English involvement on the Palatinate's behalf, and as a sympathetic recipient of exactly the kind of hawkish critique of James I that the king so disdained. According to Mede, Frederick even gave Young 'a chain of gold with his own image upon it'.[53] Young's potential opposition to the English Church's official policy of non-involvement in the Thirty Years' War, again, need not imply that Young's relationship with the church itself was fraying, any more than did Joseph Hall's opposition to the church's official policy in that respect. Yet a divide was indeed opening up in the church, one that led many conformable puritans to feel that their religion had been alienated and betrayed, and it is not hard to determine the side of that divide on which Young fell, and, critically, on which he was perceived by the likes of Frederick V and Joseph Mede to fall. A degree of growing disaffection on Young's part may be sensed in a letter that he wrote on 4 April 1626 to Patrick Young, a possible relation and the royal librarian. The letter plaintively stresses that 'the condition of the reformed Church in Germany, reformed away from the Popish shit' [*stercus Pontificium*], is far worse than has been reported: 'everyone observes that the church has been sadly rent asunder, and is nearly exhausted, by battles of combat and of opinions (battles in the name of which its safety is now thrown into the utmost jeopardy, while the church's most hostile Popish enemies foster, and by their cunning devices augment, them').[54]

Young's letters to Milton, at least one of which was written around this same time, do not appear to have survived, but his correspondence with Patrick Young may give a clue as to what some of their contents might have been. The elegy that Milton sent to Young in the spring of 1627 included multiple references to the Thirty Years' War, wherein Milton prayed for the safety of his former tutor in an embattled land, 'a pastor famous for his honouring of the primitive faith' (*antiquae clarus pietatis honore/Praesul*).[55] He seems to have intended the poem, at least in part, not just as a response to one of Young's previous letters but as a token of his appreciation for the Hebrew Bible that Young had evidently enclosed with it.[56] Both gifts, the poem and the Bible, accord nicely with our understanding of each man. Years later, however, Milton appears to have repaid Young's gift more in kind by giving him a copy of Thomas Cranmer's *Reformatio Legum Ecclesiasticarum* (1571), and this gift, by contrast, in many respects does not (Fig. 7).[57] In the 'Postscript' to Smectymnuus's *An Answer*, likely written around the very same time in which he gave Young the book, Milton rebukes Archbishop Cranmer, by name, for his 'deficiencie of zeale and courage', presenting him as a testament to the fact that even the 'best Bishops' in England's past balked at reforming the church to the fullest.[58] Yet this apparent discontinuity can be resolved by recognizing that Cranmer's *Reformatio*—perhaps especially as edited for posthumous publication by John Foxe, who supplied the work with its title—symbolized something else entirely besides the Church of England's commitment to the episcopal office of its primary author. It represented the church's historical commitment to the cause of anti-popery and Reformation, and to a corresponding vision of international Protestant unity which Cranmer had famously tried to promote.[59] In other words, it

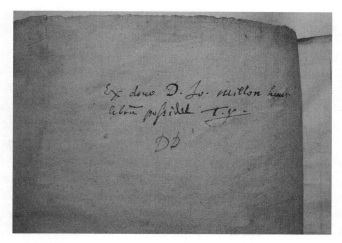

Fig. 7. Jesus College, Cambridge, book inscription from Cranmer's *Reformatio*

reflected the church's past dedication to the very ideals espoused by Young to Frederick V, to Patrick Young, and perhaps (as the gift may suggest) to the young Milton himself.

Thomas Young's responses to the Thirty Years' War nevertheless provide the first signs of conflict between him and the official policies of the English Church. During the 1630s, as the power of the Laudian authorities increased, those tensions began intensifying into opposition. In a 19 May 1631 letter written by Gataker in Rotherhithe and sent to Samuel Ward in Cambridge, Gataker reported that Young had returned from Germany and had requested that a copy of certain 'considerations' of his be sent along to Ward:

I have sent a copy of those considerations leaft with me by the Scottish minister, who is returned againe. He told me that he heard that you had ben in town, & that he had repaired unto you, had he known it before your departure. The man seemeth to be much affected with the busienes, & desirous by any meanes or paines he can to promote it. But I feare there are so many difficulties in it, that we shal hardly be so happy as to see it donne in our days.[60]

Unfortunately, Gataker did not specify 'the busienes' with which Young's considerations were concerned, but there are hints. For one, there is the fact that Young wished to confer with Ward, the master of Sidney Sussex College and a puritan famous for his moderation when it came to some of the most controversial issues of the day. That moderation, indeed, helped Ward secure perhaps the two defining appointments of his career: the first as one of the King James Bible's seven translators of the Apocrypha, whose very inclusion in the Bible many puritans opposed, and the second as one of the six British delegates to the Synod of Dort, where Ward served alongside the Bishop of Llandaff, George Carleton, and the future bishops John Davenant and Joseph Hall. Ward would never waver in his support for episcopacy, maintaining friendly correspondence with bishops and archbishops throughout his life. Yet he also remained a lifelong opponent of Arminianism, the very thing he had been sent to Dort to quell, and thus the growing Arminianism of his own national church during the 1620s and 1630s increasingly placed him in opposition to its prevailing ecclesiology. Even in those years, however, Ward never felt harried into leaving Cambridge, as other puritans did, and he continued to be a close personal friend of Joseph Mede, the most influential fellow of the adjacent Christ's College and a known defender of Arminian ceremonialism.[61]

By virtue of Ward's reputation, puritans were often eager to discuss 'considerations' like Young's with him. Over the course of their long correspondence, Gataker frequently broached topics of heightened puritan concern with Ward, and by the time of the letter relaying Young's own considerations, the rise of Arminianism, both abroad and at home, had emerged as a dominant theme of those 'private discussions' between them. 'For the points of Arminianisme publiqely preached', Gataker bemoaned to Ward in a letter immediately preceding the one regarding Young, 'it is commonly bruited *that* few come up either at Court or Crosse, but *that* touch upon them'.[62] Indeed, in his letters from that time to Ward, Gataker could be near despairing when reflecting upon the entrenched Arminianism in his national church: 'At home we have little good [news]: some reports of an heavy censure his Ma*jes*tie should have lately imposed upo*n* some Oxford men for dealing in thease Arminian co*n*troversies . . . That factio*n* seeme to cary things w*i*th an high hand, & to have greate backers above.'[63] By 1633, he was lamenting that he had nothing 'to impart unto you, *that* in thease declining times might affoard any refreshing either to my self in relating or yo*u*r self in reading'.[64] Given Ward's and Gataker's own conformable puritanism, it would be unwise to presume that Young's considerations would have bespoken an implacable or 'radical' opposition to the Church of England's doctrine, discipline, or government. Almost certainly, for instance, Young's considerations were not anti-prelatical. However, Gataker's dark characterization ('much affected with the busienes, & desirous by any meanes or paines he can to promote it') together with his own blend of sympathy and pessimism ('I feare there are so many difficulties in it, *that* we shal hardly be so happy as to see it donne in *our* days') make it equally unlikely that Young's considerations voiced support for the policies and designs of the Laudian rule.[65]

By early 1636, Young's conformability had been pushed over the brink into radicalization, in that he was by then underway with committing his first unequivocally radical act. Some time around February of that year, Samuel Hartlib recorded in his diary, *Ephemerides*: 'Mr Yong adornavit egregium *Tractatum* de Sabatho *Lingua* Latina *qui dicitur* brevi imprimi curante Mr Bacon' (Mr Young has prepared an excellent Tract on the Sabbath in Latin which is said to be printed shortly under the care of Mr Bacon).[66] Ultimately published three years later, Young's tract *Dies Dominica* (The Lord's Day) advocated strict observance of the Sabbath in overt opposition to the reissued Book of Sports, which sanctioned Sunday recreation after church services had concluded. Young dedicated the tract 'To the HOLY, ORTHODOX CHURCH OF CHRIST. Happily cleansed from the filth of *POPERY*', and he went on to decry 'the abominable, and un-christian-like violation of the Lords Day', which 'doth expose the holy Worship of God Almighty to the wicked's scorn'. 'They who love it [the Lord's Day] with a sincere love do see, and lament it', Young continued, 'although they who are bewitched with the malignant spirit of Popery, see, and rejoyce at it'. Even more sharply, Young recalled the example of the sixth-century king of Burgundy Guntram who had 'reproved the Bishops which fed not with Gospel Doctrines the people committed to them' but rather 'by their profligate manners stirred up the wrath of a revenging God against him'. To keep the bishops from ever doing so again, Guntram had it 'ordained in a Council, *That the Lords day should be kept religiously*', prompting Young to declare the following:

The pattern of this most Christian King, while the victory in this our age inclineth to the enemies, perswades us devoutly to keep the L. day solemnity; for which we have sought unsuccessfully almost these twenty years, against the enemies of our liberty, that have roared in the Churches of God, to our Great sorrow. When we count the causes of this will, why should we not apply our minds with *Guntheramnus* to bewail the heynous violation of the Lords day?[67]

Young well understood the radical nature of his tract. It was published under a pseudonym, credited no printer, and did not specify a place of publication.

While Young's authorship has long been known, almost everything else surrounding the tract's production has remained unclear.[68] Hartlib's passing mention of a 'Mr Bacon' in connection with the work, however, sheds some important light on the matter. Young gave a presentation copy of the tract with manuscript corrections in his own hand to Nathaniel Bacon (1593–1660), a lawyer and politician from Suffolk. Much later, in his will dated 27 September 1653, Young named Nathaniel's brother Francis Bacon (1600–63) a trustee of his estate. (Like his brother, Francis also went on to become a member of parliament.) Given Young's associations with Nathaniel and Francis Bacon, it seems probable that one of these two men must be the 'Mr Bacon' under whose care *Dies Dominica* was allegedly being printed. (Elsewhere in *Ephemerides*, in an unrelated entry, Hartlib himself also refers to 'the 2. Bacons, Nath*aniel* and Francis'.) This links Young in the mid-1630s, along with the production of *Dies Dominica* specifically, to a family of staunch and long-established presbyterian puritans. The father of Nathaniel and Francis, Edward Bacon (1548/9–1618), had actually lived with Beza in Geneva for a brief time. The Bacons of Suffolk were appreciably more radical than puritans such as Richard Stock and Thomas Gataker, and the evidence both within and outside of *Dies Dominica* suggests that by the early days of 1636, at the latest, the same had become true of Thomas Young.[69]

Not long thereafter, the same appears to have become true of the young Milton. Scholars have often identified 1637 as a watershed year in terms of Milton's relation to the English Church, the most compelling reason being that the autumn of that year was when Milton composed 'Lycidas' (though not, it must be remembered, the explicitly anti-prelatical headnote that he later prefixed to it). Further cause to suspect that 1637 may have marked such a turning point in the young Milton's religious and political life, however, has been more recently found to lie in the record of an episcopal visitation of the Milton family's parish. Having relocated with his family from Hammersmith some time in 1636, Milton now attended the ancient Norman church of St Michael's ministered by the puritan rector Edward Goodall, who, like Young, had formerly been an assistant to Thomas Gataker in Rotherhithe, and who, like Milton, was also a Cambridge graduate. The visitation in question took place on 8 August 1637, and it resulted, among other things, in the Milton family's pew being ordered lowered, having been declared 'to[o] high', and in Goodall himself being cited for partial nonconformity. Specifically, the rector was 'admonished to read prayers following the form of the book', i.e., the Book of Common Prayer, and 'to preach with vestments over the pelisse', the clerical gown. There is also a high probability that the tombstone of Milton's mother, who had died in April of 1637, was one of the two in the chancel cited for being 'laid the wrong waye', as in not facing east.[70]

The report of the Horton visitation furnishes the earliest documentary evidence of a potential conflict between the demands of the Laudian church and the practices of Milton and his family. What it ultimately may tell us about the young Milton's own evolving puritanism remains subject to debate, and must be left for future studies. This essay concerns the puritanism of the clergymen with whom the young Milton came in contact, and significantly, with regard to Edward Goodall, the visitation report reveals him in the end to have been practicing his ministry not as a radicalized puritan but as a conformable one. The report notes with approval, for instance, the presence of 'a convenient kneeleing bench before the Railes' of the altar, the imposition of altar rails being one of the most controversial of the Laudian reforms.[71] Moreover, Goodall *responded* to the visitation as a conformable puritan: he conformed. Goodall was to certify soon thereafter that the recommended changes had been made, and this he evidently did. On 21 February 1638, the diocesan church court records note that 'mr Goodall hath cutt his seate & so hath mr Milton'.[72]

Further indication of Goodall's conformability may be glimpsed in relation to the practices of his father-in-law, the puritan clergyman Thomas Valentine, who in 1635 had been suspended from his living at Chalfont St Giles by Laud himself for opposing the reissued Book of Sports, the very element of Laudian reform to occasion Thomas Young's *Dies Dominica* around the exact same time. Specifically, Valentine refused to read the Book of Sports to his congregation.[73] Goodall's close, personal connection to a nonconforming puritan like Valentine is, of course, significant. Yet it is most significant perhaps not for suggesting a possible affinity between Goodall and his father-in-law but rather for accentuating a crucial difference between them. In the face of Laudian censure, Goodall conformed; Valentine did not. This point needs to be made in light of the speculation that Goodall may have sympathized with his father-in-law's nonconformity. If he did, he did so privately. On record, Goodall maintained his living in Horton continuously and, outside of the August 1637 visitation, without incident during the most intolerant years of Laudian rule.[74]

Considering Valentine in relation to Thomas Young, at the same time, also helps throw into relief the fact that the line between a conformable puritan and a radical one became much less stark over the course of the early seventeenth century, as Laud and his ilk increasingly denied there to be any line between the two at all. Further, it shows that the line was not one a puritan necessarily crossed all at once. Though the 1633 Book of Sports compelled him to write the radical *Dies Dominica*, Young otherwise seems to have retained his commitment to conformability and to working within the Laudian Church of England through the 1630s. Like Gataker and Goodall, he withstood the immense pressure exerted upon conformable puritans during that decade either to become conformists or to be cast out as radicals. He was never cited for nonconformity or ever deprived of his ministry by Laudian authorities.[75] At least in the case of Young's conformability, however, the strain proved finally buckling. By 1640, he was meeting with the men who would band together to write the Smectymnuan tracts. There in attendance at those meetings may have been the no longer young, and certainly no longer conformable, Milton.[76]

IV. Milton's elegy for Andrewes and some final thoughts

Some time in the late autumn or early winter of 1626, the undergraduate Milton composed a Latin elegy for Bishop Lancelot Andrewes, who had died on 25 September of that year. A number of things about the poem, particularly its dedicatee, place the elegy at a conspicuous variance with the reformist puritanism that would come to be stridently advocated by Milton in his anti-prelatical tracts of 1641–2. Indeed, in *The Reason of Church-Government*, Milton took aim at Andrewes explicitly, devoting multiple chapters in the work to his confutation. As is perhaps too well known, Andrewes was one of the most influential forbears of the Caroline church's Arminian ceremonialism. In 1625, Richard Montagu, writing in defence of his incendiary tract *A New Gagg for an Old Goose* (1624), claimed precedence for some of his controversial positions in the prior work of Andrewes, whom Montagu twice referred to as 'our GAMALIEL'.[77] Laud, who it has been said regarded Andrewes 'as a model and an inspiration', co-edited the most important, and most aggressively anti-Calvinist, collection of Andrewes's sermons—

published posthumously as *XCVI Sermons* (1629)—under the authorization of Charles I himself.[78] Nor was Andrewes's special significance to Laudianism lost on that movement's opponents. In 1637, Robert Baillie groused that the Laudians treated Andrewes as 'the semigod of the neu faction'.[79]

Milton's Elegy III, first printed in the 1645 *Poems*, addresses the late Andrewes as 'worthiest bishop' (*dignissime praesul*) and 'the great glory of Winchester' (*gloria magna Wintoniae*), Winchester having been the location of Andrewes's see.[80] Not only does Milton accentuate Andrewes's status as a bishop multiple times, including with the poem's full title (*Elegia Tertia. In Obitum Praesulis Wintoniensis*), he concludes the poem with a vision of Andrewes being embraced by angels and received into heaven clothed in the ceremonial vestment of an alb (51–68). Primarily for these reasons, aligning the elegy with the young Milton's supposed puritanism has long seemed to pose problems for commentators. The most common solution has been to distance Milton from the work. One eighteenth-century editor of Milton's poetry, for instance, declared that 'Milton, as he grew old in puritanism, must have looked back with disgust and remorse on the panegyric of this performance'.[81] Others, though, have been tempted to construe even Milton's elegy for Andrewes as the work of a young puritan radical, notwithstanding. Perhaps most notably, Barbara Lewalski, inaccurately describing the poem as 'pointedly silent about [Andrewes's] episcopal office', has maintained that even it shows Milton 'attempting to find a poetic voice consonant with his reformist views' and registering his 'reformist concerns'.[82]

In their biography, Campbell and Corns likewise address the elegy's apparent incompatibility with the young Milton's supposed puritanism. Rather than excusing or marginalizing the implied ecclesiology of the poem, however, they insist upon it. 'No evidence better establishes the ideological perspective of young Milton than the poem he wrote for Lancelot Andrewes', they write, and they go on to discuss the poem as proof that the young Milton simply could not have been a puritan (32). Yet as this essay has tried to show, Milton's elegy for Andrewes need only be seen as antithetical to Milton's having been a puritan if one believes that supporting episcopacy and endorsing the church's ceremonialism were necessarily antithetical to being one. In other words, while Milton's elegy for Andrewes may be problematic for those who would construe the young Milton as a young puritan radical, it only frustrates the belief that Milton was a young puritan for those who regard 'puritan' and 'radical' as one and the same.

There is nothing in the elegy to Bishop Andrewes which would preclude a young, conformable puritan in 1626 from having written it. Richard Stock, as we have seen, both self-identified as a puritan, and on various, public occasions celebrated bishops and defended the Church of England from radical, reformist attacks on its ceremonial discipline—and Stock did so much more directly and boisterously than did the young Milton. Moreover, Andrewes's significance as the banner carrier of Arminian ceremonialism was hardly codified at the time of his death.[83] Laud's selected edition of Andrewes's sermons, the work that did the most to fix Andrewes as 'the founding father of English ceremonial Arminianism', did not appear until three years *after* Milton composed his elegy.[84] Relatively little of what we now regard as Andrewes's substantial oeuvre, in fact, had been published prior to his death in 1626. It is certainly the case that some of his posthumously published writings had circulated in manuscript during his lifetime; however, by the time of Milton's elegy, Andrewes's most famous works unquestionably remained his defences of James I and the English Church against the attacks of Cardinal Bellarmine. Tellingly, both times that Montagu adduced Andrewes as the church's Gamaliel in *Appello Caesarem*, it was Andrewes's *Responsio ad Apologiam Cardinalis Bellarmini* that he referenced in the margin.[85]

As has been noted, Bellarmine loomed over English Protestantism throughout Milton's youth. Many of Milton's countrymen published notable works of anti-Bellarmine polemic, from Stock and Andrewes to James I, and many more kept theological commonplace books arranged in opposition to Bellarmine, from Samuel Ward to Milton himself.[86] Given all this, it at least would not have been unusual if the young Milton had chiefly thought of Andrewes more in anti-Catholic than in anti-Calvinist terms, not as a supporter of Arminian ceremonialism but rather as one of the great defenders of England's embattled Protestant church and state. Milton, indeed, would characterize Andrewes in much this way in *The Reason of Church-Government*, referring to him as a 'famous Protestant Bishop', one 'so much bruited for learning'.[87] Of course, in the tract, that praise served a very backhanded purpose, similar to Milton's characterization of Cranmer as one of England's 'best Bishops' in *Of Reformation*. Yet, as we have seen, just as Cranmer's *Reformatio* almost certainly stood for something beyond episcopacy when Milton gave a copy of that work to Thomas Young, so too Andrewes well could have stood for something quite besides Arminian ceremonialism when Milton wrote his Elegy III. Even after Laud's edition of Andrewes's sermons had appeared in 1629, certain puritans continued to find in Andrewes something other than a proto-Laudian. In 1642, John Jackson, who would serve with Gataker and Young as a member of the Westminster Assembly, published an edited collection of some of Andrewes's lectures and sermons through which Andrewes was presented, among other things, as having been a proponent of strict sabbatarianism and a supporter of further church reform along puritan lines. The work included a frontispiece portrait, adjacent to the title-page, depicting Andrewes in his vestments and encircled by the appellation of 'Most Reverend and Most Learned Bishop' (*Reverendissimus et Doctissimus Episcopus*). A brief poem by the puritan George Wither appeared beneath it.[88]

While Milton's elegy for Andrewes thus does not preclude the young Milton from having been a conformable puritan, neither does it constitute evidence in and of itself that he was one. The poem's placement in the 1645 *Poems*, however, may be yet another indication of the conformable puritanism around which Milton had been raised and to which he had been intimately connected throughout his youth. In the collection, the elegies for Andrewes and Thomas Young that Milton had composed within a year of each other at Cambridge would appear back-to-back.[89] By understanding more fully the puritanism of the young Milton's earliest and most influential clerical contacts—and, in the process, by recovering a category of puritanism, *conformable puritanism*, long denied to and in Milton scholarship—what can otherwise seem incongruous with the puritanism of Milton's youth may be found rather to be a fitting testament of it.

Notes

I would like to thank Edward Jones, Francis J. Bremer, Nick Hardy, and Peter Lake for reading versions of this essay in draft and responding with generosity. This essay owes most, however, to William Poole and Thomas Roebuck. Finally, it could not have been written without the support of Magdalen College, the Rhodes Trust, Amy Bregar, and my parents. I dedicate it to Kirsty Milne.
1. Barbara K. Lewalski, 'How Radical was the Young Milton?', in Stephen B. Dobranski and John P. Rumrich (eds.), *Milton and Heresy* (Cambridge, 1998), 50.
2. Darbishire, 2. On Young and Essex, see Edward Jones, '"Ere Half My Days": Milton's Life, 1608–1640', in Nicholas McDowell and Nigel Smith (eds.), *The Oxford Handbook of Milton* (Oxford, 2009), 7–8.
3. *CPW*, i. 540, 602.
4. Lewalski, *Life*, 1.

5. Campbell and Corns, 15–16.

6. It is telling, indeed, that Peter Lake's classic study of *Moderate Puritans and the Elizabethan Church* (Cambridge, 1982) appears neither in the bibliography for Lewalski's biography of Milton nor in the one compiled by Campbell and Corns. Other studies by Lake that have served to enhance our understanding of the early modern period's broad spectrum of puritans, non-puritan Calvinists, and Arminians include his 'Moving the Goal Posts? Modified Subscription and the Construction of Conformity in the Early Stuart Church', in Peter Lake and Michael Questier (eds.), *Conformity and Orthodoxy in the English Church, c. 1560–1660* (Woodbridge, 2000), 179–205; 'Reading Clarke's *Lives* in Political and Polemical Context', in Kevin Sharpe and Steven N. Zwicker (eds.), *Writing Lives: Biography and Textuality, Identity and Representation in Early Modern England* (Oxford, 2008), 293–318; and *The Boxmaker's Revenge: 'Orthodoxy', 'Heterodoxy' and the Politics of the Parish in Early Stuart London* (Manchester, 2001). Important studies by other scholars to have done the same would include John Coffey, *John Goodwin and the Puritan Revolution: Religion and Intellectual Change in Seventeenth-Century England* (Woodbridge, 2006); Patrick Collinson, *Godly People: Essays on Protestantism and Puritanism* (1983) and his *The Religion of Protestants: The Church in English Society 1559–1625* (Oxford, 1982); David R. Como, *Blown by the Spirit: Puritanism and the Emergence of an Antinomian Underground in Pre-Civil-War England* (Stanford, Ca., 2004); Kenneth Fincham, 'Clerical Conformity from Whitgift to Laud', in Peter Lake and Michael Questier (eds.), *Conformity and Orthodoxy*, 125–58; Anthony Milton, *Catholic and Reformed: The Roman and Protestant Churches in English Protestant Thought, 1600–1640* (Cambridge, 1995); Jean-Louis Quantin, *The Church of England and Christian Antiquity: The Construction of a Confessional Identity in the 17th Century* (Oxford, 2009); Nicholas Tyacke, *Anti-Calvinists: The Rise of English Arminianism, c. 1590–1640* (Oxford, 1987); and Tom Webster, *Godly Clergy in Early Stuart England: The Caroline Puritan Movement, c. 1620–1643* (Cambridge, 1997).

7. It should be noted that some puritans were in fact Arminians, as John Coffey, cautioning against the hoary tendency to define puritanism 'as militant Calvinism', reminds us. Still, that particular species of puritan was unusual enough for most early moderns (along with most modern scholars) to treat the possibility of an Arminian puritan as a contradiction in terms (*John Goodwin and the Puritan Revolution*, 10).

8. Francis J. Bremer, *Puritanism: A Very Short Introduction* (Oxford, 2009), 2; Lake, *Moderate Puritans*, 10-15, and 'Reading Clarke's *Lives*', 293–303.

9. Record of these sermons survives in British Library MS Egerton 2877, the commonplace book of Gilbert Frevile, with the passages quoted from here appearing on fos. 145v, 141v, and 120r. They form part of a series of 'Notes taken, at .61. seuerall sermons of one Mr Richard Stock in London. A°. 1606. & 1607', which occupies a sizable portion of the manuscript. Since Frevile, of Bishop Middleham, County Durham, was not one of Stock's parishioners, Frevile's commonplace book gives some indication of the reach of Stock's significance, beyond what Stock's slim published output might otherwise suggest.

10. Lake, *The Boxmaker's Revenge*, 12–13.

11. Lake, 'Reading Clarke's *Lives*', 296. Lake, indeed, designates managing to remain continuously in one's ministerial post a defining characteristic of 'classic moderate puritans'.

12. Kenneth Fincham, 'Episcopal Government 1603–1640', in Kenneth Fincham (ed.), *The Early Stuart Church, 1603–1642* (Basingstoke, 1993), 77; Fincham, 'Clerical Conformity', 151–53; Webster, *Godly Clergy*, 83–84, 157–67, 335.

13. Richard Montagu, *Appello Caesarem* (1625), 308. Quoted by Fincham, 'Clerical Conformity', 151.

14. See esp. Fincham, 'Clerical Conformity', 125–26, 138–58; Lake, 'Moving the Goal Posts?', *passim*; Webster, *Godly Clergy*, 250–51.

15. *The Registers of All Hallows, Bread Street, and of St John the Evangelist, Friday Street, London*, ed. W. Bruce Bannerman, *Publications of the Harleian Society*, 43 (1913), 16.

16. Thomas Gataker, *Abrahams Decease . . . Delivered at the Funerall of that Worthy Servant of Christ, Mr Richard Stock, Late Pastor of All-Hallowes Bread-street* (1627), 4. Stock catechized 'the *males* apart one day, and the *females* another; the *riper* and *forwarder* first in the *presence* of the *ruder* and *rawer*, and the *ruder* and *rawer apart* by themselues after the *departure* of the former, that they might both *reape* what *fruit* might bee by *hearing* them, and yet *receiue no discouragement* by *being heard* of them' (12).

17. Bannerman, *Registers*, 169. Stock succeeded Edmonds as rector upon the latter's death.

18. See, for example, Campbell and Corns, 15–16; Lewalski, *Life*, 4, 549n18; Millar MacLure, *The Paul's Cross Sermons, 1534–1642* (Toronto, 1958), 90, 95.

19. Richard Stock, *A Sermon Preached at Paules Crosse* (1609), 15–16, 19.

20. Anthony Milton, *Catholic and Reformed*, 94–95; Stefania Tutino, *Empire of Souls: Robert Bellarmine and the Christian Commonwealth* (Oxford, 2010), 117–58.

21. George Downame, *Two Sermons, The One Commending the Ministerie in Generall: The Other Defending the Office of Bishops in Particular* (1608), sig. ¶2r. In this essay, I retain the most common early modern spelling of Downame's name.

22. See George Downame, *A Defence of the Sermon Preached at the Consecration of the L. Bishop of Bath and Welles* (1611); Paul Baynes, *The Diocesans Tryall*, ed. and with a preface by William Ames ([Amsterdam], 1621); and Andrew Melville, 'A Schort Confutation of D. Downames apologetick Sermon maid for the dignitie of the episcopall office', Edinburgh University Library, Dc.6.45, 1–7. On Downame's sermon and the history of *iure divino* arguments for episcopacy in England, see Anthony Milton, *Catholic and Reformed*, 454–61. On Melville's tract, which was never published, see James Kirk, 'Andrew Melville', *ODNB*.

23. Asterisks form part of the signatures for the work's introductory pages, encompassing the title-page, the dedication to Montagu, and a brief epistle to the reader. The text of the sermon itself commences on sig. A1r, which is numerated as page 1.

24. Quoting MacLure, *The Paul's Cross Sermons*, 95.

25. Peter E. McCullough, 'James Montagu', *ODNB*.

26. James Montagu, 'The Preface to the Reader', in James I, *The Workes of the Most High and Mightie Prince, Iames by the Grace of God, King of Great Britaine, France and Ireland, Defender of the Faith, &c.*, ed. James Montagu (1616), sigs. d3v, e2r. See also Anthony Milton, *Catholic and Reformed*, 57, 94.

27. Lake, *Moderate Puritans*, 58–65, 74–75, 93–115, 169–200, with the quote from Whitgift appearing on p. 59. See also C. S. Knighton, 'William Whitaker', *ODNB*. Though no doubt apocryphal, the report in fact circulated during the early modern period that Bellarmine kept a picture of Whitaker hanging above his desk, in honor of Whitaker's being in Bellarmine's own estimation the best of all his Protestant adversaries.

28. Lake, 'Moving the Goal Posts?', 203.

29. Samuel Clarke (ed.), *The Lives of Thirty-Two English Divines, Famous in their Generations for Learning and Piety, and Most of them Sufferers in the Cause of Christ*, 3rd edn. (1677), 61. The biography of Stock in Clarke's *Lives* is taken substantially from the eulogy delivered by Gataker at Stock's funeral and later published in Gataker's *Abrahams Decease*. It seems fair, therefore, to attribute Stock's entry in Clarke's *Lives* to Gataker in the main, though Stock's entry is itself unattributed, and some of the contributions to it may not be Gataker's.

30. Quoting Lake, *Moderate Puritans*, 59. See also William Whitaker, *An Answere to the Ten Reasons of Edmund Campian*, trans. Richard Stock (1606), a full translation of William Whitaker, *Ad Rationes Decem Edmundi Campiani . . . Responsio*, 2nd edn. (1581), with the margins filled by an abridged translation of William Whitaker, *Responsionis ad Decem illas Rationes . . . Defensio contra Confutationem Joannis Duraei Scoti, Presbyteri, Iesuitae* (1583).

31. Lake, *Moderate Puritans*, 61.

32. Campbell and Corns, 15.

33. Webster, *Godly Clergy*, 82–86; Anthony Milton, *Laudian and Royalist Polemic in Seventeenth-Century England: The Career and Writings of Peter Heylyn* (Manchester, 2007), 25–29.

34. See, for example, Campbell and Corns: 'Stock was never accused of nonconformist practices in his church, *but* in 1625 he was to align himself with the puritan cause by becoming one of the founding Feoffees for Impropriations [emphasis added]' (15). There are a couple of important things to note here. Firstly, there is the characteristic slippage between 'nonconformist practices' and 'the puritan cause', as opposed to the nonconformist or *radical* puritan cause. Secondly, there is the clear suggestion that Stock's connection with the Feoffees cuts against his never having been accused of nonconformity, as opposed to going hand in hand with it. In essence, as I argue here, the conjunction between Stock's apparent conformity and his association with the Feoffees should be 'and', not 'but'.

35. Webster, *Godly Clergy*, 83–85.

36. See Edward Jones, '"Church-Outed by the Prelats": Milton and the 1637 Inspection of the Horton Parish Church', *Journal of English and Germanic Philology*, 102 (2003), 56–57; Paul S. Seaver, *The Puritan Lectureships: The Politics of Religious Dissent, 1560-1662* (Stanford, Ca., 1970), 166; Brett Usher, 'Richard Stock', *ODNB*.

37. See *The Articles and Charge Proved in Parliament Against Doctor Walton, Minister of St Martins Orgars in Cannonstreet* (1641): 'Hee neither preacheth nor catechiseth on Sundayes in the afternoones, nor will permit the Petitioners to procure a Preacher, though at their owne charge'. This is noted by D. S. Margoliouth, rev. Nicholas Keene, 'Brian Walton', *ODNB*, but the title of the work is there incorrectly given.

38. National Archives, PROB 11/149, fo. 6v. This information is slightly misquoted in Usher, 'Richard Stock', *ODNB*.

39. The parish register of All Hallows notes that a daughter of one of the parishioners was buried near '*Ser Henerey Yellvertones pewe*' (Bannerman, *Registers*, 178). Gataker dedicated *Abrahams Decease* to Yelverton, noting that Yelverton's '*speciall interest* in that *worthy Seruant of Christ* [*sc*. Stock], whom this *weak work* concerneth, by your *singular fauours* to him and his deseruedly procured, cannot but giue you *interest* in the *worke* itself before any'. 'Vnto your *Worship* therefore I addresse and direct it', Gataker continued the dedication, 'as to one that may iustly lay *best claime* to it' (sigs. A3r-v). Yelverton's eldest son, Christopher, by then a former student of Preston's, was married at All Hallows by Stock on 29 September 1620 (Bannerman, *Registers*, 105). On Yelverton, see also S. R. Gardiner, rev. Louis A. Knafla, 'Sir Henry Yelverton', *ODNB*; Usher, 'Richard Stock', *ODNB*.

40. See Campbell and Corns, 26–27, 67–68.

41. Richard Stock, *A Stock of Divine Knowledge* (1641), 184.

42. Richard Stock, *A Learned and Very Usefull Commentary upon the Whole Prophesie of Malachy*, [ed. Samuel Torshell] (1641), ii. 217.

43. Edward Jones, 'Thomas Young', *ODNB*. On Melville's reform of St Andrews, see James Kirk, '"Melvillian" Reform in the Scottish Universities', in A. A. MacDonald, Michael Lynch, and Ian B. Cowan (eds.), *The Renaissance in Scotland: Studies in Literature, Religion, History and Culture Offered to John Durkan* (Leiden, 1994), 276–300.

44. Gataker preached Bradshaw's funeral sermon on 16 May 1618, at St Luke's, Chelsea, before a large, puritan crowd (Stock, in all likelihood, among the attendees). For Gataker's biography of Bradshaw, see Clarke (ed.), *The Lives of Thirty-Two English Divines*, 25–60. Therein, the respective biographies of Bradshaw and Stock appear back-to-back. On Bradshaw's relationship with Gataker, see also Victoria Gregory, 'William Bradshaw', *ODNB*.

45. See William Bradshaw, *The Unreasonablnes of the Separation*, ed. Thomas Gataker (*s.l.*, 1640).

46. Lake, 'Reading Clarke's *Lives*', 301.

47. Lake, *The Boxmaker's Revenge*, 245. On Gataker, see also Brett Usher, 'Thomas Gataker', *ODNB*, and Diane Willen, 'Thomas Gataker and the Use of Print in the English Godly Community', *Huntington Library Quarterly*, 70 (2007), 343–64, who quotes Lake's labeling of Gataker as '*the* quintessential moderate puritan minister [emphasis added]' and declares that Gataker—'Always the moderate'—'exemplifies what has now become a historiographical staple: a moderate Puritan who managed to operate within the Jacobean broad Calvinist consensus' (344, 354, 363).

48. *CPW*, i. 808–9.

49. See *CPW*, i. 315. On Young having been the author of the Smectymnuan tracts 'for the most part', see Robert Baillie, *The Letters and Journals of Robert Baillie*, ed. David Laing, 3 vols. (Edinburgh, 1841–42), i. 366. Few of the more than a hundred biographies of Milton fail to discuss Young's association with him. Jones's entry on Young in the *ODNB* provides most of the details contained in this paragraph, with others easily found in Parker, Darbishire, and Campbell's *Chronology*.

50. See Campbell and Corns, 37–38. On Young's time in Hamburg, see also William Riley Parker, 'Milton and Thomas Young, 1620-28', *Modern Language Notes*, 53 (1938), 399–407.

51. On Young and Gataker at the Westminster Assembly, see Chad van Dixhoorn and David F. Wright (eds.), *The Minutes and Papers of the Westminster Assembly, 1643–1652*, 5 vols. (Oxford, forthcoming 2012).

52. See Anthony Milton, *Catholic and Reformed*, 504–7. By contrast, Campbell and Corns write that opposition to James I's policy of non-involvement was felt and voiced '[a]mong particularly the zealous and puritanical' (38). Lewalski likewise construes support for English involvement in the Thirty Years' War as a sign of militant radicalism. She calls 'support for Protestant internationalism and English militancy in the Thirty Years' War' one of 'the defining features of oppositional politics in the 1620s', and regards Milton's closeness 'with militants opposed to Stuart pacifism in the Thirty Years' War' as a telling example 'of his early oppositional associates and attitudes' ('How Radical', 50).

53. Thomas Birch and Robert Folkestone Williams (eds.), *The Court and Times of James the First*, 2 vols. (1848), ii. 240-1. The quotations come from a letter sent by Joseph Mede to Sir Martin Stuteville on 24 March 1620/21.

54. Johannes Kemke (ed.), *Patricius Junius (Patrick Young) Bibliothekar der Könige Jacob I. und Carl I. von England: Mitteilungen aus Seinem Briefwechsel* (Leipzig, 1898), 56–7: 'Caeterum, quae sit Ecclesiae a Pontificio stercore reformatae in Germania conditio, non est, quod tibi, cui prius quam mihi innotuit, pluribus exponam: saltem eam misere contentionum et opinionum pugnis dissectam et pene exhaustam, (quarum nomine in summo jam ejus versatur salus discrimine, dum eas Pontificii ecclesiae hostes infestissimi fovent, suisque technis adaugent) nullus non observat.'

55. Elegy IV, ll. 17–18, in John Milton, *Complete Shorter Poems*, ed. Stella P. Revard (Oxford, 2009), 158. The translation is my own.

56. See *CPW*, i. 311–12.

57. Edward Jones, 'The Wills of Edward Goodall and Thomas Young and the Life of John Milton', in Kristin A. Pruitt and Charles W. Durham (eds.), *John Milton: 'Reasoning Words'* (Selinsgrove, PA, 2008), 71–72. The Cranmer volume resides in the library of Jesus College, Cambridge, and bears the inscription, though not in Milton's hand: 'Ex dono D. Jo. Milton hunc librum possidet T. Y. D D'. The volume's publication date (1640) makes clear that Milton did not send it while at Cambridge but probably during the period of time when he and Young were preparing their respective anti-prelatical tracts.

58. *CPW*, i. 974.

59. Indeed, Diarmaid MacCulloch writes in *Thomas Cranmer: A Life* (New Haven, Conn., 1996), that at the time of the Foxe edition, Cranmer's *Reformatio* had become 'a symbol of dissatisfaction with [the Elizabethan] Church settlement, and it was a sure sign of the cast of mind which was now labelled Puritanism' (611). On the *Reformatio*, see also Paul Ayris, 'Canon Law Studies', in Paul Ayris and David Selwyn (eds.), *Thomas Cranmer: Churchman and Scholar* (Woodbridge, 1993), 316–22; and Diarmaid MacCulloch, 'Thomas Cranmer', *ODNB*.

60. Gataker to Ward, 19 May 1631, Bodl. MS Tanner 71, fo. 92r. This connection between Ward and Young has previously been unknown. The 'Scottish minister' is unquestionably Young. Thomas Young had, indeed, only recently 'returned againe' to England from Hamburg, this time once and for all. (He had made temporary trips back to England before that point, as described in Parker, 'Milton and Thomas Young', 399–407.) Moreover, Gataker further reported to Ward in the letter that this same Scottish minister had also happily confirmed to him that it was 'not so' that the Marques of Brandenburg had 'turned Lutheran' and 'had discharged his Calvinist Preacher & took *one* of the other side in his roome', a rumour which had recently been making the rounds in England. This Scottish minister was apparently returning from someplace near enough to Brandenburg to be able to offer a more reliable account of what had allegedly transpired there. To Gataker, of course, Hamburg would have certainly qualified as just such a place.

61. For two excellent discussions of Ward, see Quantin, *The Church of England and Christian Antiquity*, 176–91; and Margo Todd, 'Samuel Ward', *ODNB*. On Ward and the Apocrypha, see also Gordon Campbell, *Bible: The Story of the King James Version 1611–2011* (Oxford, 2010), 52–3. On Ward and the Synod of Dort, see Anthony Milton (ed.), *The British Delegation and the Synod of Dort* (Woodbridge, 2005).

62. Gataker to Ward, 17 February 1630/31, Bodl. MS Tanner 71, fo. 68r.

63. Gataker to Ward, 2 September 1631, Bodl. MS Tanner 71, fo. 102v.

64. Gataker to Ward, 10 October 1633, Bodl. MS Tanner 71, fo. 170r.

65. In light of this finding, the suggestion by Campbell and Corns that Young would only 'turn against the Laudian church in the late 1630s' bears qualifying (37).

66. Samuel Hartlib, *Ephemerides*, Sheffield University Library (hereafter SUL), Hartlib Papers, 29/3/63B. In the adjoining margin, Hartlib further identified the entry as one concerning 'Bacon Yong./ Sabath MS.' The editors of the online edition of the Hartlib Papers expand Hartlib's abbreviation 'q. d.' as '*qui debet*', which would change the sense of the passage to be 'Mr Young has prepared an excellent Tract on the Sabbath in Latin which ought to be printed shortly under the care of Mr Bacon.' This would not substantially alter the primary implications of the entry, but the abbreviation 'q. d.' is in general more likely to be an abbreviation for 'qui dicitur' than it is 'qui debet', and in this instance specifically 'qui dicitur' makes greater contextual sense. Regarding the dating of the entry to early 1636, the entry on Young's *Dies Dominica* is contained in the 1635 bundle of *Ephemerides* (29/3/1A–65B). However, the editors of the online edition of the Hartlib Papers specifically

date the range of pages in which the Young entry falls (29/3/50B-65B) to *c.* November 1635 - *c.* February 1636. Furthermore, the entry on Young appears on a page that follows one (29/3/53B) containing an entry in which Hartlib refers to the Church of England's *Articuli de quibus Convenit inter Archiepiscopos, et Episcopos utriusque Provinciae, et Clerum Universum in Synodo, Londini. An. 1562* (Oxford, 1636), and it appears on a page that immediately precedes one (29/3/64A) containing an entry in which Hartlib records that '[Caspar] Streso, 11 February 1636 writes thus.'

67. Throughout this paragraph, I quote from the early modern English translation of Young's *Dies Dominica*: [Thomas Young], *The Lords-Day*, trans. Anon, ed. Richard Baxter (1672), sigs. A7r, b1v, b2v-3v. For the passages in Young's original Latin, see [Thomas Young], *Dies Dominica* (*s.l.*, 1639), sigs. a3r, a4r-v.

68. Robert Baillie, for example, knew 'Mr. Thomas Young' to be 'the author of *Dies Dominica*' (Baillie, *Letters and Journals*, i. 366).

69. On the presentation copy of *Dies Dominica* given by Young to Nathaniel Bacon, see David Laing, *Biographical Notices of Thomas Young* (Edinburgh, 1870), 11, 24. On Young naming Francis Bacon a trustee of his estate, see Jones, 'Wills', 67. For the quotation from Hartlib's *Ephemerides* concerning 'the 2. Bacons,' see SUL, Hartlib Papers, 28/2/23B. On the Bacons, see respectively John M. Blatchly, 'Francis Bacon', *ODNB*; Janelle Greenberg, 'Nathaniel Bacon', *ODNB*; and A. Hassell Smith, 'Edward Bacon', *ODNB*.

70. Jones, 'Church-Outed', 42–58, with a transcription of the visitation record found at 49–50, from which I quote. The admonishment of Goodall both to pray following the Book of Common Prayer and to preach wearing the proper vestments, however, appears in Latin, as follows: 'Dominus monuit Magistrum Goodall ad legendum preces iuxta formam libri et predicandum indutis super pellicio.' In the text, I have slightly modified Jones's translation. On the visitation, see also Campbell and Corns, 95–6.

71. Jones, 'Church-Outed', 49–50; Fincham, 'Clerical Conformity', 148. Here it should also be noted that Goodall was not cited for allowing 'the preaching of non-licensed, and not reported, ministers', as Jones writes (56). Rather, the entry 'Strange preachers' in the visitation record refers to the book wherein the names of all visiting preachers were supposed to be kept. It is indeed unclear whether the citation indicates that the church lacked such a book or in fact possessed one.

72. Jones, 'Church-Outed', 54.

73. See Edward Jones, '"Filling in a Blank in the Canvas": Milton, Horton, and the Kedermister Library', *Review of English Studies*, 53 (2002), 42.

74. See Jones, 'Wills', 63.

75. See Jones, 'Thomas Young', *ODNB*.

76. See Campbell and Corns, 137.

77. Richard Montagu, *Appello Caesarem*, 215, 265.

78. Quoting Quantin, *The Church of England and Christian Antiquity*, 158. See also Lancelot Andrewes, *XCVI Sermons . . . Published by His Majesties Speciall Command*, ed. William

Laud and John Buckeridge (London, 1629); Peter McCullough, 'Making Dead Men Speak: Laudianism, Print, and the Works of Lancelot Andrewes, 1626–1642', *The Historical Journal*, 41 (1998), 401–24; Nicholas Tyacke, 'Lancelot Andrewes and the Myth of Anglicanism', in Peter Lake and Michael Questier (eds.), *Conformity and Orthodoxy*, 6–7.

79. As quoted in McCullough, 'Making Dead Men Speak', 423.

80. Elegy III, ll. 13–14 in Milton, *Complete Shorter Poems*, 154. Citations from this edition of the poem appearing in the text are to line numbers. The translations are my own.

81. John Milton, *Poems upon Several Occasions*, ed. Thomas Warton (London, 1785), 450.

82. Lewalski, 'How Radical', 51–2. See also Lewalski, *Life*, 24.

83. See Quantin, *The Church of England and Christian Antiquity*,158–59; Tyacke, 'Lancelot Andrewes', *passim*.

84. Quoting Campbell and Corns, 32.

85. See Richard Montagu, *Appello Caesarem*, 215, 265. For Lancelot Andrewes's responses to Bellarmine, see his *Tortura Torti: sive, ad Matthaei Torti Librum Responsio, qui nuper Editus contra Apologiam Serenissimi Potentissimique Principis, Iacobi, Dei Gratia, Magnae Britanniae, Franciae, & Hiberniae Regis, pro Iuramento Fidelitatis* (1609) and his *Responsio ad Apologiam Cardinalis Bellarmini* (1610). As the *English Short Title Catalogue* indicates, extant copies of these two works far outnumber those of any other by Andrewes in Cambridge college collections, the *XCVI Sermons* included. On the circulation of Andrewes's writings in manuscript, see McCullough, 'Making Dead Men Speak', 419.

86. On Milton's anti-Bellarmine *Index Theologicus*, which is not known to survive, see Gordon Campbell, 'Milton's *Index Theologicus* and Bellarmine's *Disputationes De Controversiis Christianae Fidei Adversus Huius Temporis Haereticos*', *Milton Quarterly*, 11 (1977), 12–16; William Poole, 'The Genres of Milton's Commonplace Book', in Nicholas McDowell and Nigel Smith (eds.), *The Oxford Handbook of Milton*, 368; Jeffrey Alan Miller, 'Reconstructing Milton's Lost *Index Theologicus*: The Genesis and Usage of an Anti-Bellarmine, Theological Commonplace Book', *Milton Studies*, 52 (2011), 187–219.

87. *CPW*, i. 768, 771.

88. Lancelot Andrewes, *The Morall Law Expounded . . . That is, The long-expected, and much-desired Worke of Bishop Andrewes, upon The Ten Commandements: Being his Lectures many yeares since in Pembroch-Hall Chappell, in Cambridge, which have ever since passed from hand to hand in Manuscripts, and beene accounted one of the greatest Treasures of private Libraries, but never before this, published in Print. Whereunto is annexed nineteene Sermons of His, upon Prayer in Generall, and upon the Lords Prayer, in Particular. Also seven Sermons upon our Saviours Tentations, in the Wildernesse*, ed. John Jackson (1642), sig. A1v. See also Tyacke, 'Lancelot Andrewes', 7–10; McCullough, 'Making Dead Men Speak', 421.

89. See John Milton, *Poems of Mr. John Milton, Both English and Latin, Compos'd at Several Times* (1645), ii. 16–24.

Part II

Latin Experiments and Accomplishment

5

John Milton and Charles Diodati: Reading the Textual Exchanges of Friends

Cedric C. Brown

In his last and probably best Prolusion at Cambridge, on the theme 'That knowledge renders man happier than ignorance', the young Milton boldly proclaimed that there was not as commonly thought a contradiction between the learned life and sociability.[1] The man immersed in study may be 'less expert in the nicer formalities of social life' but

if such a man once forms a worthy and congenial friendship, there is none who cultivates it more assiduously. For what can we imagine more delightful and happy than those conversations of learned and wise men, such as those which the divine Plato is said often to have held in the shade of the famous plane-tree.[2]

In fact, fit society was not so easily found in Milton's life, though the search for it was advertised in his writings. Perhaps there was always a mismatch between humanist idealism and normal sociability. Many scholars reading this Prolusion, delivered during Milton's period of study before his MA, have thought of his special friendship with Charles Diodati, which had been conducted with great enthusiasm in the years before. They have also often wondered whether any friendship in Milton's life ever rivalled the intimacies of this one, so important in his years of development.[3]

This essay looks closely at all forms of textual exchange between Milton and Diodati, whether in letters or gift-verses, whether published or in manuscript. It also examines the way in which the relationship seems to have changed with time and, once Diodati had died, was then framed in the memory by Milton in preserved documents, printed collections of poetry, publications at the end of his life, and in particular the extraordinary gift-memorial of the *Epitaphium Damonis*. The last was specially printed and seems to have been sent to friends at home and abroad, at least fifteen months after Diodati's death.[4] Taken with the Italian journey, this poem has been seen as coming at a time of transition, looking forward and back.[5]

The first two parts of this essay review the extant textual exchanges before the Italian journey, noting some changes between the texts of the student years and the letters of 1637, after an apparent period of silence. The third part focuses on the posthumous *Epitaphium*. The last parts then turn to interwoven issues of self-presentation and addresses to different readerships, and to matters of selectivity and textual survival, necessary for a proper assessment of the whole record.

In method, much of what follows is an examination of the discourses of friendship. This is part of a larger project on friendship exchanges in a variety of social situations, exploring how they develop so as to enable each writer to anticipate the reactions of the other, show anxiety about maintaining the relationship, sometimes manipulate whilst protesting not to, and in general testify to the immensely rich but still patchily understood bonds of amity in early-modern society. Engagement with these wider themes will be evident, particularly with regard to ritualized exchange, ideal prescriptions of friend-ship, manipulation, and so-called 'gift theory'.

Scholarly discussion of the Milton–Diodati friendship has already tried to read its psychological importance. Suggestions have been made about a homoerotic charge. It is a considerable matter to understand some of the Platonic or 'erotic' language used by Milton in his letters to Diodati in 1637 in the context of complex Renaissance codes of ideal male friendship, codes that were in the public sphere as well as the private. A language carrying an erotic charge was not at all unfamiliar in male–male friendship in earlier centuries.[6] I express some reservations about reading this discourse too simply within twentieth-century conceptual frameworks. The direction of this study is somewhat different: it recognizes both a need for friendship and a fierce vocational idealism, seeking recognition. It also pays special attention to ritual exchange, the decorum of exchange discourse and the obligations of generosity and reciprocity in gift-exchange. I do not mean simply allowing something for convention: I take it that these codes do much to govern the discourse.

In the analyses that follow, close attention is also paid to some linguistic and literary detail. This friendship between young humanists displays shared scholarly interests, multilingual experiment, a playfully competitive element, and a search for identity through dialogue. The media need to be appreciated as well as the culture of friendship. In general, too, considerable challenges of reading exchange texts like these need to be acknowledged at the outset. For example, in friendship exchanges repetitions of role-play and teasing often provide a ritual security. In reading the textual remains of such exchanges, the reader in later centuries, unfamiliar with some of the codes of friendship or habitual play established between the friends, and unsure of the decorum of the time, may feel uncertain when faced for example with the likelihood of irony.[7] Irony and role-playing, assuming easy recognition by the recipient, are key features of this series. There is also a concern especially with texts belonging to the earlier years to match up to social expectations of manliness.[8] In later publication Milton provided explanatory contexts for some texts.

Despite all the difficulties and its fragmentary nature, the Milton–Diodati exchange is fascinating in itself and for the wider issues it raises, presents writing of more life and subtlety than is sometimes recorded, and figures special friendship in remarkable ways. What is more, *Epitaphium Damonis*, a text of greater significance than is often allowed, demonstrates an idealistic code of loving-giving in such a way as to make it arguably a reference point, perhaps to be considered alongside Montaigne's essay-tribute to Etienne de La Boëtie, the famous essay on friendship.

I. The role-play of the friends in student years

Textual gift-exchange can take many forms. In exercising their linguistic skills, the two young students often wrote in verse, thus raising the level of difficulty in congenial competition. Both surviving letters from Diodati, prose in fair hand, are in Greek, and Milton sprinkles his letters with

Greek and describes key qualities of his friend and friendship in Greek in Letter 7. Near the end of *Epitaphium Damonis* (210) he allows the name Diodati, which makes easy sense in Latin/Italian, to transmute into the Latinized Greek poetic epithet *Diodotus*, meaning god-given, or heaven-sent. In this linguistic play, it looks as though there might have been some association between Diodati and Greek in Milton's mind, possibly captured also in the 'Attic wit' attributed to him in *Epitaphium Damonis* (56). The staple written language, however, was Latin, and Milton's first and sixth elegies, addressed to Diodati, are verse letters in Ovidian elegiacs. Also addressed to him, Sonnet 4 is in Italian, the ancestral Diodati tongue. There is a particular resonance in that Italian connection. Milton also showed him English poems. In all this, I assume that the multicultural exchange went beyond texts addressed to him and look not just at Sonnet 4 but the whole Italian group, and more speculatively at other texts.

It may be helpful to offer a quick chronological and contextual review for the early period. Special friendships were usually, though not exclusively, between people of similar social class.[9] Diodati was the son of a well-heeled immigrant Protestant Italian doctor (though with an English mother) and part of a small Italian immigrant community in London; Milton was the son of a quite well-known, fairly prosperous London scrivener. Both boys were sent to St Paul's School, but Diodati moved through the educational stages faster. Although he was actually younger by some months, perhaps even by a year, he left the school two years earlier and was a young student (possibly only 12 years old) at Oxford from early 1622, staying until summer 1628. Milton went up to Cambridge in early 1625, aged 16, and left in summer 1632. After St Paul's the friends would have met mainly during vacations around London.

The largest group of extant communications comes in fact from the university years, though it is still not large. The first datable text is from 1626: Elegy I may be of early April, sent from London as Milton was expecting to return to Cambridge. Neither of the two short, lively Greek letters from Diodati is dated;[10] scholars usually place them between 1626 and 1630. Then, the Italian Sonnet 4, with the others in the set, may come from late 1629. Milton's Elegy VI dates from the end of December 1629 and is a reply to a lost letter with verses from Diodati. This series is incomplete, with some texts identified but missing, but it is self-consistent, perhaps partly, as we shall see, because it is incomplete. It gives clear evidence of role-play between the friends, shown also in the two texts from Diodati, to which I turn first.

Written in spring or summer when he was in or near London, Diodati's first letter, headed 'Diodati to Milton, to cheer up', seems to be checking that Milton still intends to come for a walk, despite poor weather. The air, sun, river, trees, birds, and men will laugh and even (dare he say it?) dance as they make holiday.[11] The tone is playfully provocative. He teases Milton with a quotation from the *Iliad* (2.408) comparing him with Menelaus eagerly joining his brother Agamemnon. (In a discourse of friendship, the brotherly identities might still be noted.) John Rumrich has drawn attention to the apparent presence of desire in the language, as Diodati 'yearns for your company' (ἐπιθυμῶ τῆσ σῆσ συνδιαιτῆσεωσ). There are also other features to note. Diodati himself uses the language of feasting—'so that we might feast on [ἐνωχωμεθα] one another's philosophical and well-bred words'—just as Milton's own documents associate his sociable friend with kinds of feasting. Intriguingly, Diodati's most provocative suggestion for having a good time seems to be the dance. Is this a cultural comment, or a teasing of his friend? Overall, for Milton, the memorial value of the text might have been considerable. It recorded a very lively friendliness, a solicitous but playful conviviality, and a therapeutic and mischievous cajoling away from excessive book study. The last may of course be a part of Milton's own role-play, and by adopting it, even jocularly, Diodati offers a form of recognition to his friend. The letter offers characteristic language of feasting and dancing, too, though applied to nature and cultural exchange. Studiously, however, perhaps typically, Milton makes one grammatical correction to Diodati's enthusiastic Greek—his scholarly meticulousness is not to be forgotten (see Fig. 8).

The depiction of Milton's grinding at the ancients in Diodati's second Greek letter is also high-spirited. Writing from the country amongst flowers and birdsong, Diodati gallantly states that the scene lacks only Milton's company. Get a better work/play balance, he says, and signs off with another sexually provocative irony: John must loosen up, but not like Sardanapalus, the depraved, effeminate Assyrian king. No danger of that with John, though there could be a mischievous glance at his fastidiousness. Nevertheless, this is a kind of compliment as well as genial play: his friend will field the allusion. More importantly, contrasting roles are rehearsed, as recognition within a ritual of friendship. To keep this letter was also to preserve a memorial to solicitous friendship conducted with some panache.

Taken together, these extremely valuable surviving documents from Diodati evidence a friendship discourse featuring playful but sympathetic

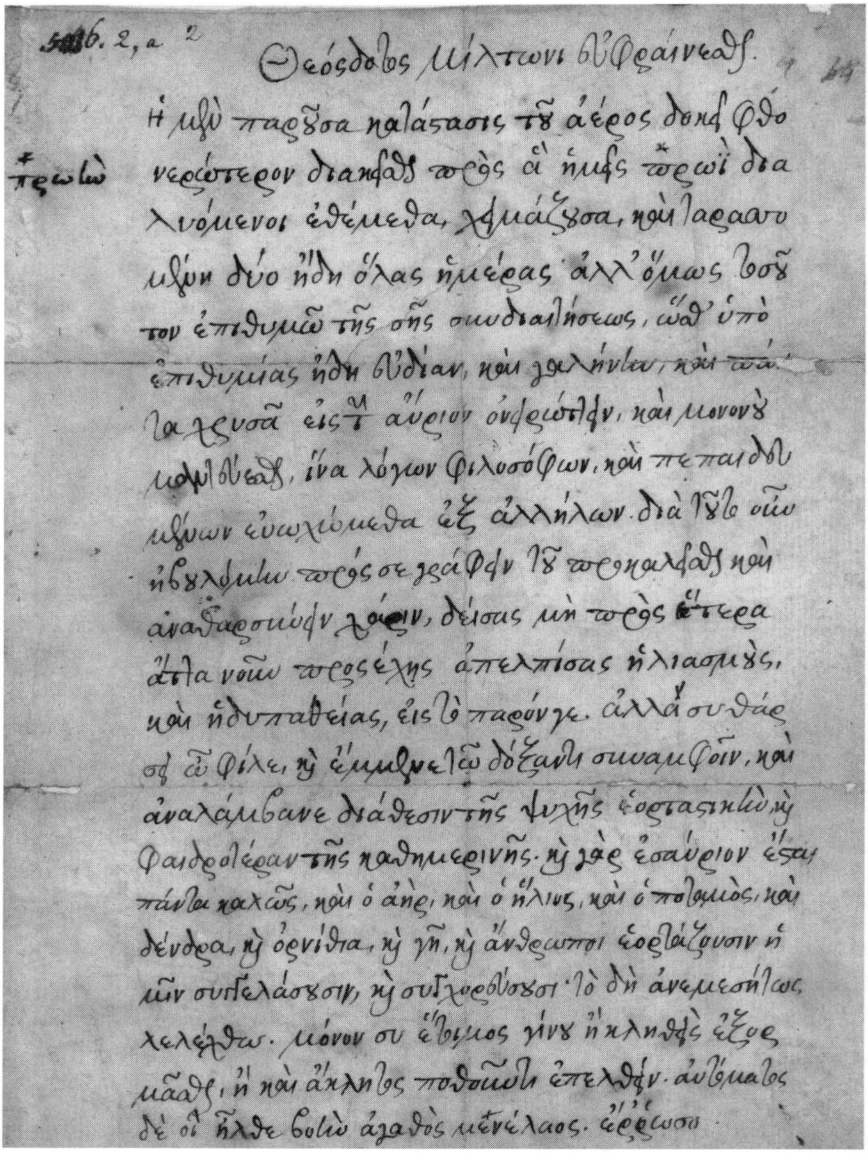

5016. 2, a 2

Θεόδοτος Μίλτωνι εὐφραίνεσθαι.

Ἡ μὲν παροῦσα κατάστασις τοῦ ἀέρος δοκεῖ φθο-
νερώτερον διακεῖσθαι πρὸς ἃ ἡμεῖς πρωΐ* δια-
λεγόμενοι ἐθέμεθα, χειμάζουσα, καὶ ταράττου-
σα μὲν δύο ἤδη ὅλας ἡμέρας· ἀλλ' ὅμως τοσοῦ-
τον ἐπιθυμῶ τῆς σῆς συνδιαιτήσεως, ὥσθ' ὑπὸ
ἐπιθυμίας ἤδη εὐδίαν, καὶ γαλήνην, καὶ τὰ
τα χρυσᾶ εἰς τὴν αὔριον ὀνειρώττειν, καὶ μόνον οὐ
μαντεύεσθαι, ἵνα λόγων φιλοσόφων, καὶ πεπαιδευ-
μένων εὐωχώμεθα ἐξ ἀλλήλων. διὰ τοῦτο οὖν
ἠβουλήθην πρός σε γράφειν τοῦ προκαλεῖσθαι καὶ
ἀναθαρσυνεῖν χάριν, δείσας μὴ πρὸς ἕτερα
ἄττα νοῦν προσέχῃς ἀπελπίσας ἡλιασμοῦ,
καὶ εὐπαθείας, εἰς τὸ παρόν γε. ἀλλὰ συνθάρ-
σει ὦ φίλε, καὶ ἐμμελετῶ δόξαντι συναμφοῖν, καὶ
ἀναλάμβανε διάθεσιν τῆς ψυχῆς ἑορταστικὴν καὶ
φαιδροτέραν τῆς καθημερινῆς. καὶ γὰρ ἐς αὔριον ἔσται
πάντα καλῶς, καὶ ὁ ἀὴρ, καὶ ὁ ἥλιος, καὶ ὁ ποταμὸς, καὶ
δένδρα, καὶ ὀρνίθια, καὶ γῆ, καὶ ἄνθρωποι ἑορτάζουσιν ἡ-
μῖν συγγελάσουσι, καὶ συγχορεύσουσι· τὸ δὴ ἀνεμεσήτως
λελέχθω. μόνον σὺ ἕτοιμος γίνου ἢ κληθεὶς ἐξορ-
μᾶσθαι, ἢ καὶ ἄκλητος ποθοῦντι ἐπελθεῖν. αὐτόματος
δέ οἱ ἦλθε βοὴν ἀγαθὸς Μενέλαος. ἔρρωσο.

*πρωΐ

Fig. 8. BL Add MS 5016*. Undated letter in Greek from Charles Diodati to John Milton.

support on Diodati's side, and also suggest that it was articulated through the behavioural extremes of festive sociability, on the one hand, and disciplined, often solitary, study on the other. That is embedded in their stereotypical ritual play. Scholars had seen Diodati depicted as particularly genial and outgoing, and a contrast with Milton has often been seen. But we are not so much assessing character as reading the playful rituals of friendship exchange in two young men growing up. As Ronald Sharp wrote many years ago, 'friends invent and play the most serious games. These games explore, hypothesize, interpret, test and validate their players' experiences, identities and values.'[12] Sharp also describes a high-spirited exchange with his own best friend: 'never breaking from our assumed roles . . . we performed this formal dance, weaving in and out of our own brand of irony and solemnity, silliness and seriousness.' Such characteristics are familiar in anthropological studies of special friendship. It seems to me that Diodati's little Greek letters give us evidence of a ritualized exchange that was important to Milton as a special resource in his development.

In Milton's two elegies to Diodati 'playing with Ovid' cuts across the habitual role-playing of the friends, and 'Ovidian banter' merges with affectionate teasing.[13] From vacation in London, Elegy I reports university life unfavourably to his more advanced friend, picturing a pastoral landscape without pleasure, an unrewarding teaching system (15–16), and too much noise.[14] On this slanted account, Christ's College did not supply the best development community for the aspiring humanist poet. But this is in confidential mode, and exaggerations and reversals beg to be recognized. The text says that his Cambridge rooms are forbidden to him at the moment (*vetiti mi*), that he resists a harsh tutor and there are other things his spirit will not bear (*Caeteraque ingenio non subeunda meo*), but the idea of exile is expressed conditionally (*Si sit hoc exilium . . .*) and comically inverted, as many have noted. Ovid was banished from cultivated Rome to barbarous and swampy Tomis; Milton's Tomis is his and Diodati's London, full of pleasures. Beyond study and poetry (25–6) he claims to vary his diet with plays and watching the girls in the suburbs, rosy-cheeked and fair-haired, the match of any. So, John shows himself as a regular guy. Nevertheless, does he now need to return to Cambridge, out of temptation—should he now *self-exile*? A balance is struck between distaste and deprivation, being patronized as a child, and too much adult temptation. For all its commonplaces, this poem presents a pack of irony in elegiacs from a youth engaging a friend in the matter of growing towards the desired manliness. It was also a generous text-gift, and to conventional expressions of obligation it adds a loving heart (*pectus amans*) and loyal mind (*fidele caput*), as Charles is *lepidum . . . sodalem*, a boon companion full of charm. The comic rewriting of Ovid also displays full trust in Diodati as reader.

Elegy VI shows Milton's practice of submitting poems for Diodati's comments, something that became very important. In a considerable exchange Diodati has just sent him more than one of his own, sadly not extant. Milton's generous reply in kind plays liberally with ironies and extremes, whilst the headnote for later readers provides the context of winter festivities in the country:

To Charles Diodati, staying in the country. He had written on 13th December and requested that his poems might be excused if they were not up to the usual standard, because, amid all the magnificence with which he had been received by his friends, he had been unable, he declared, to devote himself sufficiently or fruitfully to the Muses. This was the reply he received.

Ad Carolum Diodatum ruri commorantem. Qui cum idibus Decemb. scripsisset, & sua carmina excusari postulasset si solito minus essent bona, quòd inter lautitias quibus erat ab amicis exceptus, haud satis felicem operam Musis dare se posse affirmabat, hunc habuit responsum.

A playful spirit is to be expected, and evidence appears immediately in the contrast between Diodati's distended stomach and Milton's 'not full', *non pleno ventre* (1). A Roman richness in feasting is set against a water-drinking Pythagorean asceticism for the aspiring poet, historical references exaggerating their roles. Unable to match the manly feasting, his *aemulatio* shows ample knowledge of literary sources. Generously defending Diodati's verses from bibulous weakness, he compares his friend with ancient wine-inspired poets, like Pindar, way beyond reason. He trusts him to field half-truths, as in the mock complaint that his own muse has been denied a wished-for obscurity—sham modesty ironically introducing the news that he has been busy with the Nativity Ode, not to mention other pieces he wants Diodati to read. The examples of sternly disciplined ancient poets and seers tease with regard to age: old Tiresias and old Orpheus (68–70) are not models for a young man. He trusts Diodati, too, to see the contradiction of Horace on Homer and water-drinking (71). Commentators note playful fabrication in these proof-texts.[15]

After this play, the real point of the season is revealed: inspiration to present a gift to his Lord at Christmas. Even this news is coyly introduced, with the conditional *si* (if) sound repeated: *At tu si quid agam, scitabere (si modo saltem | Esse putas tanti noscere siquid agam)* (But if you seek to know what I am doing [if at least you deem it so important to learn of anything I may do]) (79–80). By 1629, mastery of Ovidian elegiac style sits easily with the role-play and the manner of a familiar letter to a friend. Teasing and serious revelation go together. I am inclined to think that Hale, taking up a suggestion made by John Carey,[16] is right about the low-key signing off referring to the Italian sonnets, a verse-gift other than the Nativity Ode, something more personal left for Diodati's view: *Te quoque pressa manent patriis medidata cicutis, | Tu mihi, cui recitem, iudicis instar eris* (For you personally, too, there are waiting less elevated verses composed on native pipes; for me you will be like the judge to whom I may recite them) (89–90). *Quoque* ('too') seems to refer to different verses from the Nativity Ode, previously described, and *patriis* ('native') seems to be attached to *te*.[17] However that crux is to be interpreted, *Te quoque pressa manent* provides a conversational close, and the poem ends as it began, familiarly, with more textual exchange and a celebration of Diodati as a favoured multilingual reader as well as companion and confidant.

The lines also allude to style and mode. *Cicutis* (hemlock or shepherds' pipes), from Virgil's second eclogue (36), signals pastoral. Though distinct pastoral configuration only comes with the shepherdess in Sonnet 3, there is a general equivalence between modest Italian sonnets and eclogues, and pastoral was often used, as by the Spenserians, to describe social groups and cultured friendships. Both Virgilian eclogues and sonnets sometimes provided models for the expression of *amicitia*. Like eclogues, too, these sonnets introduce 'singers' within a community of friends. The Virgilian context in Eclogue II is one of hope that young men will maintain the tradition of poetry, a reference suiting apprentice pieces on youthful themes in an established poetic medium. Also, if the meaning of plain or unadorned is taken in *pressa*, as well as that of concise, it supports a contrast with a more elevated ode. Though developing Petrarchan tropes, the sonnets are not elevated in style.

There is in a sense no need to try to prove a reference to the Italian sonnets in Elegy VI, because the desire for Diodati as sympathetic reader is shown in the sonnets themselves. Their lady is Emilia; the only named reader, in the conventional role of male addressee (in 4), is Diodati. Sonnet 4 has to be read in context, so he was probably shown the set. This is a dialogue between young men. Love and poetry entwine, and 2, 3 and the

Canzone announce a linguistic project. Italian is unknown to his country-men (though not to the expatriates gathered in the French/Italian Protestant church meeting in the Mercers' chapel in Cheapside).[18] Sonnet 3 also confides that religious study may have been neglected. From 3, the Canzone picks up the puzzlement of other young people and explains that the language suits the theme. His Lady gives this literary answer. Sonnet 5, describing the lover's feelings, is by general consent the most artificial, the return of Dawn at the end, after a night of rain-tears and sighs freezing in the air, concluding the poem in an old-fashioned way. The last sonnet memor-ializes *ingenium*, courage, the lyre and the Muses. His Lady is dark-featured, proudly demure, bilingual—*Parole adorne di lingua piu d'una*—and a good singer. The gift of his heart looks like a literary dedication, as to a muse.

Sonnet 4, addressed to Diodati, can also be read in cumulative context, relying on memory. Years before, Diodati had received Elegy I, lauding rosy-cheeked, fair-haired English girls, a stereotype displaced now by a foreign type: *sotto nova idea | Pellegrina bellezza*, a foreign beauty, after a new fashion. Who better to relish the playful change than half-Italian Charles? The confession about neglecting religious reading also fits, both friends having been thought of for the ministry. So does the bold literary exploration: Diodati, friend of multiculturalism, stands out from the sceptical, more insular others. There may be self-reflexive revelation in the series, and Diodati, from the commu-nity that probably supported Milton's Italian studies when he was immersing himself in Italian sonnets,[19] may be the supportive reader best placed to understand.

II. After a silence: friendship resumed and theorized in the letters of 1637

Letters and the like are mainly necessary when friends are apart, the texts providing presence by proxy. In the early 1630s we have neither exchange texts nor much to prove that Milton and Diodati were often meeting. This apparently long gap is puzzling and may be somewhat misleading; I comment on it later from the point of view of the selection and survival of texts. If after graduating from Oxford Diodati was in the London area there would have been opportunity to meet until early 1630, but from April 1630 to at least September 1631 he was at the Calvinist Academy in Geneva, though leaving without completing his religious studies. At some time thereafter, he prepared for a medical career, like his father. A good deal earlier, the Diodati family had established a base in the Chester region, and certainly after Geneva Charles seems to have been usually on the western banks of the Dee, east of Wrexham, south of Chester.[20] His brother John was, however, still London-based, providing a communication point for Milton, who completed his studies at Cambridge in summer 1632 and was then at the family homes outside London until the Italian journey in 1638. The friends would presumably have met when Diodati had his Oxford degree incorporated at Cambridge at Commencement on 7 July 1629, but on the whole meeting up seems to have become difficult in later years, needing effort to organize or special occasions to bring them together in town. From the period after Geneva nothing survives from Diodati, and nothing from Milton either until September 1637, with the two texts later printed as Familiar Letters 6 and 7 (probably wrongly dated September in the edition of 1674).[21] As far as we can tell from these, and what can be deduced from them about Diodati's lost reply between the two letters, the nature of the discourse had changed somewhat. Familiar trust and affection are reaffirmed, and codes of friendship certainly obtain, but the years of youthful exploration of identity have passed. Something more theoretically weighted is now evident in Milton's texts.

Perhaps because they come after long silence, Milton's two remarkable letters of late 1637 show a concern that the friendship should continue and in doing so they define retrospectively, and more maturely, Milton's idea of what it had been. That is, they display the role of memory, test and theorize former experience against elevated ideas of friendship value, and give evidence of the special importance of Diodati as intellectual companion and corresponding friend. But we might first pause on the question of what kind of texts these letters are.

Milton's selection of familiar letters, the *Epistolarum Familiarium Liber Unus*, was published in 1674, at the end of his life. Such publications advertised humanistic standing and provided models of composition as much as biographical records. For the first period of Milton's life up to the Italian journey of 1638 letters were included to just three men, all of whom must have been in the reader community that was important for Milton in his student years and aided his development: Thomas Young, erstwhile special tutor, nearly a generation older; Alexander Gil Junior, teacher at St Paul's School, neo-Latin poet and friend, about ten years older; and Diodati. Two are notable Protestant-humanist educationalists, and all three provide opportunities for polyglot exchange and critical improvement. They are all good for display in a humanist book of familiar letters, because they provide recognition of John Milton, scholar-writer. Yet only the letters to Diodati represent something like the special friendship celebrated in Cicero's hugely influential *De Amicitia*.

Cicero confided to Atticus that what he most wanted was not general company, as in the forum, but someone to joke with and sigh to. He wanted relaxed freedom within confidentiality.[22] The Diodati exchanges from the student years show strong attraction to character and close interaction and play out rituals of friendship, in teasing, complaining, cajoling, or sharing concern and support. Across the exchanges, some scholars have also seen a homoeroticism; others have resisted reading the language of Renaissance friendship in terms of post-Freudian psychology.[23] In the 1637 letters to Diodati Milton seems to have wanted to sustain a supportive special friendship, exchanging new confidences and using Diodati as an understanding reader. Adolescent play-rituals, however, were no longer so appropriate; now he more seriously theorized his feelings along Platonic lines. He intellectualized attraction.

Familiar Letter 6 is much about re-establishing contact and begins with a rebuke. Diodati is now based in the north. Milton complains that his friend, usually so quick, has not been in touch. He knows he has been writing to the bookseller and his brother John Diodati in London, could have sent greetings, and also promised to call in, but did not. Recent enquiries based on rumours of his being in the area have led to nothing. After enquiring about his friend's well-being, he plays jealous: 'Are there up in those parts any slightly learned men [*erudituli*] with whom you can feel at home and chat, as we used to do?' Hyperboreans, even south of Chester, must furnish less fully formed companions than John Milton, of London. Despite the anxiety, each communication has humour, and companionship and shared learning go together. Meanwhile, when is Charles back? There is so much to tell him.

A reply came between Letter 6 and Letter 7. Written twenty-one days later, it was evidently a solicitous reply with many wishes for good health, perhaps compensating for neglect. Milton responds with multiplications of his own, the re-bonding producing more laconic play. He attributes the many health enquiries to Diodati's new medical profession, then resumes the basic ground— 'I did indeed, *since it had been so agreed* [my emphasis], long expect letters from you'—*Literas quidem tuas, quoniam ita convenerat, diu expectabam*. He reassures Diodati that his old affection had not cooled. There is a lasting ideal: 'once begun on sincere and sacred grounds (*sinceris, & sanctis rationibus*), it [friendship] should, though mutual good offices should cease, yet be free from suspicion and blame all life long'. The evidence of real friendship must also be distinguished from mere formal acts of greeting: 'I would not have true friendship tried by the test of letters and good wishes. . . . For its nurture the written word is less essential than a living reciprocal recollection of virtues. (*quam vivam invicem virtutum recordatione*)' It is the cherished *idea* of the other that sustains, held in the memory on both sides and tested by experience.

During the silence Milton has preserved that idea, on his side: 'Your probity writes to me in your stead, and inscribes true letters (*verasque literas*) on my inmost consciousness, your frank innocence of character (*morum simplicitas*) writes to me, and your love of the good (*recti amor*); your genius also, by no means an ordinary one, writes to me and commends you to me more and more.' As in many friendship discourses showing the influence of the *De Amicitia* and other ancient authorities, true friendship is defined by a matching of virtue, but the terms in which Diodati is praised as embodying the idea of the lovable beautiful mind (τον καλου ἰδεαν), obviously betray Platonic influence:

Lest you should threaten me too much, it is in fact impossible for me not to love those like you, for though I do not know what else God may have decreed for me, this is certain: *he has instilled into me, if into anyone, a vehement love of the beautiful*. Nor is Ceres said, according to the fables, to have sought her daughter Prosperina so arduously, as I am wont, day and night, to search for the idea of the beautiful, as if for some most fair image amongst all the forms and appearances of things ('*for many are the shapes of things divine*'); day and night I pursue it as if it were leading me along with some clear tracks. So it happens that if I find one who spurns the base opinions of common men, and dares to feel, speak, and be that which the wisest minds throughout the ages have taught to be the best.

Ego enim ne nimis minitêre, tui similes impossibile est quin amem, nam de caetero quidem quid de me statuerit Deus nescio, illud certe; δεινον μοι ἐρωτα, ἐιπερ τω ἀλλω, του καλου ἐνεσταζε. *Nec tanto Ceres labore, ut in fabulis est, Liberam fertur quæsivisse filiam, quanto ego hanc* του καλου ἰδέαν, *veluti pulcherrimam quandam imaginem, per omnes rerum formas et facies:* (πολλαι γαρ μορφαι των Δαιμονιον)[24] *dies noctesque indagare soleo, et quasi certis quibusdam vestigiis ducentem sector. Unde fit, ut qui, spretis quae vulgus pravâ rerum æstimatione opinatur, id sentire et loqui et esse audet; quod summa per omne ævum sapientia optimum esse docuit illi me protinus . . . necessitate quâdam adjungam.*

The searcher for truth must bind himself to someone of such special qualities. As presented here, the friendship defines a task for them both of special refinement. Whatever characteristics of temperament and behaviour are implied in the pursuit of the idea of the Good or Beautiful, they sit side by side with aspirations for Milton's poetry, and are part of the same drive towards moral-aesthetic objectives.

The love of the beautiful also 'foretells a Christian process'.[25] Idealism may be grounded in a robust and possibly erotic language of tracking down (*indagare . . . sector*), but whereas in Plato's *Lysis* (206A, 218C), if one were to go all the way back to that through ancient descriptions of male friendship, the language of hunting is used to describe the gaining of the sexual favours of a young lover-friend, in Milton's theoretical passage the pursuit is in the intellectual process itself, in the moral and aesthetic search for the idea.[26] The exclusivity conferred on Diodati therefore also expresses the writer's character, as one who seeks above all beauty of mind. Only after renewing the friendship bond does he confide his plans: he has been composing verse (probably 'Lycidas') and has reached early medieval Italy in his historical reading. But how long will Diodati stay up there? Would he consider wintering in London amongst friends? Finally, can he lend him Giustiniani on the Venetians? Bookish friends remember such things, and text- and book-exchanges go together.

The Platonic quest, expressive of Milton's obsessive vocationalism, has been much remarked, but the reciprocal moves of friendship exchange itself also need to be recognized. In these courtesies, playfulness is still key, but it is also manipulative. As in Natalie Zemon Davis's neat formula, picking up anthropological theory after Mauss in *The Gift*, gratitude has engendered obligation; or, to put it in Derrida's cooler terms, a new 'performative chain' of promises has been inaugurated.[27] Familiar Letter 6 required a response; that response was then used to draw a reaffirmation. Letter 6 then made it easy for Diodati to establish 'normal' relations by showing playfulness in self-deprecation and teasing exaggeration, followed by the light tone of the beginning and end of Letter 7. But by making the declarations in Letter 7 Milton also puts pressure on Diodati to respond—and we have no reply. Letter 7 also prefigures the kind of remembering that will take place in *Epitaphium Damonis*. These idealizations and negotiations Milton chose to include in his collection of letters as an old man, thus suggesting for posterity their whole-life significance, a special friendship glimpsed amongst documents showing the early development of the poet and scholar. However, the greatest act of loving-giving was still to come.

III. Special friendship enacted: *Epitaphium Damonis* and generous gifts

Diodati died in August 1638, in London, possibly of the plague, while Milton was away in Italy. Milton visited Lucca, the Diodati hometown, and Charles's theologian uncle Giovanni in Calvinist Geneva on the way home. These look like acts of *pietas*, but we cannot be sure when he learned of the death. What the death produced, however, was the specially printed posthumous tribute, *Epitaphium Damonis*, of late 1639 or 1640. The poem addresses Diodati as if he were still living, and in offering the poem to new friends spreads the spirit of friendship itself.

Anthropologists note that the death of a special friend often occasions an extraordinary performance in tribute from the surviving friend.[28] *Epitaphium Damonis*, the most ambitious of his Latin poems and almost his last Latin composition, is exquisitely crafted, as it should be in a gift-act to a dead friend, and the *pietas* of this text, its sense of appropriateness and duty, is remarkable.[29] What is more, its terms of celebration spring explicitly from the generosity and religious underpinning of the friendship code.

The poem is a gift in several senses, not just a great last gift-tribute to Milton's friend but also a kind of response to new friends made in Italy, especially some academicians in Florence, and to hospitality and gifts furnished in Naples by Giovanni Battista Manso, former patron of Tasso and Marino and friend to poets. It is possible that poems to Diodati were among those Milton read to Italian academies, and his contacts with expatriate Italian communities were almost certainly revealed in some of those circles, in explanation. Readers are told in the *Argumentum* about Milton's being in

Italy when his Italian-English friend died. The Italian connections may help to explain the printing for special presentation, a gift-act preferred to scribal reproduction. Whoever received those printed copies of *Epitaphium Damonis* formed a select readership community.

Latin was the natural medium, given the audience, but Italian connections are also woven in. In treating youthful companionship and responsibility in learning, the *Epitaphium* notes that Damon was faithful to the Protestantism of his exiled family—*priscamque fidem coluisse, piumque* (33). As for the mourning shepherd-singer, melancholic or depressed, worrying those around him, he has lost the encouraging support of a special confidant. The select readership of the printed gift-text has in some way to compensate for that loss.

Epitaphium Damonis represents a gift-act made in the context of a developed friendship exchange. The general idea of Diodati as reader-friend is conveyed in the headnote, the *Argumentum: ingenio, doctrina, clarissimisque caeteris virtutibus, dum viveret, iuvenis egregius*, a young man, while he lived, richly endowed with talents, learning, and other most exemplary gifts. More importantly, the quality of Diodati as friend is celebrated liberally in the poem itself, though accompanied by pain. The friendship is *fidus*, faithful (37), offering constant support through all situations, figured in the pastoral language as through both winter and summer (38–42). It is always comforting and enjoyable: 'Who will bring the day to rest with talk and song?'—*Quis fando sopire diem cantuque solebit?* (43). As special friendships should, it deals in open confidentiality: 'To whom shall I open my heart?'—*Pectora cui credam?* (45). Like no other friendship recorded by Milton, it is therapeutic, easing of fears: 'Who will teach me to sooth eating cares and to cheat the long night with pleasant conversation?'—*Quis me lenire docebit | Mordaces curas, quis longam fallere noctem | Dulcibus alloquiis*—despite the roaring of the elements outside (45–9). Or, in the middle of a summer day, 'Who will bring back to me your blandishments, your laughter, your Attic wit, and your elegant humour'—*Quis mihi blanditiasque tuas, quis tum mihi risus, | Cecropiosque sales referet, cultosque lepores?* (55–6). This eloquent passage is supported by later lines, as Diodati is celebrated in 108 as the sole kindred spirit among thousands, in 118 as charming companion sharing grace and charm with his other Tuscan friends in 127 (*His Caris, atque Lepos; et Tuscus tu quoque Damon*), as having 'sweet and holy simplicity' and 'clear white virtue' in lines 199–200 (*dulcis . . . | Sanctaque simplicitas . . . candida virtus*), and finally as pure in conduct in lines 203–4—*purum colit aethera Damon | Aethera purus habet.*

This is a generous rehearsal of cherished memories. It also tends to celebrate some of the intimacies of their early years. In the letters of 1637, memory had been key, too, but whereas Letter 7 tended towards an intellectual capture, the eloquent and moving expressions of *Epitaphium Damonis* find ways of figuring the whole emotional experience. Many echoes can also be found of other passages associated, or possibly associated, with Diodati. Loyalty was a theme found in the elegies and *Letter 7* as well. Diodati's therapeutic lightness of discourse, calming easing cares, is like the sportful language of 'L'Allegro', and the two preserved Greek letters had displayed blandishments and humour. Those two letters from Diodati are matched in the *Epitaphium* by rests at high noon and charming talk, laughter, wit, and cultured pleasantries. As in Diodati's second letter and Milton's self-defence in Elegy I, this also recalls how young men needed to get out and about. The puzzlement of the girls at his unusual behaviour in the *Epitaphium* (88–90) parallels that of young acquaintances in the Italian poems. The combination of friendship and virtue resembles the love of the beautiful in *Letter 7*. The confiding of large literary ambitions (162–78), based after Italy on a clear aim to write in English on heroic national subjects, had been prefigured, for that time, in Elegy VI. The exchange of news recalls what they used to do, and what some of the documents preserve. As for his own literary plans, they can be shared with his new Italian friends, too, and the situation is full of ironies: the exchanges are in Latin, developments have been clarified by Italy, and lines 162–78 outline a Trojan-British epic. The stories connect with Rome, but his future audience is English-speaking, bounded by the Ouse, Humber, Trent, Thames, and Tamar. Multilingual facility had always been a theme of the Diodati exchanges.

Although readers since the eighteenth century have found Renaissance pastoral an artificial medium, the fluent inventiveness of Milton's figures (across Latin and English) is remarkable. As in landscape paintings classical and local features combine, so that Pan is asleep under the shade of an oak in the middle of a summer's day, but the farm labourer just snores under the hedge (52–4). Within that broad language of pastoral we might pick up one particular memory from the early texts: a delight in stimulating companionship in the open air. Diodati's Greek letters had celebrated the therapeutic pleasures of the outdoors, and as if in answer the ironic-laconic Elegy I had pictured Cambridge failing the test, with its bare fields and lack of shade. Winter scenes are included in the *Epitaphium*, just as they were in the festivities enjoyed by Diodati in Elegy VI, but in the memories of the mood-lightening Diodati there is a special association with the summer outdoors as a site of restorative conversation and cultured pleasure. Accordingly, when in a painful moment Milton fondly imagines meeting up again, it is either by the banks of the river Colne near Horton, or in the countryside behind, given its ancient British association: *Heus bone numquid agis? Nisi te quid forte retardat, | Imus? Et arguta paulum recubamus in umbra, | Aut ad aquas Colni, aut ubi iugera Cassibelauni?* (147–9) ('Hallo, there, old friend! What are you up to? If there's nothing important to detain you, shall we go and recline for a while in the rustling shade, either by the waters of the Colne, or where once there were the acres of Cassivelaunus?') The reminiscence of cultured talk with Diodati on the banks of an English river is however counter-pointed against the memories of the wonderful experiences in Florence, stretched out by the cool, murmuring Arno (*gelidi cum stratus ad Arni/Murmura* [129–30]). Each scene is characterized by pleasure and generous exchange; each is a kind of Italian encounter. He would have told Diodati of his elation and pride as he was allowed to hear the friendly contests in poetry in the academies, Lycidas and Menalcas singing, even daring to join the competitive enterprise (*ausus*) himself (132–3). What is more, his own poems were duly admired, and he received gifts (*munera*) of recognition, figured pastorally (135) as reed baskets, bowls, and shepherds' pipes with waxen stops, and Dati and Francini mentioned his name, or perhaps their names (*nostra . . . nomina*), in their poems (136–8).

There is a speculation about 'our names' in line 136: is this merely a poetic plural for Milton's own name, or is it actually a plural, signifying that Milton and Diodati together, as friends, were memorialized? Haan, following the sense of Hale's paraphrase, is interested in this interpretation,[30] suggesting that Milton not only explained to the Italians his friendship with Diodati and the Italian circle in London, but also included one of the elegies to Diodati in his recitations. Whether he did or not, there can be no doubt that the Diodati friendship and the Italian experience are put side by side, and that shared value is celebrated: congenial competition, generous recognition, and a wonderful proliferation of acts of giving, in such a society of friends. Milton sent the printed text of *Epitaphium Damonis* to the Florentine academicians, seeking to perpetuate the cycle of giving.[31]

The most extraordinary effect of memorial celebration is, however, in the perhaps over-debated ending of the *Epitaphium*, with its vision of Bacchic mysteries in heaven, but where there may also be a special memory of his friend. Furthermore, that apotheosis is prepared for by other acts of recognition and gift-exchange, in a second reminiscence of his Italian experiences, this time of his being generously hosted by Count Manso in Naples. If he could, John would have shown Charles the two wonderful cups (*pocula*, 181) given him as parting presents. Recollection of the generous, hospitable gift-act by the Neapolitan scholar-patron begins the final sequence and suddenly appears to provide the terms for the last celebration of his dear friend. The poem seems to work by accumulating instances of generosity in friendship.

Manso's cups provide yet another instance of intricate pastoral configuration in the *epitaphium*. Each cup has a quite elaborate description, or *ekphrasis*. In terms of event, the usual assumption is that what is recalled is the gift of two of Manso's own books, ingeniously figured in the pastoral. Manso often presented his books as gifts. Scholars have worked out that the two most likely are the *Poesie Nomiche*, a book which concludes with an Italian version of Claudian called 'La Fenice', thus giving opportunity for Milton's description of the Phoenix; and the *Erocallia*, about theories of love, thus giving possible occasion for Milton's picturing of the celestial *amor*/Cupid in the second description.[32] Milton has found a fitting way of recording his gratitude for Manso's gracious behaviour whilst telling his friend of his excitement at being so generously treated by the aged count, the creator of another academy. This was another wonderful occasion of being recognized amongst humanists.

The pastoral figure itself conveys the values of generous giving. Hospitality and friendship are allied: a pair of cups symbolizes friendship in shared drinking. The descriptions of the cups then allow the value system to be further celebrated, as they are used to reveal its religious underpinning, in the ultimate gift-sacrifice. After that revelation, the *Epitaphium* can be resolved into consolation and new celebration.

Two scenes are depicted, paired in subject (*gemino . . . argumento*, 184). One scene, of the Phoenix, is of earthly delights but suffused with the hope of rebirth:

in the middle, the waves of the Red Sea, odoriferous spring, the long shores of Arabia, and woods dripping with balsam, amongst these, the Phoenix, the divine bird, unique on earth, shining deep blue and with multicoloured wings fixes its eyes on the dawn rising from the glassy waves (*Auroram viteis surgentem respicit undis*) (185-9).

Red Sea, rising dawn, and Phoenix convey providence and resurrection. The attentive gaze in the single delayed active verb *respicit* records a special ability of the bird: like the eagle it can look directly at the sun, here a sun rising. Even amongst earthly delights resurrection is the focus of attention before the second scene.

That scene shifts straight to the heavenly Cupid and a syncretistic vision of divine love, such as inspires disciplined and refined spirits like Diodati:

In another part, the boundless sky and great Olympus, and—who would think it?— here too is Cupid, pictured in a cloud, with his quiver gleaming arms, torches, and arrows tipped with bronze; neither weak spirits, nor the breasts of the ignoble vulgar does he strike from there, but turning about with flaming eyes raised always on high, he scatters his darts through the world, never wearying, and never seeks to aim his blows downwards. Hence holy minds and the forms of the gods themselves are inflamed with love. (190–7)

The whole sequence springs out of a celebration of gifts, using symbols of friendship, and through the programme on the cups generosity and art are brought together, as they are in the *Epitaphium* itself. The lamenting refrain ceases, and the name Damon, famous for a friend from the story of Damon and Pythias, is joined by his heavenly name, also the real family name, though presented in poetic form. Diodotus, one given by God and now back to God, is finally inscribed in the memorial. As in *Letter 7* love is defined as that which turns the mind heavenwards.

It is difficult to judge neo-Latin poetics by the conventions of English poetics, but issues of decorum have been raised about the syncretism of the last two lines. Even the sympathetic Hale has the poem ending 'noisily, downright corybantically'.[33] The language recalls Revelation, the undefiled wearing crowns of glory at the marriage of the Lamb, but also the Bacchic mysteries: *Cantus ubi, choreisque furit lyra mista beatis, | Festa Sionaeo bacchantur et orgia thyrso* (218–19) ('Where there is singing, and the lyre rages in the midst of blessed dances, and under the thyrsus of Sion the festal orgies are revelling'). In the last line *Sionaeo* is so placed between *festa* and *bacchantur* as to put immediate qualification on *orgia*. That is, the festivities have the intensity of Bacchic rites, but express a Christian joy, implying disciplined order, not abandon.

It is a bold ending. Stella Revard suggests that it refers back to youthful exchanges.[34] It is worth considering how this part of the poem may also bear treasured memory. Elegy VI had light-heartedly rehearsed the link between Bacchus and poetry, just as in this poem the Phoenix enjoys earthly delights, whilst fixing its eyes on eternity. Diodati's first letter had anticipated a feast of cultured exchange and teased with dancing, to show youthful high spirits. In the *Epitaphium* (85), where reminiscences of Diodati often recall youthful times, dances are cited with sports and love as typical behaviour of happy youth. The last lines immortalize youthful exuberance, with the character of his extrovert friend affectionately displayed. That Charles combines joy with virtue in a sociable afterlife any reader will grasp, but if the pretence of the poem is followed, with Diodati as imagined reader, his friend would recognize features of their own youthful role-play. That would make the keepsake value of Diodati's two Greek letters all the greater.

In the whole exchange series, especially perhaps in the early texts and the posthumous *Epitaphium*, role-playing is as important as the confidences: rituals of form celebrate the friendship, maintain its easiness, and preserve the idea of the other, especially after a period of silence. These codes may indeed provide 'something that promotes rather than obstructs intimacy', and it may be short-sighted to ignore the power of ritualized expression in judging that the *Epitaphium* 'remains reticent about his affection for Diodati'.[35] As for the turn in the *Epitaphium*, the recollection of one marvellous generous gift, from Manso, suddenly provides the terms for the final celebration of his lively, generous friend, and social and religious values run together, as friendship reveals scenes of divine love, allowing acts of selfless love to resume.

In this deeply meditated final gift-tribute, expensively distributed to humanist friends, all friendship is celebrated in the act of celebrating one friendship, just as in Montaigne's essay the celebration of all friendship fuses with the celebration of the one dead friend. Like Montaigne's essay, which has become the standard reference for special friendship in this period, Milton's poem should perhaps be a classic reference point, though figuring it in a different way. In such celebrations, gift-acts beget new gift-acts, in a widening circle of remembrance, obligation, and affection. For each new friend who reads the text the challenges may be not just to sympathetic understanding but also to emulation of that spirit.

If we consider the range of Milton's memorial acts, they may seem smaller than Montaigne's for his friend, but they are more focused. With an intense friendship of four years before death at a mature age, and the legacy of La

Boëtie's library and what we would call literary executorship, Montaigne undertook to celebrate his dear friend by writing of ideal friendship in the essay published as long as seventeen years later and also to edit his writings into publication: sonnets, Latin poetry, and translations from Greek, Latin, and Italian. This was a various set of activities over a long period. Doing this, and developing his description of twin souls and the sharing of possessions, he often fused identities: the sonnets appeared amongst his own essays. Against that, Milton's is a less various set of activities, and Italy, linked though it was with the friendship, also provided a termination, at least after *Epitaphium Damonis* had been written and distributed. But both writers figure special male friendship in the light of ancient thought, something beyond *ces autres amitiés communes*,[36] ordinary friendships, that is, those more widely shared, and I can think of two ways in which Milton's poem demands special attention alongside Montaigne's famous essay.

To begin with, a remarkable feature of *Epitaphium Damonis* is that it *enacts* the spirit of friendship by building up a web of memories of generosity, linking different parties together, then allowing one act of hospitable friendship by another party to reveal the means of celebrating the special friendship in question, and consequently spreading that understanding to the friends to whom the generous gift-text was sent. Montaigne had achieved a combination of effects, too, by inserting La Boëtie's sonnets into the *Essais*, thus adding a new act of service by illustrating the fusion of identities described in *De l'Amitié*.[37] Montaigne disliked the calculating use of gifts; service to a friend beyond death provided opportunity for giving without manipulation of the other party. But *Epitaphium Damonis* makes the more dramatic enactment and its significance in Milton's oeuvre may also be registered by observing how strongly it engages with larger Christian-humanist ideas of the graces of giving.

In a second, very important way Milton's *Epitaphium Damonis* and the other exchange-texts provide a model for special friendship that differs in emphasis from Montaigne's celebration and might be thought to take up a more generous position. Whereas Montaigne fuses identities and makes his twin souls alike, Milton's texts, delighting in roles featuring opposites, appreciates differences in temperament in close friendship. A view expressed by Sharp might be remembered here: 'the ideal of two separate identities freely giving is considerably loftier than some imagined fusion into perfect unity'.[38] To celebrate temperamental difference is another act of generosity.

IV. Later perspectives, retrospective manipulation, and reading communities

But how did the Diodati friendship, as idealistically celebrated by Milton, actually travel through the rest of his life, and what manipulation can be seen in the expression of the ideals of the friendship code as released to a reading public? After glancing at the obvious general importance of ideas of friendship and codes of generosity elsewhere in the oeuvre, I want to turn back to the series itself to analyse matters of retrospective presentation, both in the way the record has been managed and in issues of changing readership and context.

Connections tempt between the lofty ideals of generosity in friendship in the Diodati texts and Milton's other writings. Critics have sometimes seen them preserved in other depictions. Rumrich, for example, encourages a search for echoes of the Diodati friendship through the rest of Milton's life. He and Gregory Chaplin suggest a link with the unusual stressing of intellectual and social companionship in marriage, a key point in Milton's polemics about divorce.[39] A comparison also beckons with the role of Raphael in *Paradise Lost*, teasing in the use on both occasions of the symbol of the sexually ambiguous, perhaps asexual, Phoenix. Karen Edwards has even speculated that Raphael may constitute a new act of memory for Diodati, a fulfilling of the vow made in the *Epitaphium* to keep the memory of his friend alive.[40] A real heavenly spirit stands in that sociable space at the heart of the epic, discoursing alfresco in perpetual summer and joining generous service to ideas of divine love. But caution is needed. There is an obvious association between guiding spirits and idealized teachers: Raphael does not 'need' a Diodati explanation. Broader ideas of friendship are also engaged. It could be argued for example that many instances of false or self-interested friendship are also instructive, by negation expressing ideals of giving: most memorably, Satan's key fault (*PL* iv. 46-7) is an inability to receive gifts.

Friendship is nevertheless a vital issue. The Diodati experience seems to have crystallized the need for recognition in a supportive, intellectual companionship. Later, Milton considered affiliating to learned societies, having loved his visits to Italian academies, recorded friendships with European men of letters, and as a blind man celebrated in gift-poems a congenial society coming to his London house, including quite close friends like Cyriack Skinner. Eventually he provided Adam with companionship in his conversational epic in the form of two impeccably mannered angelic instructors, a divine voice discussing 'solitude and fit society' (Argument, Book 8), and an interlocutive wife. The lack of 'fit society' is always dreaded, whilst friendship amongst learned men is advertised as the greatest of pleasures, as optimistically declared in Prolusion VII and as repeated in acts of self-presentation. These broader self-defining connections are, however, beyond the scope of this study.

The depiction of the Diodati friendship in the exchange series itself depends on how the documents are preserved, selected, and presented to later readers. Subsequent memorial functions, as constructed in published collections, are different from those in the original exchanges, and each publication has its own agenda. The incorporation of letter and gift-texts to Diodati is managed differently in *Epistolarum Familiarum Liber Unus* and in *Poems*, the two collections involved, and the different management of memory draws out issues of readers and reader communities.

The twin-volume *Poems* of 1645 is the simpler case.[41] There the presence of Diodati is substantial, perhaps iconic. Finely crafted poems are more likely to be kept and displayed than letters. The evidence of the Trinity College Manuscript supports an assumption that there is usually a close relationship between verse texts preserved there and what appeared in print. There may be a further significance, too, in the position given the *Epitaphium* in 1645. Because the ancient languages part comes after the modern languages part, *Epitaphium Damonis* is last of all in the twin volumes. With its survey of future poetic plans and its inclusion of Milton's new Italian friends, it seems to collect the valuables of the past and anticipate the future, for his poetry. The poem is partly self-promotional, and Diodati is given a special place, as the friend with whom plans were shared. Amongst the growing political activism of the mid-1640s, he may be a surrogate, too, for the desired sympathetic reader of Milton's verse.

But the story is far less straightforward with the familiar letters published at the end of Milton's life. The two 1637 letters to Diodati are, as we have seen, already retrospective, seeking to theorize the experience of earlier years, but the 1674 volume of familiar letters containing that pair creates a new temporal perspective from a very long time after the student experiences. Scholars today might also wonder how much a fashioning by *selection* has taken place for posterity. It is the biographer, creating differently, not the writer, who thinks that everything should be kept.

The matter of selection in the 1674 volume of letters is acute. An indication of the possibilities can be gained from other series. For example, strict selectivity is evident with the correspondence with Hermann Mylius, the Oldenburg envoy. He communicated with Milton in the early 1650s in the latter's roles as secretary to the Council of State and scholar. The Staatsarchiv preserves seven letters from Milton; only one substantial letter appears in the 1674 volume, as XI.[42] Assuming a selectivity in other sets in 1674, it would be logical to ask whether for the period before Italy Milton really had only two letters to Diodati, two to Young, and three to Gil to choose from. Were there no letters exchanged with Diodati between 1629–30 and late 1637? Was there no exchange about his being in Cambridge for the incorporation of his MA in July, 1629? Was there nothing in 1634, despite the fact that the Earl of Bridgewater's family was entertained in houses near Diodati's 'Hyperborean' base? And so on. Is it significant that the only letters printed were those of more mature years, more juvenile texts perhaps not being chosen for this end-of-career showpiece volume?

These questions raise others about how letters were archived.[43] Did Milton, like many scholars, keep letter-books, from which selections were made for publication, with the help of his amanuensis assistants? Whatever his practice, it may have been affected by the onset of blindness in 1652 and the need to employ those assistants. We also do not know how he archived copies of letters to him, especially since very little has survived from Diodati. The issue of survival has been opened up by surprising discoveries: that of copies, now in the New York Public Library, of the candid 1647 exchange with Carlo Dati, for example, one letter from each, both autograph,[44] and the striking case of the two Greek letters in the British Library from Diodati himself.

In its presentational aspects, the 1674 book of letters foregrounds intellectual exchange and bookish companionship on an international scale. Lifelong contacts are to be shown. The correspondents are the likes of Italian academicians, admiring European scholars or scholar-diplomats aware of Milton's anti-monarchical triumphs, and young men whom he had helped as tutor or who had helped him as assistants in the years of blindness. The common denominators are companionship, discussions of books, and above all, recognition of Milton as scholar, writer, and teacher. He seems seldom to have initiated exchange, typically responding to approaches from others, probably craving that recognition. The 1674 collection is about recognition in select company. Some texts show anxiety about the lack of continuing intellectual companionship: the long, frank letter to Carlo Dati in 1647 for example, shows relief that he has not been forgotten by his Florentine academician friends and confesses his current despair, being *in perpetua fere solitudine*, in almost complete solitude, despite (or because of) having a house full of his wife's relatives.[45]

With its emphasis on the impact of Milton's public, political works on the European stage, *Epistolarum Familiarium Liber Unus* displays an agenda far beyond the discourse of the young friends. Even the title of the book implies the existence of other familiar letters. The original intention was to publish familiar and state letters together; perhaps this selection of familiar letters was made with state letters in mind. In all this, the two Diodati letters displayed provide relatively mature expressions of the early friendship, but their impact is limited and their concern with developing plans for poetry sets a different agenda from that in most of the other letters in the volume.

In all this, for understandable reasons, an important aspect of Diodati's presence in the published volumes may be only half articulated: the degree to which he might have been a favourite reader of Milton's early poems, whether addressed to him or not. In text after text, we see him cast as reader, one whose reactions are welcome: *Tu mihi . . . instar iudicis eris*. Here is the charismatic, encouraging companion apparently preferred in early years to those by the reedy Cam. The definition of the reader by the writer is in fact a key issue with many of these texts, as frequently when 'private' commu-nications have other lives for other audiences. Even the posthumous elegy presents a specific version of the problem. *Epitaphium Damonis*, celebrating a friend and friendship itself, was sent first to a special group of friends. In that sense the publication illustrates the desired effects of the spirit of friendship, but the coercive implication is also clear: the poem asks that its readers become friends, too.

If Diodati is cast as a most welcome reader, and we do not have all the exchanges between the friends, questions follow about how many other texts, beyond those addressed to him, were submitted to his judgement or written partly with his reading in mind. The Nativity Ode and 'Lycidas' are mentioned by Milton in the letters, but as far as close fit is concerned, there is one obvious speculation: how much there was a connection between this friendship discourse and the discourse of the twin poems 'L'Allegro' and

'Il Penseroso'? From an appropriate period (1629–31), these inventive poems with flexible movement, triumphs of English versification with Italian titles, share many coordinates with the Milton–Diodati exchanges. A full discussion also requires more space than is appropriate here, but it is a fair thought that Diodati might have been in mind as an ideal reader.

Implicitly, both presented characters in the twin poems are playful affectations. The implicit grounding is probably that of rational religion such as might supposedly be shared between two scholars at some point thought of for the church. The melancholy man slides, but with beguiling cunning, into old monkishness; the mirthful man luxuriates, but with what charm, in the wishful fantasies of youth. It is an attractive imaginative exploration, and the terms of reference overlap the role-play of the friends during the exchanges of their student years. But this is not as simple as biographical identification, with the gregarious Diodati *as* the mirthful man and the studious Milton *as* the melancholic. Handel's setting of the companion poems inadvertently makes the point, when he rounds them off with a balanced third term, Il Moderato. An *articulated* third term destroys the play. In Milton's poems each character lacks grounding, and is revealed using discourse created with gentle mischief, dealing in extremes and asking for humorous recognition. Without that sense of play, there is a less inventive music. The exploration of roles, both in the twin poems and the early friendship discourse, looks like a youthful exploration of identity. But most of all there is trust in the reader to see the play; that is perhaps what is most crucially similar to the Milton–Diodati texts, written for the most welcome and intimate reader-friend.

Notes

1. For an appreciation of this Prolusion, see John K. Hale, *Milton's Cambridge Latin: Performing in the Genres, 1625–1632* (Tempe, Ariz., 2005), 91–106.
2. This text follows the translation in *CPW*, i. 295. Elsewhere, the translations from Latin and Italian in the Milton and Diodati texts are my own, because fresh analysis of stylistic detail has often been involved. I would like to thank Hugo Tucker for much help with this linguistic work. Unless otherwise indicated, all numbers in the main text that appear in parentheses refer to line numbers in Milton's or Diodati's writing.
3. For example, Campbell and Corns opine that Diodati 'may have been the closest friend that Milton ever had' (22).
4. The date of the original printing of *Epitaphium Damonis* is not known. The one usually hazarded is in the closing months of 1640, because the poem's ninth line says that

two harvests have passed since Diodati's death in August 1638, though that could also mean late 1639 or some time in 1640. But Harris F. Fletcher, 'The Seventeenth-Century Separate Printing of Milton's *Epitaphium Damonis*', *Journal of English and Germanic Philology*, 61 (1962), 788–96, posited a date as late as 1646, assuming that the printing derived from the 1645 edition of the poems. John T. Shawcross, however, in 'The Date of the Separate Edition of Milton's *Epitaphium Damonis*', *Studies in Bibliography*, 18 (1965), 262–5, re-established the earlier date. For the purposes of this essay, a distribution as late as 1646 would make the widening friendship effect very remote in time.

5. John P. Rumrich, 'The Erotic Milton', *Texas Studies in Language and Literature*, 41 (1999), 128–41; rpt. in J. Martin Evans (ed.), *John Milton: Twentieth-Century Perspectives* (2002), 32–45.

6. See Alan Bray, *The Friend* (Chicago, Ill., 2003): 'The inability to conceive of relationships in other than sexual terms says something of contemporary poverty' (6).

7. Bray poses much the same question (*Friend*, 164–74).

8. 'Arguably what is common to all these jokes is not sexuality but manliness' (Bray, *Friend*, 168).

9. Keith Thomas, *The Ends of Life: Roads to Fulfillment in Early Modern England* (Oxford and New York, 2009), 196.

10. These letters can be found in BL Add MS 5061*, fos. 5 and 71.

11. Campbell and Corns see a 'playful erotic charge' and a 'sexual frisson' in these letters (31–2), but do not relate them to epistolary and social conventions of the time.

12. Ronald Sharp, *Friendship and Literature: Spirit and Form* (Durham, N.C., 1986), 14, 34. This not very well-known essay-book is an enthusiastic study of ritual form in male friendship exchange, partly following Lewis Hyde.

13. See John K. Hale, *Milton's Languages: The Impact of Multilingualism on Style* (Cambridge, 1997), 33–7; and 'Milton Playing with Ovid', *Milton Studies*, 25 (1989), 3–19.

14. Following the now accepted view of Campbell and Corns that Milton's 'exile' is simply a reference to the vacation, not to a possible rustication (32).

15. See the scholarship reported in *A Variorum Commentary on the Poems of John Milton*, gen. ed. Merritt Y. Hughes, 6 vols. (New York, 1970–), i/1, 122–3.

16. John Carey, 'The Date of Milton's Italian Poems', *Review of English Studies*, 14 (1963), 383–6. The idea has been contested by Douglas Bush in A *Variorum Commentary*, i/1, 126 and by Lewalski, *Life*, 557–8.

17. John K. Hale, 'The Audiences of Milton's Italian Verses', *Renaissance Studies*, 8 (1994), 76–88: '"Te *quoque* pressa manent" must mean poems *other* than the Ode [surveyed in 79–88 preceding]; and why should stress be placed on such "other" poems being in *English* when the Ode already is? Similarly, the prominent initial "te" draws "patriis" to itself, connecting the first words of each hemistich, so as to herald a change of topic and reference, very suitably for the close of a verse-letter about personal matters to a friend. "Tu" similarly dominates the next line, the last of the poem. Correspondingly, the double and equally prominent "illa" of the preceding couplet . . . reads as the end of a distinct topic' (77).

18. Stefano Villani, 'The Italian Protestant Church of London in the 17th Century', in Barbara Schaff (ed.), *Exiles, Emigrés and Intermediaries: Anglo-Italian Cultural Mediations* (Amsterdam and New York, 2010), 217–36.

19. In December 1629 Milton acquired *Rime e Prose di Giovanni della Casa* (Venice, 1563), now in the New York Public Library (Rare Book Room *KB 1529), bound with Dante's *L'Amoroso Convivio* (Venice, 1529) and Benedetto Varchi's *Sonetti* (Venice, 1555).

20. The location echoes that given at the beginning of Elegy I.A leasehold on lands in the parish of Marchwiel in the names of Charles and his brother is noted in A. N. Palmer, 'The Broughtons of Marchwiel: A Contribution to the History of the Parish of Marchwiel', *Y Cymmrodor*, 14 (1901), 45–8. See also J. Karl Fransen, 'The Diodatis in Chester', *Notes and Queries*, 234 (1989), 435. On Theodore and Charles Diodati, see also the *ODNB*.

21. See Campbell and Corns, 100.

22. Apart from Plato and Cicero in *De Amicitia*, commonly cited ancient authorities on friendship include Aristotle, *Nicomachean Ethics* 8 and 9, *Eudemian Ethics* 8, *Magna Moralia* 2.11-16; Plutarch, *Moralia* 48e–74, 94a–97b; Seneca, *De Beneficiis*, *Ad Lucilium Epitulae Morales*, 3, 9, and 25; and Cicero, *De Inventione* 2.55, *De Finibus Bonorum et Malorum* 1.20, 2.24–6.

23. Notably, John T. Shawcross diagnosed homosexual experience in 1628–9, followed by an estrangement, in 'Milton and Diodati: An Essay in Psychodynamic Meaning', *Milton Studies*, 7 (1975), 127–64, revised in *John Milton: The Self and the World* (Lexington, Ky., 1993), 43–59. Most subsequent commentators have noted attraction but doubted sexual experience: see William Kerrigan, *The Sacred Complex: On the Psychogenesis of Paradise Lost* (Cambridge, Mass., 1983), 49 and Rumrich, 'The Erotic Milton', 130–2.

24. From Euripides, a sentence used at the end of several plays.

25. Gregory Ronald Chaplin, 'One Flesh, One Heart, One Soul: Renaissance Friendship and Miltonic Marriage', *Modern Philology*, 99 (2001), 266–92.

26. For a brief summary of the reorientation of the Platonic *mores* in the Renaissance, see Jill Kraye, 'The Transformation of Platonic Love in the Italian Renaissance', in Anna Baldwin and Sarah Hutton (eds.), *Platonism and the English Imagination* (Cambridge, 1994), 76–85.

27. Natalie Zemon Davis, *The Gift in Sixteenth-Century France* (Oxford and New York, 2000), 14, but see also the whole introduction for a good summary of twentieth-century gift theory; Jacques Derrida, *The Politics of Friendship*, trans. George Collins (1997; New York, 2005), 9. The observation could be replicated in many other places.

28. See, for example, Robert Brain, *Friends and Lovers* (New York, 1976), discussing the archetypal friendship of David and Jonathan: 'The intense friendship of the two Israelites, lasting till death, depended on the complete willingness of each man to give for that which is received, to forgo self-interest, to convert separate identities into togetherness. As is frequently the case . . . the most splendid occasion for the demonstration of love was the death of one of them' (28).

29. Hale is particularly good on this. See *Milton's Languages*, 58–9.

30. See Hale, *Milton's Languages*, 58 and Estelle Haan, *From Academia to Amicitia: Milton's Latin Writings and the Italian Academies* (Philadelphia, Pa., 1998), 24.

31. That a copy of *Epitaphium Damonis* was received in Florence is known from Milton's correspondence with Carlo Dati. Haan persuasively argues that the text or texts were sent to the Svogliati Academy, rather than simply to Dati personally. See *From Academia to Amicitia*, 53–60.

32. Michele de Filippis, 'Milton and Manso: Cups or Books', *PMLA*, 51 (1936), 745–56; Ralph W. Condee, 'The Structure of Milton's *Epitaphium Damonis*', *Studies in Philology*, 62 (1965), 577–92.

33. John K. Hale, 'Sion's Bacchanalia: An Inquiry into Milton's Latin in the *Epitaphium Damonis*', *Milton Studies*, 16 (1982), 115–30 at 129.

34. Stella P. Revard, *Milton and the Tangles of Neaera's Hair: The Making of the 1645 'Poems'* (Columbia, Mo., 1997), 235.

35. The first remark is from Sharp, *Friendship*, 9. The second judgement, not focussed on the power of ritual form but on the issue of suppressed homosexuality, is that of Campbell and Corns, 136. In this context, Sharp is worth quoting at greater length: 'I have been trying to demonstrate that concealment can be the agent of intimacy, that distance can create closeness, and that formality can provide a vehicle for intimacy' (62).

36. The latest edition of Montaigne's essays with apparatus is *Les Essais*, gen. ed. Jean Balsamo (Paris, 2007).

37. Remarkably, a similar thing happened with Montaigne's own literary legacy at the end of his life: the young Marie de Gournay was given and saw through the press the revised text of the *Essais*.

38. Sharp, *Friendship*, 91.

39. See notes 5 and 25 above.

40. Karen L. Edwards, 'Raphael, Diodati', in Donald R. Dickson and Holly Faith Nelson (eds.), *Of Paradise and Light: Essays on Henry Vaughan and John Milton in Honor of Alan Rudrum* (Newark, Del., 2004), 123–41.

41. On Milton's arrangement of the 1645 *Poems*, see Stella Revard's essay in this volume.

42. For a full account of the Mylius correspondence, see Leo Miller, *John Milton and the Oldenburg Safeguard* (New York, 1985). There is an overlap in this section with 'The Letters, Verse Letters and Gift Texts', in Stephen B. Dobranski (ed.), *Milton in Context* (Cambridge and New York, 2010), 35–45. I am grateful for the permission to use the repeated material.

43. See Robert T. Fallon, *Milton in Government* (Philadelphia, Pa., 1993) for a discussion of how Milton may have filed the 155 Letters of State that were later transcribed into the Columbia Manuscript (221–38). See also J. Milton French and Maurice Kelley, 'That Late Villain Milton', *PMLA*, 55 (1940), 102–18 for Daniel Skinner's involvement with Milton's manuscript copies.

44. New York Public Library, MSS Col 2011.

45. Letter 10 in the *Epistolarum Familiarium*; *CW*, xii. 44–53. On the Dati exchanges and other material on exchanges with the Italians, see Haan, *From Academia to Amicitia*.

6

Milton and the Idea of the University

Sarah Knight

Of the parade of mourners who lament for the 'sad occasion' of Edward King's death in Milton's 'Lycidas' (1637), perhaps the most impassioned in his sorrow is the river-god Camus, standing for the River Cam and the university of Cambridge:

> Next Camus, reverend sire, went footing slow,
> His mantle hairy, and his bonnet sedge,
> Inwrought with figures dim, and on the edge
> Like to that sanguine flower inscribed with woe.
> Ah; who hath reft (quoth he) my dearest pledge? (103–7)[1]

This detailed portrait of Camus is Milton's invention.[2] He was not the first to associate the Cam with the students who lived near it, but although writers such as Giles Fletcher the younger had already invoked a 'greene Muse, hiding her younger head / Vnder old Chamus flaggy banks',[3] anticipating by nearly thirty years the association 'Lycidas' makes between the Cam and 'greene', 'younger' poetic composition, Milton's personification of the river is more meaningful. 'Lycidas' is Milton's most sustained work in the mode of academic pastoral, defined here as the use of rural metaphors and topographies to represent university life and the educational process.

Eighty years ago, E. M. W. Tillyard observed that 'Lycidas' is really about Milton, and poetry, rather than about King.[4] But it is also about Cambridge, and this chapter will trace Milton's writing about the university he attended, both as he experienced it as a student, and as he attributed it with different meanings throughout his career. Written five years after he had left Cambridge, 'Lycidas' marked a pivotal moment in Milton's representations of the university: the poem both develops attitudes he had articulated in his student Latin poems and orations of the late 1620s and early 1630s, and points towards his discussions of higher education in the early 1640s prose, particularly *An Apology* (1642) and *Of Education* (1644). Interwoven into these varying pictures of academia is an ongoing exploration of how misguided epistemological training can adversely affect intellectual and literary ability later in life. Barbara K. Lewalski has written that Milton was 'disappointed by and sharply critical of the education he received at Cambridge University',[5] but he did not always write critically of the university: in *An Apology*, for instance, he fondly recalled his tutors and his own 'honest and laudable courses, of which they apprehended I had given good proofe'.[6] Milton's representations of his education varied widely, and so we cannot argue for a tidy, coherent perspective on the university in Milton's writing, only attempt to disentangle the intricacy of his perspectives.

A consideration of how Milton figured the university illuminates not only how his thinking about ancient and contemporary epistemological and pedagogical models developed, but also how his political perspectives changed. The emphasis in Milton's portraits of Cambridge shifted along with his political and ecclesiastical affiliations during the late 1620s, 1630s and 1640s. Thomas Corns and Graham Parry have suggested that while he was a student, Milton was more conservative—or, at least, less anti-episcopal and parliamentarian—than he became in the two decades following his graduation, and Campbell and Corns have argued further for this early relative conservatism.[7] Besides political changes, two other events seem also to have influenced his subsequent representations of education: while touring Europe in 1638–9 Milton attended several Italian academies, and on his return to London he began work as a schoolmaster to his nephews Edward and John Phillips. During these years, Milton moves from depicting himself as a student, as someone embedded within the university, to positioning himself as an observer and commentator on university life from outside its walls.

After some years as a schoolmaster, Milton wrote his fullest exploration of pedagogy, invited by the educational reformer Samuel Hartlib.[8] In *Of Education* he states his interest in the '*Idea*' of a perfect education:

that voluntary *Idea*, which hath long in silence presented it self to me, of a better Education, in extent and comprehension farre more large, and yet of time farre shorter, and of attainment farre more certain, then hath been yet in practice.[9]

'*Idea*' is a significant term for an author who had been as infused with Platonic philosophy during his university career as Milton had.[10] Irene Samuel traces the concept of the Platonic 'Idea' throughout Milton's writing and argues that Milton used the term variously, and 'more vaguely in earlier years, more distinctly later' he came to a 'belief in the clearly defined and unalterable nature of moral truth'.[11] In *Of Education* Milton specifically uses the term to describe his own pedagogical ideals and to offer practical guidance for the implementation of a perfect concept of education. His assertion that this '*Idea*' has 'long in silence presented it self' suggests that educational ideals have been a preoccupation long before he came to write the treatise. The implication of long pondering is supported, in fact, by a rhetorical question posed in the seventh Prolusion, written while he was still a student in about 1630:

Quis enim rerum humanarum divinarumque ἰδέας intueri digne possit aut considerare, quarum ferme nihil nôsse queat, nisi animum, per artem & disciplinam imbutum & excultum habuerit; ita prorsus ei cui Artes desunt, interclusus esse videtur omnis aditus ad vitam beatam . . .[12]

(For who can appropriately consider and ponder the *Ideas* of human and divine things, about which almost nothing can be known, if he does not possess a mind infused and refined by art and training?)

Here, Milton addresses the most difficult question about education as an '*Idea*': we can only think about ideal forms with the human mind, and if that mind has been imperfectly trained, through a flawed pedagogical system, then how can we ever hope to understand education in its ideal form? John Hale reads the seventh Prolusion in part as an 'attack' on the Cambridge curriculum,[13] and certainly in his speech Milton criticizes current university teaching of grammar, logic, and law. Yet this formal declamation is also constructive in its discussion of epistemological and educational concerns, first raising the problem that Milton would go on to explore throughout his writing life, that 'errours' of the curriculum (as he describes them in *Of Education*) need to be *corrected* before one can arrive at a pedagogical '*Idea*'.

Milton's preoccupation with the '*Idea*' continued throughout the 1630s. Estelle Haan has also noted how, in a 1637 letter to Charles Diodati, Milton declared his search for 'the idea of the good (or "beautiful"' [τοῦ καλοῦ

$\mathit{i}\delta\acute{\epsilon}\alpha\nu).$[14] Haan relates this declaration to Milton's self-immersion in Italian culture immediately before his visit, and argues that while in that country 'Milton would witness and participate in the rebirth of a particularly Platonic Idea of the Good—the institution of the Academy'.[15] When he wrote *Of Education* in the early 1640s, Milton may well have had the academies in mind as an ideal intellectual society, 'that voluntary *Idea* . . . of a better education', and it may be these evoked in his ever-classicizing imagination the original Ἀκαδημία in Athens, 'the olive-grove of Academe' bewitchingly evoked by Satan in *Paradise Regained*.[16] Yet the rhetorical question he poses in the student Prolusion suggests that it was not just the Italian academies that made him associate epistemology with the Platonic '*Idea*' and the 'mind infused and refined by art and training', but that he was already thinking about education in Platonic terms while at Cambridge.

I. Nursed upon the self-same hill

We return to 'Lycidas'—written in the same year as the letter to Diodati—and to the river-god Camus. An apparently minor revision of the poem's text in the Trinity College Manuscript, Milton's poetic notebook of the 1630s, touches directly on two important facets of Milton's representations of the university.[17] The revision concerns Camus's 'Bonnet sedge, / Inwrought with figures dim': the notebook records an initial reading 'Scrawled o'er with figures dim', but this has been changed to 'Inwrought', as printed in the 1638 *Justa Edovardo King Naufrago* and the 1645 *Poems*. The alteration is significant for the line's meaning: in the late 1630s, as now, 'scrawled' conveys puerility and haste, while 'inwrought' describes an elaborate pattern worked into expensive fabric. Milton's search for a felicitous verb might seem incidental at first glance, but when read within Milton's depictions of academic activity elsewhere the manuscript revision becomes more intriguing. While 'scrawled' suggests an association between the university and childishness, the 'inwrought' Milton eventually selected implies the university's ability subtly to engrave its pedagogical priorities onto the young male mind. So we might ask whether, in 'Lycidas', Milton intended to depict the university as a very early formative stage of human development, or to associate higher education with serious thought and right-thinking practice.

The poem's account of Cambridge life engages with this debate, as Milton's involvement in the university anthology pulled him back into recalling his student days, caused him to alight on his own literary activities and those of his contemporaries, to remember what he and they had been writing in the late 1620s, and to consider how he had participated in the university's cultural life. A closer investigation of the academic pastoral mode of 'Lycidas' reveals how Milton developed a pre-existing student literary tradition and pushed this mode in new directions. Milton figured Cambridge as a 'hill' on which he and King were 'nursed', two shepherds who 'fed the same flock' (23–4). By situating Cambridge within this pastoral world, Milton followed several other student and graduate writers who represented the university as a questionable *locus amoenus*. These writers moved beyond the commonplace association of Parnassus as home of the Muses and metonym for poetry—made explicit in titles like Robert Allott's 1600 anthology *Englands Parnassus: or the Choysest Flowers of Our Moderne Poets*—by associating the fabled mountain directly with the university, and with Cambridge particularly from the end of the sixteenth century onwards.

The association between Cambridge and Parnassus is most fully realized in a trilogy of comedies performed at St John's College between 1598 and 1601, *The Pilgrimage to Parnassus* and the two parts of the *Return from Parnassus*, which represent two young Cambridge students as 'pilgrims to Parnassus mount'.[18] These plays established many of the conventions of academic pastoral, with which 'Lycidas' directly engages. At the start of the trilogy, before the 'pilgrimage' (i.e., BA degree) begins, all is idyllic: Consiliodorus, an aged educational optimist, figures Cambridge as an idyllic site for learning how to compose poetry:

> You twoo are Pilgrims to Parnassus hill
> Where with sweet Nectar you youre vaines may fill,
> Wheare youe maye bath youre drye and withered quills
> And teache them write some sweeter poetrie
> That may heareafter liue a longer daye. (36–40)

Consiliodorus furthers the ancient Greek topographical conceit on which this comparison rests, arguing that time spent at Cambridge/Parnassus will give the two students Orphic powers: 'There maye you bath youre lipps in Helicon / ... And teache them warble out some sweet sonnets / To rauishe all the fildes and neighboure groues' (41–4). By the end of the trilogy, though, these 'sweet sonnetes' have been trodden in the mud, while the relationship between academic life and the pastoral mode has been seriously called into doubt. A Cambridge degree has not, in fact, taught 'sweeter poetrie', but only bitterness and disappointment. The university continues to be an *alma mater* to one 'still happy' Academico, who finds peace on the banks of its river: another less lucky character caustically tells him: 'When thou repayr'st vnto thy Grantaes streame, / Wonder at thine owne blisse' (2175–6). But most of the other characters hold the same perspective as the satirist Ingenioso, who laments that, 'had not Cambridge bin to me vnkinde, / I had not turn'd to gall a milkye mind' (2180–1). Rendering the pastoral conceit uncomfortably literal, the two students retire to become shepherds in Kent: their Orphic ambitions remain—'The woods and rockes with our shrill songs weele blesse' (2104)—but their poems will now be elegiac: 'Weel chant our woes vpon an oaten reede, / While bleating flock[s] vpon their supper feede' (2157–8). The *Parnassus* trilogy can be read as a sustained interrogation of the value of a humanist education, and as a response to the employment crisis facing late Elizabethan graduates.[19] These plays established a distinct literary phenomenon of academic pastoral, offering student writers a set of conventions for representing the university as a place of pastoral retreat, but also as only a very dubious site of intellectual and social formation.

Like the students in the *Parnassus* trilogy, who 'chant [their] woes vpon an oaten reede', the pastoral register compels the speaker of 'Lycidas' to rely on his own 'Oate' to create poetic reminiscence, and the 'oaten flute' also animates the Cambridge students' 'rural ditties':

> Meanwhile the rural ditties were not mute,
> Tempered to the oaten flute,
> Rough satyrs danced, and fauns with cloven heel
> From the glad sound would not be absent long
> And old Damaetas loved to hear our song. (32–6)

At this stage in the poem, the speaker is involved in this activity—'old Damaetas loved to hear *our* song'—but he soon diverges from this communally shared music of the 'oaten flute' to the singular: 'But now *my* Oate proceeds' (88) [my emphasis]. As the poem moves forward, so the speaker disassociates himself from the 'rural ditties'. His decision to distance himself and his individual 'Oate' from this milieu of academic composition prompts us to read his characterization of fellow-students as 'rough satyrs' as implying crudeness and lack of sophistication, rather than as nostalgia for uncontrived youthful naturalism. John Spencer Hill has argued that the speaker's self-representation as an 'uncouth Swain' figures him as a writer 'rude but full of promise', aligning his 'unreadiness' with 'the promise of future achievement'.[20] But this 'promise' lies only in that final movement towards 'fresh Woods, and Pastures new', not on the 'self-same hill' of Cambridge, and that movement away from the hill and the 'rough satyrs' strongly suggests that he will not remain 'uncouth' for long. If 'Lycidas' is a poem about moving on from the university, the progression towards 'pastures new' might well represent a movement from the official, constrained world of the college anthology to a new kind of poetic composition.

The speaker of 'Lycidas' argues strongly for individual work over collective 'rural ditties', an extraordinary claim to make in a polyphonic college anthology. We should bear in mind that 'Lycidas' was written after a period of private study, the retirement to Horton 'to read good Authors'.[21] Yet while the insistence in 'Lycidas' on solitary self-improvement might reflect its author's self-imposed retirement, we again find similar emphasis on individual work ('*my* Oate') in poems Milton wrote as a student. 'Il Penseroso' forcefully evokes the appeal of solitary contemplation: most likely written during the summer of 1631, before Milton had completed his MA,[22] this poem dramatizes a gradual retreat from communal 'studious' and religious activity towards near-monastic isolation. Milton locates his speaker within an [an academic context]—'But let my due feet never fail / To walk the studious cloister's pale' (155–6)[23]—but emphasizes the devotional as well as collegiate meaning of 'cloister' as the speaker moves from monastery to hermitage: 'And may at last my weary age / Find out the peaceful hermitage, / The hairy gown and mossy cell' (167–9). The speaker leaves behind 'the high embowed roof' (157) of the 'studious cloister' he inhabits, its 'storied windows richly dight' (159), 'pealing organ' (161) and 'full-voiced choir' (162), to move into contemplative solitude.

The heady whiff of incense in this poem has prompted Graham Parry to observe that 'it is hard to think of a more complete Laudian moment in poetry than this';[24] Thomas Corns and Annabel Patterson have also located Laudianism in this poem, and it is difficult to disagree with these readings.[25] Yet perhaps more striking than the profound appreciation of religious music befitting a poem written by a composer's son is the yearning for solitude that compels the speaker to abandon the 'antique pillars massy proof' and

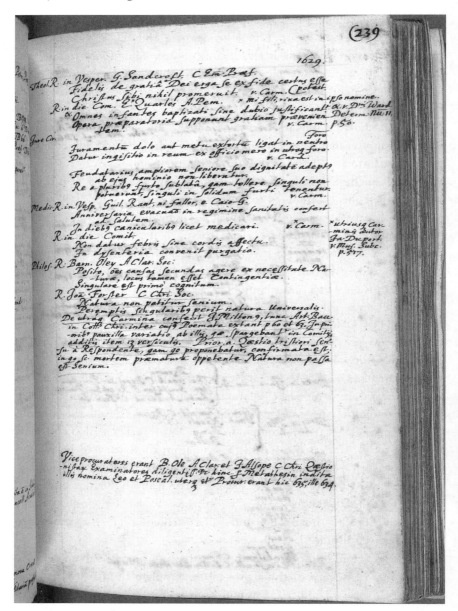

Fig. 9. Lambeth Palace Library MS 770.

'service high' for the 'mossy cell' of the hermit. We know that Milton had more sympathy for high church worship as a student than at any other time in his life: we also know that when he had just started his MA in autumn 1629, he wrote two poems for a royalist showcase arranged at Cambridge for the benefit of the new Chancellor, Henry Rich, Earl of Holland, and the French ambassador (see Fig. 9).[26] 'Il Penseroso' might suggest, though, that by 1631 the 'mossy cell' of solitary intellectual labour might have presented itself as an appealing alternative to the high church conventions of Caroline Cambridge. We could read the speaker's transition from an impassioned wish to melt into the 'service high' of the 'studious cloister'—'Dissolve me into ecstasies' (165)—to his intention to 'find out the peaceful hermitage' (168) as another version of leaving behind the 'rural ditties' of the university, and moving on to 'pastures new'.

II. Vocal reeds

The speaker of 'Il Penseroso' eventually dons the 'hairy gown' of a hermit, anticipating the 'mantle hairy' (104) Camus wears in 'Lycidas', but while the earlier poem might make us think of a saintly hair-shirt, Camus's mantle both recalls a scholar's furred robe and mirrors the texture of his reed-adorned 'bonnet sedge'. Within the poem's pastoral topography, as we have seen, Cambridge is linked with Parnassus; Milton also uses its river and reeds as a shifting metaphor for literary activity at the university. Edward King's ship capsized in the Irish Channel, and 'Lycidas', like all the other poems in the *Justa*, is an anthem for drowned youth, making the poem's fixation on the river particularly apt, but the portrait of Camus is also woven into a larger conversation with classical predecessors, situating the Cam somewhat bathet-ically alongside bigger, quicker, more venerable rivers. Milton mentions Camus *et al.* shortly after his invocation to two classical sources of inspiration: 'O Fountain *Arethuse*, and thou honoured flood, / Smooth-sliding *Mincius*, crowned with vocal reeds' (85–6), and the university river suffers by compari-son. Rivers are powerfully meaningful in Miltonic pastoral: a few years previously, in the entertainment *Arcades* (1633), he had referred to Arethusa, the fountain in Siracusa associated with the Sicilian originator of pastoral, Theocritus, as 'that renown'd flood' (29), and the similarly impressive 'smooth-sliding *Mincius*' refers to the modern River Mincio, which Milton associated with Virgil's home town of Mantua. In Book 10 of the *Aeneid*, Virgil describes the Mincio as *uelatus harundine glauca* / *Mincius infesta* (205–6),[27] translated by Dryden as 'Mincius, with wreaths of reeds his forehead cover'd o'er', recalling Camus's 'bonnet sedge'. Milton's evocation of the Virgilian river-god at the moment of 'Lycidas', shortly before the appearance of Camus, cannot be coincidental, not least because the *Aeneid* is doubly present in this portrait of Camus.

Just as the Cam 'footing slow' contrasts unfavourably with the 'smooth-sliding' Mincio, Milton's Camus is a deliberate echo of Virgil's Tiber in Book 8 of the *Aeneid*. The river-god appears to Aeneas in a dream, and Milton borrows Virgil's physical description (in Dryden's translation, 'An azure robe was o'er his body spread, / A wreath of shady reeds adorn'd his head').[28] Yet while Camus can only somewhat passively lament, the Tiber urges Aeneas, overwhelmed by the imminent prospect of war in Latium, on to hope and courageous acts. Milton's portrait of the river-god compels us to think of how Camus evokes vanished expectations, in comparison with Virgil's Tiber's promise of future glories. 'Lycidas' further reinforces this sense of contemporary Cambridge as unequal to the classical literary past: the speaker invokes Arethusa and Mincius only to note sadly that 'That strain I heard was of a higher mood' (87), and returns to the instrument of an earthbound *academic* pastoral: with a sense of resignation, he returns to the 'rural ditties' with which the poem opened, and the description of Camus 'footing slow'. The Cam and the 'rough ditties' heard along its banks, then, are clearly unequal to the rivers of the *Aeneid*.

Alongside Milton's personification of rivers to stand for university life, the reeds growing along their banks also assume figurative weight. Reeds are neither thrilling nor picturesque, but 'Lycidas' bristles with them, as we have seen. The reeds, sedge, and the 'oaten flute' that Milton, King, and other Cambridge poets play are all entangled with the *arundiferum Camum*, the 'reedy River Cam' first mentioned in Elegy I (1626?).[29] This poem is our earliest instance of Milton using the pastoral landscape of the university town to reflect a perceived crudeness and rusticity in its cultural life: the choked Cam is unfavourably compared with London, the *dulcis patria* (sweet homeland). The speaker wittily dismisses the university as sequestered and provincial, just as we would expect in such an exercise in Ovidian urbanity,[30] but at the same time we get a sense of precisely *why* Cambridge could be so unsatisfactory. In

Elegy I, for instance, the metropolitan young speaker represents the university as a stern, stark place:

> Iam nec arundiferum mihi cura revisere Camum,
> Nec dudum vetiti me laris angit amor.
> Nuda nec arva placent, umbrasque negantia molles,
> Quam male Phoebicolis convenit ille locus!
> Nec duri libet usque minas perferre magistri
> Caeteraque ingenio non subeunda meo. (11–16)

(I am not anxious to revisit the reedy Cam. I am not pining for my rooms, long forbidden to me. Bare fields which offer no gentle shades do not attract me. How badly that place suits the worshippers of Phoebus! I do not like having always to stomach the threats of a stern tutor, and other things which my spirit will not tolerate.)[31]

That 'long forbidden to me' has been interpreted as a reference to rustication, but it may simply mean the length of the university vacation: it is difficult to be certain.[32] In any case, the forbidden rooms, plus the reed-choked river, bare fields, and stern tutor, add up to a particularly unenticing picture of the university as a place where freedom of movement is impossible. The speaker's *exilium* (17) to London is no exile at all: he wishes that Ovid had been so lucky in *his* place of exile, emphasizing through this happy 'exile' that he is unhappy in that town where he is *meant* to be, in pursuit of his education. Cambridge, the speaker exclaims, simply does not suit *Phoebicolis*, the devotees of Phoebus, an association which suggests that from his earliest writing onwards, even as an undergraduate, Milton could not depict the university without reaching for allusions to Phoebus and the pastoral mode. Elegy I may have been at the back of Milton's mind when Phoebus 'touched' the speaker's 'trembling ears' (77) in 'Lycidas', animating him to reconsider how he 'tends the homely slighted shepherds trade' (65) and compelling him towards those 'pastures new', away from the university where *Phoebicoli* are unwelcome.

III. Vomited out thence

If we move from poetry to prose, from pastoral to polemic, we gain new insight into Milton's university. *An Apology* offers perhaps the most autobiographical account of Milton's academic experience:

[Joseph Hall's attack[33]] hath given me an apt occasion to acknowledge publickly with all gratefull minde, that more then ordinary favour and respect which I found above any of my equals at the hands of those curteous and learned men, the Fellowes of that Colledge wherein I spent some yeares: who at my parting, after I had taken two degrees, as the manner is, signifi'd many wayes, how much better it would content them that I would stay; as by many Letters full of kindnesse and loving respect both before that time, and long after I was assur'd of their singular good affection towards me. (*CPW*, i. 884–5)

We need to keep in mind the treatise's rhetorical purpose: Milton defends himself against Joseph Hall's calumny that he was 'after an inordinat and riotous youth spent at *the Vniversity*, to have bin at length *vomited out thence*', so it is of course in his interest to stress the regard in which he was held among his tutors. At the same time, this praise of those 'ingenuous and friendly men', Milton's tutors, recalls the role played both by 'old Damaetas' and by Camus in 'Lycidas'; in *An Apology*, too, all of these encouraging, affectionate old men— and the institution they stand for—have to be abandoned if the student is to move on. In *An Apology* Milton goes further in articulating a dislike of what Cambridge has become, making it clearer than he has yet done what he thinks of Caroline institutional interference. He picks up on Hall's purgative meta- phor—that he has been '*vomited out*' from Cambridge—and argues that despite the continuing presence of its kindly old tutors, it is now only 'the worser stuffe' that the university 'strongly keeps in her stomack':

As for the common approbation or dislike of that place, as now it is, that I should esteeme or disesteeme my selfe or any other the more for that, too simple and too credulous is the Confuter, if he thinke to obtaine with me, or any right discerner. Of small practize were that Physitian who could not judge by what both she or her sister, hath of long time vomited, that the worser stuffe she strongly keeps in her stomack, but the better she is ever kecking at, and is queasie. She vomits now out of sicknesse, but ere it be well with her, she must vomit by strong physick. (*CPW*, i. 885)

This 'worser stuffe' refers to the 'young Divines' Milton goes on to criticize, remembering them in the undignified postures of a college play:

when in the Colleges so many of the young Divines, and those in next aptitude to Divinity have bin seene so oft upon the Stage writhing and unboning their Clergie limmes to all the antick and dishonest gestures of Trinculo's, Buffons, and Bawds; prostituting the shame of that ministery which either they had, or were nigh having, to the eyes of Courtiers and Court-Ladies, with their Groomes and *Mada-moisellaes*. (*CPW*, i. 887)

We are reminded here of the inept, sprawling clergymen St Peter attacks in 'Lycidas': both the poem's pastoral register and its academic setting prompt us to think of these 'Blind mouths! That scarce themselves know how to hold / A sheep-hook' (119–20) as Cambridge students or recent graduates: the 'rural ditties…tempered to the oaten flute' (32–3) have become 'lean and flashy songs / [which] grate on their scrannel pipes of wretched straw' (123–4). The speaker of 'Lycidas' expressly defines himself against these individuals, glossed in the retrospective 1645 phrasing as 'our corrupted clergy then in their height';[34] it is just as important for *An Apology* as it is for the earlier poem that Milton figures his student self as an onlooker rather than a participant, disdainfully separate from his student peers: 'There while they acted, and overacted, among other young scholars, I was a spectator; they thought themselves gallant men, and I thought them fools' (887).[35]

IV. *Juvenes ornatissimi*

Both in 'Lycidas' and in *An Apology*, Milton represents his fellow-students in critical terms, for specific reasons that have to do with an increasingly politicized attitude towards the Caroline university. But in Milton's under-graduate and postgraduate writing, too, and especially in the Latin Prolu-sions, he demonstrates a sharp consciousness of his fellow-students as malleable figures to be represented according to his particular rhetorical purpose at any one time, ascribing certain values not only to the university, but also to the young men who attended it. In the Prolusions we see the same emphasis on singularity as we have noted in 'Lycidas' and *An Apology*, although in these early Latin orations that emphasis seems more provisional. In the first Prolusion, Milton the student orator describes himself as poised 'on the very *threshold* of the speech' (*in ipso Orationis Limine* 118), and the Prolusions constantly move between expressions of precocity and assurance, and a kind of tentativeness, a sense of uncertainty on the part of the speaker. Similarly, the student audiences are figured as *juvenes ornatissimi* and 'innumerable companies of the ignorant' by turns. The university itself, similarly, is sometimes exalted, filled with the *Libris & Sententiis doctissimorum hominum* ('books and opinions of most learned men' 248) and sometimes figured as a dreadful place that is so hidebound that it still teaches scholasticism. Sometimes, as at the start of the first Prolusion when the orator is feeling particularly grandiloquent, his fellow Christ's students are a 'great assembly' (*in hoc tanto concursu*), accorded the double roles of *Academici* ('Scholars') and *Auditores* ('Listeners' 118); at other times, as in the third Prolusion, they are complimented as *juvenes ornatissimi* ('most distinguished young men' 162); in the sixth Prolusion, they become sterner than the judges of the Underworld, waiting to dispatch the young speaker to Elysium or Tartarus: 'Aeacus and Minos would be kinder judges than any one of you' (206). Part of the reason for this, of course, is due to Milton's use of the *captatio benevolentiae* device: he is not going to capture much goodwill by insulting his audience, so to some extent the praise is predictable.

Yet elsewhere the mask slips, and in the Prolusions, too, we find that sharply critical—or, at best, ambiguous—characterization of fellow-students as unrefined intellects prone to crude behaviour, 'Rough satyrs'. In the first Prolusion, for example, identifying the few supporters he sees (*sparsim video*) in the audience, he then spends far more time listing the failings of those young men who manifest the worst aspects of juvenile literary and rhetorical activity, the 'innumerable companies of the ignorant' (*ab innumeris imperitorum Centuriis*) who make up the bulk of his audience: these students are boastful (*sese venditantibus*); they rely on patchwork quotations from modern authors (*emendicatos ab novitiis Authoribus*); finally, they draw in their horns like snails when they have exhausted their 'frail supply' or words (120). The third Prolusion offers a similarly critical view: although the speaker initially addresses his audience as *Juvenes ornatissimi*, he makes it clear that some among them are 'rustic, and obviously hairy-chested' (*agrestis, & hirsuti plane pectoris*), and he draws once again on the link between the university and the home of the Muses: 'There never was a place for them on Parnassus' (162). This association of rural labour with ignorance—in contrast with the idealizing tendency of classical pastoral to represent shepherds as uncommonly articulate—seems to have been a habit for Milton: in the sixth Prolusion, too, he declares that he has never lain on his back in the midday sun like a 'seven year-old cattledriver' (240). Although he may have been 'nursed upon the self-same hill' as his student audience and more than once had complimented them shrewdly, Milton still seems eager to differentiate himself from his peers, to assert his own place on Parnassus while he questions his fellow-students' right to be there too.

V. Private academies and preposterous exactions

This disregard for his student peers becomes more starkly engraved in the polemic of the early 1640s, as we see in the carefully pitched disgust that he directs in *An Apology* towards the fellow-students 'writhing and unboning their Clergie limmes' on the college stages. Yet although Milton's growing impatience with church and state does seem to have tainted his sense of the university's involvement with both institutions, an additional factor that had altered his view of the university was his recent travels to Italy, and, in particular, his experience of the Italian academies. These were not institutions of learning directly comparable with the Cambridge he had attended, but nonetheless offered Milton a new perspective on how ideas might be exchanged and literary endeavours discussed within a gathering of cultured intellectuals. Barbara Lewalski has also made the point that his previous 'isolation of solitary study' would have made Milton even more appreciative of 'the attractive social and intellectual life of the Italian academies'.[36] Perhaps by the late 1630s Milton was ready to abandon the 'mossy cell', particularly for Italy, and the sociability he encountered must have seemed all the more appealing when his writing was apparently so warmly received there. 'Whatever the reason', conclude Campbell and Corns, paraphrasing the poem Milton had written a couple of years earlier, 'he decided to explore fresh woods and pastures new'.[37] A continental journey may not have been one of Milton's immediate plans when he wrote the poem, but the restlessness articulated at the poem's end, and throughout its characterization of student life, anticipates the trip abroad.

In the immediate aftermath of his visit, Milton's first reminiscences emphasize these learned societies' exclusivity and refinement. His recollections of the 'privat Academies of *Italy*, whither I was favour'd to resort' are telling: for Milton, the Italian academies are highly selective, 'privat', and his 'favour'd' admission to them was a mark of his reputation. In 1638, for instance, Milton visited the Accademia degli Svogliati in Florence, and read some of his Latin poetry to the assembly: Estelle Haan has traced this visit and persuasively argues that Milton was glowingly received, and 'surpassed normal expectations' of an English visitor's literary efforts.[38] Haan notes Milton's discussion of this visit in an autobiographical section of *The Reason of Church-Government*. Milton wrote this a couple of months before starting on *An Apology* in early 1642: perhaps his warm reminiscence about his experience of the Italian academies while constructing the argument of *The Reason of Church-Government* was still glowing when he came to *An Apology*, causing him to reflect unfavourably on the English university by comparison. His Italian experience is the source of fond memory in *The Reason of Church-Government*:

But much latelier in the privat Academies of *Italy*, whither I was favour'd to resort, perceiving that some trifles which I had in memory, compos'd at under twenty or thereabout (for the manner is, that everyone must give some proof of his wit and reading there) met with acceptance above what was lookt for; and other things which I had shifted in scarsity of books and conveniences to patch up amongst them, were receiv'd with written Encomiums, which the Italian is not forward to bestow on men of this side the *Alps*. (*CPW*, i. 809–10)[39]

As well as causing him to define the English universities unfavourably against the Italian academies, this passage also shows that Milton continued to be proud of his student work a decade after he left Cambridge, if we read this description of his earlier work as 'some trifles', best fit for 'proof of his wit and reading', as an elegantly self-deprecating effort to make it seem as though he just showed up in Italy, dredged up his student works from memory, and delivered them to the enchantment of the academies. In any case, as Haan and Anna Nardo have argued, Milton's Italian experience profoundly altered his views of English higher education.[40] His reception during and after his Italian academic visits marked Milton's acceptance into the continental *respublica litterarum*, and functioned, in Nardo's words, as 'a kind of initiation into the ranks of international scholars'.[41] If we accept Milton's statement in *The Reason of Church-Government*, that this European reputation was initially based on works 'composed at under twenty or thereabout', then Milton's student writing becomes more than just the impressive juvenilia of an adolescent prodigy; it becomes the carefully selected ticket of admission into an intellectual elite far removed from the reedy river Cam.

On his return from Italy, and his entry into a schoolmaster's life, Milton continued to meditate on student experience, and his thoughts reached their fullest fruition in *Of Education*. The argument animating this treatise is that contemporary educational provision in England is inadequate: it does not form correct habits of mind, and is both outdated and unsophisticated. Milton's reforms relate both to school and to university; he makes it clear that common pedagogical 'errours' are shared by both kinds of institution: 'these are the errours, and these are the fruits of mispending our prime youth at the Schools and Universities as we do, either in learning meere words or such things chiefly, as were better unlearnt' (*CPW*, ii. 376). We think again of his avowed commitment to the 'voluntary *Idea*...of a better Education', and it seems likely, as he worked on this treatise, that Milton was accumulating examples of 'errours', bad pedagogical practice, from his own memories of school and university. Milton reserves some of his most savage criticism for those who seek to frogmarch the youth through academic exercises prematurely, describing these exercises 'preposterous', meaning indecorous and inappropriate (in the etymological sense of 'back to front'[42]). Such exercises, Milton argues, constitute:

a preposterous exaction, forcing the empty wits of children to compose Theams, verses, and Orations, which are the acts of ripest judgement and the finall work fill'd by long reading, and observing, with elegant maxims, and copious invention. (*CPW*, ii. 366)

We might recall the 'forced fingers rude' (4) with which the speaker of 'Lycidas' begins the poem, and align those with this 'forcing the empty wits of children'. Such observations reflect unfavourably on how Milton himself had been trained to write: did he regard 'Orations' such as the Latin Prolusions he had himself composed and delivered, or the 'Theams, verses' he had composed while at Cambridge, for instance for the 1629 visit, as exercises for 'empty wits'? Ought we to interpret this argument as evidence that Milton had come to view his own rhetorical beginnings as somewhat artificial, 'forced'? The institution described in *Of Education* is so different from the reality of Caroline Cambridge that it is difficult not to see this difference as oppositional and even corrective.

As we have seen him do throughout his Latin poems, and particularly in 'Lycidas', in *Of Education*, too, Milton inscribes his ideas about the university and the intellectual and literary activities he deems appropriate for students onto the landscape of the text. Having located 'Lycidas' on the 'self-same hill' of Cambridge five years previously, in *Of Education* he develops the image of an educational institution as a Parnassus-like location still further, claiming that his treatise will act as a map:

I shall detain you now no longer in the demonstration of what we should not doe, but strait conduct ye to a hill side, where I will point out the right path of a vertuous and noble Education; laborious indeed at the first ascent, but else so smooth, so green, so full of goodly prospect and melodious sounds on every side, that the harp of *Orpheus* was not more charming. (*CPW*, ii. 376)

Here, finally, the educational institution has become the *locus amoenus* that it was not permitted to be in any of the earlier poems: we seem closer to the 'Parnassus hill / Where with sweet Nectar you youre vaines may fill' glimpsed in *The Pilgrimage to Parnassus*, and far from the bare, flat fields and reed-choked Cam of Elegy I, as well as from the 'rural ditties' of 'Lycidas'. *Of Education* can be read as an effort to define a pedagogical '*Idea*' *against* the experience of its author, and Milton's use of language makes this contradistinction clear: as the Yale editor has observed (*CPW*, ii. 377n54), Milton uses similar terms for his attack on *scholasticism* in the third Prolusion—where he states that the scholastic philosopher *humana pectora spinis & sentibus implevit* ('has stuffed human breasts with thorns and briars' 166)—as he does for the educational process *in its entirety* in *Of Education*:

I doubt not but that ye shall have more adoe to drive our dullest and laziest youth, our stocks and stubbs from the infinite desire of such a happy nurture, then we have now to hale and drag our choisest and hopefullest wits to that asinine feast of sowthistles and brambles which is commonly set before them, as all the food and entertainment of their tenderest and most docible age. (*CPW*, ii. 376–7)

In the Prolusion, as we have seen, scholasticism is banished from Parnassus, unless to some 'uncultivated, unpleasant corner at the foot of the hill, thick and bristling with thorns and thorn-bushes' (162). In *Of Education*, Milton goes much further: rather than consigning a discipline he does not admire to a rough patch at the base of Parnassus, he instead conducts the reader to a *different* hill side of a 'vertuous and noble Education', in which no compromises are made and no subjects permitted of which he does not approve. In figuring the educational process as a journey up a hill, Milton recalls the Parnassus plays; he also creates a similar scenario to that imagined by a Cambridge author of the previous century, the rhetorician Gabriel Harvey. Harvey characterized learning as an 'ascent' in his *Ode Natalitia* (1575), which figures a Ramist university curriculum as a young man's journey to the homes of Apollo and the Muses under the direction of the character 'Methodus'.[43] Milton's less mythologically fanciful but just as pedagogically optimistic account becomes his '*Idea*': *because* it ultimately depicts only an imaginary academy, *Of Education* is the nearest to a Platonic form of education that Milton ever offered.

VI. Vain wisdom all, and false philosophy

Milton's two pictures of academia in *Paradise Lost* and *Paradise Regained* build on his previous explorations of 'the *Idea* . . . of a perfect education', but when we look at the poems in parallel, it becomes clear that the pedagogical '*Idea*' is no longer merely secular, as in *Of Education*, but has become fundamentally associated with religious doctrine. The hills and streams of the pastoral landscape that we have examined throughout Milton's academic figurations appear again in the two late epics, but this time used to strongly negative effect. In Book 2 of *Paradise Lost*, we see a savagely parodic version of academic debate enacted: uncomfortably evoking *Of Education*'s 'smooth' and 'green' 'hill side', Belial's companions sit 'on a hill retired', recreating in Hell the kind of academic philosophical debates in which Milton had himself participated at Cambridge:

> Others sat apart on a hill retired,
> In thoughts more elevate, and reasoned high
> Of providence, foreknowledge, will, and fate,
> Fixed fate, free will, foreknowledge absolute,
> And found no end, in wandering mazes lost.
> Of good and evil much they argued then,
> Of happiness and final misery,
> Passion and apathy, and glory and shame,
> Vain wisdom all, and false philosophy. (557–65)[44]

Milton's irony here is caustic: retirement to a hill in Hell for the purposes of debate, reasoning 'high', does *not* lead to 'thoughts more elevate', but rather to wasting time 'in wandering mazes', and finding 'no end' in refining and quibbling over abstract definitions: the fallen angels' debates may precisely have defined 'fate' as 'fixed fate', 'will' as 'free will', and 'foreknowledge' as 'foreknowledge absolute', but these precise theological definitions cave in under the weight of their immediate predicament and their own self-interest:

this conversation only reminds them of their own loss, disorientation and self-pity. The hill-top debate occasions only 'false philosophy' for the followers of Belial: apparently lofty at first, the intellectual confusion and ultimate pointlessness of their activity soon become clear.

Milton's picture of academic life darkens still further in *Paradise Regained*, and in this later poem, the replacement for the '*Idea*' of a secular education becomes clearer. In Book 4, in an apparent masterstroke of bookish temptation, Satan characterizes Athens as a site of pure scholarship, intended to divert Christ from his mission and faith:

> See there the olive-grove of Academe,
> Plato's retirement, where the Attic bird
> Trills her thick-warbled notes the summer long,
> There flowery hill Hymettus with the sound
> Of bees' industrious murmur oft invites
> To studious musing; there Ilissus rolls
> His whispering stream. (244–50)

Here, again, scholarly pursuits are mapped onto the topography of the academic city, its hills and streams, and as we have seen throughout Milton's work, the descriptions of these local features are subtly telling. While several of Satan's words imply rigorous intellectual activity—'industrious'; 'studious'—this implied diligence is only on the surface of his description, while a stronger verbal undercurrent pulls towards sensuous languor—'retirement'; 'murmur'; 'musing'; 'whispering'. Although in this city, 'mother of arts / And eloquence' (240–1), the hills and rivers appear to invite study, we learn that the city's real power to allure stems from more sensual, even soporific enticements: 'thick-warbled' birdsong, summer heat, the scent of flowers and hum of bees on Mount Hymettus, the river Ilissus's 'whispering stream'. Christ 'sagely' picks up on this immediately, asserting that the 'mellifluous streams' (277) of Greek philosophical debate become—when set against the blazing illumination of Christian doctrine, 'Light from above, from the fountain of light' (289)—simply 'false, or little else but dreams, / Conjectures, fancies, built on nothing firm' (291–2). Christ then proceeds to demolish the tenets of Platonic, Sceptic, Epicurean, and Stoic philosophy in turn, chiselling away at the value of the classical philosophies which Milton's two degrees had sought to inculcate.[45]

By the end of his life, in his religious poetry, at least, Milton suggests that the only true '*Idea*' possible in educational practice is Christian doctrine. But

his late publishing history in the early 1670s, particularly, serves to complicate this perhaps too teleological interpretation of how Milton had come to
represent the university in his late poems. We recall Irene Samuel's discussion of how Milton used the term '*Idea*' differently throughout his career,
and how he eventually came to a 'belief in the clearly defined and unalterable nature of moral truth'.[46] Yet while Milton may have resolved that in
contrast with 'light from above' all other learning was 'false philosophy', his
actual publications of the last half-decade of his life diverge to some extent
from this theological and epistemological resolution. The publication of
Accedence Commenc't Grammar (1669), the *Artis logicae plenior institutio* (1672), and
the *Prolusions* in 1674 demonstrates 'Milton's enduring interest in pedagogy', as
Stephen Dobranski has observed.[47] The emphasis of these works, particularly
the *Accedence Commenc't Grammar*, is practical rather than hypothetical, fore-
grounding hard terrestrial study rather than 'light from above'.

All three works relate to Milton's educational experience: the *Accedence*
proposes a new way of teaching Latin, the Prolusions are student orations,
and the *Ars Logicae* crystallizes Milton's theories of this central discipline of
the *trivium*. Although the printer's letter to the 1674 *Epistolae Familiares* and
Prolusions is somewhat ambivalent about the motives for publication,
implying that commercial concerns were uppermost, the fact remains that
Milton had kept hold of his student orations and was apparently not
embarrassed to have such juvenilia published late in his life.[48] The method
and definitions of the *Ars Logicae* also hearken back to Milton's Cambridge
career, and the Ramist methodology he absorbed there, as Emma Wilson has
convincingly argued.[49] The title page of *Accedence Commenc't Grammar* appeals to
a developmentally wide-ranging, expediently minded readership: 'For the
use of such (Younger and Elder) as are desirous without more trouble then
needs to attain the Latin Tongue; the Elder sort especially, with little
Teaching, and their own Industry'.[50] In the light of Milton's long-held
institutional scepticism, that final phrase echoes his implications in the
Prolusions and *Of Education* that being 'desirous' of learning and capable of
'Industry' is more important than (usually problematic) institutional
instruction, and that the 'mind infused and refined by art and training'
described in the seventh Prolusion can in effect be attained 'with little
Teaching'. In *Accedence Commenc't Grammar*, as in *Of Education* twenty-five years
earlier, Milton continues to use the metaphor of the journey or ascent to
describe the educational process, in this case, through teaching Latin in

English, 'whereby the long way is much abbreviated' (sig. A2r). These publications cumulatively suggest that Milton had not, in fact, given up on the '*Idea* . . . of a better education . . . then hath been yet in practice', and by publishing examples of his own 'practice' in the traditional disciplines of the *trivium*, Milton must have seen his own writing on logic, grammar, and rhetoric as still possessing pedagogical value and still offering potential help, even within a flawed educational system.

Notes

1. John Milton, *Complete Short Poems* (hereafter *CSP*), ed. John Carey, 2nd edn. (Harlow, 1997), 237–56.
2. *A Variorum Commentary on The Poems of John Milton*, gen. ed. Merritt Y. Hughes, 6 vols. (New York, 1970–). See ii/2, *The Minor English Poems*, eds. A. S. P. Woodhouse and Douglas Bush, 671–2.
3. Giles Fletcher, *Christs Victorie, and Triumph in Heauen, and Earth, ouer, and after Death* (Cambridge, 1610), 83.
4. E. M. W. Tillyard, *Milton*, rev. edn. (1956), 80; see also David Norbrook, 'The Politics of Milton's Early Poetry', in *Poetry and Politics in the English Renaissance*, rev. edn. (Oxford, 2002), 252–3.
5. Lewalski, *Life*, 15.
6. Milton's term 'courses' probably just means 'studies', but might also invoke the Latin *cursus*, meaning a race or movement along a career path; see *CPW*, i. 884.
7. See Thomas N. Corns, 'Milton before "Lycidas"', in Graham Parry and Joad Raymond (eds.), *Milton and the Terms of Liberty* (Cambridge, 2002), 23–36; Graham Parry, *The Arts of the Counter-Reformation: Glory, Laud and Honour* (Woodbridge, 2006), 154–6; Campbell and Corns, 43.
8. See Timothy Raylor, 'New Light on Milton and Hartlib', *Milton Quarterly*, 27 (1993), 19–31.
9. *CPW*, ii. 364.
10. For discussion of the philosophy curriculum at Milton's Cambridge, see Harris Francis Fletcher, *The Intellectual Development of John Milton*, 2 vols. (Urbana, Ill., 1956–61); Victor Morgan, 'Volume 2: 1546–1750', in Christopher N. L. Brooke (ed.), *A History of the University of Cambridge*, 4 vols. (Cambridge, 1988–2004), ii. 511–19; Irene Samuel, *Plato and Milton* (Ithaca, N.Y., 1947); see also William T. Costello, *The Scholastic Curriculum at Seventeenth-Century Cambridge* (Cambridge, Mass., 1958). Mordechai Feingold's work on the contemporary Oxford curriculum is also relevant. See 'The Humanities', in Nicholas Tyacke (ed.), *The History of the University of Oxford* (Oxford, 1997), iv. 211–359 (esp. 215, 258–9).
11. Samuel, *Plato and Milton*, 131–49 (see 145).
12. *CW*, xii. 254. The translation is mine.

13. See John Hale, 'Milton's Last Declamation, Prolusion VII', in *Milton's Cambridge Latin* (Tempe, Ariz. 2005), 91–106 (see 103).

14. *Familiar Letter* 7 in *CW*, xii. 26.

15. Estelle Haan, *From Academia to Amicitia: Milton's Latin Writings and the Italian Academies* (Philadelphia, Pa., 1998), 3.

16. For different perspectives on the historical relationship between the Italian academies and the Platonic Academy, see 'The Italian Academies', in Frances A. Yates, *Renaissance and Reform: The Italian Contribution* (1983), 6–29; James Hankins, 'The Myth of the Platonic Academy of Florence', *Renaissance Quarterly*, 44 (1991), 429–75; David S. Chambers, 'The Earlier "Academies" in Italy', in David S. Chambers and F. Quiviger (eds.), *Italian Academies of the Sixteenth Century* (1995), 1–14.

17. Although C. F. Stone III does not discuss the Camus passage, he considers other Trinity College Manuscript revisions in 'Milton's Self-Concerns and Manuscript Revisions in *Lycidas*', *Modern Language Notes*, 83 (1968), 867–81.

18. *The Pilgrimage to Parnassus*, in *The Three Parnassus Plays*, ed. J. B. Leishman (1949), 95 (Prologue).

19. Studies of this employment crisis that have proved particularly influential include: Mark H. Curtis, *Oxford and Cambridge in Transition, 1558–1642* (Oxford, 1959) and 'The Alienated Intellectuals of Early Stuart England', *Past and Present*, 23 (1962), 25–43; Lawrence Stone, 'The Educational Revolution in England 1560–1640', *Past and Present*, 28 (1964), 41–80; Christopher Hill, *Economic Problems of the Church: From Archbishop Whitgift to the Long Parliament* (rev. edn., Oxford, 1956) and his *Intellectual Origins of the English Revolution Revisited* (Oxford, 1997).

20. John Spencer Hill, 'Poet-priest: Vocational Tension in Milton's Early Development', *Milton Studies*, 8 (1975), 40–69 at 59.

21. *CPW*, i. 885.

22. See Campbell and Corns, 60–1.

23. *CSP*, 151.

24. Parry, *Arts of the Counter-Reformation*, 156.

25. Corns 'Milton before "Lycidas"', 31–2; Annabel Patterson, '"Forc'd fingers": Milton's Early Poems and Ideological Constraint', in Claude J. Summers and Ted-Larry Pebworth (eds.), *'The Muses Common-Weale': Poetry and Politics in the Seventeenth Century* (Columbia, Mo., 1988), 9–22 at 14.

26. See my 'Royal Milton', *Times Literary Supplement*, 5 February 2010, 15 and 'Milton's Student Verses of 1629', *Notes and Queries*, 255 (2010), 37–9.

27. See P. *Vergili Maronis Opera*, ed. R. A. B. Mynors (Oxford, 1969), 339.

28. *Aeneid* viii. 31–4, ed. Mynors, 283: *huic deus ipse loci fluuio Tiberinus amoeno* / *populeas inter senior se attolere fronts* / *uisus (eum tenuis glauco uelabat amictu* / *carbasus. et crinis umbrosa tegebat harundo).*

29. *CSP*, 19–24.

30. Cedric C. Brown, 'The Legacy of the Late Jacobean Period', in Thomas N. Corns (ed.), *A Companion to Milton* (Oxford, 2003), 109–23 (see 118).

31. *CSP*, 20 (Latin) and 23 (English translation, cited here).

32. See *CSP*, 19; Campbell and Corns, 32.

33. In his chapter 'The Literature of Controversy', Joad Raymond offers a useful overview of the 'Smectymnuus' dispute: see Corns, *A Companion to Milton*, 191–210 at 195–6; see also Richard McCabe, 'The Form and Methods of Milton's *Animadversions upon the Remonstrant's Defence against Smectymnuus*', *English Language Notes*, 18 (1981), 266–72; Campbell and Corns, 137–50.

34. *CSP*, 243; see also Neil Forsyth, '"Lycidas": A Wolf in Saint's Clothing', *Critical Inquiry*, 35 (2009), 684–702 at 697.

35. For discussion of Milton's attitudes towards student drama, see Alan H. Nelson, 'Women in the Audience of Cambridge Plays', *Shakespeare Quarterly*, 41 (1990), 333–6 at 335, and David Masson, *The Life of John Milton Narrated in Connexion with the Political, Ecclesiastical, and Literary History of His Time* (1859–94), i. 186.

36. Lewalski, *Life*, 87.

37. Campbell and Corns, 103.

38. Haan, *From Academia to Amicitia*, 22.

39. See also Haan, *From Academia to Amicitia*, 22.

40. Haan, *From Academia to Amicitia*, 10–28; Anna K. Nardo, 'Academic Interludes in *Paradise Lost*', *Milton Studies*, 27 (1991), 209–41.

41. Nardo, 'Academic Interludes', 216.

42. See Patricia Parker, 'Preposterous Reversals: *Love's Labour's Lost*', *Modern Language Quarterly*, 54 (1993), 435–82.

43. See my 'Flat Dichotomists and Learned Men: Ramism in Elizabethan Drama and Satire', in Steven Reid and Emma Wilson (eds.), *Ramus, Pedagogy and the Liberal Arts* (Aldershot, 2011), 53–4.

44. Milton, *Paradise Lost*, ed. Alastair Fowler, 2nd edn. (Harlow, 1998), p. 137.

45. See also Donald Swanson and John Mulryan, 'The Son's Presumed Contempt for Learning in *Paradise Regained*', *Milton Studies*, 27 (1991), 243–61.

46. See note 11.

47. Stephen B. Dobranski, *Milton, Authorship, and the Book Trade* (Cambridge, 1999), 176.

48. See Sarah Knight, 'Milton's Forced Themes', *Milton Quarterly*, 45 (2011), 145–60.

49. Emma Annette Wilson, 'The Art of Reasoning Well: Ramist Logic at Work in *Paradise Lost*', *Review of English Studies*, 61 (2010), 55–71.

50. *Accedence Commenc't Grammar* (1669).

7

Obituary and Rapture in Milton's Memorial Latin Poems

Noam Reisner

Critical estimates of Milton's Latin poetry have begun to turn away from the traditional view of these compositions as laboured neoclassical exercises cluttered with classical and mythological allusions. What was once a seemingly indecorous mixing of classical and Christian themes is now viewed as a feature of Milton's ingenuity, even if the end result is not always pleasing. It is now fully accepted, moreover, that it is precisely Milton's effortless command of the Latin language and the sinewy control he demonstrates over his classical materials that allow his singularity as a poet to emerge, even in his earliest work.[1] Consequently, the voice that speaks in these poems is one that we are all now trained to recognize as distinctly young Milton's: rigorously dialectical but playfully so, anxiously ambitious, and searchingly self-referential. Notwithstanding these advances, some of the Latin poems remain relatively neglected by critics outside specialized neo-Latinist circles, and broader discussions of Milton's bilingualism and neoclassical humanism. The four obituary poems marking the death of university dignitaries, composed in a burst of activity in Milton's second year at Cambridge, tend to fall through the net and are usually passed over very quickly as interesting but forgettable formal experiments in a variety of classical metres, most notably the Ovidian elegy and the demanding Horatian Alcaic strophe. The most that has been ventured in their way have been analyses focusing primarily on issues of style and Milton's creative imitation of his classical sources, or on topical allusions to current events at home and abroad which highlight young Milton's ideological commitment to militant Protestantism.[2]

Whatever scholarly interest the four obituary poems have attracted so far, it has rarely been focused upon what these poems are actually about. That is, the occasion and subject which gave birth to these poems have been deemed relatively unimportant when compared to the style and manner in which Milton rose to the occasion and tackled his subject in each instance. In his recent survey of the four obituary poems in their Cambridge context, John Hale has clarified much about the nature of the funerary occasion in question. He has made a strong case for seeing the four obituary poems as an artistic 'group' in which Milton produced 'four attempts at a single sort of occasion and its decorum . . . cultivat[ing] variety within the broad similarities of occasion'.[3] According to Hale, the absence from the obituary poems of young Milton's more familiar modesty claims about being unready as a poet is a sign of 'only a small personal engagement, and hence more likely to be an impersonally couched claim to public attention'.[4] However, the four poems also merit close examination of how the process of mourning public dignitaries sets the teenage Milton's neoclassical baroque imagination in motion. It is my contention that it is possible and indeed worthwhile to consider the four obituary poems as a group united by subject matter and thematic concerns with rape and rapture, subjects that reveal that what was at stake for the young Milton were not only matters of performance and public recognition, but subjects of deeply personal interest. It is not simply a case, as some have noted, of Milton transforming rather violently in these poems Ovidian erotica into visions of Christian consolation,[5] but of Ovidian energies of metamorphosis and rape competing with Christian notions of rapture at these poems' deepest rhetorical and creative levels. The Latin *funera* reveal that even as a very young poet, still unsure of his calling, Milton seized on the opportunity occasioned by the death of university dignitaries to explore the vocational conceit that it is always at an imaginary point of rapture between the fallen and the beatific worlds that the most sublime poetry is born. This is not an argument in favour of a young prophetic Milton, but of a young Milton audaciously experimenting in heavenly poetic flight. In 'At a Vacation Exercise in the College', written probably a few years later,[6] Milton promises his raucous audience of Cambridge undergraduates to reserve the poetic pursuit of 'some graver subject' (30)[7] for use of his English poetry, but the truth of the matter is that in his early Latin poems, even at his most playful, Milton is in fact already hard at work looking for the materials to be reworked into such future gravity. The four Latin *funera*, with their extraordinary visions of heaven and deeply allusive erotic subtexts about death and rapture, offer as a group a revealing Miltonic narrative about this youthful exploration after graver subjects, where 'the deep transported mind may soar / Above the wheeling poles, and at heaven's door / Look in, and see each blissful deity' ('At a Vacation Exercise', 33–5).

Despite considerable speculation, we will never know why Milton decided suddenly in his second year at Cambridge to make a modest name for himself among his peers as a Latin poet by joining in the public lament for not one, but four university dignitaries who died in close succession in the last months of 1626: Lancelot Andrewes, the Bishop of Winchester and a former Master of Pembroke college on 25 September; Richard Ridding, the Cambridge University Beadle a day later; Nicholas Felton, the Bishop of Ely and also a former Master of Pembroke on 5 October; and John Gostlin, the Vice-Chancellor and Regius Professor of Medicine, on 26 October.[8] As Campbell and Corns note in their recent biography of Milton, we should probably not read too much into the fact that a 'scrivener's son' in his first year as an undergraduate did not participate in the outpouring of memorial university verses on the death of James I and the panegyrics for the coronation of Charles I a year earlier.[9] However, it does seem significant that when the opportunity did present itself the next year, Milton chose to eulogize not just the university Beadle and Vice-Chancellor, but also Bishops Andrewes and Felton, both of whom were known at the time for their Arminian leanings and preference for high church ceremonialism.[10] The political subtext, however, is finally of lesser consequence in this case, though it does of course raise tantalizing questions about Milton's early radicalism or lack thereof. While it is in fact quite plausible that Milton felt genuine grief for the passing of Andrewes (who was not just a bishop but also a celebrated classical scholar, theologian, and linguist with a reputed command of fifteen languages, and a man noted for his charitable work around London as Royal Almoner), it is finally irrelevant, not to say unknowable, whether Milton felt genuine heart-rending grief for any of these dignitaries and whether his decision to mourn them in verse was somehow politically motivated. The tears Milton claims to burst into are not any more or less real than the poetic verses produced on the occasion of the four dignitaries' deaths, where the formal posture of poetic lament recommends itself as art worthy of literary consideration precisely because of its impersonal, highly stylized positioning within an established classical poetic tradition of *lacrimae* (laments) and the corresponding university tradition of Latin memorialization.

Even a quick glance at the four poems soon reveals that Milton's imagination on this occasion was drawn to other subjects entirely. The four poems do not in fact mourn the passing of specific individuals at all, so much as the general condition of human frailty and mortality which the death of these dignified, Christian individuals opens up to almost by way of allegory. Elegy II, on the late Beadle, begins with and is conducted under the formulaic cry against *saeva Mors* (fierce or violent death), itself a sort of beadle of the afterlife, 'who does not favour even members of her own office' (*officio nec favet ipsa suo*, 5). The obituary to the Vice-Chancellor plays on the central conceit of personified death avenging a surgeon who saved so many from its 'black jaws' (*atris | Faucibus eripuisse mortis*, 39–40), while the obituary to Felton contains a shrill invective against a reconstituted mythological apparatus of death, who is neither daughter of Night, nor of Erebus, nor a Fury, nor born of Chaos, but the divine agent 'sent from the starry heavens to collect everywhere the harvests of God' (*Ast illa caelo missa stellato, Dei | Messes ubique colligit*, 35–6). Similarly, Elegy III begins again not with an actual encomium of the late bishop and his many possible virtues, but with the macabre universal image of Libitina, goddess of corpses, cutting a path of carnage hand in hand with 'horrid Death with her sepulchral torch' (*Dira sepulchrali mors metuenda face*, 6) through plague-struck London and the grim battlefields surrounding Breda, which fell to the Catholics with the loss of many Protestant lives in 1625.

The funerary occasion of having to confront poetically life's inevitable transience gave the young Milton the opportunity to test the waters of public acclaim as a poet interrogating a worthy classical-Christian *topos*. Much in Milton's treatment of the subject is admittedly formulaic and unexceptional, but as Hale and Le Comte have shown, there is considerable variety of diction and tone as well as a great deal of technical ingenuity within the group as a whole. In this regard one of the most daring and striking thematic features of these poems that makes them stand out in the context of Milton's early vocational narrative is the way in which the speaking poet anxiously associates in them the *idea* of overcoming death in an absolute Christian sense with physical as well as spiritual rapture and ecstasy. The clichéd Christian *memento mori* theme which governs in different ways the structure of all four obituary poems is complicated by elaborate baroque allusions to classical myth and erotica where death is re-inscribed as a mark of absence and silence around which human agency and creativity perpetuate themselves. The resulting clash of Christian and classical themes about death, rapture, and transience, therefore, is not inadvertent or merely conventional but carefully calculated. It dramatizes, through a meditation on erotic Ovidian flux and metamorphosis, Milton's anxious resistance as a promising young poet to the violent loss of voice implicit in the platitudes and self-effacing abstractions of a Christian afterlife.

Allusions to Ovid far outweigh any other classical reference in Milton's early Latin poetry, and this is especially true of the four *funera*. Moreover, most of these allusions specifically point to Ovidian tales of rape and unrequited desire. In the elegy on the university Beadle, for example, we read how death snatches, *rapit*, one of its fellow Beadles. Any translation of *rapit* as 'snatches' or 'seizes', while correct, disarms the sexual overtones of the Latin verb *rapere* which Milton himself seizes on as he laments in the next lines, thinking of Ovid:

> *Candidiora licet fuerint tibi tempora plumis*
> *Sub quibus accipimus delituisse Iovem,*
> *O dignus tamen Haemonio iuvenescere succo,*
> *Dignus in Aesonios vivere posse dies,*
> *Dignus quem Stygiis medica revocaret ab undis*
> *Arte Coronides, saepe rogante dea.* (5–10)

(Although your brows shined whiter than the swan's down beneath which, as we are told, Jove lurked, you nevertheless deserved to be made young again with a Haemonian potion; you deserved to be able to live the length of Aeson's days; you deserved to be called back from Stygian waters through the medical art of Coronides and the frequent pleas of a goddess.)

In their respective commentaries, Carey and Bush draw our attention to the echo of Ovid's *Heroides* viii. 67–8 in Milton's *plumis* / *Sub quibus accipimus delituisse Iovem* ('the swan's down beneath which, as we are told, Jove lurked').[11] Milton's *accipimus* (literally meaning 'as received by us') is not merely a nod to the well-known mythological story of Jove raping Leda disguised as a swan. It is in fact a calculated literary nod to Ovid's Hermione, herself a victim of rape and a forced marriage, seeking true happiness with Orestes and release from her inexorable fate of anguish and ravishment as the daughter of Helen. But Milton does not stop here; even his subsequent references to the myths of Aeson and Asclepius (Coronides)—both memorably rendered by Ovid—as if to wish the late Beadle that he might have lived and become young again through the intervention of ingenious human art, not to say magic, also evoke the elaborate myths associated with these mythical characters and the torrid love affairs and tragedies at their core. Medea's witchcraft and Asclepius's medicinal art alluded to here are intimately related with violent forces of creation and flux which in Ovid's poetry, and by extension Milton's as well, animate the poetic creative process itself.

It is precisely by way of such playful mythic allusions that Milton draws attention to himself as a poet in command of his craft, but also points to what we know from later works to be a very personal vocational anxiety which the themes of violent rape and illicit, potentially sinful powers of poetic suggestion dramatize. Having reflected rather dryly on the late Beadle's virtues in the execution of his office, Milton is finally moved to address the 'great queen of tombs', who is 'too cruel to the Muses', and asks: 'why do you not snatch away (*rapias*) those who are a useless burden to the earth, for there is a mob of these for you to assault with your arrows' (*Quin illos rapias qui pondus inutile terrae,* | *Turba quidem est telis ista petenda tuis,* 19–20). While sounding formulaic, this complaint is quite daring in that it flouts traditional classical-Christian consolations where death is presented as the great equalizer which precisely does not distinguish between rich and poor, useful or useless man. The equanimity and traditional *contemptus mundi* of Ecclesiastes is replaced here with the indignation of a Ciceronian humanist lamenting the death of a virtuous man in the Roman sense of the term. However, the more we dwell on the potential novelty of these ideas, the more the image of the Beadle grows dim and a Miltonic persona begins to shine through. The late Beadle, presiding over the gowned assembly of 'Pallas's flock' (*Palladium . . . gregem,* 2), may symbolize in a very general sense a university community of educated and therefore virtuous people, but the reference specifically to the Muses hints that Milton may already be thinking about the fate of poets and of himself especially. This is borne out within the poem itself, when Milton concludes the elegy in its last four lines by turning to address the university community directly as if assuming the Beadle's office; bound by the same virtuous fate, poet and university official become one. The poet instructs his fellow-students how to mourn and lament as if the process of rehearsed grief has conferred on him authority. Just as the Beadle was a virtuous man who did not deserve to die, so the poet, now assuming the Beadle's role, asserts his privileged and therefore fragile status as someone who has much yet to achieve but also to lose. This sense of usurped authority, however, is nevertheless qualified by the shadow of violent rape and metamorphosis introduced into the elegy as decorative embellishments. The thought begins to creep in that the only place in which the Beadle Esquire might live again is in the Ovidian *eros* animating the pathos of Milton's lament, but it is a life won through Miltonic ingenuity asserting itself violently at the expense of voice—both the Beadle's and potentially in the future of the poet as well.

This theme is carried over into the metrically different but thematically comparable obituary to another university official, this time John Gostlin, the Vice-Chancellor and Regius Professor of Medicine. Here, however, the more elaborate scheme results in a deepening of its thematic implications. The opening tone of the Horatian ode lamenting the Vice-Chancellor is far more sombre, but also more mythologically remote. We are transported to a pagan world of death and violence where the university becomes a Mount Helicon or Delphi and the late Vice-Chancellor a mythic healer who could even boast Apollo as his student. The vast bulk of the ode (40 of its 48 lines) is made up of a dark and wild mythic catalogue of heroes and heroines who notwithstanding their powerful desire and will to live could not outwit the 'laws of fate' (*fati . . . legibus*, 1) and outsmart death. In this case, Homer's *Iliad* competes with Ovid's *Metamorphoses* for the abundance of allusions, but the Ovidian sentiment of death as change of form prevails. Milton's imagination ranges erratically from the story of Hercules's horrific death after being tricked by his vengeful wife to wear a shirt poisoned with the blood of the centaur Nessus, through the tragic but heroic deaths of Hector and Sarpedon during the Trojan War, to the ineffective witchcraft of Circe and Medea and the hubristic medical skills of the centaur Chiron and Asclepius, both of whom met with violent deaths as a price for their art. This catalogue gives a wonderful sense of dire inevitability: we open with Hercules dying from the poisoned blood of one mythic centaur, and we end with Hercules slaying a different centaur with the poisoned blood of the hydra. The relentless progression from one myth into the other and the growing subtext of violent desire which defines this catenation of myths are Ovidian par excellence, as is the emerging audacity of the poet creating the links in this chain, slowly asserting his authority.

One of the most intriguing conceits in this respect is the explanation offered towards the end of the poem for the now mythic death of the Vice-Chancellor, whose thread of life, we learn, was cut in anger by Persephone (here assuming the role of the goddess of death) because Gostlin saved so many from 'death's black jaws' (*atris* | *Faucibus eripuisse mortis*, 39–40). As Carey and Bush note in their commentaries, it appears to be Milton's novel idea to associate Persephone with Atropos, the third of the three dreaded Fates who traditionally cuts the threads of life. It is highly unlikely that Milton made a schoolboy's error of mistaking Persephone for Atropos, and it is only marginally more probable that he needed 'Proserpina' merely for metrical reasons. It is far more likely that his was an intentional move which becomes all the more cogent when we consider that Persephone also carries with her one of the most famous myths about rape and abduction in the classical corpus, memorably rendered by Ovid in *Metamorphoses* v. 385–424. Persephone performs in Milton's poem the function of a death goddess through no wish of her own; she was coerced into this unhappy role after being abducted by Pluto, god of the underworld, who fell madly in lust with her, and she is meta-poetically coerced again, it seems, by Milton. It is almost as if, by way of an ingenious conflation of myths, Milton inscribes the idea of violent rapture and the ecstatic loss of identity it brings into the idea of death itself—a carrying over into a nameless eternity the thought of which can move only the anxious poet to pray that the Vice-Chancellor may walk about 'in Elysian fields among the eternally blessed' (*Interque felices perennis* | *Elysio spatiere campo*, 47–8).

Strangely, however, the seemingly formulaic concluding prayer for the Vice-Chancellor's happy afterlife veers from the accepted formula as it asserts the power of Milton's Ovidian art to triumph over eternity. The narrowing of focus in the poem from the plight of all presumptuous humans, the 'descendants' or 'sons of Japetus' (*Iapeti . . . neopotes*, 4), to the late Professor of Medicine crossing the Styx on Charon's boat raises again the issue of vocation. Just as Gostlin must have been struck down for his astounding medical skills, other exceptionally gifted humans like our poet must also have cause to worry. Milton likens the Vice-Chancellor to

Asclepius who was struck down by Jupiter for presuming to bring the dead to life with his skills, but reanimation through art is also the task of the lamenting, memorializing poet erecting a perpetual monument on the Vice-Chancellor's behalf. Milton's use of Ovidian energies and themes to animate this monument becomes therefore doubly significant. He is responding chiefly to Ovid's relentless exploration of 'Eros' as a force of attraction which animates the world and dictates its rhythms of life, ecstasy, and what all English poets patently influenced by Spenser thought of as the Ovidian paradox of 'eterne in mutabilitie'. Spenser coined this phrase in his mytho-poetic creation of the 'garden of Adonis', where 'All be he subiect to mortalitie, / Yet is eterne in mutabilitie, / And by succession made perpetual, / Transformed oft, and changed diuerslie'.[12] The young Milton was clearly captivated by the Spenserian notion of a blissful earthly paradise in which the forces of life, death, and mutability are locked, paradoxically, into the perpetual rhythms of immanent, as opposed to transcendental, eternity. The yearning for such an Ovidian, anti-Platonic paradox—for the wish to recuperate the consolation of beatific eternity *in* the mutable world and not beyond it—animates the lament for the Vice-Chancellor which concludes with what is in fact a decidedly un-formulaic Spenserian prayer (filtered through Ovidian mythology and Horatian diction) that may 'roses and marigolds and the crimson mouthed hyacinth spring' (*Crescant rosae, calthaeque busto,* / *Purpureoque hyacinthus ore,* 43–4) from the Vice-Chancellor's grave *as* he walks in Elysian fields. As the Vice-Chancellor enjoys a perpetual afterlife of bliss, new life will spring in this world from his grave in a form of meta-poetic flowering which is 'eterne' precisely for being a function of Milton's artificial and therefore timeless art.

The proverbial tension between the mutability of material forms and the permanence of artifice in Milton's Cambridge *funera* finds expression then in the play of 'amorous' Ovidian forces of attraction and resistance to attraction which are destructive and violent but also give release to the poet's creativity. It is at the erotic core of the obituary poems (as it is, for example, in the agon between the chaste Lady and Comus in the later *Maske*) that the unfolding narrative of spiritual rapture and the chaste resistance to physical rapture takes place. The point of rapture itself, of the carrying over from this world to another, from self control to ex-stasis, from controlled voice to the effable remoteness of what Milton alludes to in the Nativity Ode as 'the unexpressive notes' (116) of heavenly music (and again in 'Lycidas' as 'the unexpressive nuptial song', 176), is the structural and thematic point around which Milton often tended to construct and project his singular poetic persona. That Milton does so in the invocations of *Paradise Lost* is well known, but remarkably he can be seen already experimenting with such structures of self-fashioning as early as the Latin *funera*. This is especially noticeable in the obituary poems on the two bishops, where the intense and seemingly inappropriate eroticism is not just a superficial function of Milton playing fast and loose with the erotic energies he finds in his Ovidian model, at least not eventually, but a function of the young poet's corresponding obsession with chastity as a way to shield himself from vocal dismemberment and contamination.

The move to the more overtly religious laments for the two bishops alerts us that the link between physical and spiritual 'rape' is not merely etymological but heavily weighted theologically. In the Western Christian tradition such links have their roots in the conventions of Christian apophatic mysticism, which seeks to secure the promise of the *visio Dei* through various gestures of ascetic self-abandonment and self-cancellation and a giving over of oneself to God passively, as one taken over, or 'rapt', into the divine, or holy. For the young, humanistic Milton, contemplating divine calling as a poet, the promise of the fifth Beatitude, 'Blessed *are* the pure in heart: for they shall see God' (Matt. 4:8), is understood as the promise of singular poetic achievement for those who remain chaste and pure in the fallen world. Moreover, such a promise must be realized, or is at the very least engendered, in the impossible meeting point between the vatic, pagan poet's desire, as Horace says in *Ode* I.i, to strike the stars with an uplifted head (*sublimi feriam sidera vertice*, 36),[13] and the Pauline stance of one who has been caught up passively into the third heaven and hears 'unspeakable words which it is not lawful for a man to utter' (2 Cor. 12:2). What attracts both the young and older Milton intellectually about the impossibility of reconciling these two models of creative poetic agency is the rhetorical paradox of passive inspiration. The bliss of the afterlife, as 'At a Solemn Music' for example indicates, promises harmonious union with the 'undisturbèd song of pure concent' (6) of the angelic choirs and divine beatitudes, but also signals the death of the merely human poet and his artifice. To live with God and sing 'in endless morn of light' ('At a Solemn Music', 28) is not to sing in the mutable here and now. In other words, to confront the unsayable at the heart of any religious or beatific mystery is to confront the radical otherness of the supernatural, and to wish to lose oneself in it is to wish not to be human anymore.[14]

Milton, however, is no mystic. Even as a young man he subverts the conventions of apophatic mystical writings in converting the incoherence of quivering rapture into the *plenum* of assured and commanding poetry. The link with sexual rapture as creative poetic process is the key here. Felton's obituary, written in brisk alternating lines of trimeter and dimeter iambics, is a formal complaint against death—indeed, it begins with the energy of someone heaping curses on death, as the poet says, more dreadful than those Ovid conceived in the deepness of his heart on Ibis (*Nec vota Naso in Ibida | Concepit alto diriora pectore*, 18–19). There are no overt references to Ovidian rape and metamorphosis in the emerging tirade, but there is extreme violence nonetheless. Milton in fact goes out of his way to conjure images of distressing unfulfilled erotic desires where none are in fact justified as a matter of decorum. As if to lend support to the formality of his grief-struck shrill tone, Milton reflects how 'far more moderate was the Greek poet who cursed Lycambes' shameful fraud and his fiancée Neobule' (*Graiusque vates parcius | Turpem Lycambis execratus est dolum, | Sponsamque Neobolen suam*, 20–2). This negative comparison, which seems to suggest that a distraught Milton is more upset about Felton's death than the Greek poet Archilochus of Paros who, according to the story recorded in Horace's *Epistle* I.xix, drove both father and daughter to hang themselves with his deriding satires when his marriage proposal was refused, is very revealing in its absurdity. Milton wants to reach for a certain *gravitas* but ends up conjuring images of a vengeful poet using his art to destroy those who would deny his desires. Admittedly, a certain learned precociousness in this and the other *funera* no doubt expects a discerning readership to complete from memory these oblique allusions and perhaps smile with irony at the exhibition of wit, if not even parody, but the resulting thematic implication is entirely serious. The allusion to the potential power and violence of poetry allows Milton to invest the passive model of biblical prophecy otherwise dominating the poem's Christian sensibility with an active and potentially violating voice which brazenly insists on its own *ingenium* rather than self-deprecatingly playing down its limited human range when faced by divine subject matter.

The conceptual axis around which Milton arranges these themes is again to be found with the Latin verb *rapere*. Throughout Felton's obituary, classical images of chthonic powers conspiring against a fragile humanity whose souls are 'buried beneath a mass of flesh' (*mole carnae reconditas*, 37) are balanced with the scriptural-mystical image of the vatic poet rising to the stars as that 'old prophet who was rapt to the sky, riding a chariot of fire' (*vates ut olim raptus ad coelum senex / Auriga currus ignei*, 49–50). Milton's Latin here perfectly retains a sense of elusive ambiguity which holds in tension the idea of the *vates* as an active, ambitious poet and the idea of the *vates* as the passive mouthpiece of divine inspiration, for which Elijah, the 'old prophet', functions as a nameless type. On the one hand the *vates* in question is passively *raptus* (rapt) into heaven, but he does so while actively 'riding' (*currus*) a chariot of fire. This chiastic movement normally works in traditional apophatic discourse to silence the speaker, but Milton insists that it allows for the movement of speech across the human–divine gulf implied in the poem. A few lines earlier, as the poet hurls his abuses on personified death, wishing, Donne-like, that death itself shall die (*imprecor neci necem* 24), he on a sudden hears whispered syllables which turn into a voice urging him to cease his pointless tirade against death: 'rapt in a frenzy I seemed to hear sounds such as these carried on a gentle breath beneath the wind' (*Audisse tales videor attonitus sonos / Leni, sub aura, flamine*, 25–6).[15] These whispered words, carried to the poet-prophet from the other side of heavenly beatitude on a gentle breath, are reminiscent in their otherworldly quality of the 'still small voice' Elijah hears on Mount Horeb:

And, behold, the LORD passed by, and a great and strong wind rent the mountains, and brake in pieces the rocks before the LORD; but the LORD was not in the wind: and after the wind an earthquake; but the LORD was not in the earthquake: And after the earthquake a fire; but the LORD was not in the fire: and after the fire a still small voice. (1 Kings 19:11–12)

If Milton knew his biblical Hebrew, and it is still mooted that he did,[16] it is tempting to think that he would have been aware that the word *kol* in Hebrew, translated above as 'voice', is in fact a homonym which can mean both 'speaking voice' and 'sound' more generally. 'Still small voice' is in any case a very interesting mistranslation of what should be rendered literally from the Hebrew as 'a faint sound of silence'.[17] Given the overall prophetic mystique surrounding the emerging *consolatio* of the Felton obituary and Elijah's muted appearance several lines later, it seems inescapable that Elijah's encounter with divine silence on Horeb functions as a silent backdrop to the emerging neoclassical lament. A force of divine inspiration grips the poet at the exact moment when his hyperbolic tirade risks breaking into incoherent rage, calming it down through the agency of gentle and somehow unspeakable sounds. This move does not silence, however, the Miltonic poet, causing an outpouring of paradox, but gently gives him the prop of divine authority as we realize that the limits of human art and representation have not been transgressed, but merely temporarily obscured.

It finally emerges, therefore, that the redirection of illicit erotic energies and the violence of rapture, especially in the beatific obituary poems for the two bishops, points to the emerging mysterium of heavenly bliss as forbidden, because erotically illicit, mystical territory. In both poems Milton falls back on the mystical formula of conceding that the sights of heavenly beatitude are past his merely human abilities of expression and are altogether forbidden to be revealed. In Felton's obituary, the poet assumes the Pauline stance of one who has been rapt into the third heaven where he heard 'unspeakable words which it is not lawful for a man to utter' and concludes the consoling recuperation of beatific ecstasy with the self-admonition that he too must now hold his tongue:

> Sed hic tacebo, nam quis effari queat
> Oriundus humano patre
> Amoenitates illius loci, mihi
> Sat est in aeternum frui. (65–8)

(But on this matter I must remain silent, for who born of human descent is able to speak of the delights of that place? For me, it is enough to enjoy it in eternity.)

As the poet describes his mystical journey to the ineffable remoteness of an indefinite, transcendental 'that place', he fills the emerging gap with a tedious mythological account of the landmarks of his ascent as he passes by the various zodiac signs, Boötes, the Scorpion, Orion, and the Milky Way. We may wish to forgive the young Milton this sudden lapse in imaginative flight, but it is a very adequate lapse: in the absence of the beauties of that *other* place, what else can remain but the conventional yearning of an astrological star-gazer?[18]

A similar stance of mystical *occupatio* recurs at the beatific core of the Ovidian elegy lamenting the passing of Bishop Andrewes as well, where the poet, struggling to find the words to communicate his dream vision, cries out, 'Alas I have not the talent to relate what I saw' (*Heu nequit ingenium visa referre meum*, 38). What ensues is an elaborate depiction of a rosy, sun-drenched paradise with flowering gardens, silver streams, and blossoming meadows. This imagined paradisal vista, structured as a negative simile, transcends its classical-mythological registers as we learn that the dreamed-of place is *not* like the gardens which Chloris 'decked' (*ornavit*, 43) or the gleaming sands of 'Hesperian Tagus' (46). Like the *visio Dei* of recondite Christian mysticism, Milton's dream-vision falls short of its meaning as it describes the forbidden sight through negation which is self-referentially inadequate. Having described what this imagined paradise is not, the poet immediately concedes that if it is *like* anything, it is like the 'imagined house of royal Lucifer on the mouth of the Ganges in faraway lands' (*Talis in extremis terrae Gangetidis oris | Luciferi regis fingitur esse domus*, 49–50). The raw materials of classical mythological allusion—in this case alluding to depictions of the house of the sun thought by Ovid to be in India—serve a double purpose: they allow the young Milton to exhibit his poetic-humanistic credentials as a craftsman in command of his classical materials, but they also point to their own pagan inadequacy as mere figments of the imagination which undergo a process of Christian chastening in Milton's poetry. However, as already hinted above it is not a simple process where pagan classical materials are reworked into sober, Christian themes, but of the idea of erotic voyeurism and illicit sexuality animating poetically the Christian promise of rapturous beatitude. As we are invited to share with the poet the sights and sounds of his forbidden, ineffable vision we see the apotheosized bishop, 'his god-like head...encircled with a white band' (*Infula divinum cinxerat alba caput*, 56) walking amid harping and singing angelic choirs. The imagery, which Milton will revisit again for the conclusion of the far more personal *Epitaphium Damonis*, gathers tremendous ecstatic force as the sedate but highly eroticized classical registers of pastoral meadows and Elysian fields give way to a vision of explicitly sexual rapture allegedly chastened not—as is often assumed—by its sudden elevation to a Christian register of heavenly bliss but conversely for being merely the echo of an unrequited erotic dream. Echoing Ovid's *Amores* I.v in 'may such a midday often revisit me' (*proveniant medii sic mihi saepe dies*, 26),[19] Milton expresses the similar wish, 'may such dreams often come upon me' (*talia contingant somnia saepe mihi*, 68).

However, it is not simply a matter of a faint echo in the final line of Milton's Ovidian obituary poem suddenly translating an erotic daydream about lovemaking into a sober Christian dream about heavenly bliss centred on the vision of a deceased clergyman. As Le Comte has shown, there is a strange and mesmerizingly assonant Ovidian play throughout the *consolatio* of Andrewes's elegy on colours, garments, and body parts which complicates any notion of Milton simply turning Ovidian sexual frivolity into sacred Christian meditation and renders the echo of Ovid's *Amores* I.v inescapable. Milton picks up Ovid's *candida*, used to describe the whiteness of Corinna's neck, only to locate it in the robes, *vestis*, draping the body of the saintly Andrewes, while the *vestis* itself stands in all-too-suggestive a contrast to Corinna's *tunica*, which the enraptured daydreaming poet imagines tearing off her body. The transmutation of the object of Eros into an object of death and transcendence thus takes place quite literally in the transformation of one imagined body into another: Ovid's Corinna is not replaced in Milton's imagination by Andrewes—she metamorphoses into him. The sober Christian reader of Milton will be quick to point out at this point the obvious and important departures from Ovid. In Ovid's poem, the modest Corinna coyly holds on to her tunic only to succumb finally as the poet reveals her forbidden nakedness and begins to enumerate, as in a blazon, her various naked body parts. In Milton's elegy on the other hand the white robe, which hides more than it shows, completes the iconic image of Andrewes's distinctly chaste sainthood, whose face shines with a 'starry brightness' (*Sydereum nitido*, 54). Indeed, it might be argued that at the very point Andrewes makes his Corinna-like appearance, Ovidian erotica melts away leaving only the calm of chaste Christian modesty.

This last assertion, however, is deceptive. As the enraptured poet lowers his averted gaze in reverence, he notes underneath the hem of the white robe Andrewes's bare feet. Andrewes's Christ-like holiness strangely extends, as with Ovid's Corinna, from the luminous detail of a naked body part: Andrewes's feet are not just bare, but are in fact 'golden' (*auratos*). This remarkable flight of classical imagination bears closer scrutiny. In much classical Latin poetry, 'golden', 'yellow', and their cognates are the stock adjective for describing fair hair, or tresses, and it is also commonly found as the stock epithet of Cupid and his golden wings, where 'gold' suggests not just a colour, but also a sort of sheen or golden radiance. However, the image of 'golden feet' is far more unusual and in fact mythologically and culturally specific. Golden feet recur in classical Latin poetry as an erotically charged image associated specifically with the consummation of matrimony. Hymen, the god of marriage, is often portrayed as wearing golden slippers and this can be transferred, as in Catullus 61, to the description of the bride's feet as the poet bids her walk into the groom's bedroom in anticipation of sexual intercourse, where 'golden' (*aureolos*) stands as metonymy for her bedazzling footwear:

> *transfer omine cum bono*
> *limen aureolos pedes,*
> *rasilemque subi forem.* (159–61)[20]

(Lift up your golden feet across the threshold with good luck, and enter through the polished door.)

Given the Ovidian context of Milton's elegy, however, it is far more likely that Milton was thinking here, as Douglas Bush suggests in his *Variorum* commentary, of *Amores* III.xiii which describes with great mystique the marriage rites of Falerian maidens under the auspices of Juno:

> *virginei crines auro gemmaque premuntur,*
> *et tegit auratos palla superba pedes* (25–6)[21]

(The maidens' tresses are braided with gold and gems, and the splendid palla covers golden feet.)

By transferring the *auratos pedes* of Ovid's maidens (whose feet also incidentally peer beneath the hem of a long gown, or *palla*) to the image of Andrewes, Milton insists on the nuptial qualities of his beatific vision even as he retains its erotic undertones: physical and spiritual rapture are consummated in the heavenly marriage act which unites the beatific soul with God in the fruition of everlasting life. Milton's ingenious play with Ovidian sensibilities thus transposes adjectives and their erotic Ovidian connotation to create an arresting image of supernatural bliss, which is all the more arresting for its seemingly inappropriate erotic undertones. If anything, Milton deliberately intensifies the erotic power of the resulting imagery by noting how when the golden-footed bishop walks along the heavenly ground his footsteps cause the flowery earth to 'quiver' suggestively in a 'joyful sound': *Intermuit laeto florae terra sono* (58). It is true that Milton sublimates Ovidian erotic energies in this sequence, but he does so by redirecting these energies towards a moment of creative and poetic rapture, not emptying them of their erotic content. Such energies are vital for the elegy's exploration of forbidden rapture and ecstasy which is, again, like Ovid's stolen moment with Corinna, finally not to be spoken of. As Ovid says, leaving the act of imagined sexual consummation unspoken, 'the rest, who doesn't know?' (*cetera quis nescit?*, 25); but the paradox remains that both poets' words vividly show and enact what they claim their words cannot and should not say.

Milton's beatific dream-vision in Elegy III concludes with the poet over-hearing the blessed spirits greeting new arrivals with a generic, scriptural benediction uttered on 'gentle lips' (*placido ore*, 62) echoing Revelation 14:13: 'Come, my son, and blessed take possession of the joys of the Father's kingdom; from here on be forever free my son from hard labour' (*Nate veni, et patrii felix cape gaudia regni,* | *Semper ab hinc duro, nate, labore vaca*, 63–4). An obituary poem which began with the grim abstractions of plague and war ends with the transcendental abstractions of eternal bliss. The poet's elusive Ovidian singularity emerges against the background of such abstractions. A sense of identity with fallen, specifically English Protestant humanity distils into the very specific and exceptionally singular intimacy of a dream. Con-templating the fallen world and its ills, the poet withdraws into himself so that he might finally in an indefinitely differed future rise and melt away ecstatically in the abstractions of another, higher order. This future is always deferred, but its promise gives Milton's poetry its sense of direction. It is a constant movement in Milton's religious and theological poetry, and in many respects it also informs much of his political poetry as well. Such a movement, however, finally requires a source of inspiration or the agency of a transcendental creative power to act on Milton's behalf. It is in this respect ultimately that it is best to understand the function of Felton or Andrewes—the objects of the laments—not as biographical entities but as conceptual, vatic ones where the persona of the bishop anchors Miltonic aspirations. The deceased bishops embody a mixture of Christian but also poetic ideals of sacral vocation and a specifically Protestant sainthood. In a revealing line in Elegy III, Milton refers to Andrewes as a man possessing a 'half divine soul' (*Semideamque animam*, 30). It has been missed that this form of praise partly echoes Horace's praise of Virgil in *Ode* I.iii as 'half of my own soul' (*animae dimidium meae*, 8)[22]—praise which the young Milton reserves far more explic-itly to Thomas Young in Elegy IV: 'that man even means more to me than one part of my soul' (*Ille quidem est animae plusquam pars altera nostrae*, 19).[23] It may well be that in the case of Andrewes the impersonal 'half divine soul' alludes, imprecisely, to little more than the Neoplatonic concept of the tripartite soul one-third of which (not half) is divine in its rational yearning for God. However, what is lost in the English translation is retained in the assonance of the Latin where *Semideamque animam* echoes *animae dimidium meae*: Andrewes is not just semi-divine in his own right, but also, as Virgil was to Horace, a source of poetic inspiration for Milton. What is remarkable about Andrewes and Felton, and in a more limited sense the Beadle and Vice-Chancellor as well, is how they finally metamorphose and apotheosize into an unnamed muse. Just as Milton translates the inspirational friendship with Thomas Young or Charles Diodati into meta-poetic explorations of his vocational calling, so imagined or superficial relationships with, say, a deceased bishop or a fellow student like Edward King may serve the same purpose.

What triumphs in either case is the peculiarly Miltonic creative process where diffuse materials are given their unique specificity within a poem through, of all things, the urge to abstract. The Latin construction in Elegy III alluding to Andrewes's 'half divine soul' in fact hovers on the edge of abstraction, since, again, it is not finally about Andrewes at all but about a general condition of mortality. Milton questions obliquely personified death's penchant for wanting to pierce with its 'unerring darts a noble breast and chase away a half divine soul from its abode' (*Nobileque in pectus certas acuisse sagittas, | Semideamque animam sede fugasse sua?*, 29–30). The context implies that this is yet more hyperbolic praise of the late bishop, but the syntax retains the apparently rhetorical question in the realm of general speculation. The question, indeed, is not only rhetorical but finally metaphysical. It queries not only why Andrewes was victimized by death, but why more generally 'noble breasts' are the victims of mortality. We are back then with the sentiment of guarded elitism that we find in the shorter, more secular lament for the late Beadle, and what is finally remarkable about such sentiments is the manner in which they allow the poet's singular voice to vent personal anxieties through communal or even universal concerns.

The physical–spiritual dialectic implied in Milton's obituary poems between quiet acquiescence and violent rapture defines therefore in many ways what would become the driving impetus of Milton's early poetic ambitions: Milton's conceptual desire to lose himself in heavenly rapture and abstractions must be deferred until he can prove his worth as a holy poet in a very particular sense, and in order to prove his individual worth he must *not* lose himself in any form of earthly 'frenzy' or physical ectasy. Such resistance to rapture for the young Milton is enacted in the personal, experiential dimension of poetic affect and is generated by it, but it achieves its fuller conceptual significance ultimately in the emergence of abstract and therefore impersonal ideas, not to say ideology. Indeed, once the Cambridge obituary poems are considered for their subject matter, it seems that the final line of Elegy III—'may such dreams often come upon me'—carries with it both the promise and the anxieties of Milton's future poetic achievements.

Notes

1. We owe much of this understanding to the complementary scholarship of Stella Revard, John K. Hale, and Estelle Haan. All three have been especially instrumental in shedding much-needed light on Milton's multilingual ingenuity when practising imitation in his Latin poetry. See Revard, *Milton and the Tangles of Neaera's Hair: The Making of the 1645 'Poems'* (Columbia, Mo., 1997); Hale, *Milton's Languages: The Impact of Multilingualism on Style* (Cambridge, 1997), 19–50, and *Milton's Cambridge Latin: Performing in the Genres* (Tempe, Ariz., 2005), 127–46; and Haan, *From Academia to Amicitia: Milton's Latin Writings and the Italian Academies* (Philadelphia, Pa., 1998), but more relevant to the obituary poems which predate Milton's Italian journey, see her '"Both English and Latin": Milton's Bilingual Muse', *Renaissance Studies*, 21 (2007), 679–700.

2. Of the four obituary poems, Elegy III on the death of Lancelot Andrewes, the Bishop of Winchester, has attracted relatively the most attention, but even here concerns with style, genre, and imitation have always been the focus of analysis. Such analyses always stop by noting the rather random manner in which Milton yokes Christian subject matter onto pagan classical models. Hale, for example, notes how multilingualism in the elegy on Andrewes allows Milton to transform, or 'translate', Ovidian erotic bliss into heavenly bliss (*Milton's Languages*, 35). In a similar vein see also Michael West, 'The Consolatio in Milton's Funeral Elegies', *Huntington Library Quarterly*, 34 (1971), 233–49, and Edward S. Le Comte, 'Sly Milton: The Meaning Lurking in the Context of His Quotations', rpr. in Le Comte, *Milton Re-Viewed: Ten Essays* (New York, 1991), 51–82. Haan, however, provides a different perspective on Milton's indebtedness in two of the obituary poems to contemporary Italian humanist writings in 'Milton and Two Italian Humanists: Some Hitherto Unnoticed Neo-Latin Echoes in *In Obitum Procancellarii Medici* and *In Obitum Praesulis Eliensis*', *Notes and Queries*, 44 (1997), 176–81.

3. Hale, *Milton's Cambridge Latin*, 131.

4. Hale, *Milton's Cambridge Latin*, 128n5.

5. See Hale, *Milton's Languages*, and West and Le Comte, 'Sly Milton'.

6. For new conjectures about the dating of Prolusion 6 to which 'At a Vacation Exercise' belongs, see Campbell and Corns, 58–9.

7. All references to Milton's poetry other than to *Paradise Lost* are to *Milton: Complete Shorter Poems* (hereafter *CSP*), ed. John Carey, 2nd edn. (1997). All translations of the Latin, both of Milton's poetry and his classical sources, are my own.

8. The order of composition probably does not correspond to the order of the deaths. Milton most likely wrote first the Ovidian elegy on the university Beadle, followed by the Horatian lament to the Vice-Chancellor, where it has been suggested that Milton reworked an older exercise in the Horatian alcaic strophe written perhaps a

year earlier. Then came probably the Ovidian elegy on Andrewes, followed finally by the more formal complaint against death couched in the lament for Felton, written in alternating lines of trimeter and dimeter iambics. See Lewalski, *Life*, 23–4, and Hale, *Milton's Cambridge Latin*, 136. Carey, however, in his headnote to Elegy III, questions whether any of the assumptions about the chronology of the funeral poems are reliable (*CSP*, 51). The matter is not addressed by Campbell and Corns.

9. Campbell and Corns, 29.

10. While Milton of course would grow to despise bishops, and would even directly attack the late Andrewes in *The Reason of Church-Government* (1642), in 1626 a much younger Milton appears not to have thought so. Given that Milton hails Felton in his obituary poem—one assumes without irony—as 'king of the sacred rites in that island which is known by the name of Eel' (*rex sacrorum illa fuisti in insula | Quae nomen Anguillae tenet*, 13–14), it is quite evident that there was nothing particularly unchristian about the idea of bishops for the nearly eighteen-year-old Milton.

11. See *A Variorum Commentary on the Poems of John Milton*, gen. ed. Merritt Y. Hughes, 6 vols. (New York, 1970–), i/1.

12. Edmund Spenser, *The Faerie Queene*, ed. A. C. Hamilton (Harlow, 2001), III.vi.47, 3–6.

13. Horace, *The Odes*, ed. Kenneth Quinn (1996), 4.

14. See in *How Milton Works* (Cambridge, Mass., 2001), Stanley Fish's analysis of the lines 'till God ere long | To his celestial chorus us unite, | To live with him, and sing in endless morn of light' ('At a Solemn Music', 25–8): 'Properly understood, then, the wish that we be united with God's celestial 'consort' (at once a musical term and a reference to the mystical marriage) is a wish that we not be heard, that we utter sounds in such a way as to remain silent. The man who wants to sing alone is like a man who wants to stand alone, raised by his own merit to some bad eminence' (312). On the active–passive dialectic of Milton's prophetic and poetic personae see also William Kerrigan, *The Prophetic Milton* (Charlottesville, Va., 1974), 17–82 and more recently Stephen M. Fallon, *Milton's Peculiar Grace: Self-Representation and Authority* (Ithaca, N.Y., 2007), 39–44.

15. The participle *attonitus* (from *attonare*) literally means 'struck by thunder' and hence more generally to be stunned or terrified. But there is also a sense of *attonitus* to be found both in Virgil and Horace of a prophet (*vates*) 'frantic with divine inspiration'. Given the context of the line in the poem, 'rapt in a frenzy' is therefore a justified translation.

16. Golda Werman, *Milton and Midrash* (Washington, D.C., 1995), 42–74, casts doubts on Milton's knowledge of Hebrew, whereas Jason P. Rosenblatt, Mary Ann Radzinowicz, Jeffrey S. Shoulson and others, in a number of significant publications, seem to think that while Milton probably did know just about enough Hebrew to read the Bible, it may well not have been good enough to understand the finer details of actual rabbinical sources. Rosenblatt's recent book, *Renaissance England's Chief Rabbi: John Selden* (Oxford, 2006) has demonstrated, for example, that Milton mostly relied on the Hebrew scholarship of others, in this case of John Selden, when

approaching rabbinical sources. See also Douglas A. Brooks's introduction to *Milton and the Jews* (Cambridge, 2008), 4.

17. The Authorized Version's translation is also retained in the Revised Standard English Bible, and is partly based on the Geneva Bible's 'stil and soft voyce'.

18. In *Paradise Lost*, star-gazing is presented as a muddled, satanic activity. In this respect, the identification in the invocation of Book 7 of *Paradise Lost* to the heavenly muse as 'Urania', the ancient goddess of astronomy, is misleading. As Regina Schwartz has shown in *Remembering and Repeating: On Milton's Theology and Poetics* (Chicago, Ill., 1993), Milton in fact associates Urania (whose meaning, not the name, he invokes) with the allegorical Wisdom of the Book of Proverbs, which was present at the moment of creation and is 'qualified to offer knowledge, not rumor or quaint opinions of it...Milton thereby converts star-gazing, the emblem of presumptive curiosity, into a divinely sanctioned quest' (59).

19. Ovid, *P. Ovidi Nasonis: Amores, Medicamina Faciei Femineae, Ars Amatoria, Remedia Amoris*, ed. E. J. Kenney (Oxford, 1961), 12.

20. C. J. Fordyce, *Catullus: A Commentary* (Oxford, 1961).

21. Ovid, *Ovidi Nasonis*, ed. Kenney, 97.

22. Horace, *Odes*, 6.

23. See *A Variorum Commentary*, i/1, 82. Bush notes this was a common formula of praise to be found also in Ovid and in the neo-Latin poems of Buchanan and Castiglione.

8

Milton on Tragedy: Law, Hypallage, and Participation

Andrew Zurcher

In some ways, Milton's literary output over four decades was dominated by the tragic genre. Although it was only in 1671 that he would put his name to a published tragedy, nonetheless from his earliest Latin and English poems—many of them university exercises—the conventional philosophical preoccupations and the structures of thinking characteristic of tragedies permeated as much his poetry as his prose. It is well known that the Trinity College Manuscript of Milton's early poems contains substantial notes for tragedies he planned, at some stage, to write, including the closet drama *Adam Unparadiz'd*, which appears to have been abandoned (though not forgotten) in favour of *Paradise Lost*.[1] The same manuscript also contains copious detail for other biblical tragedies, not only on Samson but on the subjects of Abraham's sacrifice of Isaac and the destruction of Sodom; and the notes towards Anglo-Saxon and Scottish history, apparently compiled at some point in the 1630s, dwell suggestively on the tragic fates of most of the royal remembered.[2] These were to be Milton's tragedies; but, for the present acknowledging the one exception, tragedy largely filtered into Milton's literary composition, throughout the forty years between his Latin elegies and the publication of *Samson Agonistes*, as a continuously catalysing set of conventions—as influential in his writing as the storm to the sailor, or the wolf to the shepherd. The traces indelibly left on Milton's composition by these conventions are to be found at large in his laments and elegies; in the extended anti-masque of *A Maske*, and the decisively unresolved threat of materiality and embodiment that it admits;[3] and in the structure and meaning of *Paradise Lost*, where tragedy hovers as a tempting generic herme- neutic by means of which the reader may elegantly perjure his or her soul. But it persists, equally if not more conspicuously, in the way in which Milton thought and wrote, throughout his career, about law both human and divine, about materiality and form, and about language. Probably the best evidence we have of Milton's early attitudes to tragedy—and particularly the Old Testament tragedies sketched in the notebook—comes (anachronisti- cally) from *Samson Agonistes*. This essay will start there, before returning to three early student poems, *Naturam Non Pati Senium*, *De Idea Platonica*, and 'On Time'.

Although evidence survives of Milton's extensive and careful reading of Greek tragedies,[4] his ultimate attitude to the genre, as a Christian, was probably hostile. In his prefatory remarks to *Samson Agonistes*, Milton makes no secret of his antipathy to seventeenth-century English tragedy, which by 'intermixing comic stuff with tragic sadness and gravity... by all judicious hath been counted absurd' (29–31).[5] But he appears, in the same epistle, to take a much different view of Attic drama, or 'tragedy, as it was anciently composed', which 'hath been ever held the gravest, moralest, and most profitable of all other poems' (1–2). At first glance, Milton's apparent intention to 'vindicate' the dignity and value of tragedy upon an ancient model seems clear enough; but the particular words that Milton selects to extol his Greek models, and the many words he does not use, may suggest otherwise. Tragedy's worth as a genre rests on its cathartic power:

[It is] said by Aristotle to be of power by raising pity and fear, or terror, to purge the mind of those and such-like passions, that is to temper and reduce them to just measure with a kind of delight, stirred up by reading or seeing those passions well imitated. Nor is nature wanting in her own effects to make good his assertion: for so in physic things of melancholic hue and quality are used against melancholy, sour against sour, salt to remove salt humours. (3–9)

In his apparent rehabilitation of the genre, Milton cites St Paul, who himself once cited Euripides and Gregory of Nazianzen, the Bishop of Constantino- ple who was thought to have written the fourth-century tragedy *Christus*

Patiens. But when it comes to the mechanics of a shift from pagan Greek to Christian tragic matter, Milton skirts the consequences of his own account of tragedy's cathartic power. Should a zealous Christian really seek to 'purge the mind' of pity and fear—or even soften them to 'just measure' by an admixture of delight? If so, what subject would be appropriate to inspire this effect? If sour and salt are used to purge sour and salt, then by Milton's own metaphor extremity should provide the cure for extremity. But if the Christian tragedian should compose a tragedy on a Christian subject, would he or she not run the risk of inciting not catharsis, but admiration and imitation?[6] Milton addresses none of these issues in his epistle; instead, perhaps pointedly, he occupies himself with comments on the form and 'modelling' of his poem, in which 'the ancients and Italians' are to be followed.

The problem of the Christian tragic subject, and the inscrutability to which it leads in our understanding both of *Samson Agonistes* and of Milton's purpose, may well be the poet's primary preoccupation in the work as a whole. In his account of Milton's reception of the genre, Northrop Frye argued that, for the Greeks,

> tragedy was primarily a vision of law, of the nemesis that follows pride, of the social contract that replaces the fury of revenge in Aeschylus' *Oresteia*. For a religion concerned with deliverance from the law, the source of tragedy comes to be thought of as increasingly cruel and malignant.[7]

The way in which *Samson Agonistes* mystifies its hero's *ethos*, leaving the reader to choose between two equally plausible but diametrically opposed accounts of Samson's only action, testifies to Milton's ambivalence about the usual conventions of the genre: if Samson experiences an *anagnorisis*, it is not one in which we do, or can, participate. The final speech of the Chorus may seem at first to dispel lingering doubts about the rightness (rather than the righteousness) of Samson's action, but its careful composition may, on closer scrutiny, further complicate those doubts:

> All is best, though we oft doubt,
> What the unsearchable dispose
> Of highest wisdom brings about,
> And ever best found in the close.
> Oft he seems to hide his face,
> But unexpectedly returns
> And to his faithful champion hath in place

Bore witness gloriously; whence Gaza mourns
And all that band them to resist
His uncontrollable intent,
His servants he with new acquist
Of true experience from this great event
With peace and consolation hath dismissed,
And calm of mind all passion spent. (1745–58)

On the face of it, this passage appears to find means to reconcile human law to the tragic catharsis that, in Milton's prefatory remarks to the poem, he had promised: the Philistines having been massacred, and their society with them, the Jews are by Samson's life and death freed not only to triumph in God's 'unsearchable dispose', but to live by their own laws. The cathartic purgation of the final line develops from the graded trio of rhyme words that precedes it—'resist', 'acquist', 'dismissed'—so that the tragedy's 'calm' can be seen to arise from God's interposition of an 'acquist', or acquisition, between the resistance of the Philistines and the (triumphant) dismissal of the Jews. It is of considerable significance to the passage that Milton reaches for a technical legal term such as 'acquist', attested most frequently, in this period, by lawyers and political philosophers in their efforts to describe the way in which political sovereignty can be gained over land through conquest, purchase, or treaty.[8] The use of this term activates the peculiarly legal sense of 'uncontrollable intent' in the previous line, which to a common lawyer in this period would have meant, roughly, 'sovereign juridical power', or power to determine law not open to contest or revision.[9] The luck and arbitrariness characteristic of the presentation of the gods in Greek tragedy is here completely displaced, in favour of a God whose lawgiving power trumps (and consoles) the human forms of law that normally order the broken remnants of tragic catastrophes. The mourning Philistines find themselves forever expelled from the play's tragic consolation, and the Jews conclude the play not surrendering to the unknowability of a recedent divine will, but glorying in the full expression and conviction of its proffered face. Their 'calm'—a kind of calm inimical to tragedy—is one of righteousness, and their law as unknown and 'uncontrollable'—literally, as unverifiable—as ever.

What is perhaps most interesting about the Chorus's final speech, from a poetic perspective, is its syntactical disarray: even given Milton's tendency to exploit the stylistic effects of hyperbaton and associated figures of syntactical displacement, this speech seems slightly anomalous. The first quatrain of the famous 'sonnet' is constructed around its adversative intermediate clause, so that 'All is best . . .' eventually becomes fulfilled, despite our doubt, by the 'ever . . . found' of the 'close'; this pattern of assertion, doubt, and return makes sense of Milton's use of the verbal noun 'dispose', which though it plainly means 'ordering or ordaining power', literally refers to God's ability to 'set things' (L. *ponere*) 'apart' (*dis-*). The defining or limiting nature of the 'close', which reveals the true nature of God's disposing power, is then immediately disturbed by resort to a new 'oft', which seems as if it will repeat the enclosing circularity of the comprehensive settlement of the first quatrain; but instead, Milton's God 'unexpectedly' asserts himself, suddenly transcending the 'oft' to bear witness to his 'faithful Champion' here, in this instance, in Gaza—'in place'. This sudden emergence into place, both of God's power and of the syntax that describes it, is short-lived: Milton immediately appends two clauses conspicuous for the way in which they split heavy groups ('whence Gaza mourns, / and all that band them to resist . . .'; 'his servants he . . . with peace and consolation hath dismissed / and calm of mind . . .').

Given the context of a passage that continues to suffer from a displaced syntax, God's unexpected appearance 'in place' seems loaded, as if Milton were drawing attention to the unusualness of the material and revelatory specificity of God's intervention in human affairs. In a sense this specialness of God's emplaced witness is only natural, for God's serial interventions in Old Testament history are, to our experience, remote. But the emphasis on placement here seems particularly fraught because it gives rise to another kind of displacement, this time not by hyperbaton but by the more specialized figure of hypallage. Quintilian, following Cicero, considers hypallage to be another name for metonymy, and discusses it as such in the *Institutio Oratoria*.[10] By the sixteenth century, the term had come to be restricted to instances of 'exchange' in a phrase or sentence, where one word swapped places with another. In synthetic languages like Greek and Latin, where syntactical organization depends less on word order and much more on inflexions, the Renaissance understanding of hypallage—a deformation of the sense by the 'exchange' or alteration in the order of the words—might rarely if ever arise. But in an analytic language like English, where word order almost exclusively determines syntactical relationships, changing the order of words would most likely alter the sense, often with absurd or comical results. So George Puttenham illustrates the figure in his *Arte of*

English Poesie by adulterating a dinner invitation: by hypallage, 'for *come dine with me and stay not, come stay with me and dine not*'.[11] To more serious effect, Spenser and Shakespeare used hypallage in their poetry to endow material objects or physical actions with human characteristics, especially volition. Thus in a typical instance in *The Faerie Queene* (III.i.62), Spenser writes that Malecasta's brethren 'rashly out of their rouzed couches sprong', applying 'rouzed' to the couches rather than to the men springing from them. Shakespeare's interest in the transferred epithet, as this kind of hypallage has come to be known, is less allegorical than psychological, as in Antony's famous claim that Brutus's was 'the most unkindest cut of all' (*Julius Caesar*, 3.2.181). As these examples show, the sensitive relations between English syntax and meaning left the figure of hypallage in a taxonomical limbo, neither purely a figure of words nor purely a figure of thought. Instead the materiality of English syntax meets in examples of hypallage the strangely porous nature of, for example, causation, intention, or guilt. At the end of *Samson Agonistes*, the materiality of hypallactic displacement participates in a larger philosophical and theological vanishing act. Saints are said to 'bear witness' when they die for God, and of course are called martyrs (from Gr. *martyros*, 'witness') for this reason; the martyr in Samson's story is not God but Samson, the glorious act not God's but Samson's. We might thus expect lines 1750–2 to read, 'But unexpectedly returns / To whom his faithful champion hath in place / Bore witness gloriously'. But at the moment of his unexpected return, it is to God that Milton attributes both the action of 'bearing witness' and its adverb, 'gloriously'; one might even say that God's unexpected return is constituted by his assumption of authority for the witness and its glory. In an exchange of grammatical subject typical of hypallage, God's emplacement is achieved at the expense of Samson's displacement.[12]

Whether Milton can (or will) be said to have transferred the application of 'gloriously', here, from Samson to God depends, of course, on the reader's theology. Axiomatic to and pervasive in Calvinist doctrine is the necessity and sufficiency of grace to election; Calvin argues in Book II, chapter 2 of the *Institutes of the Christian Religion* that *non suppetere ad bona opera liberum arbitrium homini, nisi gratia adiuuetur, & gratia quidem speciali, qua electi soli per regenerationem donantur* ('free will is not sufficient to enable man to do good works, unless he be helped by grace, indeed by special grace, which only the elect receive through regeneration').[13] While he insists that grace is indispensable, at first Calvin seems to accommodate free will—though insufficient to election, it is not an impediment. But this apparently tolerable hybridity between free will and special grace breaks down completely as Calvin continues his argument, until the two become virtually mutually exclusive:

Quod tamen initio huius capitis præfatus sum, cogor rursum hic repetere, Vt quisque maximè a suæ calamitatis, inopiæ, nuditatis, ignominiæ conscientia deiectus est & consternatus, ita optimè in sui cognitione profecisse. Non enim periculum est ne sibi nimium adimat homo, dummodo recuperandum in Deo discat quod sibi deest. At sibi ne tantillum quidem sumere vltra ius suum potest, quin & inani confidentia se perdat, & diuinum honorem ad se traducens, immanis sacrilegij reus fiat. Et sanè quoties hæc libido mentem nostram incessit vt aliquid nostram habere expetamus, quod in nobis scilicet potrus quàm in Deo resideat, cogitationem hanc non ab alio consiliario sciamus nobis suggeri, quàm qui primos parentes induxit vt dijs esse similes vellent, scientes bonum & malum.

(Nevertheless, what I mentioned at the beginning of this chapter I am compelled here to repeat once more: that whoever is utterly cast down and overwhelmed by the awareness of his calamity, poverty, nakedness, and disgrace has thus advanced farthest in knowledge of himself. For there is no danger of man's depriving himself of too much so long as he learns that in God must be recouped what he himself lacks. Yet he cannot claim for himself ever so little beyond what is rightfully his without losing himself in vain confidence and without usurping God's honour, and thus becoming guilty of monstrous sacrilege. And truly, whenever this lust invades our mind to compel us to seek out something of our own that reposes in ourselves rather than in God, let us know that this thought is suggested to us by no other counsellor than him who induced our first parents to want to become like gods, knowing good and evil.)[14]

The binarist Calvinist position on the authority for good works would, then, suggest that Milton's syntax has nothing to do with hypallage: the witness is God's, the glory God's.[15] And yet Milton has selected, in the story of Samson, an Old Testament narrative as yet untouched by anything more than the promise of redemption through Christ, which creates for the reader a dilemma: should Samson be considered one of those select few Old Testament heroes and prophets, the fate of whose souls was reserved from the common punishment of original sin? That Milton self-consciously worried about just this problem, in the development of the plans for his Old Testament tragedies, is suggested by the curious note he attached, in his manuscript for the original draft of the tragedy of *Paradise Lost*. Moses, in his prologue to the tragedy, was to recount:

how he assum'd his true bodie, that it corrupts not because of his wit[ness of] god in the mount declares the like of Enoch and Eliah, besides the purity of ye pl[ace] that certaine pure winds, dues, and clouds præserve it from corruption whence [he de-] parts to the sight of god . . .[16]

Moses, Enoch, and Elijah, by virtue of their direct encounter with God, have been justified and purified; of Samson, in the perplexity of his Miltonic blindness, we can be less sure. But the witness of Milton's notebook indicates something important about how we may construe the dilemma of the hypallage at the end of *Samson Agonistes*, or about how that dilemma may help us to understand Milton's early response to tragedy. The materiality on which Moses insists in the early draft of the tragedy of *Paradise Lost* is matched, in 1671, by the material ontology of hypallage. The exchanged meanings that hypallage can create can arise only from thoughts materialized in words; if thoughts do not exist in forms (words) to be moved, the structure of meanings that they create cannot by hypallage be altered. Similarly, the operation of hypallage on the thoughts signified by those words acts—like an acknowledgement—as a fixer of the materiality of the thoughts. To attribute to God a glorious mode of action is to suppose, by the back door, his material agency, and perhaps even a material existence.[17]

Milton's consummate coordination of syntax, rhetoric, law, and theology in this passage from *Samson Agonistes* suggests a considered integrity to his thought on these subjects. The studied way in which Milton connects the return of God's materiality—his 'face'—to the material intrusion of language—through syntactical displacement and hypallage—seems to result in a distinctively Miltonic implication: what distinguishes true Christian faith is its readiness to see the tragedy of a linguistic materiality as the opportunity to live by an inscrutable and paradoxical divine law. This suggestiveness of the Chorus's closing lines, though, leaves open a number of questions, above all the degree to which, by 1671, this suggestiveness could be thought a coherent coda to a life's work around (if not in) tragedy. But when we return to Milton's earliest poetry, in both Latin and English, it is clear that the connections established in *Samson Agonistes* among law, theology, language, and time were long-standing preoccupations; long before the composition of *Paradise Lost*, it was Milton's reading in and thinking about materiality, error, and language in tragedy that structured the distinctive, almost reflexive, associations he would eventually make in his two greatest works. The important early influence of Milton's reading in tragedy emerges clearly in three short, early poems—*Naturam Non Pati Senium*, *De Idea Platonica Quemadmodem Aristoteles Intellexit*, and 'On Time'. These three poems function, indeed, as a kind of index by means of which we may understand and assess the nature and philosophical vigour of Milton's later interventions in both tragic modality, and (in *Samson Agonistes*) tragedy proper.

Perhaps the first explicit reference to a tragedy in Milton's extant poetical writings appears in the Latin poem *Naturam Non Pati Senium* ['That Nature does not suffer old age'], probably written in 1629.[18] In the poem's opening lines, Milton offers a kind of *moralitas* through which the rest of the poem's rhetoricized anxiety over the relation of Nature to God must be viewed:

> *Heu quam perpetuis erroribus acta fatiscit*
> *Avia mens hominum, tenebrisque immersa profundis*
> *Oedipodioniam volvit sub pectore noctem!*
> *Quae vesana suis metiri facta deorum*
> *Audet, et incisas leges adamante perenni*
> *Consilium fati perituris alligat horis.* (1–6)

(Ah! How perpetual are the errors which drive man's restless mind to exhaustion! How deep the darkness which swallows him when he harbours in his soul the blind night of Oedipus! In his madness he dares to measure the deeds of Gods by his own, to make those laws which are cut in everlasting adamant of no more account than his own laws, and to link that decree of fate which no age will ever wear away to his own dwindling hours.)[19]

Milton's ostensible point, in this introduction to the theme of Nature's self-generating renewal, is to assimilate all mortal experience to the tragic condition of Oedipus, who is held up as an example of the blind human prone to project his limitations onto the eternal and immutable nature of the divine. Most English translations of the original Latin poem, like that cited above, introduce into its syntax a temporal-conditional clause ('when he harbours in his soul . . . '), which seems to indicate that human experience is subject to error in this way when, and only when, the individual falls into an Oedipal blindness; but this is not present in the original, where Milton simply imagines the *mens hominum* in its tendency to meditate on (*volvere*) the darkness of Oedipus. The rest of the poem that follows, then, makes good sense as an example of the way in which, as mortals, we have erred and mistaken the nature of things again, as Oedipus before us: Nature cannot be anthropomorphized, nor the fates of God or of time itself considered by any human frame. Should we persist in such an unsound opinion, we risk a tragic limitation and fate.

Such a reading of the poem overlooks two aspects of Milton's invocation of Oedipus. The first, more obvious, is not at first fatal to the reading. If we take Oedipus's error, in Milton's allusion, to be his attempt to evade his fate, the lesson that his tragedy must teach us is that these inscrutable and 'uncontrollable intents' cannot be avoided. The point of rehearsing the *moralitas* at the opening of the poem would seem to be that it primes us to join Milton, after line 6, in rejecting with contempt the ridiculous claim that Nature does, in fact, suffer old age. By contrast, the force of the allusion at the centre of the *moralitas* seems to make our collapse into error ineluctable, and thus to promise not spiritual catharsis, but serial catastrophe. This may help to explain the abrupt and confusing *volte face* that the poem produces for its close. Having insisted, by means of a pageant of classical allusions, on the constancy and immutability of nature, Milton concludes:

> *Sic denique in aevum*
> *Ibit cunctarum series iustissima rerum,*
> *Donec flamma orbem populabitur ultima, late*
> *Circumplexa polos, et vasti culmina caeli;*
> *Ingentique rogo flagrabit machina mundi.* (65–9)

(In fact, then, the process of the universe will go on for ever, worked out with scrupulous justice, until the last flames destroy the globe, enveloping the poles and summits of vast heaven, and the frame of the world blazes on one huge funeral pyre.)[20]

The long middle section of the poem, which insists on the unchanging nature of the fabric of being and of time, is here entirely overturned. In a sense our Oedipal night (*Oedipodioniam . . . noctem*) turns out to have been right all along, though with a crucial difference: when at last the universe is consumed in its *flamma . . . ultima*, it will be the result of a *series iustissima*—the most just possible order. The poem as a whole self-consciously echoes Edmund Spenser's *Two Cantos of Mutabilitie* (1609), and nowhere more so than in this conclusion, where a vision of uncontrollably stable process is seen, as in Spenser's poem, to leap without explanation into finality. Our inability to understand this *volte face*, as in the *Cantos*, stems again from the ineluctable limitation of our tragically mortal perspective.

But Milton also writes into his allusion to Oedipus another, more profoundly subversive idea. When he speaks of the *errores* under which human minds, like Oedipus's, may travel, Milton seems to be talking about Oedipus's mistakes about fate and his own agency, taking *errores* in a metaphorical sense. But the reference to the *Oedipodioniam . . . noctem*, given the history of Oedipus's catastrophe, pulls in quite another, literal direction. Milton seems by this pairing to extend the possibility that the *errores* afflicting humankind are to be joined not (only) to Oedipus's metaphysical misprisions, but to his physical wanderings once exiled from Thebes. This of course makes good sense of the way in which Milton also imagines Oedipus's fault as one of hubristic anthropomorphization, by which he assumes that the doings of gods are to be reckoned by his own, that the heavenly state is to be governed by his laws, and that divine time is to be judged by his mortal temporality. For the end of Sophocles's play *Oedipus Tyrannus* centres on the impious way in which Oedipus, *after* his various crimes and their ultimate exposure, *after* Jocasta's death, and *after* his blinding, seeks dispensation from the temporal ruler, Creon, and in despite of the divine ordination of his instant death, to be allowed to wander. When Oedipus demands that, as a parricide (πατροφόντης), he be cast out of his paternal city (πατρῴονᾰστυ), Creon asks him to be ruled by the god, and offers to send to the priest for guidance:

CREON   This would I have done, be thou sure, but that I craved first to learn all my duty from the god.

OEDIPUS   Nay, his behest hath been set forth in full,—to let me perish, the parricide, the unholy one, that I am.

CREON   Such was the purport; yet, seeing to what a pass we have come, 'tis better to learn clearly what should be done.

OEDIPUS   Will ye, then, seek a response on behalf of such a wretch as I am?

CREON   Aye, for thou thyself wilt now surely put faith in the god.[21]

At this Oedipus seems to agree, acknowledging his duty to divine dispose, but within a few lines he has returned to his plea, and demands, ἀλλ᾽ ἡ μὲν ἡμῶν μοῖρ᾽, ὅποιπερ εἶσ᾽, ἴτω ('Let my fate go whither it will', 1458). The close juxtaposition of the two verbs here (εἶσ᾽, ἴτω) joins the going to the impulse to go, insisting on an automaticity that leaves no place for Creon's pious motions towards divine authority. While the nature of μοῖρα (fate) is such that Oedipus's apparent wilfulness is equivocal—he seeks to ignore the gods in order to fulfil their decree—by the time he has seen Ismene and Antigone, he has refigured his plea as an appeal to Creon's earthly authority. When he demands, again, to be sent away from Thebes, Creon answers, τοῦ θεοῦ μ' αἰτεῖς δόσιν ('Thou askest me for what the god must give', 1518).[22] The end of Sophocles's play, as Milton must well have known, allows Oedipus to equivocate on this issue of his reconciliation to the god; but, on balance, it appears that Oedipus's *errores*—the subject of the opening of *Oedipus at Colonus*—are the outgrowth not of the god's will, but of his own construction of his fate: ἡ . . . ἡμῶν μοῖρα.

The importance of the conclusion of Sophocles's play to Milton's poem lies in the way that, by choosing *acta . . . avia*, Oedipus literalizes his *errores* and his *nox* not only by blinding himself, but by setting off on a wandering journey. The exchange between Creon and Oedipus at the end of the play seizes into the human sphere a *series iustissima* that—as both the end of Spenser's *Cantos* and the end of Milton's Latin poem make clear—ought to remain entirely between the protagonist and the inscrutable, 'uncontrollable intent' of the divine power. Oedipus's repeatedly declared preference for the dispensation of the human power and the human law, over the appeal to the god's instruction, performs explicitly the damning comparison of which Milton writes at the opening of his poem. In other words, what Milton recognizes as tragic in Oedipus's narrative is precisely the way in which Oedipus remains resistant to divine order—paradoxically, by insisting on a knowable, human ruling on his condition and future. With that superb irony that would come, forty years later, to define the paradox of Samson's assertive self-displacement, Milton characterizes Oedipus's choice for *legibility* (knowability through *lex*, the law) as one of darkness and night, revolved *sub pectore*.

It is no accident that Milton turned to Spenser's *Cantos of Mutabilitie* in his defence of Nature in *Naturam Non Pati Senium*: the *Cantos* function as Spenser's abjuration of allegory in the same way that Milton's poem functions as an abjuration of tragedy, and for the same reasons. Indeed, the links between tragedy and allegory are closer than generally recognized and subsist exactly in these preoccupations of both genres with the relation of the temporal to the eternal, the material to the essential, or the instance to the law. The move that Milton makes at the beginning of *Naturam Non Pati Senium*—to condemn Oedipus (and through him, tragedy) for the way in which he sets up a false idol in the heavens—is also the move that Nature makes in the *Cantos* when she condemns Mutabilitie for claiming precedence over Jove. Nature's judgement insists that the forms or 'estates' that lie behind the temporal manifestation of those forms, in instances, are not subject to change precisely because they comprehend change; it is thus possible that all the instance-forms taken by matter in its temporal course represent 'dilations' of a 'first estate'—here not a temporally prior, but a formally precedent estate.[23] Likewise, Milton's allusion to Sophocles's *Oedipus Tyrannus* cannily picks up on the way in which Oedipus's bid to be judged and determined by human dispensation must result in plurality and extension, both of errors (wanderings) and of depths (turnings *sub pectore*). In the verb *volvere* that he uses to describe the mental state of the Oedipal mind, Milton tracks not the turn and return of the primary forms, through their temporal pilgrimage, to their eternal nature, but a tragic parody of this proliferation: the assertion of a divine warrant for human fate might seem a consoling guarantee of the nature of what is, but when that divine warrant is modelled, as in *Oedipus Tyrannus*, on the appetite and limitation of the human subject, 'desire' leads simply to 'decay'. Milton recognizes that the aftermath of the Oedipal tragedy is as ontologically unstable as the proliferation of forms threatened by Spenser's Mutabilitie. Spenser closes down his allegory to contain the twin dangers of autogenesis and recursive regression; through Oedipus, Milton turns away from a tragic vision because its errors are wide, and its shadows deep.

Gordon Teskey has written persuasively on the ontological peril of the medieval (Dantean) allegory that Spenser perfected. The two poles of Spenser's *allegoresis*, what Teskey calls capture and personification, are perched precariously on opposed edges of 'the rift', a source of allegorical imagery that, like the paradox at the centre of Samson's assertive displacement, can be neither seen nor questioned.[24] Personification is the name given to that operation by which a universal is predicated of itself, as when (Teskey notes) justice is said to be just. Capture, by contrast, is 'the point of contact between allegory and violence', 'the creative exertion of force' that takes place when something that is 'intolerably other' is made to become a transcendental other—that is, when something that has its own absolute and unassimilable meaning is made to carry 'instrumental meaning'.[25] Teskey singles out a particular danger arising from personification, which threatens not only our understanding of things as they are, but also those things themselves (that is to say, it is both an epistemological as well as an ontological problem): the attempt to personify a form in a figure, by giving to that form some shape, extent, and temporal instance, leaves the allegory susceptible to the charge that *some other* more precedent form must lie behind both and all the instances of which it is the form. This problem, for Teskey, is illustrated in the moment that Guyon meets Shamefastnesse: when Alma tells the knight that he participates in shamefastness, but that standing before him is Shamefastnesse herself, we are of course immediately invited to speculate about that in which *she* participates (see *Faerie Queene*, II.ix.40-4).[26] This is the problem known to Aristotelian metaphysics as the Third Man, after Aristotle's serial consideration of it, in this form, in several of his works.[27] The original statement of the problem occurs in Plato's *Parmenides*, a dialogue on the nature of being and the one as popular in the Renaissance as it was among the Platonists of the early Christian era. In this work Plato shows Parmenides discussing the Third Man argument with a young Socrates not in connection to man, but (as Milton would have found it) in connection to τὸ μέγα, 'the great'. "'I fancy your reason for believing that each idea is one is something like this"', says Parmenides:

'when there is a number of things which seem to you to be great, you may think, as you look at them all, that there is one and the same idea in them, and hence you think the great is one.'

'That is true,' he [Socrates] said.

'But if with your mind's eye you regard the absolute great and these many great things in the same way, will not another great appear beyond, by which all these must appear to be great?'

'So it seems.'

'That is, another idea of greatness will appear, in addition to absolute greatness and the objects which partake of it; and another again in addition to these, by reason of which they are all great; and each of your ideas will no longer be one, but their number will be infinite.'[28]

Teskey notes how personification is vulnerable to the Third Man (or the Infinite Greatness) argument, but does not discuss how what he calls 'capture' is similarly at stake in the same passage from the *Parmenides*. The reason why Parmenides and Socrates take up the Third Man argument, as Parmenides asserts here, is to show that the principle of similarity—which is our only evidence for the participatory nature of instances in forms—will lead not to a reduction of complexity, but to a proliferation of complexity in forms. The Third Man unseats personification, but it similarly unseats capture. This is why the replacement of Law by law, in *Naturam Non Pati Senium*, results in an infinite dilation (*erroribus*) as well as an infinite immersion (*tenebris*).

As it happens, of course, Milton composed a poem on the Third Man problem at about the same time as *Naturam Non Pati Senium*. *De Idea Platonica Quemadmodem Aristoteles Intellexit* ('On the Platonic idea as Aristotle understood it'), also a Latin poem from the *Sylvarum Liber* and first published in 1645, satirizes its own persona of the youthful Aristotle, challenging Plato over his theory of forms. In Milton's poem, Aristotle avoids the Third Man problem by conceiving of an individual man who is at once both the idea, and a universal, but also existent in space and through time: *Sed quamlibet natura sit communior, | Tamen seorsùs extat ad morem unius, | Et, mira, certo stringitur spatio loci . . .* (13–15) ('But howsoever he is by nature general, nevertheless [O wonder] he exists apart as an individual, and is confined to an exact portion of space.') The nonsense that Milton attributes to Aristotle here bears a close relation to his discussion of Oedipal hubris in *Naturam Non Pati Senium*. The ascription of an individual nature to any Platonic idea violates one of the fundamental principles of Socratic forms, articulated by his *Parmenides* immediately before the Third Man argument:

And even if all things partake of both opposites, and are enabled by their participation to be both like and unlike themselves, what is there wonderful about that? For if anyone showed that the absolute like becomes unlike, or the unlike like, that would, in my opinion, be a wonder; but if he shows that things which partake of both become both like and unlike, that seems to me, Zeno, not at all strange, not even if he shows that all things are one by participation in unity and that the same are also many by participation in multitude; but if he shows that absolute unity is also many and the absolute many again are one, then I shall be amazed.[29]

Socrates's argument here, sometimes by historians of philosophy called the principle of purity, insists that the form of an idea cannot be contradictorily composite. The instability of the unity of Oedipal hubris is implied in *Naturam Non Pati Senium* by both of the verbs Milton uses in his opening rejection of tragedy: *Heu quam perpetuis erroribus acta fatiscit | Avia mens hominum, tenebrisque immersa profundis | Oedipodioniam volvit sub pectore noctem!* (Ah! How perpetual are the errors which drive man's restless mind to exhaustion! How deep the darkness which swallows him when he harbours in his soul the blind night of Oedipus!) Both *fatiscere* (literally 'to come apart into pieces') and *volvere* ('to turn, revolve') show how the replacement of a Law by a law leads to an untenable and exhausting compositeness (i.e., one that immediately becomes discomposite). Thus *De Idea Platonica*, though it ostensibly has little if anything to do with tragedy, comes at the same concerns that, in his other contemporary reference to the ontological problem of the tragic outlook, had defined the representation of tragedy. Moreover, in this account of the Third Man problem, Milton explicitly links the Aristotelian evasion of tragedy to both law and to poetry:

> *Dicite sacrorum præsides nemorum deæ*
> *Tuque O noveni perbeata numinis*
> *Memoria mater, quæ in immenso procul*
> *Antro recumbis otiosa Æternitas,*
> *Monumenta servans, & ratas leges Jovis,*
> *Cælique fastos atque ephemeridas Deûm . . .* (1–6)[30]

(Declare, O goddesses that guard the sacred groves, and you, O Memory, blessed mother of the ninefold deity, and you, Eternity, who in some vast cave far-off lie stretched at ease, guarding the chronicles and the unalterable laws of Jove, recording the festivals of heaven and the daily life of the gods . . .)

It is the business of poets to make monsters (Milton's *monstra* [36]) punning on Aristotelian demonstrations) like the composite one–many man, just as it is the business of Eternity to guard both the laws and the chronicles. For this reason, Milton's poem ends with an absurd and sarcastic recall of the poets to Plato's republic, for their proliferating forms turn out to be exactly those many–one ideas which, in a more logical time, Plato had expelled from the state.

It is important to recognize that Milton's presentation in *De Idea Platonica* of the union between the universal and the individual is absurd not because it is repugnant to logic, or to faith—indeed, Milton would make very similar claims for the Son as an individuated, temporally existent creature of God's making in the *De Doctrina Christiana*,[31] where he also argues for the nature of God as *natura simplicissima SPIRITUS*:

God in his most simple nature is a SPIRIT . . . From this it may be understood that the essence of God, since it is utterly simple, allows nothing to be compounded with it, and that the word *hypostasis*, Heb. i. 3, which is variously translated *substance*, *subsistence*, or *person*, is nothing but that most perfect essence by which God exists from himself, in himself, and through himself . . . *Hypostasis*, therefore, is clearly the same as essence, and in the passage cited above many translate it by the Latin word *essentia*. Therefore, just as God is an utterly simple essence, so he is an utterly simple subsistence.[32]

What makes the attack on Plato absurd in Milton's parody of Aristotle is precisely Aristotle's confidence that he can demonstrate the monstrousness of Plato's theory; *monstra* are the problem, because, here as later in Milton's poetry, the mystery of God's *certo . . . spacio*—what would become, in *Samson Agonistes*, a glorious witness 'in place'—is something that can neither be seen nor understood by human observers. As Milton puts it in the passage above, though God is 'an utterly simple subsistence', that subsistence 'is nothing but that most perfect essence by which [he] exists from himself, in himself, and through himself'. This emphasis in Milton's early poetry on the way in which eternity and instant, the one of God's omnipresence and the many of particular body and space, can meet only through the power and in the sight of God, is the central point of the second half of Milton's Spenserian poem 'On Time',[33] also published in 1645:

> For when as each thing bad thou hast entomb'd,
> And last of all, thy greedy self consum'd,
> Then long Eternity shall greet our bliss
> With an individual kiss;
> And Joy shall overtake us as a flood,
> When every thing that is sincerely good
> And perfectly divine,
> With Truth, and Peace, and Love shall ever shine
> About the supreme Throne
> Of him, t' whose happy-making sight alone,
> When once our heav'nly-guided soul shall clime,
> Then all this Earthy grosnes quit,
> Attir'd with Stars, we shall for ever sit,
> Triumphing over Death, and Chance, and thee O Time. (9–22)

The persistence of the individual in this confrontation with the divine sits uneasily with Milton's satire of Aristotle in *De Idea Platonica* unless we recognize the importance of the limiting clause in line 18: 't' whose happy-making sight alone'. The spatial gradation implied in 'clime', like the persistence of identity after the exhaustion of time itself, can be distinguished from the fallacies of tragedy only by this limitation of a solitary, divine comprehension. It is fitting, then, that, just as in the crucial concluding sonnet of *Samson Agonistes*, Milton should turn in this poem to the possibility of hypallage. The attribution of individuality to Eternity's kiss depends on the individuality of the man—say, Milton—who stands before God and all time, and it is from this mortal's individuality that the individuality of the kiss is derived, or transferred. Against this individuality Milton immediately rears the prospect of Parmenidean participation, as, having been kissed, the individual is 'overtake[n]' by Joy 'as a flood'—a neat analogue for the example Socrates offers, in the *Parmenides*, of day, a thing that can befall us in one place, and yet be everywhere at once.[34] The materiality of hypallage, importing its ontology of a placing displacement, reaches its consummation in this collectivizing image of the flood. Oedipus does not impose his laws on God; rather, God bestows on Milton, but inscrutably, his blissful individuality, even as Milton finds himself dissolved in the universal good.

But this divine composite of the flooding kiss has one more suggestive offering to throw up, which plays back into the way Milton, a young man of about 20 years when he composed these poems, asserted his displacement just like another young man of the same age, thousands of years before him:

'Then will it be possible for God to know human things, if he has absolute knowledge?'

  'Why not?'

'Because,' said Parmenides, 'we have agreed that those ideas are not relative to our world, nor our world to them, but each only to themselves.'

  'Yes, we have agreed to that.'

'Then if this most perfect mastership [δεσποτεία] and this most accurate knowledge are with God, his mastership can never rule us, nor his knowledge know us or anything of our world; we do not rule the gods with our authority, nor do we know anything of the divine with our knowledge, and by the same reasoning, they likewise, being gods, are not our masters [δεσπόται] and have no knowledge of human affairs.'

'But surely this,' said he, 'is a most amazing argument, if it make us deprive God of knowledge.'

'And yet, Socrates,' said Parmenides, 'these difficulties and many more besides are inseparable from the ideas, if these ideas of things exist and we declare that each of them is an absolute idea. Therefore he who hears such assertions is confused in his mind and argues that the ideas do not exist, and even if they do exist cannot by any possibility be known by man; and he thinks that what he says is reasonable, and, as I was saying just now, he is amazingly hard to convince. Only a man of very great natural gifts will be able to understand that everything has a class and absolute essence, and only a still more wonderful man can find out all these facts and teach anyone else to analyse them properly and understand them.'

'I agree with you, Parmenides," said Socrates, "for what you say is very much to my mind.'[35]

Milton's anti-tragic project, as it is shadowed in these early poems, was not designed to drive an unbridgeable rift between God and humanity, but to assert the precise conditions, and ways, by which the human might access, know about, and be assimilated to the divine. The hypallactic unknowability of Milton's glorious and individual witness is the solution to a terrible problem— one that, Plato gives us to understand, had stood before Socrates in his youth, and stood still before Milton in his. It is curious, and suggestive, that, as David Norbrook has noted, Milton shows in his marginal annotations to his copy of Euripides's plays a particular interest in the Greek word δεσπότης and its derivatives, given that the word shows up with considerable force in *Samson Agonistes*, *Of Reformation*, and *The Tenure of Kings and Magistrates*.[36] It is also central to this passage from Plato's *Parmenides*, where—as a synonym for the 'control' or 'controlment' with which Milton concluded his *Samson Agonistes*—it similarly describes the way in which the true mastership of one power (e.g., the gods, or God) derives from its ability to match (here, by knowing) another power (e.g., that of humanity); Plato's gods confer their knowledge with that of humanity, and can rule us, it seems, only if the two records are alike.[37] For Milton, ultimately, Oedipus's inability to impose his laws on God did not correlate with God's inability to impose his δεσποτεία upon us and the things of our world; indeed, as the conclusion to *Samson Agonistes* demonstrates, God's δεσποτεία, a hypallactic mastership as inimical to tragedy as to the Greek language of its origin, must be as absolute as his power. In these three early poems, each of them in a different way labouring under the example of Spenser and the problems of materiality raised by Spenser's allegorical language, we witness Milton beginning that response through, and eventually to, tragedy.

Notes

1. See Trinity College, Cambridge MS R. 3. 4, published in facsimile, with a transcription, as *Milton: Complete Shorter Poems* (Menston, 1970), hereafter designated TMS. The notes on *Adam Unparadiz'd* in the Trinity College Manuscript end with Milton's note to himself, 'compare this with the former draught' (40). This former draft is presumably that appearing five pages earlier where the tragedy is given the title *Paradise Lost*. The manuscript also contains plans for plays on *The Deluge*, tentatively titled *Sodom* and/or *Dinah* (see 36, but also 39–40 where the material is given another working title); *Asa, or Aethiopes*, based on 2 Chronicles 14 (36); *Abram from Morea, or Isack redeemd* (39); and *Baptistes*, a dramatic account of the sentencing and death of John the Baptist (39). Brief notes survive for *Moabitides or Phineas* (41), concerning

Phineas's murder of Zimri in Numbers 25:6–15, and *Christus patiens*. The transcription supplied in the Scolar facsimile is in places poor, and should not be trusted.

2. See TMS, 37–8 ('British Troy') and 41 ('Scotch stories or rather brittish of the north parts'). That Milton intended these notes towards some dramatic composition is suggested by the character of the notes, e.g., the final comment on the history of Macbeth: 'the matter of Duncan may be express't by the appearing of his ghost' (41).

3. In 'Milton's *Comus* as a Failure in Artistic Compromise', *ELH*, 16 (1949), 104–19, D. C. Allen suggests that 'the pallium of classical tragedy covers the whole poem', a pallium chiefly to be discerned in its prologist, its 'antistrophic choral of Comus', and its *deux ex machina* conclusion (112).

4. Bodleian Library, Oxford Don. d. 27–8 is a bilingual edition of the complete plays of Euripides, with annotations in Milton's hand: *Euripidis Tragoediae quae extant* (Geneva, 1602). For Milton's debts to Euripides, see P. W. Timberlake, 'Milton and Euripides', in Hardin Craig (ed.), *Essays in Dramatic Literature: The Parrott Presentation Volume* (Princeton, N.J., 1935); William Riley Parker, *Milton's Debt to Greek Tragedy in 'Samson Agonistes'* (Baltimore, Md., 1937); and David Norbrook, 'Euripides, Milton, and *Christian Doctrine*', *Milton Quarterly*, 29 (1995), 37–41.

5. All quotations from Milton's shorter poetry are taken from *Poems of Mr John Milton* (1645); English translations of the Latin poems are taken from *Milton: Complete Shorter Poems*, ed. John Carey (1968), hereafter designated *CSP*. Line numbers are noted parenthetically in the text.

6. This obvious line of questioning leads directly to the critical debate that has dominated the recent reception of *Samson Agonistes*. For an introduction to the key points of contention, see Joseph Wittreich, *Interpreting 'Samson Agonistes'* (Princeton, N.J., 1986).

7. Northrop Frye, 'Introduction to *"Paradise Lost" and Selected Poetry and Prose*', in Angela Esterhammer (ed.), *Northrop Frye on Milton and Blake* (Toronto, 2005), 15.

8. The Latin verb from which 'acquist' is, by the past participle 'acquestum', derived is *adquirere* or *acquirere*, than which there is, simply, no more important verb in the civil or native English common law of *dominium*; see for instance Henry de Bracton (?), *De Legibus et Consuetudinibus Angliae*, ed. Samuel E. Thorne, 4 vols. (Cambridge, Mass., 1968), ii. 42ff. (Section 2: *De adquirendo rerum dominio* [Of acquiring the dominion of things]). 'Acquest' or 'acquist' is a key term in John Selden's 1636 work on English rights to dominion over the sea, *Mare Clausum, seu De Dominio Maris*; Marchamont Nedham's 1654 English translation of the work is fronted by an English poem, 'Neptune to the Common-wealth of *England*', the fifth stanza of which spells out the lawyer's traditional distinction between rights acquired by inheritance and acquest:

> If little *Uenice* bring's alone
> Such waves to her subjection as in the Gulf do stir;
> What then should great *Britannia* pleas,
> But rule as Ladie o're all seas, and thou as Queen of her.
> For Sea-Dominion may as well bee gain'd
> By new acquests, as by descent maintain'd. (sig. p1v)

Selden also quotes directly from a medieval libel asserting the dominion over the sea of the kings of England, and collocates 'acquest' with 'forfeiture' (425).

9. 'Intent' was a common substitute, or even form, in this period for the equally common legal term, 'intendment' or 'entendment'. As John Cowell defines it in *The Interpreter: Or Booke Containing the Signification of Words* (Cambridge, 1607), '*Entendment*, commeth of the French (*entendement. i. intellectus, ingenium.*) It signifieth in our common lawe so much, as the true meaning or signification of a word or sentence' (sig. Bb3v). The etymology of the verb 'control', from the Fr. *contrôler* or *contreroller*, clearly continued to impinge on the usage of the verb and its derivatives during the early modern period. Originally used to describe the way in which a judge's clerk verified, legitimated, or supervised official entries in legal registers or rolls (literally by applying these entries to the 'counter-roll'), the verb continued during the seventeenth century to be associated with distinctively legal forms of supervision and oversight. Shakespeare's use of the word, for example, frequently draws on its technical legal origins, as in the famous common law couplet to Sonnet 125 ('Were 't aught to me I bore the canopy'): 'Hence, thou suborned informer: a true soul / When most impeached, stands least in thy control.' See William Shakespeare, *Complete Sonnets and Poems*, ed. Colin Burrow (Oxford, 2002), 630–1.

10. See Quintilian, *Institutio Oratoria*, VIII.vi.23; and Cicero, *De Oratore*, xxvii.93.

11. George Puttenham, *The Arte of English Poesie* (1589), 143.

12. The importance of hypallage to an understanding of these final lines can be better discerned if they are compared to the close of Book I, canto xi of Spenser's *The Faerie Queene*—a parallel idea expressed by resort to a similar rhetorical strategy. Here Spenser writes of Una congratulating Redcrosse on the slaying of the dragon: 'Then God she praysd, and thankt her faithfull knight, / That had atcheiude so great a conquest by his might' (*Faerie Queene*, I.xi.55.8–9). Spenser leaves ambiguous the subject of the verb ('had atcheiude') controlling his final line, as well as the antecedent of 'his'; though the rhyme may seem to call the might the knight's, the poem has already insisted upon Redcrosse's complete surrender to, and rebirth in, God's purpose and power. Milton's account of Samson differs from Spenser's of Redcrosse in three ways. First, he goes beyond Spenser, who is merely ambiguous, by completely effecting a shift from Samson's to God's agency—a full exchange takes place. Second, his lines explicitly foreground the materiality of this displacement (in 'returns', 'in place') as it occurs, forcing us to attend to it *as* displacement. And third, the exchange is effected by the shifting of particular words (e.g., 'to' in 1751) which, though having become detached from their natural grammatical relations, still retain a kind of magnetism for them (e.g., the latent phrase, 'But unexpectedly returns *to his faithful champion*'). The persistence of a 'natural' ordering of the words behind their actual order marks this passage as an instance of hypallage.

13. See John Calvin, *Institutio Christianae Religionis* (1576), 110. The English translation supplied here is that of Ford Lewis Battles, in John T. McNeil (ed.), *The Institutes of the Christian Religion*, 2 vols. (Philadelphia, Pa., 1960), i. 262.

14. Calvin, *Institutio* (2. 2. 10), 112; i. 267–8.

15. Milton's essentially Arminian position on the ability of the human to resist special grace—clearly articulated in *De Doctrina Christiana*, ch. 4, and shadowed in the closing lines of *Samson Agonistes*, where the Philistines 'band them to resist' God—does not undermine the fundamentally Calvinist choice between God and Samson in this instance.

16. TMS, 35. I have supplied in square brackets [ ], by guesswork, words lost in damage to the margin of the manuscript.

17. The threat of this back-formation of God's materiality was of such moment that Moses Maimonides, in his twelfth-century masterpiece *The Guide of the Perplexed*, trans. Shlomo Pines, 2 vols, devoted an entire and uncharacteristically digressive chapter to refuting it. Maimonides's project, the harmonization of Aristotelian metaphysics with the Torah, uses the conventions of allegorical interpretation to reject the material and temporal existence of God. Ultimately his only concession to the knowability of the divine comes in his account, in the 54th chapter of the first book, of Moses's vision of God at the tabernacle by Mount Horeb (Exod. 33:11–23). In Maimonides's account, when Moses asked God 'to let him know His attributes', and further 'His essence and true reality', God promised him:

> to let him know all His attributes, making it known to him that they are His actions, and teaching him that His essence cannot be grasped as it really is. Yet He drew his attention to a subject of speculation through which he can apprehend to the furthest extent that is possible for man. His request regarding the knowledge of [God's] attributes is conveyed in his saying: *Show me now Thy ways, that I may know Thee, and so on.* Consider the wondrous notions contained in this dictum. For his saying, *Show me now Thy ways, that I may know Thee,* indicates that God, may He be exalted, is known through His attributive qualifications; for when he would know the *ways,* he would know Him. Furthermore his saying, *That I may find grace in Thy sight,* indicates that he who knows God *finds grace in His sight* and not he who merely fasts and prays, but everyone who has knowledge of Him. Accordingly those who know Him are those who are favored by Him and permitted to come near Him, whereas those who do not know Him are objects of His wrath and are kept far away from Him. For his favor and wrath, His nearness and remoteness, correspond to the extent of a man's knowledge or ignorance. (i. 123–4)

The connection between Moses's witness of God on Sinai, on the one hand, and Maimonides's emphasis on knowledge and approach to God through an understanding of his 'ways', on the other, clearly suggests Milton's study of the work, which he almost certainly knew in the Latin translation by Johann Buxtorf: *Doctor Perplexorum* (Basel, 1629). Maimonides's emphasis on knowledge of God through his 'ways' may, similarly, have influenced Milton's emphasis on knowing God through his external efficiency in *De Doctrina Christiana*, Book 1, chaps., 3, 5–8. Milton's knowledge of Maimonides was probably mediated by his study of and respect for the Hebraist and lawyer John Selden, who quotes heavily from Maimonides in *Uxor Hebraica* (1646), a key source for Milton's *De Doctrina Christiana*; see Jason Rosenblatt, *Renaissance England's Chief Rabbi: John Selden* (Oxford, 2006); and Matthew Biberman, 'Milton, Marriage, and a Woman's Right to Divorce', *Studies in English Literature 1500– 1900*, 39 (1999), 131–53. The quoted passage from Maimonides appears in the two-volume edition of *The Guide of the Perplexed* (Chicago, Ill., 1963) translated by Shlomo Pines.

18. On the recent re-dating of these two poems, see Sarah Knight, 'Milton's Student Verses of 1629', *Notes and Queries*, 255 (2010), 37–9.
19. Carey, *CSP*, 61–5.
20. Carey, *CSP*, 65.
21. Sophocles, *Oedipus Tyrannus*, ed. R. C. Jebb (Cambridge, 1893), 1438–45. I have used Jebb's text and translation because, although archaic, it best preserves the literal sense and grammatical relations of the original.
22. Note that Jebb translates the verb αἰτέω here as 'ask', when its resonance in Greek is more in the spirit of 'claim'—that is, a legal claim, as in its close derivative, the noun αἰτία, 'charge, accusation'—or 'claim'. Sophocles's point in this passage must be that Oedipus claims by human law that which he ought to recognize as the privilege of the gods.
23. See Edmund Spenser, *The Faerie Queene*, VII.vii.58–9.
24. See Gordon Teskey, *Allegory and Violence* (Ithaca, N.Y., 1996), 5–8.
25. Teskey, *Allegory and Violence*, 5–6.
26. The importance of this moment in *The Faerie Queene* to an understanding of Spenser's reception of Plato's and Aristotle's views on the theory of forms was recognized before Teskey. See Kerby Neill, 'Spenser's Shamefastnesse, *Faerie Queene*, II.ix.40–44', *Modern Language Notes*, 49 (1934), 387–91. For Teskey's discussion, see *Allegory and Violence*, 22–3; as he writes, 'personification has been regarded as the sine qua non of allegorical expression. But if this is so, then it is not because personification reveals what is essential to allegory but because it hides what is essential so well' (22).
27. Aristotle mentions the Third Man in his *Metaphysics*, 990b17 (a passage repeated at 1079a13), and describes it at 1039a2 briefly, but adequately enough to make it clear that he was considering this and not another problem.
28. Plato, *Parmenides*, trans. H. N. Fowler (Cambridge, Mass., 1926), 217–19 (132a–b).
29. Plato, *Parmenides*, 207–9 (129b). It is curious that neither of the standard twentieth-century studies on Milton and Plato—Irene Samuel's *Plato and Milton* (Ithaca, N.Y., 1947) and Stephen M. Fallon's *Milton among the Philosophers: Poetry and Materialism in Seventeenth-Century England* (Ithaca, N.Y., 1991)—mentions the *Parmenides*.
30. Carey, *CSP*, 68.
31. See *CPW*, vi. 203–80 (Book 1, chapter 5, of Milton's *Two Books of Investigations into Christian Doctrine*).

32. John Milton, *De Doctrina Christiana (A Treatise of Christian Doctrine)* ed. Charles R. Sumner (Braunschweig, 1827), 15, and *CPW*, vi. 140–2.
33. The unusual form of Milton's poem, which Fletcher has connected to Pindar, is more immediately an echo, and revision, of the eighteen-line stanza form of Spenser's *Epithalamion* (1595), which employs a similar combination of pentameter and short lines, with a similar rhyme scheme. Milton has in mind a different kind of marriage, and makes a monument to longer time.
34. See Plato, *Parmenides*, 215 (131b).
35. Plato, *Parmenides*, 227–9 (134d–135b).
36. See Norbrook, 'Euripides, Milton, and *Christian Doctrine*', 39–40. The use of δεσπότης is roughly equivalent to L. *dominus* (and δεσποτεία to L. *dominium*), and like the Latin term indicates a mastery that shades into, and derives its force from, absolute ownership, as that of a master of his slaves.
37. The origins of δεσποτεία in the οἶκος (house) are important here: the political idea of absolute sovereignty, like the word itself, was originally imported from the domestic sphere, in which the δεσπότης ('master of the house') ruled absolutely precisely because his relationship to the family and slaves was one of ownership. The Greek adjective for 'domestic', οἰκεῖος, also means 'proper, fitting', or—for Plato in the *Parmenides*—'belonging to, conformable to the nature of a thing'. Milton absolutely denies the conformability of God's knowledge with our own, and yet still insists on God's δεσποτεία.

9

The Design of the 1645 *Poems*

Stella P. Revard

In 1695, a little over twenty years after Milton had reissued in 1673 the second edition of 1645 *Poems*, Jacob Tonson brought out the third edition of Milton's *Poems upon Several Occasions*. However, whereas in 1673 Milton, even with his additions of sonnets, psalms, and some earlier pieces, kept carefully the order of the 1645 volume, Tonson deliberately sets forth a different sequence. 'Lycidas' has pride of place as first poem followed by 'L'Allegro' and 'Il Penseroso' and then the Ludlow *Maske* and 'Arcades'. Not until after this display of what we might call Milton's greatest hits does the Nativity Ode appear followed by the poems of the 1673 volume in a descending order with the psalms last as in 1673. Tonson seems more or less to be making a case for Milton's shorter poems by putting his so-called best poems forward first in a sequence climaxing with *A Maske*. He does not rearrange the *Poemata*, however, keeping 1673's organization and even publishing, as Milton had, the *Testimonia* before the book of Elegies.[1] When the fourth edition appeared in 1707, the arrangement Tonson had set forth twelve years earlier reappears. And even ninety years later in 1785 in an edition by Thomas Warton, Tonson's rearrangement of Milton's 1645 *Poems* prevails. Readers are introduced to Milton's shorter poems with 'Lycidas', the twin odes, and *A Maske*, which by now had assumed its popular title *Comus*.[2] The editor Thomas Warton was a passionate defender of Milton's earlier verse and includes elaborate notes on the poetry, together with English translations of the

Latin verse. Most interesting for us is his assertion that Milton's earlier poetry has been neglected; this is the reason that he puts forth 'Lycidas', 'L'Allegro' and 'Il Penseroso', and *Comus* first, for in the eighteenth century they had become widely known in musical settings rather than in their own right.[3] The practice of placing the best-known shorter poems first continues into the nineteenth century. In the third volume of his Milton edition, William Pickering organizes the shorter poems according to popularity, with *Samson Agonistes* first, then *Comus*, 'Lycidas', 'L'Allegro' and 'Il Penseroso', 'Arcades', and finally the miscellaneous poems in chronological order.[4]

By the twentieth century the norm for organizing Milton's poetry is by date of composition. Only a few modern editions present Milton's English poems and *Poemata* in the order of Milton's 1645 volume—principally, John Leonard's Penguin edition, Roy Flannagan's Riverside edition, and my own 2009 Blackwell edition.[5] In 1951, however, Brooks and Hardy published an edition of the 1645 English poems with accompanying essays which argued for reading the English poems in their original setting.[6] Nevertheless, chronological order remained the norm for most modern editions, including Merritt Hughes's *Complete Poems and Major Prose*, John Carey's *Complete Shorter Poems*, and *The Complete Poetry and Essential Prose*, edited by William Kerrigan, John Rumrich, and Stephen Fallon. In these editions and many others, the poems are arranged in an approximated order of composition with the English and Latin, usually mixed together.[7]

Although there is some argument for reading the shorter poems in appropriate chronological order, to do so is to miss the experience that Milton specifically intended when he designed his editions in 1645 and 1673. Thus, there are compelling reasons for following his order—for reading the English poems of the first volume in the order in which Milton arranged them and correspondingly, when coming to the *Poemata* as the second part of this double book, to observe not only their arrangement, but how the second volume works as a complement and contrast to the first. In each volume Milton carefully chooses a signature poem—the Nativity Ode and Elegy I to Charles Diodati respectively—and then arranges the poems following in ascending order. He concludes both English and Latin volumes respectively with his pastoral laments—'Lycidas' and *Epitaphium Damonis* as the penultimate and ultimate poems, thus providing a complementary ending for each volume. The English and Latin volumes are designed as both contrasting and complementary experiences. To read the 1645 volume in Milton's arrangement is a quite different experience from reading it in Tonson's 1695 arrangement, where the reader would come first on 'Lycidas', the twin poems, and *A Maske*, and then experience the other poems in descending order almost as afterthoughts.

Although Milton did not arrange the 1645 *Poems* in exact chronological order, he did place early poems in the first half of each volume and the most recent poems toward the end of each book. However, clearly his principal intent was to create something like a cumulative experience for the reader. Each poem or group of poems is affected by what has come before and prepares for what follows. Moreover, the *Poemata* function to complement or to contrast with the English poems, so as to produce a unique sort of symmetry in the double book. Indeed Milton has given us some clues on how to read the 1645 *Poems* in *Ad Joannem Rousium*, the Latin ode composed for John Rouse, the librarian of the Bodleian, and dispatched with a volume of the book to replace one lost in transit. In the ode he begins by telling Rouse that the book is a twin volume, both joined together with a single binding but separated with its double title pages. It is a young book (*juvenilis*) and with this word he is remarking not only upon the number of juvenilia composed in his teens and early twenties that he has included in it but also on the attitudes of a confessedly young poet just starting out. He also gives special attention to the sense of play within the volume, a sportiveness deliberately indulged. He has composed the poems, he tells Rouse, with a meticulous, but unlaboured elegance and with a carefree joy, his foot barely touching the ground. He gives equal value to native English and Latin verse, referring thus to the languages of the poems—English, Italian, Latin, and Greek—and to the locales in which he composed them—the English and the Ausonian or Italian fields.

Milton's comment on the playfulness of the book would certainly apply to poems such as 'L'Allegro' and 'Il Penseroso' and some of the sportive elegies, particularly those addressed to Charles Diodati. But it would hardly seem to describe the *funera* of the *Poemata* or serious odes such as the Nativity Ode or the laments for the Marchioness of Winchester or for Edward King. Indeed, in the double book the sportfulness of Latin Elegy I is balanced by the solemnity of the Nativity Ode, as though Milton were deliberately trying to show off different sides of his poetic persona in the poems that begin both volumes. Both poems function as introductory pieces for their volumes. Also both come chronologically at important moments in the poet's life, Elegy I in spring 1626 when he was either on vacation or in rustication from Cambridge University, or possibly a year later when he was in London taking part in business transactions arranged by his father. The Nativity Ode was composed in December 1629 at Christmastide.[8] In the elegy to Diodati, he adopts a distinctly Ovidian tone and persona, putting forth literary tastes that range from Roman comedy to Greek tragedy and also expressing preference for British girls over those Latin beauties who might have graced Pompey's colonnade. In the Nativity Ode the ranging poetic personality of Elegy I is replaced by a poet who has chosen a serious path—to lay his poetic offering at Christ's feet and to claim his title as a divine poet—one who, as he states in Elegy VI, has decided to sing of heaven and hell with a voice and vocation devoted only to God.[9] The dichotomy between the poet of the English poems and the *Poemata* is not fully realized throughout the respective books, for there is sportiveness in the English poems and visions of heaven and hell in the Latin works. However, it is interesting that Milton chooses in the respective books to introduce himself to his readers in contrasting ways. Furthermore, no matter how earnestly Tonson has put it forward, 'Lycidas' is simply not an introductory piece, as the Nativity Ode and Elegy I are. Milton chose more wisely than did the editors who follow him.

Assuredly both the English book and the *Poemata* are miscellaneous collections, each in its own right. But in each Milton approaches their miscellaneousness in a different way. In the *Poems*, he is intent to support the genre of the Nativity Ode by placing serious poems after it. Thus immediately following are two psalm translations probably completed at St Paul's School, which separate 'The Passion' from the Nativity Ode. Had 'The Passion' been the successful poem Milton had hoped for, it might have followed directly after the Nativity Ode. However, as C. W. R. D. Moseley has pointed out, the placement of the two early psalm translations here has significance in 1645 in the wake of the victory of parliamentarian forces at Naseby.[10] As I have argued, the dismissal of the pagan gods in the Nativity Ode signalled Milton's desire to purge the English Church of idolatry, which, as he clearly notes in the headnote to 'Lycidas' has been accomplished with the fall of the corrupted clergy earlier at their height.[11] Psalms 114 and 136 are psalms of deliverance that rejoice at Israel's escape from Egypt and its deliverance into Canaan. The placement of these psalms immediately after the rout of the pagan gods in the Nativity Ode could hardly have failed to have special resonance among puritans in 1645, as

Milton would have well known. The first eight poems of the 1645 volume are all on religious themes; Milton places after 'The Passion' three successful mini-odes composed about three years after it—'On Time', 'Upon the Circumcision', and 'At a Solemn Music'.[12] Just as these three odes belong together in our reading sequence, they serve both as contrasts and complements to the Nativity Ode. Like the Nativity Ode, these brief odes have apocalyptic overtones and depict present time in relation to eternal time that stretches from the Creation to the Last Judgement. 'On the Circumcision' treats, like the Nativity Ode and 'The Passion', an event in the liturgical calendar, and it might have been intended with them as part of a projected sequence on liturgical events. Music is important in these odes, sounding forth in the Nativity Ode with joy and called upon in 'The Passion' and 'On the Circumcision' to mourn. 'At a Solemn Music' invokes the Sirens, Voice, and Verse, as personifications of sacred vocal music and poetry, and is set in antiphonal form with the second part responding to the first. Milton has placed these three odes after the Nativity Ode and 'The Passion' to reinforce the resemblance between their themes, and he placed 'At a Solemn Music' last of the three as the most joyous affirmation of its religious theme. The first section of the English poems comes to a climax with a final ode, the 'Epitaph on the Death of the Marchioness of Winchester', which presents the Marchioness as a 'new-welcomed saint' crowned in heaven.[13] With the two short pieces—'On May Morning' and 'On Shakespeare'—we completely change pace as we are led into a group that climaxes with 'L'Allegro' and 'Il Penseroso'. But more of that later. When Milton decided in 1673 to publish 'On the Death of a Fair Infant' in the second edition of his 1645 collection, he specified that it should appear in this early group that culminates with the epitaph for the Marchioness. Both poems share the theme of early death and employ as a figure the blossom untimely plucked. Its placement further indicates that Milton cared about the order of his poems.

The Latin volume—*Poemata*—works in a slightly different way from the English volume, for it is clearly divided into two books—*Elegiarum Liber* and *Sylvarum Liber*. On the one hand, the division is dictated by its different metrical types. The sequence of elegies and epigrams of the *Elegiarum Liber* is grouped together because they are all composed in elegiac couplets. The *Sylvarum Liber* contains poems of diverse metres—hexameters, stanzas, iambics, and scanzons. On the other hand, the two books are divided by theme. The seven elegies of *Elegiarum Liber* are of three types—two *funera*, three personal epistles, and two genre pieces on the coming of spring and on a visitation by Cupid.[14] The epigrams that conclude the first book are contrasted by theme and subject. The first four epigrams are early pieces written in 1625–6 on the subject of the Gunpowder Plot; the second three are a mature trilogy, honouring the Italian singer Leonora Baroni whom Milton heard in Rome in 1638–9.

Although the elegies of *Elegiarum Liber* fall into different types, in all we hear the distinctive voice of the young poet, introduced to us in his opening elegy to Charles Diodati. It is for us an unusually personal voice that complains of the harshness of a tutor, unfolds his delight in books, and expresses a warmth of personal friendship. Friendship is the theme of several of the elegies. Elegy VI is a second poetic epistle to Charles Diodati and Elegy IV a poetic epistle to his former tutor, Thomas Young, who was then living in Hamburg.[15] While the themes of the Latin poems appear in the English poems, few of the English poems—perhaps only the sonnets—possess the personal voice that we hear throughout the Latin corpus. Even though 'L'Allegro' and 'Il Penseroso' celebrate Milton's love of books and describe Tragedy and Comedy as admired genres, Milton does not celebrate them personally as he does in Elegy I, calling books his very life (*Et totum rapiunt me mea vita libri*—'and books, my life, possess me wholly').[16] In the twin poems comedy is used to characterize the cheerful man, tragedy the pensive man. They are not as they are in Elegy I the tastes of a single young man, our poet, exiled from studies in Cambridge.

It is almost as though Milton at this stage at least felt easier unlocking his heart in Latin, and it is perhaps for this reason that he composed the personal poems such as the elegies, as well as *Ad Patrem* and *Epitaphium Damonis*, in Latin rather than in English. Only in Sonnets 1 and 7 and in the Italian sonnets of the first volume do we hear the voice of the young poet who so often in the *Poemata* complains in Latin. However, the funeral pieces constitute one link between *Elegiarum Liber*, the *Sylvarum Liber*, and the English poems, several of which are placed strategically early in each volume. The epitaph for Jane Paulet, the Marchioness of Winchester, appears early in the English poems and is a formal poem that expresses regret for her early death, but refrains from personal expressions of grief. Even the Marchioness's translation to heaven is effected with restraint, as she sits with Rachel like a bright saint high in glory. In contrast, both the *funera* for the Bishops of Winchester and of

Ely begin with elegiac tears and end with exaltation. Though we may question whether the young Milton felt real grief for either bishop's death, in 1626 he writes in the first person to express sorrow, describing how he dissolves into tears at the news of each death, particularly since the death of Ely came so soon after Winchester's. Although not without classical underpinnings these are Christian poems that form a contrast with the opening sequence of religious poems found in the English volume. Both excoriate Death as a cruel goddess; both conclude with visions of the bishops being translated to an Elysium-like heaven. Milton certainly learned something from these early *funera*, for in both 'Lycidas' and *Epitaphium Damonis* he refrains from denouncing the goddess Death, directing his sorrow and anger at other targets. However, these early elegies build, as do later 'Lycidas' and *Epitaphium Damonis*, toward ecstatic visions of heaven, and thus provide a link between the beginning and end of Milton's *Poemata*, as well as that of his English book.

The two Hobson epitaphs follow not long after the epitaph for the Marchioness of Winchester, the latter's serious figures contrasting with the puns of the former. However, there is nothing else quite like the Hobson poems in the English volume.[17] We must turn to the *Poemata* to find *funera* that combine regret for a death with a jocular attitude toward death. Elegy II for the Beadle of Cambridge University and the iambic verses for the physician John Gostlin rely, as do the Hobson poems, on the departed men's profession for the relentless punning that makes up most of all four poems. Just as Milton's verses on Hobson jest that Death has carried away the carrier and laid him in a slough, the elegy for the Beadle Richard Ridding jests that Death proves a more forceful Beadle than the Cambridge official, and the verses for Gostlin suggest that Death, having been cheated of so many victims, gained through the physician's death, a sense of satisfaction. Milton decorates both Latin poems with classical references, the first to heralds in antiquity from Mercury to Eurybates and the second to famous surgeons of antiquity, who like Gostlin, finally fell prey to Death. The wit that characterizes the *funera* of the *Poemata* and epitaphs on Hobson in the English poems is quite different from the *jeux d'esprit* of the twin odes 'L'Allegro' and 'Il Penseroso' that immediately follow the twin Hobson poems in the English volume. In neither ode does Milton indulge the outrageous puns of the Hobson poems.

The dominant poetic form in the English book is the ode, but Milton rings the changes on this poetic form, producing both the brief odic salute to flowery May, as well as the solemn Nativity Ode, the lamenting ode or monody 'Lycidas', and the joyous twin odes. Probably 'L'Allegro' and 'Il Penseroso' with their elaborate invocations of Euphrosyne and the muse-like Melancholy are, as I have argued, the closest thing Milton composed to the classical hymn to the deity.[18] Of course, the odes actually concern not the twin goddesses but their devotees, the happy and the thoughtful man. Milton places these odes at the centre of his first volume, emphasizing not only their contrasts and counterparts with one another, but also the contrasts with the poems that precede and follow them. They face in opposite directions. 'L'Allegro' turns away from the serious religious poems of the first part of the volume to sudden joy. In a similar way in the *Poemata*, Elegy V on the coming of spring uplifts the mood after the funeral poems and the serious epistle to Thomas Young. 'Il Penseroso' faces in the opposite direction and after its solemnity we have the collection of sonnets that turns the mood from the studious cloister and solitary hermitage to the only set of poems in the first book where the poet engages with other persons and unfolds his mind and heart as he does in the *Poemata*. In the Italian sonnets he speaks as a lover for the only time, but one, in his entire poetic corpus, telling how he is entranced not by the English girls he viewed in Elegy I in the fields outside the city or by the girl in Elegy VII glimpsed briefly, then lost, but by a dark-haired, dark-eyed Italian beauty. Is it not strange that the young Milton can only dally with the opposite sex in a foreign language? But then, as he confesses, Italian is the language of love. Sonnets 9 and 10, to a virtuous young woman and to Lady Margaret Ley, are addressed to women, to be sure, but with a formal tone. As such, they contrast with the familiar tone Milton employs in the *Poemata* for the verse to Diodati, Young, or for that matter to his Italian acquaintances. The epigrams for Leonora Baroni placed at the end of the *Elegiarum Liber* balance in some way these sonnets to women in *Poems*, for they too have a formal air. We might almost argue that it is vocal music rather than the singer herself that inspired the epigrams. The epigrams express, as Milton had in 'At a Solemn Music', how Leonora, like the twin-borne Sirens, possesses in her voice the very essence of the heavenly third mind and brings down to earth that music of the spheres, so often alluded to in the English poems.

Aside from the Italian sonnets, Sonnets 7 and 8 are the only really intimate poems that Milton includes in the English poems. However, unlike Elegies I and VI, in which Milton confides his poetic aspirations to his friend Diodati, Milton speaks to himself in Sonnet 7, 'How soon hath time'. He regrets that he has not yet attained the accomplishment as a poet that should attend maturity and at the same time determines to devote himself 'To that same lot, however mean or high, / Toward which Time leads me, and the will of Heav'n' (11–12). Sonnet 8, composed when Charles's army threatened the city of London, expresses a different kind of confidence in the poetic vocation, less personal, but still idealistic, that poetry (as two classical allusions illustrate) has a power to transcend politics.

The personal poems of the *Sylvarum Liber* employ a markedly different voice from the elegies to Diodati and Young in the *Elegiarum Liber*. They differ from the jocular epistle to a friend or the obsequious letter to a former tutor with its apologetic starts and stops, and are the assured and urbane addresses to poetic peers met during the Italian journey. Milton had matured as a Latin poet in the ten or so years following these early elegies. He experiments with scanzons in his verses to Salzilli and exchanges the elegiac couplets of the first book for the hexameters he uses for the final poems of the *Sylvae*. Prefacing, as it were, the poems composed in Italy is the hexameter poem to his father, which Milton places strategically to introduce this final group of Latin poems.[19] Composed probably not long before his departure for Italy, *Ad Patrem* is as close as Milton ever came to an apology for poetry, for in it, while thanking his father for his education and his father's paternal indulgences, he passionately defends poetry as a vocation. Apollo is the ruling deity of the poem, as he is also in the verses to Salzilli and Manso. In an affectionate gesture to his father's accomplishments as a musician, Milton wittily proposes that father and son have divided the god between them. But Milton's chief concern in this poem, and what links it to the poems to Manso and to his dead friend Diodati, is his projection of future achievement as a poet. He moves beyond that nervous anxiety of the sonnet on his twenty-third year and expresses in *Ad Patrem* the confidence that these verses to his father will survive, assuring his father's fame together with his own. It is a hope he voices even more confidently in the ode to John Rouse composed after the publication of the 1645 *Poems*, where he consigns his newly completed book to the Bodleian Library to reside beside the Greek and Latin classics.

These final Latin poems, composed in Italy or soon after his return to England, supply more specifically and in greater detail Milton's future plans as a poet. The scanzons to Salzilli and the hexameter poem to Manso, it is true, offer thanks for friendship and hospitality extended, but they do much more. Milton recalls in his poem to Salzilli that the Roman poet had in an epigram (actually published in the *Testimonia* prefaced to the *Poemata*) extravagantly praised Milton as the equal of Homer, Virgil, and Tasso. Moreover, in thanking Manso, patron of the poets Tasso and Marino, for his hospitality, Milton includes himself among those poets Manso had encouraged. More importantly Milton confides to Manso his plans to compose an English epic, praising the deeds of King Arthur. Although *Epitaphium Damonis* is primarily a pastoral lament for Milton's closest friend, Charles Diodati, it also affectionately remembers Manso and Milton's Florentine friends while confiding his plans, now to the dead Diodati, for undertaking the epic for the English people.

Not all the poems of the *Poemata* connect neatly with poems of the English book. The philosophical exercises—*Naturam Non Pati Senium* and *De Idea Platonica* and the Greek verses, *Philosophus ad Regem*—have no counterparts in English. Although Milton includes in the *Poemata* a Greek translation of Psalm 114, made many years after the English translation of this same psalm placed after the Nativity Ode, it is not placed in the Latin book so as to recall the earlier translation nor does it especially connect with the other Greek poem that follows it. Other poems in both books have no real counterparts. *In Quintum Novembris* has no true English opposite, and 'Arcades' and *A Maske* no Latin equivalents. However, *In Quintum Novembris*, the longest poem of the *Sylvarum Liber*, is connected with the gunpowder epigrams of *Elegiarum Liber*, Milton's shortest verse, composed probably at the same time as the mini-epic and on the same subject, the Guy Fawkes conspiracy of 1605.[20] Both possess a mordant wit and openly ridicule the Pope and the Gunpowder conspirators. Their wit might be compared with the ridiculing scorn that Milton employs in his prose tracts to respond to the attacks of his enemies, but is nothing like the clever wit of the Hobson poems or the Latin *funera*. Even so, the epigrams stand apart from *In Quintum Novembris*, for the latter is the only long narrative piece of the 1645 collection and is Milton's earliest attempt at the hexameter verse that he uses more successfully in the final poems of *Sylvarum Liber*.

However, the final poem of the *Poemata*, *Epitaphium Damonis*, and 'Lycidas', the penultimate poem of the English volume, as has been long recognized, are inextricably connected and must surely have been placed in their respective volumes in their climactic position with each in mind of the other.[21] In chronological terms, *Epitaphium Damonis* is, except for the final three sonnets, the latest composed poem of the entire book and one of the few that was published before its appearance in the 1645 volume.[22] Therefore, we ought to look on it, not just as a contrast to 'Lycidas' but as a kind of follow-up or sequel, for in it Milton takes the lament for a friend in quite a different direction than he had in the previous poem. True, of course, both poems are pastorals and both exploit the generic characteristics of the pastoral tradition, some the same, and some quite different. The uncouth swain of 'Lycidas' is never named or indeed directly connected with Milton himself but Thyrsis in the later poem is named and clearly identified as Milton in the opening frame of the eclogue. Nor does Thyrsis, long before the climactic passage that places Damon under the auspices of the bacchic Sion, ever doubt that Damon is in heaven. However, in 'Lycidas' it takes the whole long poem for the shepherd-swain to rescue Lycidas from the whelming tide and resurrect him in heaven at the wedding feast of the Lamb. Moreover, in 'Lycidas' the shepherd speaks for the community, but in *Epitaphium Damonid* for himself. In the first he says, 'Who would not sing for Lycidas?' (10) but in the second 'What will become of me?' (*At mihi quid tandem fiet modo?* [37]). So what I am suggesting is that Milton expects us to move on from the earlier monody and by placing *Epitaphium Damonis* last of the Latin poems, he is making a statement not just for the *Poemata* but for the entire volume. The thyrsus of Sion belongs not just to Damon, but also to those, who may be consoled, as the poet is, in personal grief and in expectation of heavenly joy.

That leaves the question of Milton's *A Maske Presented at Ludlow Castle* placed, clearly out of its order of composition, as the final work of the English volume. The usual explanation for its position in the volume is simple: printers' convention placed masques last in a miscellany of collected poetry. But that explanation is not good enough. Certainly, in 1695 in his reprint of the 1645 *Poems*, Tonson had no such compunction and freely moved *A Maske* to the beginning of the volume. In my view, however, Milton had a definite design in positioning his masque last. As Moseley has commented, *A Maske* is, if not the final composition of the volume, the most comprehensive and ties together the separate pieces of that volume. In 1645 it would resonate, as 'Lycidas' does, with political and religious implications that in the 1634 performance or even in its 1637 printing would not have been immediately apparent. Further, *A Maske* realizes the fullest conceptual expression up to that time of Milton's notions of virtue, human suffering and trial, God's providence, and the interactions of the divine and human. Steadily throughout the English book from the Nativity Ode to the *Maske*, Milton arranges poems to build to this climax.

First of all, the Attendant Spirit is a development of the Genius of 'Arcades', but in *A Maske*, he is not a spirit who descends from the skies to praise a lady, but is the protector of the virtuous woman. Throughout the volume, however, Milton has included figures like the Attendant Spirit, who link heaven and earth. Such, for example, are the sphere-born sirens of 'At a Solemn Musick'. Through such figures connected with music or through music itself, Milton often suggests that corrupt earth will be purged and rejoin heaven, an idea first expressed in the Nativity Ode but lastly also at the end of *A Maske*. The Lady's singing suggests even to Comus divine ravishment, and she herself invokes Echo as the 'Daughter of the Sphear' to be translated to the skies. Like the lady of the Italian sonnets, the Lady of *A Maske* 'could steer / the weary moon down from the mid-hemisphere' (Sonnet 4, 11–12). These ladies anticipate Sabrina, another siren voice, and also are connected with another singer, Leonora Baroni. In the Latin epigrams of the *Poemata* Leonora brought down with her singing the very essence of heaven's third intelligence. Throughout these early poems music and sphere-born singers establish for Milton the connection between heaven and earth.

Other works in the volume anticipate *A Maske* in different ways. Comus as an anti-masque figure is both the opposite of Milton's Attendant Spirit and the opposite of Milton's Mirth. Comus's invitation to 'Joy, and Feast, / Midnight shout, and revelry, / Tipsie dance and Jollity' (102–4) is the inverse of Mirth's invitation to true joy—'Jest and youthful Jollity, / Quips and Cranks, and wanton Wiles, / Nods, and Becks, and Wreathed Smiles' (26–8). Mirth's 'unreproved pleasures free' (40) are quite different from 'the pleasures' Comus urges the Lady to be wise and taste. The Lady herself resembles the 'Virgin wise and pure', the idealized but unidentified addressee of Milton's ninth sonnet.

Finally, Milton has strategically placed 'Lycidas' before *A Maske*, even though it was written later, to allow both the masque and the ode to pose similar questions. The long Neoplatonic discussion of the Brothers about the dangers to Virtue has correspondence to the swain's angry indictment of the forces of nature or heaven that permitted poets such as Lycidas and Orpheus to perish. The swain's brief temptation to 'sport with *Amaryllis* in the shade, / Or with the tangles of *Neaera's* hair' (68–9) has correspondence to Comus's urging to 'mutual and partak'n bliss' (741). Comus is not only a dissolute courtier, but the offspring of Circe—from whom Milton himself flees at the end of Elegy I. Circe was a figure often associated with the Whore of Babylon and may here embody corrupt religion and the dangers of Catholicism, subjects found in 'Lycidas'. No two-handed engine crushes Comus, but he is chased from the scene and the Lady rescued. *A Maske* is a more optimistic work than 'Lycidas'. True, 'Lycidas' bids the woful shepherds to weep no more and assures us that Lycidas in heaven hears 'the unexpressive nuptiall Song, / In the blest King-doms meek of joy and love' (176–7). But *A Maske* concludes with a joyful celebration, returning the children to safety and bestowing on them 'crown[s] of deathless Praise' and rejoicing at their triumph 'o're sensual Folly, and Intemperance' (973–5). Rewards in heaven await them, but it is enough, Milton seems to say, to rejoice now in the reward of virtue on earth. The volume that began with the descent of the Christ child into the 'darksom House of mortal Clay' (Nativity Ode 14) ends with the ascent of the Attendant Spirit. Like Christ he had taken on 'the rank vapours of this Sin-worn mould' (17) as he descended, but he re-ascends with joy to the 'broad fields of the sky' (979). His final advice is fitting as a recurrent theme of this volume—'Love vertue', which 'can teach ye how to clime / Higher then the Spheary chime' (1019–21). Although *Paradise Lost, Paradise Regained,* and *Samson Agonistes* would take him further, the *Maske* in 1645 was the fullest moral and spiritual manifesto of the young Milton. As the Latin epigraph of the title page portends—'Bind my forehead with foxglove, lest evil tongues harm the future bard'—Milton was determined with the publication of the 1645 *Poems* to assume the role of England's future bard.

Notes

1. See *Poems upon Several Occasions* (1695).
2. See *Poems upon Several Occasions: English, Italian, Latin*, ed. Thomas Warton (1785).
3. The most popular eighteenth-century music settings of Milton's verse were by Thomas Arne and George Frideric Handel. Thomas Arne composed the music for *Comus* to an English libretto by John Dalton based upon Milton's *A Maske Presented at Ludlow Castle*. The work premiered at the Theatre Royal, Drury Lane in London on 4 March 1738. In 1740 George Frideric Handel composed music for 'L'Allegro' and 'Il Penseroso' to texts adapted by Charles Jennens, who added a third part, 'Il Moderato'.
4. See Volume 3 of *The Poetical Works of John Milton*, ed. William Pickering, 3 vols. (1885).

5. See *John Milton: The Complete Poems*, ed. John Leonard (1998). Leonard, however, separates the English poems from the *Poemata*, which are placed after *Samson Agonistes*. In Roy Flannagan's *Riverside Milton* (Boston, Mass., 1998), the 1645 *Poems*, both English and Latin, appear as a unit, as they also do in *Complete Shorter Poems*, ed. Stella P. Revard (Oxford, 2009). *John Milton*, ed. Stephen Orgel and Jonathan Goldberg (Oxford, 1990) also prints the 1645 English poems as a unity. The Latin and Greek poems, however, though following, only are printed in excerpt, with several important Latin poems omitted. *Milton: The Complete English Poems*, ed. Gordon Campbell (1990) prints Milton's English poems in the 1673 order. *The Poetical Works of John Milton*, ed. Helen Darbishire, 2 vols. (Oxford, 1952–5) chooses the 1673 order for both English and Latin poems. *The Student's Milton*, ed. Frank A. Patterson (New York, 1933) also chooses the 1673 order, with translations of the Latin and Greek poems printed first, with the Latin texts following.

6. See Cleanth Brooks and John Edward Hardy, *Poems of Mr. John Milton, The 1645 Edition with Essays in Analysis* (New York, 1951). See especially the essay, 'The Progress and Form of the Early Career', which speculates on Milton's reasons for omitting the 'Fair Infant' poem and the 'Vacation Exercise' from the 1645 volume.

7. See *John Milton: Complete Poems and Major Prose*, ed. Merritt Y. Hughes (New York, 1957); *Milton: Complete Shorter Poems*, ed. John Carey, 2nd edn. (New York, 1997); *The Complete Poetry and Essential Prose*, ed. William Kerrigan, John Rumrich, and Stephen M. Fallon (New York, 2007). Other editions that organize the poetry according to order of composition include *The Poetical Works of John Milton*, ed. William Aldus Wright (1903)—Wright places the Latin poems after *Samson Agonistes*; *The Complete Poetry of John Milton*, ed. John Shawcross (New York, rev. edn., 1971); *The Portable Milton*, ed. Douglas Bush (New York, 1960); *Poems and Selected Prose*, ed. Marjorie Hope Nicolson (New York, 1962); *Poems*, ed. B. A. Wright (1956)—Wright prints only the English poems.

8. For the dating of Elegy I and the Nativity Ode, see Campbell and Corns, 32, 38, 50; Lewalski, *Life*, 32, 38, 46. For additional commentary on Elegy I see the essays in this volume by Cedric Brown, Sarah Knight, and Edward Jones.

9. Elegy VI, like Elegy I addressed to Charles Diodati, was composed in either late December 1629 or possibly early January 1630. See Campbell and Corns, 50–1; Lewalski, *Life*, 37–8.

10. C. W. R. D. Moseley, *The Poetic Birth: Milton's Poems of 1645* (Aldershot, 1991). Moseley pays attention throughout his book to the way in which Milton has organized the collection.

11. See Stella P. Revard, 'Apollo and Christ in the Seventeenth-Century Religious Lyric', in John Roberts (ed.), *New Perspectives on the Seventeenth-Century English Religious Lyric* (Columbia, Mo., 1994), 143–67, reworked in *Milton and the Tangles of Neaera's Hair: The Making of the 1645 'Poems'* (Columbia, Mo., 1997).

12. Lewalski connects these three brief odes to the Nativity Ode and 'The Passion' and assigns them to early 1633 (*Life*, 62); Campbell and Corns place them in late 1632 and early 1633 (75). Drafts for the three odes appear in the Trinity College

Manuscript after the draft of 'Arcades', which would also point to 1632–3 as the date of composition.

13. Milton's 'Epitaph on the Death of the Marchioness of Winchester' was probably composed not long after the Marchioness's death in April 1631, thus before the three odes that precede it. See Lewalski, *Life*, 42.

14. The seven elegies are all youthful compositions, dating from 1626 to 1629–30. See Lewalski, *Life*, 21–32; Campbell and Corns, 32–9.

15. Elegy IV was probably written in March 1627. Young, Milton's former tutor, was serving as a chaplain to a community of English merchants in Hamburg. Milton models the letter on Ovid's *Tristia* 3 and addresses Young as though he were, like Ovid, an exile and was experiencing oppression because of his puritan views. See Lewalski, *Life*, 25–6; Campbell and Corns, 37–8.

16. Quotations of Milton's poetry are from *Complete Shorter Poems*, ed. Revard.

17. That these poems circulated in manuscript could explain in part their different flavor. See Peter Beal, 'Milton', in *Index of English Literary Manuscripts, 1625–1700*, vol. 2, part 2 (1987–93), 86, 91.

18. See Stella P. Revard, ' "L'Allegro" and "Il Penseroso": Classical Tradition and Renaissance Mythography', *PMLA*, 101 (1986), 338–50, reworked in *Milton and the Tangles of Neaera's Hair*.

19. *Ad Patrem* has been dated from 1631 to 1645. Barbara Lewalski dates it in late 1637 or early 1638 before Milton's departure for Italy (*Life*, 71–3). See also Campbell and Corns, 101–2.

20. *In Quintum Novembris* and the gunpowder epigrams are usually dated in 1626. See Lewalski, *Life*, 24–5; Campbell and Corns, 34–5.

21. Among the many essays that compare 'Lycidas' and *Epitaphium Damonis* see James H. Hanford, 'The Pastoral Elegy and Milton's "Lycidas"', *PMLA*, 25 (1910), 403–47; rpr. in C. A. Patrides (ed.), *Milton's 'Lycidas': The Tradition and the Poem* (New York, 1961); Fred J. Nichols, ' "Lycidas", *Epitaphium Damonis*, the Empty Dream, and the Failed Song', in J. Ijsewijn and E. Kessler (eds.), *Acta Conventus Neo-Latini Lovaniensis* (Leuven, 1973), 445–52.

22. *Epitaphium Damonis* was first printed in a private edition in 1640.

Part III

Early Vernacular Development

10

'Oh my simplicity': Revising Childhood in Milton's Ludlow *Maske*

Blaine Greteman

During the eighteenth and nineteenth century editors and audiences renamed Milton's *A Maske Presented at Ludlow Castle* for the figure they found most memorable—*Comus*—the glistering, romantic tempter. A member of the original audience on Michaelmas night 1634, seeking a similarly pithy encapsulation of his experience, probably would have chosen something like *Egertonis Stirpes* ('the branches of Egerton'), emphasizing that individual dramatic characters were less consequential than the way the masque showcased the lineage of Milton's patron, the first Earl of Bridgewater. *A Maske* gave the Earl's children an excuse to display their precociousness, fencing, singing, dancing, and debating as they made their way to their father's house to celebrate his public role as the Lord President of Wales. Whatever we think of the work's themes of chastity and providence, its critiques of the masque genre, or the broader court culture, this was the dominant imperative of the first performance—to show aristocratic children outstripping the expectations of their particular developmental stage. Because we continue to recast *A Maske* in terms of our own interests, the idea takes some getting used to, and partly for that reason many critics have bristled at or ignored William Riley Parker's suggestion that the performance was 'essentially a children's party'.[1] But while Parker may have misgauged the seriousness of this state occasion and its degree of sophistication, he was surely right that the children and their performance were central. For all the critical discussion about sex and scandal, faith and works, the Attendant Spirit introduces the masque's threat simply by saying that in the dark woods the children's 'tender age might suffer perill' (*BMS*, 63), and he concludes the action by returning to the parents 'three fayer branches of yor owne' and proclaiming that 'Heav'n hath timely tri'd their youth' (*BMS*, 928–38).[2]

Several critics, including Cedric Brown, William B. Hunter, and William Shullenberger, have accordingly traced the way the familial role and physical presence of the child actors inflects the masque's subject, aesthetics, and projection of gendered subjectivity.[3] But *A Maske*'s performance of childishness and precocity, which became central to Milton's own poetic development as it evolved through his lengthy revision process, remains surprisingly under-analysed.[4] What was 'timely' about the trials of youth in Milton's masque and his culture? The author, at age twenty-five, was legally adult, unlike the nine-, eleven-, and fifteen-year-old children who performed the masque. But he, too, still lived in his father's house, and for the next decade he staged a very similar sort of performance in his works—at age thirty-three, when he published *The Reason of Church-Government*, we find the solidly middle-aged writer still protesting his extreme youth, admitting that without divine assistance the work would be 'too difficult for my years' and invoking the same imagery of young shoots and buds that he used to describe the Egerton children to remind readers that he writes while 'green yeers are upon my head' (*CPW*, i. 749, 806). To make such claims obviously implies a fairly flexible notion of youth and a corresponding idea of full adulthood not as a physical or legal condition but as an earned, meritocratic achievement.[5] During the intervening period and for some time afterward, Milton's revisions of *A Maske* critically reshaped its concept of childhood along these lines, introducing serious new questions about the characters' agency, innocence, and ability to resist temptation. As he revisited the earlier versions of the masque, where passive but virtuous children are buffeted by outside forces, Milton developed the very different idea that the substance and voice of virtue arise only from temptation, trial, and resistance. As a text and a process of revision, *A Maske* both meditates on the possibility of independent voice and begins to enact that voice in a way that will indelibly mark the poet's later work. Shullenberger illuminates its mythic under-structure to argue that *A Maske* 'is not only representational but performative. It is not only *about* a young woman's passage from girlhood into womanhood; it ritually *accomplishes* that passage for a certain young woman.'[6] Its textual understructure shows that it served a similar formative function for a certain young author.

By examining Milton's revisionary process, we can profitably move past the critical debate over whether the masque is the work of a young radical or a still-conforming and essentially conservative young man of leisure—a debate that for generations has inflected and dominated discussions of everything from its form to those strangely suggestive 'gumms of glutenous heate' (TMS, 939). Admittedly, the debate has been one-sided, with the vast majority endorsing the view that *A Maske* is the work of a puritan reformer, while the occasional dissenting voice argues that Milton's work and its politics actually look very orthodox for the time.[7] In fact, both sides are right, although they are wrong to view the masque as a stable statement of Milton's reified ideology *c.*1633–4. As J. Martin Evans argues, 'the text of *Comus* is profoundly unstable. . . . [I]t seems to have been in a constant state of flux from the time it was first written down to the day it first appeared in print'.[8] S. E. Sprott documented this instability in his tri-text edition, and the precise stages of composition have been subsequently debated and refined.[9] These discussions, however, have had only a muted impact on criticism of *A Maske*, which still routinely conflates lines that first appeared in the 1645 text with a girl who took the stage in 1634 or that makes arguments about Milton's poetic development in 1634 using lines he almost certainly did not write—and perhaps could not even have conceived—until years later.[10] This essay uses Milton's extensive manuscript and print revisions of the masque to demonstrate its dynamic place in his poetry and thought, emphasizing that Milton's poetry was *radicalizing* before it was radical. I share certain assumptions with critics who, in recent years, have worked to embed *A Maske* in the network of collaborative relationships that produced it, rather than viewing it as the work of a young, independent genius.[11] At the same time, however, Milton clearly *is* a unique genius, and one who, for better or worse, constructs an image of himself as a singular, inspired author—not autonomous, because inspired by God, but not dependent on the assistance and approval of others, either. This is key to his ethical proof, and if Milton's self-representation as lone, inspired prophet is belied by the collaborative processes that his culture and his later blindness necessitated, it is also the struggle for singular voice within this framework that makes his poetry great.[12] In the revisions to *A Maske* we see that struggle play out.

I. Text and key revisions

Before I explain how Milton's revisions reshape *A Maske*'s conception of childhood and claim a voice for virtue, it will be necessary to discuss the order in which he made changes and to explain necessary caveats. The Trinity Manuscript contains the earliest extant text. At the head of the first page, Milton titled the work simply 'A maske' and dated it 1634. Presumably this is the date of composition in the notebook, just as the manuscript dates Milton's sonnet to Lawes 1645, a date borne out by certain conspicuous changes to Milton's hand.[13] Milton significantly reworks each of these texts in the TMS to such an extent that some believe the notebook contains Milton's foul papers, or his very earliest stages of revision. But while the TMS *Maske* records passages of intense revision and very tentative rewriting, it also consists of long passages that are almost completely unrevised except for word substitutions and the occasional reworked line. Such a state of the text implies that Milton copied his foul papers into the notebook, but not that those papers constituted a coherent version of the masque. Indeed Hunter suggests that the most extensive revisions in the TMS occur where Milton composed new material to join scenes and speeches he had already completed elsewhere.[14] After drafting a full version of *A Maske*, Milton made a set of revisions that consisted mostly of individual word changes.[15] The text at this point would have been copied out into a performance text, which is now lost. The Bridgewater Manuscript, now held at Bridgewater House in London, is not this performance text, as was once thought, but it seems to preserve a near relative of it.[16] A presentation copy with an elaborate title page and written throughout in a careful secretary hand, the BMS contains the closest text to that which was presented in 1634, and would have been produced soon or immediately thereafter.

BMS is very similar to the revised TMS, but it contains some conspicuous cuts, probably but not necessarily made either by Lawes or by Milton. The excised material includes a long speech by the Lady, at her most lost and vulnerable, where she begins to worry about the 'theevish night' that has stolen her brothers and then continues:

> this is [the] place as well as I may guesse
> whence even now the tumult of Loud mirth
> was rife & perfect in my listening eare
> yet nought but single darknesse doe I find[,]
> what might this be? a thousand fantasies
> begin to throng into my memorie
> of calling shaps, & beckning shadows dire
> and ayrie toungs *that lure night wanderers * that syllable mens nams
> on sands, & shoars, & desert wildernesses. (TMS, 224–32)

In the TMS, the Lady then has a vision of Faith, Hope, and Chastity, expresses her belief in divine providence, and begins to sing her song to Echo, whereas in the BMS, and presumably in performance, she moves much more directly from noting the absence of her brothers to hallowing them with her song.

Other key passages omitted from Bridgewater and examined in more detail below include Comus's famous and suggestive dissuasion from Virginity, which begins 'list Ladie, be not coy, nor be not cozen'd / with that same vaunted name virginity' and ends both by admiring the Lady's 'love-darting eyes' and 'tresses like the morne' and by warning 'you are but young yet' (TMS, 769–70, 785–7). Whether the lines were cut by Milton or a 'censor' out of concern for decorum or pacing is pure speculation, but we can say with more confidence that these all appear to be instances where the demands of performance shaped Milton's writing.

If the TMS was not originally Milton's working draft, it soon became one, as Milton returned to make revisions after the 1634 performance and before the 1637 printing. Some of the differences in the 1637 printed text merely restore lines cut for the performance and BMS—all of the passages cited above, for example, appear in 1637 as they do in the TMS. This alone would lend significant support to the argument that as Milton moves chronologically further from the performance he begins to extricate his text from the material and social conditions of its first production—even though the 1637 edition remains heavily embedded in those conditions, significantly lacking any authorial attribution to Milton but prominently featuring the names of the aristocratic performers and, on the title page, the name, rank, and position of their father.[17] But Milton also rewrites several passages and augments others around this time, evidently in preparation for the printed edition, substantially shifting the balance and emphases of some scenes. Among the most pronounced changes, Milton cancels the passage where the younger brother, in the BMS and performance, had worried that his sister 'soe fares as did forsaken *Proserpine* / when the bigg rowling flakes of pitchie clouds / and darkness wound her in' (BMS, 358–60). In place of these lines in the TMS, Milton pasted a leaf, now lost, evidently containing the language that appeared in the first printed edition and all subsequent versions, where the brother worries instead that his sister might be 'within the direfull graspe / Of Savage hunger, or of Savage heate' (*1637*, 374–5). Milton also adds to the debate between the Lady and Comus, so that she now claims both that Comus is incapable of apprehending the 'sage / And serious doctrine of Virginitie' and warns that her vocalization of this doctrine could move dumb things 'to sympathize, / And the brute Earth would lend her nerves, and shake, / Till all thy magick structures rear'd so high / Were shattere'd into heaps ore thy false head' (*1637*, 830–3). Finally, for the 1637 edition Milton rearranges the final scenes so that they reflect the TMS rather than the BMS order, taking away the brothers' incantatory role invoking Sabrina and putting all their lines in the mouth of the Attendant Spirit, who also has a much-expanded epilogue. This is not a complete list of changes— and Milton continued to revisit the TMS, with scribal assistance, to revise vocabulary, spelling, and punctuation until the final edition of his poems in 1673—but we will see that these revisions are some of the most profound, especially as they affect the masque's notion of childhood and its ceremonial function.

II. Occasion and afterlife

These changes establish that when Milton's *A Maske* was first performed it was a good deal more conventional in its adherence to typical seventeenth-century masque themes and form than the text most of us read today. We can start to see this right from the beginning of the BMS in the absolute innocence of the Lady and her lack of dramatic engagement with Comus, who in this early version cannot properly even be called her tempter. In this version, and presumably on stage in 1634, the Lady reluctantly follows the sound of 'riott and ill-manag'd merriment' (BMS, 203), although she is 'loathe' to meet the rustics she suspects of making that noise, because she needs directions to 'informe my unacquainted feete / in the blinde mazes of this tangled wood' (BMS, 211–12). She then immediately hallows her brothers with a lovely Echo song—the star turn for the young Alice Egerton. In this pared-down version, we could grant her song a kind of integrity and purity that was problematized in Milton's earlier draft and in his later versions, where the Lady begins her song only after dreamily noting that 'a thousand fantasies / Begin to throng into my memorie' (*1637*, 220–1). With those lines in place, her own song begins after she has proclaimed Comus's own orgiastic music 'rife, and perfect in my listening ear' (*1637*, 218), a phrasing that makes the Lady seem profoundly open to the night world she has entered, or that has begun to enter her. Even in later versions she is of course horrified by the uncouth revelry she hears, but she becomes somehow permeable, an indiscrete being whose memory is thronged by the 'calling shapes, and beckning shadows dire, / And ayrie tongues, that syllable mens names / On Sands, and Shoars' (*1637*, 222–4). The sense that Comus has somehow already got inside the Lady's head—that those seductive tongues belong to him—is especially pronounced if we recall that his opening recitative has used near-identical language to invoke the supernatural creatures that haunt 'the tawny sands and shelves' (*1637*, 130) while indicating his own airy nature 'of purer fire' (*1637*, 124).

With such allurement rife in her ear, the Lady's Echo song sounds uncomfortably like an echo of Comus himself, her imagery adulterated by his own powerful imaginative world: his opening recitative pictures 'Wood-nymphs' (*1637*, 133) while the Lady's song responds by invoking 'the sweetest Nymphe' Echo (*1637*, 246); he speaks of the 'dimpled brooke & fountain brim' (*1637*, 148) while she recalls the brim or 'margent' of the Meander (*1637*, 231); both Lady and tempter imagine a landscape romantically studded with caves and flowers. But none of this is an issue in the BMS. Here, where she launches more directly into her song, it seems a little less like Comus has penetrated her psyche (and implicated her morally?) with the tongues that syllable men's names or even more provocatively 'lure' them, as Milton first wrote the line (TMS, 231–2). Without the voice of Comus thronging through her memory, in the performance version, we are more free to hear the Lady's Echo song as perfectly voiceless voice—a charmingly blank or innocent display of vocal virtuosity:

> Sweete Echo, Sweetest nymphe that liv'st unseene
>   within thy ayrie shell
> by slowe Meanders margent greene
> and in the violett imbroderd vale
>   where the love-torne[18] nightingale
> nightly to thee her sad song mourneth well.
>
>   (BMS, 229–34)

Echo was an 'unsubstantial' voice of pure reflexivity, as George Sandys described her in his translation of Ovid's *Metamorphosis*, like 'the face reflected from one glasse to another, melting by degrees'.[19] This 'daughter of aire and tongue', as the Latin poet Ausonius had described her in a poem that Sandys translates, was a familiar figure for childhood and youth because of her capacity for purely mimetic, unmotivated speech, and in this way the Lady's invocation of Echo is a perfect opportunity to display the particular type of precocity demanded by the original performance.[20] Named 'The Lady' (the fair-skinned author's own nickname at Cambridge), Alice Egerton was at age fifteen the oldest of the young performers, and critics have called her 'a marriageable adult'.[21] But she would remain a legal and conceptual infant until age twenty-one—literally 'voiceless', from the Latin *infans*. Before age sixteen she was marriageable only with her father's consent and would have been recognized in the law by the appropriately ambiguous term 'woman child', while her nine- and eleven-year-old brothers were even less ambiguously situated in early childhood.[22]

To speak at this stage was, *de facto*, to echo the speech of others, and this gave the mythological figure a certain pedagogical relevance. As the minister William Thomas explained, 'the readiest way to make any Instruction take, propounds the question, and puts the Child to answer it, as the Eccho doth the Voyce'.[23] Various critics have noted that the Lady receives no answer to her Echo song, as was typical of the form, and have understood this as emphasizing her need for self-reliance or the danger of solipsism.[24] But the original audience would have expected the Lady herself to function as a kind of echo of the filial authority in which her education had immersed her. As she imagines Echo holding 'a Counterpointe to all heav'ns harmonies' as she concluded her song, the Lady's own harmonies, composed by her tutor, testify to this authority's shaping power (BMS, 242). Such a reading is foregrounded by the context of a masque featuring a powerful man's children and their tutor, making their way to their father's house, performed on a night liturgically devoted to exemplary ideas of childhood.

The Gospel for Michaelmas, the day *A Maske* was performed, was Matthew 18:1–10, in which Christ instructs his disciples to 'become as little children' to 'enter into the kingdom of heaven', and warns that 'whoso shall offend one of these little ones which believe in me, it were better for him that a millstone were hanged about his neck, and that he were drowned in the depth of the sea'.[25] As the Dean of Canterbury John Boys explained in his explication of the Michaelmas Gospel, becoming like children did not mean 'eating dirt and paddling in the mire' or emulating all the other 'ignorant' and 'inconstant' habits of children, but rather being 'chast in body, pure in mind' and utterly obedient—a lesson he believes '*state criticks*' would also do well to follow.[26] Such obedience meant becoming a kind of echo, emulating the type of reflective figure who could 'hold a Counterpointe' in the technical musical sense where a voice's melody might seem independent but was really interdependent, moving in conjunction with a dominant, higher strain (BMS, 242). This filial quietism (with corresponding political application) was endorsed widely across the theological spectrum, from the very orthodox John Boys to the nonconformist Thomas Watson, who matriculated at Cambridge three years after Milton took his MA and who perhaps put the issue most succinctly: 'A Child should be the Parents *Eccho*: When the Father speaks, the Child should Eccho back Obedience.'[27]

Despite the changes Milton had made for the 1637 edition, the printed text was itself framed as a similar sort of *mise en abyme* by Henry Lawes, in his dedication to Viscount Brackley, who played the Elder Brother:

This poem, which receiv'd its birth from your selfe, and others of your noble familie, and much honour from your own Person in the performance, now returns againe to make a finall dedication of it selfe to you. Although not openly acknowledg'd by the Author, yet it is a legitimate off-spring, so lovely, and so much desired, that the often copying of it hath tir'd my pen to give my severall friends satisfaction, and brought me to a necessitie of producing it to the publick view; and now to offer it up in all rightfull devotion to those faire hopes, and rare Endowments of your much-promising Youth, which give a full assurance, to all that know you, of a future excellence. Live sweet Lord to be the honour of your Name. (*1637*, sig. A2r–v)

Appropriately, in making a dedication to a fourteen-year-old boy, Lawes appears to have some difficulty attributing agency for the work. The youth seems to generate a poem that is also the product of larger familiar forces—forces that subsume the boy as he strives to become the honour of the name he has inherited. If the figure of the author recedes in this mirroring act, the presence of the father certainly does not.

Milton's revisions trouble and challenge these notions of childhood, but prior to a closer examination of them, it is worth highlighting how these notions were—quite literally—bound up with Milton's authorial anonymity in *A Maske*'s early versions. In the 1645 edition of his poems, Milton prefaced the masque with a letter from Henry Wotton. In the letter, Wotton praises the work, thanks Milton for sending him the 1637 edition, and then reveals that he has already read it without knowing the author: 'For the work it self, I had view'd som good while before, with singular delight, having receiv'd it from our common Friend Mr R. in the very close of the late R's Poems, Printed at *Oxford*, wherunto it was added (as I now suppose) that the Accessory might help out the 'Principal.'[28] Milton's anonymous work was apparently bound up with Thomas Randolph's *Poems with the Muses Looking-Glass: And Amyntas*, published in early 1638, at about the same time as *A Maske*. Randolph died young in 1635, but he matriculated one year before Milton, at Trinity College, Cambridge, and burned white hot for the next ten years, writing multiple plays and a royal entertainment, losing a finger in a bar fight (and promptly eulogizing the severed digit in a brilliantly witty poem), all while gaining a reputation as a fine Aristotelian scholar. In 1637 he remained a much more influential figure than Milton, and Ann Coiro has demonstrated the startling ways that Milton's work echoes Randolph's and shows the younger writer embedded in a mode of authorship that was collaborative, academic, and intimate in its coterie manuscript circulation.[29] It is easy to see why Coiro describes the echoes as 'uncanny' by looking at just one example from *The Jealous Lovers*, a play produced for King Charles at Cambridge while Milton was a student there.[30] When Randolph's heroine in the play finds herself trapped in a den of iniquity, she entreats

> Whatsoever goddess else protects
> Untouch'd virginity, shield me with your powers.
> To what a wilderness have my wandering steps
> Betray'd me![31]

As she continues to lament the 'strange fancies' that throng into her mind, the voice seems to belong to Milton's Lady with the phrases just slightly rearranged.[32] It would have been easy, in this regard, to mistake the work for Randolph's and bind it together, or simply to collect the works without regard to authorship for the way they exemplified a certain pastoral tragicomic style. I think we need to add to and slightly alter Coiro's assessment, however, by noting both that Randolph was a poet obsessed with the duties and obligations of youth and that here Milton begins to establish real differences from his predecessor.

Appropriately for someone who wrote primarily academic drama, one of Randolph's central interests in works like *The Muses Looking-Glasse* is the pedagogical function of drama and literature. In the theory of mimesis that the play sets forth, 'The soule sees her face / In Comedy', and Randolph illustrates this principle repeatedly as the player Roscius brings wayward characters onto stage and shows them his mirror so they can learn both which qualities they should avoid and which they should emulate.[33] The play's epilogue makes clear that its intended audience is the young: 'Gentle-youths', who 'we mean / Your selves unto your selves still to present.'[34] The whole trope draws on the idea not only that drama is mimetic, but that youths and children are too, and that they thus form more adult selves through a process of mirroring and reflection.[35] Young people on this view are essentially blank slates, and an exemplary child learns to reflect back the lessons of authority, as Randolph writes in one of the poems in the posthumous volume that was bound to Milton's masque:

> Honour thy Parents to prolong thine end,
> With them though for a truth doe not contend.
> Though all should truth defend, doe thou loose rather
> The truth a while, then loose their *Loves* for ever.[36]

Randolph does not seem to have had his tongue in cheek when he suggested that parents could rightly withhold their love from children who pointed out their errors. As a principle of obedience, this is identical to the unquestioning child that John Boys valorized in his explication of the Michaelmas Gospel. And like Boys, Randolph also readily draws a political analogy: 'Honour the King, as sonnes their Parents doe, / For he's thy Father, and thy Country's too.'[37]

For the Egerton children to succeed on Michaelmas night, 1634, they needed to be similarly blank, except for their capacity to echo back the lessons they had learned as they were 'nurst in princely love' (BMS, 57).[38]

Milton did not sacrifice any of the rich associations of youthful voice with Echo in 1637 when he restored the lines about 'ayrie tongues, that syllable mens names' (*1637*, 223), but the change does raise questions about who the Lady echoes and what kind of echoing might be included in the proper education of a warfaring Christian. This is a key part of the transition between *A Maske* as a performance text and as a 'Poem', as Henry Lawes calls it in his dedicatory letter (*1637*, 7). Taken on its own, admittedly, the restoration of these lines would not demonstrate a major rethinking of childhood and the path with adult voice. After all, this version of *A Maske* still ended up bound with Randolph's poems, anonymous and apparently complementary. And the lines were evidently in Milton's early draft by 1634 before being cut before the performance, so we cannot say that restoring them marks a radically altered political or pedagogical consciousness in 1637. Other revisions, however, show that at the same time Milton was recovering these lines he was discovering a new kind of story.

III. Hunger and heat

One of the most remarkable but least remarked revisions comes near the beginning of the brothers' debate, where the Younger Brother in 1634 worried that his sister 'in wild amazement, and affright / soe fares as did forsaken *Proserpine* / when the bigg rowling flakes of pitchie clouds / and darkness wound her in' (BMS, 357–60).[39] Milton ultimately struck these lines, but they remain in the Bridgewater text, and this implies both that the revision was fairly late and that the original performance included the haunting equation of the Lady's capture by Comus with Proserpine's rape by the god of the underworld. In Ovid, this is a scene of childish innocence interrupted. Proserpine is 'playing' (*ludit*), gathering flowers in her tunic with 'childish eagerness' (*puellari studio*) when the dark god Dis seizes her.[40] Calling out for her mother and her playmates, the young girl begins to cry not for her own fate but for the flowers that fall from her torn dress. 'Such', remarks Ovid, 'was the simplicity of her childish years' (*simplicitas puerilibus adfuit annis*).[41]

The moment has tremendous resonance for Milton, who returns to it decades later in *Paradise Lost*, where the garden is favourably compared to the field 'Of Enna, where Proserpin gathering flowers / Herself a fairer flower by gloomy Dis / Was gathered' (iv. 269–71). The use of Ovid's story in *Paradise Lost* underlies the insistent association of Eve with the flowers she names, tends, and weeps to leave behind, and would also seem to work beautifully in Milton's *A Maske*, where a god of darkness and night seizes the unsuspecting Lady. As poetry, there is nothing rough or unfinished about the lines, which are as lovely as anything in the masque.[42] Yet Milton revisited the passage in the TMS, cancelled the lines, and pasted in an entirely new leaf where the Younger Brother worries, instead, that his sister might be 'in the direfull graspe / Of Savage hunger, or of Savage heat' (*1637*, 374–5). Anthony Welch insightfully notes that this is perhaps the most overt example of Milton's tendency to use the Proserpine myth as 'an imaginative catalyst or trigger, at the early stages of a work', then 'to cover up its traces, to suppress his "over-exquisite" preoccupation with the goddess' rape and to write it out of his poetry'.[43] But ultimately I cannot agree with Welch's idea that Milton rewrote the lines in preparation for the first printed edition of 1637 because he found 'the overtones of sexual violence...too strong for the Egerton family'.[45] It seems highly improbable that an author backing away from an indecorous image would shift from the allusive 'pitchie clouds / and darkness wound her in' to the frankly suggestive 'Savage hunger, or...Savage heat' (BMS, 359–60; *1637*, 374–5).

If anything, the revision makes the danger more extreme and the Lady's situation more desperate, and if that is more dramatically interesting it is also, by definition, a revision to the masque form, which typically pays its compliments by using idealized aristocratic figures to foreclose or defuse dramatic tension.[44] The change also subtly raises the possibility, which has already emerged in the Lady's Echo song, that the threat she faces may be as much internal as external. To be in the grip of hunger or heat does not require the pyrotechnics of Dis and his cloudy chariot. If it seems obvious that 'Savage hunger' must refer to the threat of carnivorous beasts, as it is typically glossed, we should remember that the brothers first become separated from the Lady because they go searching for food for her, alarmed when they see her 'wearied out / With this long way' (*1637*, 197–8). And if it seems absurd that Milton could even hint of 'Savage heat' in the virginal daughter of his patron, we should remember that the food the boys are trying to bring her is 'cooling fruit' (*1637*, 201). It *would* have been absurd, and quite indecorous, to follow through the implications of that line in performance— which helps explain why the image of the Lady in 'the direfull graspe / Of Savage hunger, or of Savage heat' never seems to have occurred to Milton as he prepared his commissioned text. At least it was not recorded in any of the early drafts—but it was suggested in a subtle and inchoate form by the Lady's need for cooling fruit, a need the young girl expressed in the masque's performance and one that precipitated the work's action even in the very earliest draft.

At the very least, the change eliminates an image of absolute childish innocence from the poem. And if the new language resonates with the Lady's lines about her own hunger and heat, calling attention to her own weaknesses and desires, this does not compromise the essential childishness of Milton's lost protagonist. Instead, it simply exchanges Proserpine's innocence for a view of childhood that was both more problematic and more central to Milton's culture and his later writing. In the dominant Galenic medical discourse and the presiding Aristotelian moral universe, childhood was the time of heat and passion. As Henry Cuffe explained in his popular *Differences of the Ages*, which saw one of its many reissues the year before Milton wrote his masque, childhood 'lasteth (for the most part) until wee be five and twenty yeeres old, and this age is proportionable to the *Spring*, hot and moyst'.[46] Such an extended conception of childhood sheds some light on Milton's continual references to himself as a youth—by this definition he was still a child when writing his *Maske* about children. And Cuffe's crucial ambiguity about when childhood ends, ('for the most part') shoved into a parenthesis, sheds some light on the cultural underpinnings of the anxiety in poems like Milton's Sonnet 7 ('How Soon Hath Time').

Cuffe and his contemporaries connect developmental stages to the humoral body and its fully embodied passions: ageing was a process of cooling off and drying out, until in the final stage of life 'our strength and heat is so farre decayed, that not onely all ability is taken away, but even all willingnesse'.[47] If this made childhood a generative time, full of potential, it also made it full of danger. As their heat dissipated, old men lost their will, and by the same principle children in their fiery prime were pure wilfulness. Understanding the way this concept of childhood emerges in later drafts is necessary to understand *A Maske*'s moral and imaginative stakes. Comus knows of what he speaks when he makes his offer, which Milton carefully reworked, of 'all the pleasures / that fancie can beget on youthful thoughts / when the fresh blood grows lively' (TMS, 708–10). The child's hot, moist nature directly informs her imaginative responsiveness (or susceptibility). 'All children are naturally very greedy, and gluttenous', explained a 1612 translation of the French surgeon Jacques Guillemeau's influential work on childbirth and paediatric disease:

and this corruption growing hot by the heat and moisture of the child, it sends up vapors to the brain, from the aforesaid parts, which mingling themselves with the spirits, which are there placed, doe cause dreames, frights and startings in the sleepe, and (as *Avicen* witnesseth) makes children afraide of things which are not at all to be feared.[48]

The children of *A Maske* seem to be aware of such ideas, but this awareness still remains painfully inadequate to navigate and evaluate their visceral responses to the magical world around them. Or as Guillemeau would construe it, they continue to struggle to navigate their imaginative responses to their own bodily desires. Milton highlights the dilemma in lines he added for the Elder Brother at the same time he cut the passage on Proserpine to replace it with 'Savage heat': 'Peace brother', the boy cautions his even younger sibling, 'be not over exquisite / To cast the fashion of uncertain evils' (*1637*, 376–7). The irony here is that the Younger Brother *is not* being over-exquisite—the older child's swaggering confidence is the false imaginative construct, while his sister has in fact been abducted by a semi-divine being even more potent and menacing than the mountain bandits and rural ruffians the younger boy fears. Precocious in his academic wariness of the childish imagination, he is nevertheless susceptible to it as he spins out his own wild vision of chastity's talismanic powers, detailing his belief that the 'rigid looks of Chast austeritie' can dash 'brute violence / With sudden adoration, and blancke aw' (*1637*, 470–2). Needless to say, Comus's kind of 'sudden adoration', which includes trapping and binding the Lady in gums of glutinous heat that strikingly echo Guillemeau, is not exactly what the brother has in mind as he pictures the Lady striding past obstacles that wither before her '*Gorgon* sheild' (*1637*, 467).

At first, the Lady's response to the 'thousand fantasies' that 'begin to throng into my memorie' (*1637*, 220–1) seems similarly inapt. This intense imaginative moment—which includes visions of Faith, Hope, and Chastity in addition to her sense of disembodied voices and 'beckning shadows dire' (*1637*, 222)—prompts her to sing the song that ravishes Comus and makes him determined to take her as his queen. The impression the song makes on him is 'home-felt delight' (*1637*, 278), which editors typically gloss as 'heart-felt' or 'intimate'.[49] But considering the way the Lady's imagery echoes Comus's own, the way she responds to those airy tongues and beckoning shadows, the more obvious meaning is that the Lady's song resonates with something deep within his own nature. He says she reminds him of 'my mother *Circe*' but even more enchanting, and for a moment he seems as much a lost child as she (*1637*, 269). Together, as he hears her 'Breath such Divine inchanting ravishment' (*1637*, 261), the Lady and Comus inhabit a world of Ovidian myth and transformation full of danger and potential but shorn of Proserpine's absolute innocence. Yet for that same moment the Lady's song uses these dubious materials to seduce Comus to the good—he experiences it as a 'sober certainty of waking bliss', an understandably novel sensation for the son of Bacchus (*1637*, 279). As the Lady in Milton's later versions of *A Maske* concludes her song with an image of Echo 'translated to the skies' (*1637*, 258) her profound accomplishment is, as Shullenberger suggests, to translate her own 'potential lovelorn alienation, vulnerability, and longing for the securities of a now lost protected childhood into a maturing imaginative resource' with real ethical power and appeal.[50]

Every child, in the prevailing Renaissance conception, begins life like Comus and the members of his rout—pure pleasure principle. Indeed, Comus's pedigree as the son of Circe is significant in this regard: humanist educators from Erasmus to Ascham described the threat of incomplete or bad education precisely in terms of Circean transformation. 'If there was a Thessalian witch who had the power and desire to transform your son into a swine or a wolf', Erasmus asks, 'would you think that any punishment could be too severe for her?'[51] Of course not. Yet bad or insufficient education regularly leaves children prisoners to their own desires, transformed like Comus's entourage, 'human souls within bestial bodies'.[52] It is only half-right to say that children can devolve into such bestiality, because this, really, is their natural state. The challenge of the educator, the parent, the preacher, and poet, is to create the human out of this mass of unbounded appetite and desire.

In consequence, the child's body and mind become a tremendous moral battleground. The encyclopaedist Bartholomaeus Anglicus perfectly expresses this union of bodily and moral concerns in *De Proprietatibus Rerum*, which in its English translation remained a foundational text in the seventeenth century:

The childe is properly called *Puer*, when he is wayned from milke, and departed from the breast, and knoweth good and evill and therefore he is able to receive chastising and learning, and then he is put and set to learning under tutours, and compelled to take learning and chastising: Children of this age be hot & moyst of complection . . . able and lyght to moving, wittie to learne, & leade their lives without thought & care, and set their courages onelye on mirth and lyking, and dread no perills more than beating with a rod, and they love an apple more than golde.[53]

The desire for the apple and the ability to know good and evil mark this as a key moral moment, when the child begins to re-enact the Fall and becomes more fully human only by trading original innocence for the inheritance of Adam. The problem is that this spiritually charged development clearly begins to happen before the child has the full rational capabilities to understand its consequences. The principles that Bartholomaeus draws upon here are, not incidentally, also reflected in the legal and cultural double bind facing young people in Milton's England. They were judged utterly incompetent to manage their own affairs or property until they were quite old, but liable to be convicted as adults any time they stepped out of line. John Boys claims that young heirs were literally put to the apple test when they tried to claim their fortune if interested parties protested their competency: 'the Judge commands an *apple* or a *counter*, with a piece of *gold* to be set before him, to *try* which he will take; If he take the apple or the counter, and leave the gold, then he is cast for a *Fool*, and so held by the Judgment of the Court, as one that is unable to manage his estate.'[54] But if such simplicity precluded full adult rights, it did not preclude full adult responsibility, as the legal theorist Matthew Hale explained, drawing on the same confluence of religious and legal texts to describe the principle of *malitia supplet aetatem* ('malice supplies the age').[55] Like Adam who took the apple, a child of any age could be punished as an adult if the court could prove he had knowledge of good and evil and acted with a corrupted will.

Throughout his work, Milton is keenly aware of the way bodily appetites can rise up against us—he makes a point of Eve's real hunger when she bites the fruit in *Paradise Lost* and Jesus's when he resists temptation in *Paradise Regained*. The child's naturally unruly appetites would have made an appealing subject, and they help set *A Maske* in the line of all his great narrative works. When he forsakes the innocent, unblemished figure of Proserpine, the change helps move the masque out of the world of courtly compliment and into the world of *Areopagitica*, with its startling proclamation that 'We bring not innocence into the world, we bring impurity much rather: that which purifies us is trial, and trial is by what is contrary' (*CPW*, ii. 515). Whatever

A Maske's formal or theological commitments, this really is radical thinking, because here Milton accepts the basic concept of childhood that was central to his culture and humanist education, but he utterly rejects the corresponding idea that children must be sheltered from dangerous influences to cultivate virtue. Instead he adopts a position that would have been anathema to most good humanists, that children must be exposed to the arguments of vice to cultivate virtue—and not just straw-man arguments and negative examples paraded on stage in buffoonish form, but 'the utmost that vice promises to her followers' (*CPW*, ii. 515).

As he moves inward, abandoning the image of Proserpine taken by Dis for the more urgent but also more ambiguous hunger and heat, Milton not only revises the view of childhood at the poem's centre, but also its formal and generic allegiances. Heather Dubrow has tracked *A Maske*'s ambivalent relationship to works like Fletcher's pastoral *Faithful Shepherdess*, which counterpoints Milton's work with two virgins, one destined for marriage and one who opens the play by announcing her intention to make herself a kind of priestess of perpetual purity: 'thus I free / My selfe from all ensuing heates and fires / Of love'.[56] To Dubrow's list of striking similarities and departures could be added one more important than the way Milton questions the sufficiency of pastoral song or nature: in Fletcher's play, violence against the virgin comes wholly from without, as other characters suffering from savage lust repeatedly, and somewhat comically, injure her. In terms of dramatic action, Fletcher's play is less interested in what his heroine does than in what happens to her. The same is true of Randolph's virtuous maidens, who are utterly passive and utterly innocent figures in a comically recursive pattern of threat and salvation (and who, not incidentally, would readily serve to demonstrate the typical Protestant conception of the operations of grace on the believer). The heroines of such works beg comparison to Proserpine, as they seem to preserve a near-Pelagian innocence unclouded by heat or hunger.

Milton's Lady sounds just like these heroines, in one of Milton's earliest drafts, when she responds to her abduction with Proserpine-like *simplicitas:* 'Oh, my simplicity'! (TMS, 803). But Milton carefully cancelled this breathless innocence, scoring through the line, and even if we resist the idea that Milton's *Maske* makes its heroine more susceptible to her own bodily passions, there is no question that Milton gives her a far more active, and heated, role in fending off the threats against her (see Fig. 10). If she cannot exactly procure her own salvation, neither is she passive in defence of her

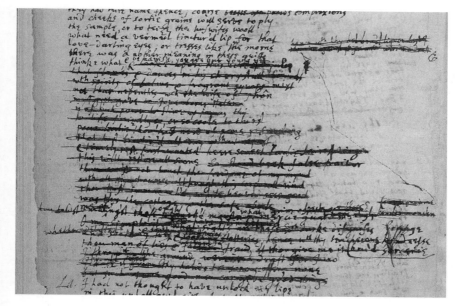

Fig. 10. Wren Library, Trinity College Manuscript, Cambridge, Trinity Manuscript

virtue and liberty, and as Milton continued to revise his work he continued to enhance the voice she used in that defence. The Lady's newly discovered eloquence is directly tied to the enhanced temptation she endures. Another echo from Randolph helps make the point. One of Randolph's favourite characters, who recurs from play to play, is Asotus, a prodigal child trained by his father to become an epicurean spendthrift—in this sense, he has a Comus-like pedigree, but unlike Comus he is utterly idiotic and repulsive. In a scene that must have echoed in Milton's memory when he crafted Comus's first encounter with the Lady, Asotus assails Randolph's heroine with assistance from Ballio, the man his father has hired to tutor him in vice:

Asotus: Hail heavenly Queen
         Of beauty, most illustrious Cupids daughter
         Was not so fair.
Ballio: His mother.
Asotus: 'Tis no matter.
         The silly damsell understands no Poetrie.[57]

Clearly Asotus is actually the one who understands no poetry, an impression confirmed as he continues to woo his would-be mistress by praising her 'azure lips' (12) to the horror of his tutor. Such a temptation, needless to say, is easy to reject, and Asotus easily fills the precepts of humanist negative example, exposing vice without making it attractive. Compare Comus, in lines that Milton restored and rewrote for the 1637 and 1645 printings:

> course complexions
> And cheeks of sorrie graine will serve to ply
> The sampler, and to teize the huswifes wooll.
> What need a vermeil-tinctur'd lip for that
> Love-darting eyes, or tresses like the Morn?
> There was another meaning in these gifts,
> Think what, and be adviz'd, you are but young yet.
>
> (*1645*, 749–55)[58]

'Course complexions' is a latter addition—Comus originally made the comparison to more basically ugly 'beetle brows' (TMS, 781) before Milton shifted the lines to reflect not merely the Lady's good looks but her deeper humoral constitution (the original meaning of 'complexion').[59] The way he describes the import of her gifts is not only erotic and poetically sophisticated but compelling on the level of basic physiology.

Only in response to such allurements does the Lady find an independent voice that is not an echo of Comus or even of her court milieu, critiquing 'lewdly-pamper'd Luxury' and making the case for 'unsuperfluous eeven proportion' (*1645*, 770, 773). Of course, we can always find a place for decorum and argue such lines imply that the Earl of Bridgewater and his clan simply had a befitting share of luxury, but it is difficult not to read the lines as an attack on the very system that supported the family's power and paid for the kind of festive entertainments of which the Lady was a part. The effect is of a voice finding itself. And this effect was enhanced in the 1637 edition, where Milton does not allow Comus to cut the Lady off at this point by dismissing her childish 'babble', as he did in the TMS and the 1634 performance (BMS, 750). Instead, Milton gave the Lady twenty-one new lines that discover a wholly new vocal power, as she claims her words could move 'dumb things . . . to sympathize, / And the brute Earth would lend her nerves, and shake' (*1637*, 830–1). Comus still attempts to dismiss her words as 'babble', but not before he admits, in a private aside, that he has been shaken to the core: 'I feele that I doe feare / Her words set off by some superior power' (*1637*, 834–5). The experience leaves him drenched in a cold sweat, as he discovers that the Lady's heat is of quite a different nature than he had expected and works to quite a different effect. She has come a long way from the lost girl invoking Echo in the forest, responding to voices and imaginations that throng irresistibly through her mind.[60]

Various critics have punctured the idea that Milton's revisions to the masque form are wholly original. However, one central difference is clear and is highlighted again by this change: both traditional and revised masques promote the idea that virtue can be assailed, but not that it needs to be developed. The kind of virtue the Lady displays as she claims this orphic power of speech, however, develops not only in the masque but through it—it is simply not a part of the original structure, which is built on the bones of masques and plays where Proserpine's innocence would be more at home. Evans has also examined changes in the final debate between Comus and the Lady to make the point that 'the 1634 text as it was actually staged at Ludlow—far from defending virginity, hardly mentions it at all. . . . The theme of the 1634 text presented to the Earl of Bridgewater and his family, then, was quite straightforward: it was temperance pure and simple.'[61] True as this may be, from his first conception Milton was also pulling back from an allegory of temperance, with the dispassionate disengagement suggested by the term since Aristotle.[62] In an early draft, Milton had indeed had the Attendant Spirit moralize the masque, as he presented the children to their parents, by noting that 'Heav'n hath timely try'd thire youth / thire faith, thire temperance, & thire truth' (TMS, 997–8), but he cancelled 'temperance' in favour of 'patience', which then remained in all subsequent versions. Like Spenser, whose Protestant knight of temperance often really embodies the Aristotelian half-virtue of continence, Milton was drawn to the idea that genuine virtue consisted not in the absence of strong passions but in the struggle to overcome them.[63]

IV. Conclusion: 1637 'yet once more'

To express such an interest, the text must focus closely on the Lady, body and mind, at her particular developmental stage, and ironically this closer engagement becomes possible only as the text becomes more distant from the performance and the actual body of Alice Egerton. But it makes perfect sense that even in the 1637 edition, which is dedicated to Lord Egerton and so in some sense still obligated to him, Milton begins to pursue poetic integrity in ways that violate or simply ignore the demands of decorous performance.[64] By 1637 Milton was, after all, becoming a profoundly different poet: the exact date of the 1637 printing is unknown, but it was likely very late in a very momentous year or very early in the next. In June, William Prynne, Henry Burton, and John Bastwick were convicted and mutilated before a crowd that dipped their handkerchiefs in their blood—an event that polarized the nation and helped force the choosing of sides. In April, Milton's mother died, and on 8 August of that year an episcopal inspection of the Horton church by the Laudian archdeacon declared that her gravestone was improperly placed, and cited irregularities regarding the Milton family pew and the rector's surplice.[65] On 10 August, Edward King died, and Milton later declared the elegy he wrote for him, 'Lycidas', a prophecy of the demise of Laud and his 'corrupted clergy'. Thomas Corns and Gordon Campbell, who are extraordinarily cautious about attributing any early radical sentiments to the young Milton, admit that the unease in this poem is 'palpable'.[66] But like most writers on the subject, they do not mention Milton's revisions to *A Maske* at this time—instead, they simply flip the tendency to read the radicalized Milton of the 1640s back into the masque, arguing that this early work is instead 'the most complex and thorough expression of Laudian Arminianism and Laudian style within the Milton oeuvre, and indeed, the high-water mark of his indulgence of such beliefs and values'.[67] As he turned to revising A *Maske*, though, just as in 'Lycidas', Milton was rethinking the relationship between form and content, between interior and exterior. As Cedric Brown argues with characteristic understatement, 'In 1637 the mind of the poet was not quite so scrupulous of the delights of the occasion.'[68]

In the ensuing years, with each publication, Milton continued to strip away the layers: in 1645, the title page retained the name of the Earl of Bridgewater, Lawes's dedication to viscount Brackley, and the names of all the aristocratic performers, but now it came after 'Lycidas' with a title page that proclaimed in bold font 'A MASKE of the same AUTHOR'; by 1673, no name of Egerton or any of the prefatory material remained.[69] Even at this late date, scribal marking in the TMS suggests that Milton continued to revisit and tweak his earlier drafts, as the characters in *A Maske* became more anonymous but also less abstract, not blanks, but embodied, passionate beings. Or at the very least, they became the rough drafts of such beings. No matter how far *A Maske* came from its original performance, Comus would always escape, the children's victory would always be marked with just a hint of failure, and they would conclude the work with measured steps calculated to please their powerful parents. Evil is always with us, *A Maske* seems to suggest, and no matter how much we revise and rewrite, no matter how powerfully we learn to speak, our ability to navigate a hostile and confusing world will continue to reflect the lessons of youth and the bonds of filial feeling.

Notes

1. Parker, i. 142. For incredulous responses to Parker see for example John Creaser, '"The Present aid of this occasion": The Setting of *Comus*', in David Lindley (ed.), *The Court Masque* (Manchester, 1984), 111–34, and Roy Flannagan, 'Introduction to *Comus*', in *The Riverside Milton* (Boston, Mass., 1998), 110.
2. Parenthetical citations to the Trinity College Manuscript (TMS), Bridgewater Manuscript (BMS), and the 1637 edition (*1637*) of *A Maske* abide by the line numbers found in S. E. Sprott (ed.), *A Maske: The Earlier Versions* (Toronto, 1973). I have also consulted Milton's original manuscript housed at the Wren Library in Cambridge and volume 1 of Harris Francis Fletcher (ed.), *John Milton's Complete Poetical Works Reproduced in Facsimile* (Urbana, Ill., 1943). Parenthetical citations to the 1645 edition (*1645*) and Milton's other poetry, unless otherwise indicated, are from Milton, *Complete Shorter Poems*, ed. Stella P. Revard (Oxford, 2009).
3. Hunter argues that the masque's topic is 'the family itself', while Cedric Brown suggests that Milton's use of children, rather than adult performers, helped move his work away from the form's 'usual mode of idolatry', although neither of these explorations of the family milieu focusses on the concepts of childhood that will be this essay's focus. Shullenberger discusses *A Maske* as an initiation ritual in ways that inform my own discussion of childhood and maturation throughout, although his method is anthropological and psychoanalytic where mine works to historicize the concepts of childhood in Milton's work and to trace their transformation through Milton's textual revisions. See William B. Hunter, *Milton's, 'Comus': Family Piece* (Troy, N.Y., 1983), 5; Cedric Brown, *John Milton's Aristocratic Entertainments* (Cambridge, 1985), 92; and William Shullenberger, *Lady in the Labyrinth: Milton's, 'Comus' as Initiation* (Madison, N.J., 2008).
4. I have addressed the critical neglect of this issue and discussed in more detail the theological and legal status of childhood in '"Perplex't Paths": Youth and Authority in Milton's *Maske*', *Renaissance Quarterly*, 62 (2009), 410–43. Here I am more interested in the way Milton's textual revisions rethink and rework the concepts of youth and authority.
5. Stephen Dobranski has argued that Milton 'disingenuously implies that he is much younger' than he really is in the pamphlet; as we shall see, however, broad

Renaissance conceptions of youth and childhood extending late into life were not uncommon and they generated genuine anxieties. See Stephen Dobranski, *Milton, Authorship, and the Book Trade* (Cambridge, 1999), 75.

6. Shullenberger, *Lady in the Labyrinth*, 15.

7. John Carey in *Milton* was among the first to argue that Milton's work was a 'masque against masquing' in a book which also appears to be the first to suggest that the gums of glutinous heat bring 'to mind the sexual heat for which Comus' enchantments are allegories' (New York, 1970) 50, 46. Other arguments for a reformed masque include David Norbrook, *Poetry and Politics in the English Renaissance* (rev. edn., Oxford, 2002) and 'The Reformation of the Masque', in Lindley, *The Court Masque*, 94–110; Barbara Lewalski calls the work 'in every respect a reformed masque, a generic tour de force' in 'Milton's *Comus* and the Politics of Masquing', in David Bevington and Peter Holbrook (eds.), *The Politics of the Stuart Court Masque* (Cambridge, 1998), 314. Diametrically opposed to such arguments are Catherine Gimelli Martin, 'The Non-Puritan Ethics, Metaphysics, and Aesthetics of Milton's Spenserian Masque', *Milton Quarterly*, 37 (2003), 215–44, and Campbell and Corns, 84. Taking a middle road, Heather Dubrow argues for a generically and politically ambivalent masque, and importantly shows that even the final version of *Comus* is much more like its predecessors than critics often acknowledge, in 'The Masquing of Genre in *Comus*', *Milton Studies*, 44 (2005), 62–83. John Creaser, '"The Present aid of this occasion"', also stakes out a subtle middle position. While both arguments are correctives, neither accounts for the way the masque evolves; both arguments depend upon a stable text.

8. J. Martin Evans, *The Miltonic Moment* (Lexington, Ky., 1998), 40. Although Evans notes the instability, it is not the central focus of his discussion, which considers Milton's revisions only as they impact the debate between Comus and the Lady—a debate I will attempt here to put into a larger revisionary context.

9. See Sprott, *A Maske: The Earlier Versions*, 3–33. Other studies of the Trinity College Manuscript and *A Maske*'s stages of composition include John S. Diekoff, 'The Text of *Comus*, 1634 to 1645', *PMLA*, 52 (1937), 705–27; John Shawcross, 'Certain Relationships of the Manuscripts of *Comus*', *Papers of the Bibliographical Society of America*, 54 (1960), 38–58; and 'Speculations on the Dating of the Trinity MS. of Milton's Poems', *Modern Language Notes*, 75 (1960), 11–17; and William Hunter, 'A Bibliographical Excursus into Milton's Trinity Manuscript', *Milton Quarterly*, 19 (1985), 61–71.

10. Ronald Corthell, for example, astutely stresses the Egerton family relationships and the actual, gendered 'body imprisoned by Comus', but he makes no distinction between the lines that Alice Egerton actually delivered in the flesh and those added later. See '"Go Ask Alice": Daughter, Patron, and Poet in *A Maske Presented at Ludlow Castle*', *Milton Studies*, 44 (2005), 113.

11. See Katherine Kellett, 'The Lady's Voice: Poetic Collaboration in Milton's *Maske*', *Milton Studies*, 50 (2009), 1–19, and Ann Baynes Coiro, 'Anonymous Milton, or *A Maske* Masked', *ELH*, 71 (2004), 609–29. Coiro brilliantly uses the text's material history—its transition from courtly manuscript, to anonymous

printed text bound with the courtly, witty, but posthumous works of Randolph, to its culminating position in the 1645 poems—to show how 'it broke away from an imitative, conventional, and collaborative past to something quite new: an autobiography told in a collected volume of his own work' (624). I hope to show that we see the pressure of this movement not only on the machinery of title pages and dedications, but on the deepest levels of plot and character.

12. For Milton's self-representations and their role in ethical proof, see Stephen Fallon, *Milton's Peculiar Grace: Self-Representation and Authority* (Ithaca, N.Y., 2007).

13. The most obvious and consistent change in Milton's hand is his increasing preference for the Italian 'e' over the Greek 'ε', which became pronounced around 1637 and predominant after his trip to Italy in 1638. The change has long been used to date Milton's handwriting, as in Helen Darbishire, 'The Chronology of Milton's Handwriting', *The Library*, 14 (1934), 229–35, and James Holly Hanford, 'The Chronology of Milton's Private Studies', *PMLA*, 36 (1921), 251–314. Shawcross uses the appearance of two instances of the Italian 'e' to argue that the entire Trinity College Manuscript of the *Maske* was composed in 1637, and the Bridgewater Manuscript subsequent to this, in 'Certain Relationships'. No one is better on tracking the changes in the manuscript and their chronology, but this thesis finally introduces an unnecessarily convoluted and improbable manuscript transmission history, since, as Shawcross himself recognizes, Milton clearly adopted the form gradually and Greek 'ε' continues to be the default character nearly everywhere in the TMS of Milton's *Maske*. There remains some uncertainty in dating the Trinity and Bridgewater manuscripts to 1634, but convincing cases are made by Sprott, *A Maske: The Earlier Versions*, 9–19, and Hunter, 'A Bibliographical Excursus', 68–71.

14. Hunter's theory seems generally credible, although I remain agnostic about its specific application. At line 92, for example, the Attendant Spirit says 'I heare the tread / of virgin steps I must be viewless now' and Milton has cancelled 'virgin' to write 'hateful'. Following Diekhoff ('The Text of *Comus*'), most critics have taken this slip as evidence that as Milton copied the completed *Maske* into his notebook he was thinking forward to another scene when the Lady enters and Comus speaks a very similar line; Hunter ('A Bibliographical Excursus') instead argues it is evidence of initial composition, as Milton originally intended to have the Lady enter at this point but then thought better of it and rearranged the pieces accordingly (65).

15. Sprott (*A Maske: The Earlier Versions*) designates the first and revised versions in the Trinity Manuscript as TMS[1] and TMS[2] respectively. It is an important distinction but one that does not need to be maintained in my analysis, which depends on the larger changes between the revised TMS, the BMS, and subsequent printed editions.

16. Diekhoff, 'The Text of *Comus*', 705.

17. See Fletcher, *John Milton's Complete Poetical Works Reproduced in Facsimile*, 263.

18. I follow Sprott in transcribing 'love-torne' here, although this reading could be disputed in favor of 'love-lorne', which appears in all other versions—the

character the scribe has written looks more like his 't' than his 'l', but really could be an atypical version of either letter.

19. George Sandys, *Ovid's 'Metamorphosis' Englished* (1628), 104.

20. Sandys, *Ovid's 'Metamorphosis' Englished*, 104. Ausonius, 'In Echo Pictam', in *Ausonius*, ed. Hugh Evelyn White, 2 vols. (Cambridge, Mass., 1921), ii.

21. Flannagan, 'Introduction to *Comus*', 111.

22. For the law governing the marriage of a 'Woman Child' see *Statutes at Large, from the First Year of King Edward the Fourth to the End of the Reign of Queen Elizabeth* (1786), ii. 499–500 (regnal year 4–5 Philip and Mary, ch. 8).

23. William Thomas, *A Preservative of Piety* (1662), 146.

24. See Stephen Orgel, 'The Case for Comus', *Representations*, 81 (2003), 40–1. For Echo as an ominous figure who dies 'withering into the ghostly voice of pure reflexivity', see Shullenberger, *Lady in the Labyrinth*, 125. For more on the rich figure of Echo and echoing as a trope in the masque see also Angus Fletcher, *The Transcendental Masque: An Essay on Milton's 'Comus'* (Ithaca, N.Y., 1972), 198–202 and Louise Simons, ' "And Heaven Gates Ore My head": Death as Threshold in Milton's *Mask*', *Milton Studies*, 23 (1987), 153–96.

25. The translation is the one found in contemporary editions of the Book of Common Prayer. For more on the relation of *A Maske* to Michaelmas, see Brown, *John Milton's Aristocratic Entertainments*, 38–40.

26. John Boys, *An Exposition of the Festivall Epistles and Gospels Used in Our English Liturgie Together with a Reason Why the Church Did Chuse the Same. The Third Part* (1615), 109–10, 111.

27. Thomas Watson, 'Epigraph: Exodus 20.12, Honor thy Father and thy Mother', *A Body of Practical Divinity* (1692), 354.

28. *CSP*, 84–5.

29. See Coiro, 'Anonymous Milton', 612–25.

30. Coiro, 'Anonymous Milton', 620.

31. Thomas Randolph, *The Jealous Lovers* (Cambridge, 1632), 49–50.

32. Randolph, *The Jealous Lovers*, 50.

33. Thomas Randolph, *Poems with the Muses Looking-Glasse: With Amyntas* (Oxford, 1638), 7. Citations of this volume refer to page numbers.

34. Randolph, *Poems*, 92.

35. To cite just a few examples: in 1592 Bishop Gervase Babington addressed the perpetual fear that 'now a dayes' youth were becoming disrespectful to their parents and recommended the Old Testament's Joseph as a 'glasse for all children to behold them selves in'; moralists regularly exhorted fathers to make themselves a 'mirrour' for their children's edification; Richard Baxter compared the process of reading about saintly biblical figures (who reveal our own filth by comparison) to the common process of showing 'a child *his face* in a *glass* when he *cryeth*, that he may see how he deformeth it'; see Gervase Babington, *Certaine Plaine, Briefe, and Comfortable Notes Upon Everie Chapter of Genesis*, EEBO (1592), 168; Thomas Watson's *A Body of Practical Divinity*, 359; Richard Baxter, *A Saint or a Brute* (1662), 366.

36. Randolph, *Poems*, 42–3.

37. Randolph, *Poems*, 43.

38. The appearance of 'love' would seem to be a scribal error for BMS and 1637 'lore', but it also appealingly reflects the work's emphasis on filial affection and duty.

39. Even Mary Loeffelholz, who argues at length that 'Milton's Lady undergoes the trials and temptations of Proserpine', does not note that Milton made this association explicit in an earlier version, before backing away from it. See 'Two Masques of Ceres and Proserpine: *Comus* and *The Tempest*', in Mary Nyquist and Margaret W. Ferguson (eds.), *Re-membering Milton: New Essays on the Texts and Traditions* (New York, 1987), 31.

40. Ovid, *Metamorphosis*, ed. and trans. Frank Justus Miller, 3rd edn. (Cambridge, Mass., 1997), v. 392–3. *Puellari* might also be rendered 'girlish', but the most important of Ovid's translators during Milton's time, George Sandys, also has 'childish care', in *Ovid's Metamorphosis Englished*, 134.

41. Ovid, *Metamorphosis*, v. 400. Sandys also emphasizes Proserpine's 'sweet Youth's simplicity' in *Ovid's Metamorphosis Englished*, 134.

42. John Diekhoff, in 'Critical Activity of the Poetic Mind: John Milton', *PMLA*, 55 (1940), argues that the lines were cut to avoid bombast and achieve clarity of thought: 'Everyone will agree, surely, that the poem is better for the absence of these lines, and because of their extravagance' (751). But I do not find the lines about Proserpine particularly bombastic or obscure, and they seem decidedly less extravagant than dozens of others that remained uncut, such as the Elder Brother's unintentionally comic 'Unmuffle ye faint stars, and thou fair Moon / That wontst to love the travailers benizon, / Stoop thy pale visage through an amber cloud, / And disinherit *Chaos*, that raigns here' (*1637*, 348–51).

43. Anthony Welch, 'Milton's Forsaken Proserpine', *English Literary Renaissance*, 39 (2009), 529.

44. Welch, 'Milton's Forsaken Proserpine', 528; Roy Flannagan ('Introduction to *Comus*') also suggests that Milton cut the lines because their imagery of sexual violence was 'extreme' (139n232).

45. The greatest example is Thomas Carew's *Coelum Britannicum* (1634) featuring the Egerton brothers as torchbearers. In Carew's masque, the gods themselves decide to emulate the court of Charles and Henrietta Maria, and accordingly purge the heavens of evil influences. In *The Stuart Court Masque and Political Culture* (Cambridge, 2008), Martin Butler makes the point that in more traditional masques 'an absence of dramatic interaction allowed the masquers' heroism to be assumed rather than demonstrated', while 'Milton created a world of conflict in which virtue was not invulnerable and its foe was formidable' (356). Although he has discussed the masque form's adaptability and relationship with post-Restoration dramatic forms, David Lindley (*The Court Masque*) also notes that 'characteristically the masque does not debate, but asserts, for all that its form appears to offer a dialectical possibility' (4). For more on the 'Neoplatonic rhetoric' of the masque form see Victoria Kahn, *Machiavellian Rhetoric: From the Counter-Reformation to Milton* (Princeton, N.J., 1994), 196–7.

46. Henry Cuffe, *The Differences of the Ages of Mans Life* (1633), 118.

47. Cuffe, *The Differences of the Ages of Mans Life*, 120.

48. Jacques Guillemeau, *Child-birth or, The Happy Deliverie of Women . . . To Which is Added, a Treatise of the Diseases of Infants, and Young Children: with the Cure of Them* (1612), 69.

49. See *John Milton*, ed. Stephen Orgel and Jonathan Goldberg (Oxford, 1991), 764n51; Milton, *Complete Shorter Poems*, ed. John Carey, 2nd edn. (Harlow, 1997), 194n261; Flannagan, 'Introduction to *Comus*', 135n171; Milton, *Complete Shorter Poems*, ed. Revard, 97.

50. Shullenberger, *Lady in the Labyrinth*, 127.

51. *Si qua Thessala mulier esset, qua malis artibus posset & conaretur filium tuum in suem aut lupum vertere, none putares nullum supplicium fatis dignum illius scelere?* My translation, from *De Pueris*, in *Desiderii Erasmi Roterdami Opera Omnia* (1703), ed. Jean Le Clerc (Hildesheim, 1961), i. 494. See also Roger Ascham's discussion of those 'who serve in Circe's court' becoming bestial through their misguided education in *The Scholemaster* in *The Works of Roger Ascham*, ed. William Aldis Wright (Cambridge, 1904), 227.

52. *animus humanus in corpore bestiae*; Erasmus, *De Pueris*, 493.

53. Bartholomaeus Anglicus, *Bateman uppon Bartholome his Booke 'De Proprietatibus Rerum'*, trans. Stephen Bateman (1582), 73.

54. John Boys, *An Exposition of the Dominical Epistles and Gospels . . . the Winter Part from the First Adventuall Sunday to Lent* (1610), 479.

55. Matthew Hale, *Historia Placitorum Coronae*, ed. George Wilson, 2 vols. (1800), i. 26, 629. For a discussion of the way the principle of *malitia supplet aetatem* crossed over into law from theological treatments of Genesis, see Anthony Platt and Bernard L. Diamond, 'The Origins of the "Right and Wrong" Test of Criminal Responsibility and Its Subsequent Development in the United States: An Historical Survey', *California Law Review*, 54 (1966), 1227–60.

56. John Fletcher, *The Faithful Shepherdess* in *The Dramatic Works in the Beaumont and Fletcher Canon*, ed. Fredson Bowers et al., 10 vols. (Cambridge, 1966–96), iii. 6–8. See Dubrow, 'The Masquing of Genre in *Comus*', 62–83.

57. Randolph, *The Jealous Lovers*, 12.

58. Revard reverts to the TMS spelling 'coarse complexions', but 1637, 1645, and 1673 all spell the word 'course'. The difference may be accidental and insignificant, but since 'course' can refer to the 'flowing' of humours through the body (*OED* 9) and the 'ordinary' way of doing things (*OED* 20), Milton's earlier spelling does not seem obviously preferable.

59. When Milton made this change is unclear. The lines do not appear in the BMS at all, and the earliest draft of TMS contains 'beetle brows'. Milton cancelled those words and wrote 'coarse complexions' in the margin in a handwriting that resembles other changes introduced in 1637 but could potentially be earlier. See Sprott, '*A Maske': The Earlier Versions*, 12–13.

60. This is where I part from Kellett ('The Lady's Voice'), who argues that the Lady's 'development of an authorial voice . . . suggests that the very reliance on other voices leads to poetic authority' (4). It is true that Milton's work shows that language is mediated, and true that *A Maske* owes much to its collaborative

production—but this crucial example of 'authorial voice' develops only as Milton begins to detach the text from its production context.

61. Evans, *The Miltonic Moment*, 52.

62. See Book 7 of Aristotle's *The Nicomachean Ethics*, trans. David Ross, rev. edn. (Oxford, 1998).

63. Many critics have noted that Spenser's knight combines temperance and continence, but see Jane Grogan, *Exemplary Spenser: Visual and Poetic Pedagogy in "The Faerie Queene"* (Burlington, VT, 2009), 97–9. When Milton calls Spenser a 'better teacher then Scotus or Aquinas' in *Areopagitica* he is embracing precisely the way *The Faerie Queene* pushes temperance towards a more typical classical definition of continence, as Guyon encounters temptation in the Bower of Bliss so 'he might see, and know, and yet abstain' (*CPW*, ii. 516). A useful comparison is offered, once again, by Randolph's *Muse's Looking Glass*, which really is about temperance pure and simple: the plot is nearly non-existent, consisting merely of various extremes that meet on stage to demonstrate that virtue consists only in the golden mean: ignorance and knowledge, prodigality and parsimoniousness, urbanity and rusticity, strict and lenient justice.

64. See Brown (*John Milton's Aristocratic Entertainments*), who argues that the heightening of Comus's 'cavalier' rhetoric in 1637 shows Milton making 'an even more independently outspoken authorial comment on the moral state of the real world about him' (137).

65. See Edward Jones, '"Church-outed by the Prelats": Milton and the 1637 Inspection of the Horton Parish Church', *Journal of English and Germanic Philology*, 102 (2003), 42–58.

66. Campbell and Corns, 99.

67. Campbell and Corns, 84.

68. Brown, *John Milton's Aristocratic Entertainments*, 141.

69. See Fletcher, *John Milton's Complete Poetical Works Reproduced in Facsimile*, 189–92, 56.

11

That Two-Handed Engine and the Millennium at the Door

John Leonard

'But that two-handed engine at the door, / Stands ready to smite once, and smite no more.'[1] The mountain of commentary about this crux is so large, and the interpretations so involved and interwoven, 'that those confused seeds which were impos'd on *Psyche* as an incessant labour to cull out, and sort asunder, were not more intermixt'.[2] Some arguments nevertheless stand out as wheat from chaff, and pre-eminent among them is David Sansone's recent suggestion that the 'two-handed engine' is the winnowing fan prophesied by John the Baptist in Matthew 3:12.[3] I shall return to Sansone's argument in due course, but first I want to note some elementary points that are often forgotten or overlooked.

A common mistake is to assume that the entire couplet is a riddle wrapped in a mystery inside an enigma. This assumption has led to two opposite errors. The first is to suppose that *every* part of the couplet requires ingenious explication. The second error is a reaction to the first. Many critics, exasperated by far-fetched interpretations, have concluded that Milton intended the mystery to be impenetrable and that it is therefore pointless to look for a specific reference. Stanley Fish takes this line when he writes: 'whatever the two-handed engine is . . . we shall never know'.[4] Christopher Hill makes the same point with a more political edge when he reminds us that 'Lycidas' was written under the shadow of the Laudian censor. 'Critics who complain of Milton's obscurity', he writes, 'forget the censorship. He could hardly say in plain terms either that Laud should be impeached (if the engine equals the two Houses of Parliament); or executed (if it is an axe, or Michael's two-handed sword).' Hill goes on to list other possible candidates, including the Old and New Testaments, and the shepherd's rod and crook, before concluding: 'The whole beauty of the pastoral mode, under a strict censorship, was that meanings could be multiple, slippery, covering an attitude rather than a precise statement.'[5] The trouble with this approach is that it obscures the fact that one part of Milton's phrase does have a simple explanation. The 'two-handed engine' is a mystery, but the words that immediately follow—'at the door'—would have been pellucid to all seventeenth-century readers. Thomas Newton explained this phrase over 250 years ago, but many recent commentators seem to be unaware of his contribution, so a reminder is perhaps called for. By reaffirming what we do know (or ought to know) about 'that two-handed engine at the door', we can gain a clearer sense of what we do not know.

It is useful to divide line 130 into three parts: (1) the demonstrative adjective 'that'; (2) the engine itself; (3) the prepositional phrase 'at the door'. Only the second of these expressions is a mystery. Let's start with 'that'. Demonstrative adjectives gesture towards something assumed to be known. The point is self-evident, but it needs to be made because many critics in the past few decades have agreed with Hill and Fish that the two-handed engine is not just unknown but unknowable. Despite Hill's assertion that Milton is not making 'a precise statement', deictic *thats* do that. Milton was especially fond of 'that' gestures. They are a characteristic feature of his style (in poetry and prose) from the beginning of his career. Bear with me while I list some of the more memorable instances. The Nativity Ode alone has five: 'That glorious form, that light unsufferable'; 'that far-beaming blaze'; 'that blast'; 'that twise batter'd god'. Five more appear in 'On the Death of a Fair Infant': 'that high first-moving Spheare'; 'that just Maid'; 'that sweet smiling Youth'; 'that crown'd Matron'; 'that heav'nly brood'. Other instances in the early poems include: 'that great Cov'nant'; 'that melodious noise'; 'that Song'; 'That fair *Syrian* Shepherdess'; 'that Golden Key'; 'that snaky-headed *Gorgon* sheild'; 'that *Nepenthes*'; 'that Starr'd *Ethiope* Queen'. Elsewhere in 'Lycidas' we have 'that sanguine flower inscrib'd with woe' and (in a cancelled draft of a different passage) 'that sad floure'. In the sonnets we find 'that same lot', 'that mark', 'that care', and 'that one Talent'. The octave alone of Sonnet 10 adds 'that good Earl', 'that Parlament', 'that dishonest victory', and 'that Old man eloquent'. Turning to *Paradise Lost*, we find: 'that Forbidden Tree'; 'that shepherd'; 'that Sea-beast / *Leviathan*'; 'that opprobrious Hill'; 'that Pigmean Race'; 'that *Serbonian* Bog'; 'that mighty leading Angel'; 'that warning voice'; 'that first Battel'; 'that faire field of *Enna*'; 'all that pain'; 'that sweet Grove of *Daphne*'; 'that *Nyseian* Ile'; 'that wilde Rout'; 'that Milkie way'; 'that bright Starr'; 'Or that, not Mystic'; 'that bituminous Lake'; 'Not that more glorious'; 'Nor that which on'; 'that sober Race'; 'that Just Man'; and 'that proud Citie'. *Paradise Regained* adds 'that fatal wound'; 'that long threatn'd wound'; 'that Spirit unfortunate'; 'that *Pellean* Conqueror'; 'that Prophet bold'; 'that first golden Monarchy'; 'that Evil one'; 'that fierce Democratie'; and 'that *Theban* Monster'. And last, but not least: 'That Heroic, that Renown'd / Irresistible *Samson*'; 'That specious Monster'; 'that fallacious Bride'; 'That invincible *Samson*'; 'that self-begott'n bird'. There are even more in the prose—so many that the editors of the Yale edition (*CPW*) despair of listing them, perhaps in the belief that this is that doom which Adam fell into.

My point in reciting this admittedly exhausting (though it is not an exhaustive) list is that every last one of Milton's other 'that' gestures points to something specific. If Hill and Fish are right, and 'that two-handed engine' points to nothing in particular, it would be the only 'that' in all of Milton's writings to fail to deliver. That is not to say that Milton's other *thats* yield their secrets immediately. Milton sometimes likes to tease (not the same as 'trap') his readers. He will use a 'that' to point towards something as if it were plain as day when he knows very well that it is not. Annabel Patterson has written splendidly about this in her essay 'That Old Man Eloquent'. Commenting on 'Sonnet 10', she notes that 'the markedly repeated "that"' provokes 'the question, "Which one?"' even as it 'operates in the confidence that the fit reader will know'.[6] Some of Milton's *thats* work like clues in a crossword puzzle. I do not mean to trivialize in putting it like that. Several of Milton's 'that' gestures work *exactly* like clues in a crossword puzzle— especially when they withhold a proper name, as in 'that fair *Syrian* Shepherdess' (Rachel), 'that Starr'd *Ethiope* Queen' (Cassiopeia), and 'that Old man eloquent' (Isocrates).[7] Even when Milton names names, he can play tricks. He sometimes surrenders a name only to snatch it back: 'Descend from Heav'n *Urania*, by that name / If rightly thou art call'd'. At other times he leads us astray with ambiguous names: 'nor that sweet Grove / Of *Daphne* by *Orontes*, and th'inspir'd *Castalian* Spring'.[8] Empson assumed that Daphne was the nymph chased by Apollo and so inferred that Milton was 'Eve-baiting'.[9] But Milton's Daphne is not the nymph in the vale of Tempe, but a laurel grove near Antioch. The '*Castalian* Spring' has also led readers astray. Patrick Hume was but the first of many annotators to direct us to the 'Fountain at the Foot of the Hill *Parnassus*'.[10] The Jonathan Richardsons get it right when they warn us that the Castalian spring in Milton's catalogue of gardens is 'not that known One at the Foot of *Parnassus*, but that of the Grove of *Daphne* which foretold *Hadrian*'s Advancement to the Empire'.[11] 'Not that known One': Milton's *thats* often challenge us to reconsider what we think we know.

To sum up my argument so far: Milton's 'that' gestures do not always point to something *obvious*, but they do (sometimes after a bit of teasing) invariably point to something *specific*. This gives me hope that there might be a satisfying explanation for 'that two-handed engine at the door'. Breakthroughs can happen. Consider the parallel case of 'Blind mouths' (119). Critics were stymied by this startling juxtaposition until Ruskin revealed the hidden wordplay. His explication is worth quoting at length:

> Of other care they little reckoning make,
> Than how to scramble at the shearers' feast.
> *Blind mouths—*

I pause again, for this is a strange expression; a broken metaphor, one might think, careless and unscholarly.

Not so: its very audacity and pithiness are intended to make us look close at the phrase and remember it. Those two monosyllables express the precisely accurate contraries of right character, in the two great offices of the Church—those of bishop and pastor.

A Bishop means a person who sees.

A Pastor means one who feeds.

The most unbishoply character a man can have is therefore to be Blind.

The most unpastoral is, instead of feeding, to want to be fed,—to be a Mouth.

Take the two reverses together, and you have 'blind mouths'. We may advisably follow out this idea a little. Nearly all the evils in the Church have arisen from bishops desiring *power* more than *light*. They want authority, not outlook.[12]

To my mind, this is the most valuable single comment ever made about 'Lycidas'. 'Audacity and pithiness' are characteristic Miltonic virtues and we should keep them in mind when interpreting 'that two-handed engine at the door'.

Ruskin offers another excellent comment on 'Miter'd locks' (112). Many critics have been puzzled by the fact that St Peter wears a bishop's mitre. Some have even inferred that the digression in 'Lycidas' is not an outright rejection of episcopacy but a final *cri de coeur* for reconciliation with the established church. Ruskin offers a different explanation:

His 'mitred' locks! Milton was no Bishop-lover; how comes St. Peter to be 'mitred'? 'Two massy keys he bore'. Is this, then, the power of the keys claimed by the Bishops of Rome, and is it acknowledged here by Milton only in a poetical licence, for the sake of its picturesqueness, that he may get the gleam of the golden keys to help his effect? Do not think it. Great men do not play stage tricks with doctrines of life and death: only little men do that. Milton means what he says; and means it with his might too—is going to put the whole strength of his spirit presently into the saying of it. For though not a lover of false bishops, he *was* a lover of true ones; and the Lake-pilot is here, in his thoughts, the type and head of true episcopal power. (27–8)

We should not leap to hasty conclusions, for the question of Milton's early radicalism is still hotly debated. But Ruskin's comment has the ring of truth. There is no contradiction between 'Lycidas' and the avowedly anti-prelatical tracts that Milton would write a few years later. His prose pamphlets repeatedly and emphatically make the point that prelates and bishops are not the same thing. Milton never attacks 'bishops'; he seeks to expose prelates as *false* bishops. When he gave his second prose pamphlet the title *Of Prelatical Episcopacy*, his point was that true episcopacy is not prelatical. For Milton, 'prelatical episcopacy' is an oxymoron, not a tautology. Ruskin's comment on 'Blind mouths' brings all this within its scope.

Having pondered 'that', let me (for the moment) overleap the engine and turn to 'at the door'. This phrase is not a problem. For informed readers it never has been. Even unimaginative seventeenth-century readers would have had no difficulty with it. Even marginal Prynne would have needed no marginal note to tell him exactly what Milton was referring to. The crucial thing to realize is that Milton is not talking about a physical door. *There is no door.* Thomas Newton made this clear in 1752, and later critics (notably Harry F. Robins) have confirmed his reading, but to this day even very good critics have hung ingenious arguments on the false belief that Milton is talking about the kind of door that swings on hinges. If we believe that, we shall become unhinged. 'At the door' is a biblical locution signalling Christ's imminent return. It locates the 'two-handed engine' in time, not space. The modern colloquial equivalent would be 'around the corner'. When a modern prophet of apocalyptic doom, speaking about global warming or economic meltdown, says 'catastrophe is around the corner', he or she is not telling us that we can find it on the corner of St Giles and Beaumont Street or at the intersection of Mulholland and Fifth. So with 'at the door'. There is, in some biblical instances of the phrase, a metaphorical suggestion of Christ *knocking* at the door, but that is still no invitation to go searching for someone else's door. The point is that Christ is coming to *your* door, and coming soon.

Countless commentators, ignoring this biblical locution (many are simply unaware of it), have embarked on quixotic quests for a mysterious portal in an as-yet-unidentified architectural edifice. So far as I am aware, Masson was the first editor to encourage readers to think of 'the door of an edifice'.[13] Subsequent critics, following his lead, have proposed numerous specific doors, gates, or wickets: the pearly gates opened by St Peter's keys, the gate to a sheepfold, and the high priest's door where Peter stood when he denied Christ are just some of the candidates proposed by twentieth-century critics. Other candidates have been proposed in the first decade of the twenty-first century. I shall briefly mention two. Within their own terms, both are intriguing, but both come to grief due to a failure or refusal to acknowledge the biblical resonance of 'at the door'.

Jonathan Sawday's *Engines of the Imagination: Renaissance Culture and the Rise of the Machine* is an excellent book that adds greatly to our knowledge of industry and technology in the early modern period. The chapter on 'Milton and the Engine' makes an especially valuable contribution by examining the semantic range of the word 'engine' in seventeenth-century English. Interpreters of the 'two-handed engine' have sometimes told us that the modern sense did not exist before the Industrial Revolution. Sawday demonstrates that both the technological sense and the technology that gave rise to it were familiar in the seventeenth century, when 'London, in particular, was a hive of mechanized industrial activity'.[14] He makes a compelling case that Milton would have seen and heard mechanical engines (including an early steam engine that was invented and operated in the Royal Ordnance works in Vauxhall). Sawday is not dogmatic and he does not deny that Milton sometimes uses 'engine' in other senses. He acknowledges that 'engine' could signify either abstract or concrete entities, and sometimes both at once:

Related to the idea of *ingenium* or human ingenuity, a seventeenth-century engine might, at almost the same instant, be understood as an artillery piece, a vast battering instrument, a clumsy crowbar, a precision apparatus, or even an idea or a text. For Milton, engines were products of ingeniousness, and hence, fittingly, they were associated with Satanic energy and inventiveness. (272)

Sawday cites several instances from *Paradise Lost*, including the brief simile likening Satan in the throes of guilty conscience to a 'devillish Engine' that 'back recoiles' (iv. 17). He is also good on Mulciber's futile attempt to save himself with 'devious and cunning engines' (270):

> nor aught avail'd him now
> To have built in Heav'n high Towrs; nor did he scape
> By all his Engins, but was headlong sent
> With his industrious crew to build in hell. (i. 748–51)

Anyone who doubts that 'Engins' is a pun need only consult Milton's seventeenth-century annotator, Patrick Hume:

By all his Engins; With all his Tricks and Contrivances: The Word seems a Derivative of *Ingenium*, Wit and Cunning, of which a great deal is requisite to find out those strange Engines, and Mathematical Machines, useful in raising great Piles and vast Weights. (48)

An excellent book, then, but even Sawday's *ingenium* avails him naught when he turns to the two-handed engine of 'Lycidas'. Having listed some old candidates ('the Old and New Testaments? A two-handed broadsword? A printer's device? The two nations of England and Scotland? The keys to heaven?'), he introduces his own:

Or rather more literally, perhaps it is simply a black-powder firearm of the type which, by the time the poem had been republished in 1645, had been deployed in the volleys of fire unleashed at Naseby and Marston Moor in the civil wars, or which had been manufactured on Milton's doorstep throughout the 1630s at Vauxhall. In the form of a matchlock pistol, which required two hands to fire, or the flintlock musket, which in the everyday guise of the fowling piece would indeed have stood 'at the door' of many a country house in the seventeenth century, this device would have been instantly recognizable to Milton's contemporary readers. (274)

The problem, of course, is 'at the door'. Sawday tells us that firearms were 'manufactured on Milton's doorstep', and he makes much of the fact that

Vauxhall was 'just a short walk down river from Milton's residence in Hammersmith in the period 1631–8' (267). But Milton did not reside in Hammersmith throughout this period. At some time in 1635 or 1636 he moved to the village of Horton, some seventeen miles west of London, sufficiently removed from the bustle of the city for his retired father to refer to his 'removal to inhabit in the country'.[15] The Trinity College Manuscript draft of 'Lycidas' is dated 'November 1637', so the Vauxhall factories were not 'on Milton's doorstep' when he made his cryptic reference to 'that two-handed engine at the door'. Sawday knows better than to offer 'doorstep' as a straightforward gloss on 'at the door', but he does direct us to a physical door when he informs us that guns disguised as fowling pieces 'stood "at the door" of many a country house in the seventeenth century'. This is true. Rousham house in Oxfordshire retains such an architectural feature. Sawday does not spell out the implications, but I take it that his point is that Milton is prophesying 'the civil wars'. Within its own terms this argument is intriguing, but Sawday goes too far when he asks us to believe that Milton's engine 'would have been instantly recognizable' as a pistol or musket.

The second recent interpretation of 'at the door' that I shall consider occurs in an important recent essay by James Kelly and Catherine Bray. They argue that the 'two-handed engine' is a printing press. They present some plausible *prima facie* evidence when they inform us that 'the common or wooden hand press of 1637 was equipped with two handles and the machine or engine was serviced by two pressmen, or press hands (beater and puller)'.[16] They also direct us to a seventeenth-century text, Joseph Moxon's *Mechanick Exercises on the Whole Art of Printing* (1683–4), that calls the wooden hand press 'an Engine'.[17] These are suggestive details, and it is easy to see their appeal. But problems remain. Firstly, the phrase 'smite once and smite no more' threatens a single stroke, not the repeated motions of beaters and pullers. Secondly, Kelly and Bray offer a strained reading of 'at the door'. Noting that cathedral doors 'operated as notice boards for the rapid dissemination of important news and protest', most famously when Martin Luther posted his *Ninety-five Theses against Indulgences* "at the door" of the Collegiate Church of All Saints, Wittenberg, on 31 October 1517', Kelly and Bray draw the bold inference that 'Milton's metaphorical use of one such door might therefore gesture at an early modern information portal': 'We suggest that the component images in line 130 converge at the Great North Door of old St Paul's where that potentially subversive entity, the press, had its main retail outlet—in booksellers' shops ranged around the Cross Yard, under the very nose of the Anglican establishment.' 'Positioning the "two-handed engine at the door"', Kelly and Bray continue, 'signifies it as a hand press as opposed to any other seventeenth-century "engine"' (127). This is fascinating, but it matters that St Paul's Cross Yard was a 'retail outlet', not a site of production. No mechanical engine actually operated 'at the Great North Door'. Kelly and Bray try to get around this difficulty by retreating into metaphor and calling the cathedral door 'an early modern information portal' (they *need* the pun). Even if we ignore the distinction between production and retail, the booksellers' shops did not in fact 'converge' at the cathedral door. As Kelly and Bray candidly admit, the shops were 'built against the Cathedral walls, the north side of the Yard, and in areas adjacent to St Paul's school where Milton was pupil'. They try to turn this picture to their advantage by adding that 'the Press had the North Door and Paul's Cross surrounded', but even this melodramatic image is powerless to conceal the fact that Kelly and Bray have exaggerated the political significance of a physical door. They seem to be dissatisfied with their own explanation, for (like Sawday) they feel the need to mention one of Milton's old doorsteps: 'His home in Bread Street was situated to the east of the north transept of the Cathedral, less than 200 yards door to door' (128).

I submit that all material doors are irrelevant. As I noted earlier, no seventeenth-century reader would have had any difficulty with 'at the door' or detected the slightest hint to go hunting for specific doors, north, south, east, or west. Let me quote four instances of the biblical locution. I quote from the Geneva Bible. At Mark 13:29 and Matthew 24:33, Jesus tells his disciples that '*the kingdome of God* is neere, *even* at the doores'. At James 5:9 we read: 'behold, the judge standeth before the doore'. The closest parallel to Milton's wording occurs in Revelation 3:20, where the Son of Man tells John to write to the church of the Laodiceans, which has become complacent with worldly riches. He says: 'Behold, I stand at the door, and knock.' It may be relevant that when the Son of Man first addresses John, 'out of his mouth went a sharp two-edged sword' (1:16). Some critics have identified 'this two-edged sword' with the 'two-handed engine'. But my immediate point is that 'at the door' is a biblical locution that denotes Christ's imminent return. Too many critics either ignore this locution or shunt it off into the margins as an unimportant detail. Kelly and Bray fall into the latter category. They finally acknowledge the biblical phrase in the closing pages of their essay and quote two biblical occurrences (Mark 13:29 and Rev. 3:20) in a footnote.[18] It is strange that they can do this and still not see that the biblical provenance of 'at the door' makes all physical doors irrelevant. At least Kelly and Bray are aware of the biblical locution. Most recent critics never mention it.

This is partly the fault of modern editions. Very few modern editors have noted the biblical provenance of 'at the door'—even when they note other biblical allusions (such as the echo of 1 Samuel 26:8 in 'smite no more'). Editors tend either to list the prime candidates (axe, sword, keys, and so on) or throw their hands up with an evasive comment such as 'variously interpreted'. Such notes have reinforced the belief that the whole couplet is impenetrable. It is not. 'At the door' *can* be explained and earlier editors did explain it. The first commentator to explain 'at the door' was Thomas Newton in 1752. He did not present the information as a eureka moment; it was more a case of reminding readers of what every Christian ought to know. But he did present one piece of information as news. He pointed out that Milton uses the same phrase in one of his anti-prelatical tracts: 'In his Animadversions upon the Remonstrants Defense, addressing himself to the Son of God [Milton] *says—but thy kingdom is now at hand, and thou standing at the door.*'[19] So far as I am aware, Newton was the first person to remark this instance in Milton's prose. Others have since noted it, but surprisingly few modern editions have picked it up. Woodhouse and Bush in the *Milton Variorum Commentary* note both the biblical locution and Milton's prose use of it, but their twenty-page entry on the two-handed engine offers so much information that Newton's contribution gets lost in the crowd.

I now come to the heart of the crux: the 'two-handed engine'. Whatever the engine is, it must be related in some way to Christ's imminent return as signalled by 'at the door'. Harry F. Robins saw this clearly. Writing in 1954, he came independently to Newton's interpretation of 'at the door', which he offered as an original discovery. Like Newton, he recognized the biblical phrase and noted Milton's use of it in *Animadversions*. He concluded that the 'two-handed engine' is an instrument of judgement. He identified this instrument as Christ himself. Here it must be admitted that Robins coarsened his own argument. He claimed that the engine is 'two-handed' because Christ is: 'I propose that the elemental sense of "two-handed engine" is an engine with two hands—a man.'[20] It is not hard to see why Robins's essay is now largely ignored. At the crucial moment, he reduces his argument to a banal syllogism: the engine has two hands, people have two hands—*ergo* the engine is a person, '—a man'. We should throw out Robins's bath-water with both hands, but we should keep the baby. He is right about 'at the door' and right to direct us to Matthew's Gospel. Two pages after presenting us with his syllogism, he quotes the following verses from Matthew 25 (they appear just one chapter after Matthew's use of 'at the dores'): 'And before him shall be gathered all nations: and he shall separate them one from another as a shephearde separateth the sheepe from the goates. And he shall set the sheepe on his right hand, and the goats on his left' (25:32–3). Astonishingly, Robins never explicitly connects 'two-handed' with Christ's division of sheep and goats on his right and left hands. Presumably, he thought the connection so obvious that there was no need to spell it out. But his argument needs all the help it can get after that gaffe about 'a man' being 'an engine with two hands'. Robins would have done better to have cut that sentence and instead emphasize the division into left and right. The *OED* might have helped. Most critics have taken 'two-handed' to mean either 'wielded with both hands' or 'composed of two parts' (both are plausible interpretations), but the *OED* admits a third possibility under the now obsolete adjectival compound 'two-hand', which it defines as follows: 'leading in two directions (right hand and left hand)' (*OED* 'two-hand' 3). If 'two-handed' includes (I am not arguing that it should be limited to) this sense, Milton's 'engine' would be an instrument of judgement that brings about a final separation.

Here it is useful to turn to Joseph Mede (or Mead), the renowned and influential theologian who was a Fellow at Christ's College Cambridge during Milton's seven years there (though he was not Milton's tutor). Marjorie Nicolson has plausibly identified him as the eponymous 'old *Damoetas*' of 'Lycidas'.[21] Mede had little sympathy with radical anti-prelatical views. Campbell and Corns tell us that he had 'secured his Fellowship through the patronage of Lancelot Andrewes, and his own inclinations were certainly ceremonial and Arminian' (28). His scholarly study of the Books of Daniel and Revelation had nevertheless convinced him that the Pope was the Antichrist, and he stood by that conclusion despite feeling

an anxiety that his insistence on equating the pope with the Antichrist perhaps made him appear to be a puritanical zealot in the eyes of those whose support he courted, though for him it was a conclusion founded on his study of the Revelation of St John the Divine.[22]

Mede's interpretation of scripture certainly appealed to those who saw prelatical episcopacy as a relic of papacy. John Rumrich notes that 'one of the first acts of the Westminster Assembly in 1641, charged with reforming the Laudian Church of England, was to have Mead's work translated into English'.[23] Mede's millenarianism—his belief that Christ would return to reign on this earth for a thousand years—helped to foster what Rumrich calls an 'apocalyptic consciousness' and so 'had great significance for seventeenth-century religious politics' (39).

Mede had an avowedly millenarian understanding of the picture of Final Judgement in Matthew 25:32–3. Writing to William Twisse from Christ's College on 18 April 1636, he offered the following gloss upon the separation of sheep from goats:

Concerning . . . *Matth.* 25 when our Blessed Saviour shall sit upon his Throne of Royalty to judge the world; I conceive a Figure to be in that expression of placing the *Sheep* on his *right hand* and the *Goats* on the *left*, borrowed from the custome of the Jews in their Tribunals, to place such as were *absolved* on the *right hand*, where stood the Scribe who took the Votes for *Absolution*; and those who were to receive the sentence of *Condemnation*, on the *left hand*, where stood the Scribe which took the Votes for *Condemnation*. Such a custom of theirs *Drusius* in his Notes upon that place observes out of *Moses de Kotsi*. That therefore nothing else is meant thereby, but that our Saviour should distinguish the world of men into two Orders; one of such as should receive the *Sentence of bliss and Absolution*, the other of such as should receive the *Sentence of Condemnation*. That he should *first* pronounce the Sentence of Absolution upon such as are to be absolved; and that once finished, then to pronounce the Sentence of Condemnation upon such as are to be condemned.[24]

This picture works very well with Robins's notion of judgement as an 'engine' that divides the human race into two categories, the saved on the right, the damned on the left. Mede did not believe that the judgement would be a quick process. He goes on to inform Twisse that 'the *Sentence of Absolution* shall continue all the time of the *First Resurrection*, that is, all the *Thousand years* long' (1031). But Christ's return will still end all earthly monarchies and some of the saved will sit in judgement with him.

By the time that he came to write *De Doctrina Christiana* Milton himself was a millenarian. We do not know when he first espoused these views, and there has been some debate as to whether he abandoned them after the Restoration had thwarted his political hopes. Stella Revard has made a strong case for believing that he was a millenarian throughout his career.[25] If she is right, we must take care to distinguish the Second Coming from the Last Judgement. Christ may be 'at the door' as returning judge, but his imminent judgement could last a thousand years. We should eschew dogmatic readings, especially when the evidence is so slender, but an awareness of the *possibility* of a millenarian interpretation adds to the difficulties attending 'that two-handed engine at the door'.

Some readers will dismiss the whole topic of right and left hands as another irrelevance, and it must be admitted that the line of argument I have been pursuing encounters an obstacle in 'engine'. That word lies at the heart of this crux, and it has brought more than a few ingenious readings to ruin. A notable exception is David Sansone's recent article in *Modern Philology*. Most of what I have to say in the remainder of this essay is offered in grateful response to Sansone's plausible and original argument that the 'two-handed engine' is the winnowing fan prophesied by John the Baptist in Matthew 3:12. While I am unconvinced by the second half of Sansone's argument (he leaves me behind when he turns his winnowing fan into an oar and paddles off into the wild blue yonder with Odysseus and Telemachus, taking detours via Theocritus and Lycophron), his basic insight that the 'two-handed engine' is a biblical implement of divine judgement is not only plausible but persuasive. Sansone makes it seem strange that no one should have suggested a winnowing fan before—and that in itself is the sign of a first-rate essay. The process of threshing and winnowing was, after all, a familiar biblical metaphor for judgement. Old Testament precedents include Jeremiah 51:33 ('the daughter of Babel is like a threshing floore: the time of her threshing is come') and Habukkuk 3:12 ('thresh the heathen'). The association of judgement with a harvest can evoke other two-handed engines, such as a scythe, and this too has biblical precedents, as in Joel 3:13 ('put in your sithes [A.V. "the sickle"], for the harvest is ripe'). Sansone nevertheless detects a specific reference to John the Baptist's prophecy of the winnowing of the wicked. John says that the Messiah 'hath his fanne in his hand and will make cleane his floore, and gather his wheate into his garner, but will burne up the chaffe with unquenchable fire' (Matt. 3:12). The separation of wheat from chaff, like the separation of sheep from goats, connects readily with the eschatological implications of 'at the door'. This gives Sansone's winnowing fan an advantage over many (though not all) other candidates for the 'two-handed engine'.

Unfortunately, Sansone misses the opportunity to drive this advantage home. Like so many before him, he fails to recognize that 'at the door' is a biblical locution and so draws the false inference that Milton is talking about a literal door. '"The door"', he writes, 'surely refers to a specific door.' Sansone identifies this 'specific door' as the gate of heaven. Ignorance of the biblical provenance of 'at the door' is fatal to many interpretations of the two-handed engine, but the true interpretation of this phrase would have helped Sansone. His argument also works well with 'two-handed', for winnowing fans are wielded with two hands and they also separate wheat and chaff into two piles. As an agricultural implement, a winnowing fan would also be more at home in a pastoral poem than (say) axe, sword, or keys.

But there are some problems. Firstly and most importantly winnowing fans do not smite. They winnow the buxom air, but they do not whack anything. Even when beating the air they do not 'smite once, and smite no more'. They fan repeatedly, creating sufficient breeze to blow the lighter chaff away from the heavier grain. Sansone is aware of the problem and confronts it honestly. 'The word "smite"', he admits, is 'not literally appropriate to the action of a winnowing fan.' Sansone thinks that Milton chose 'smite' because it 'expresses the doom that inevitably attends those sinners who are revealed by the process of threshing and winnowing' (339). There is some slippage here—and another missed opportunity. Sansone speaks of 'threshing and winnowing' as if they were a single 'process', but they are really two processes. Before the grain is winnowed, it must be threshed from the husks. Threshing used to be done with a threshing flail: two hardwood sticks joined with a short rope or chain. In some cultures threshing flails (such as the Japanese *nunchaku*) have been used as weapons. My point is not that 'that two-handed engine' is an agricultural implement used as a weapon. My point is that Sansone's argument can survive the rebuttal that winnowing fans do not smite. They do not. But flails do, and the Bible repeatedly likens divine judgement to the twin processes of threshing and winnowing. Sansone sells his own argument short when he falls back on a metaphorical reading of 'smite'. To thresh *is* 'to smite'. 'Thresh' and 'thrash' are etymologically the same word.

But there is still a problem. Threshing is arduous and repetitive. Roy Flannagan (who has first-hand experience) tells me that it is back-breaking work and that no threshing flail that he has ever worked with could 'smite once and smite no more'. Point taken. But Milton is not talking about an ordinary thresher. If Robins and Sansone are right, he is talking about the

Son of Man. 'Smite once and smite no more' would gain added point if it refers to an act that is *ordinarily* labour-intensive but is, in this instance, miraculously efficient. This would not be the first time that Milton has described a superhuman feat of threshing. Compare the lubber fiend in 'L'Allegro':

> When in one night, ere glimpse of morn,
> His shadowy flail hath threshed the corn
> That ten day-labourers could not end. (105–7)

If the lubber fiend is as quick and efficient as ten farm labourers, how much more efficient must be that ultimate thresher, Christ the Judge?

There are in fact biblical precedents for associating divine judgement with a sudden violent act that threshes and winnows at one single spectacular stroke. Sansone directs us to two such precedents. The first is Matthew 21:44, where Jesus (recalling 'the stone, which the builders refused', Ps. 118:22) threatens the priests and pharisees: 'And whosoever shall fall on this stone, he shall be broken: but on whomsoever it shall fall, it will dash him to pieces.' Sansone informs us that the Greek 'word translated "dash" is λικμήσει, the literal meaning of which is "winnow", as the note in the Geneva Bible points out' (339). The Geneva note reads: 'As chaffe useth to bee scattered with the winde, for he useth a word which signifieth properly, to separate the chaffe from the corne with winnowing, and to scatter it abroade.' Sansone's second biblical precedent is even more suggestive, for both the Geneva and King James translations use the word 'smite'. Sansone directs readers to the smashing of the image in Nebuchadnezzar's dream. Nebuchadnezzar dreams of 'a great image' whose 'head was of fine golde, his breast, and his armes of silver, his belly and his thighes of brasse', his 'legs of iron, and his feete were part of yron, and part of clay'. A stone 'cut without hands' then

smote the image upon his feete, that were of yron and clay, and broke them to pieces. Then was the yron, the clay, the brasse, the silver and the golde broken all together, and became like the chaffe of the summer floures, and the winde caried them away, that no place was found for them: and the stone that smote the image, became a great mountaine, and filled the whole earth. (Dan. 2:35)

Sansone concludes that this biblical verse, together with Matthew 21:44, provides a precedent for a winnowing fan that smites, and he quotes a number of early modern pamphleteers (including Thomas Draxe, John Knox, and William Perkins) who used the image of winnowing in just this way 'to convey the notions of destruction and instruments of destruction' (339). The point can be made even more strongly, for Milton himself is one of the pamphleteers who use this image. In *Animadversions* he makes an explicit allusion to Nebuchadnezzar's dream and associates the smashed image with prelacy. He does this just a few pages before he uses the phrase 'at the door'. Both moments have millenarian implications, for millenarians frequently read Daniel 2 alongside Revelation 20 as a prophecy of Christ's thousand-year reign on earth.

I shall return to *Animadversions* in a moment. First we need to take a closer look at Daniel. The stone that smote the image 'was cut without hands'. Christians of all persuasions took these words to be a reference to the miracle of the incarnation. But commentators disagreed as to the significance of the 'great mountaine' that the stone subsequently 'became'. Orthodox exegetes since at least the time of Tertullian had interpreted the mountain as Christ's church, spread unto the ends of the earth. This interpretation places the fulfilment of Nebuchadnezzar's dream in the past. Millenarians believed that the latter part of the dream was yet to be fulfilled. All Christians agreed that the composite 'great image' symbolized successive earthly kingdoms, but there had long been disagreement as to their number and identities. The image is composed of five materials (gold, silver, brass, iron, and clay) and so some exegetes (including many Jewish commentators) counted five kingdoms, but most Christian interpreters conflated the legs with the feet and so counted four. These were usually identified as Babylon, Persia, Greece, and Rome. Most Christian exegetes (both Catholic and Protestant) took Rome to be the ancient Roman empire and so concluded that the prophecy had been fulfilled long ago. Millenarians took a different view. They extended the Roman kingdom (the feet of iron and clay) to include the papacy (and sometimes the imperfectly reformed English Church) and so inferred that the stone was yet to strike. They identified the 'great mountaine' that would fill 'the whole earth' as a fifth monarchy: Christ's thousand-year reign on earth. The extreme Puritans active in the 1650s and known as the Fifth Monarchy Men were willing to use military force to establish Christ's kingdom. Conservative millenarians like Mede had no sympathy with this kind of radicalism, but his theories inspired those who did.

Daniel's prophecies were certainly important to Milton. He alludes to them often throughout his career, most memorably in *Paradise Regained*.

> Know therefore when my season comes to sit
> On *David*'s Throne, it shall be like a tree
> Spreading and over-shadowing all the Earth,
> Or as a stone that shall to pieces dash
> All Monarchies besides throughout the world,
> And of my Kingdom there shall be no end. (iv. 146–51)

The 'tree' is another allusion to Daniel. Jesus is recalling Nebuchadnezzar's dream of a 'great tree and strong, and the height thereof reached unto heaven, and the sight thereof to the ends of all the earth' (Dan. 4:8). Like the 'great mountaine' of Daniel 2:35, the tree provoked controversy. Orthodox commentators took it to be another prophecy of the church now existing, but millenarians took it as a prophecy of the kingdom yet to come. Stella Revard has argued that Jesus's lines in *Paradise Regained* accord with Mede's theory that both mountain and tree are prophecies of 'the future millenarian kingdom'.[26] The evidence is not conclusive, but Revard's reading makes better sense of 'shall to pieces dash / All Monarchies'. No one knew better than John Milton that earthly monarchies had *not* been dashed in his own time (though the Stuart monarchy had taken a hit). Jesus's 'shall' can be heard as a warning to complacent Royalists—and it should also serve as a warning to any Miltonist who believes that *Paradise Regained* is the work of a disillusioned quietist.

Milton was certainly no quietist in 1641 when he published *Animadversions upon the Remonstrants Defence against Smectymnuus*. Here he explicitly enlists Daniel against the prelates. Refuting the Remonstrant's argument that 'the old way was the good way', Milton likens reverence for tradition to idol worship. He does not name Daniel and he does not immediately name Nebuchadnezzar. The allusion emerges gradually from a more general statement about the folly of overvaluing 'what was done in Antiquity':

Why doe wee therefore stand worshipping, and admiring this unactive, and livelesse *Colossus*, that like a carved Gyant terribly menacing to children, and weaklings lifts up his club, but strikes not, and is subject to the muting [defecating] of every Sparrow. If you let him rest upon his *Basis*, hee may perhaps delight the eyes of some with his huge and mountainous Bulk, and the quaint workmanship of his massie limbs; but if yee goe about to take him in pieces, yee marre him.... Wee shall adhere close to the Scriptures...and with this weapon without stepping a foot further, wee shall not doubt to batter, and throw down your *Nebuchadnezzars* Image and crumble it like the chaffe of the Summer threshing floores, as well the gold of those Apostolick Successors that you boast of, as your *Constantinian* silver, together with the iron, the brasse, and the clay of those muddy and strawy ages that follow.[27]

There is much here to make a millenarian's ears prick up. The references to '*Nebuchadnezzars* Image', '*Constantinian* silver', and the 'strawy ages that follow' are not just casual metaphors. Milton's language is precise and his target clear. The reference to Constantine is especially suggestive. Milton knows that his prelatical adversaries follow Roman Catholics in identifying the millennium prophesied in Revelation 20 with the thousand years that had commenced with the conversion of Constantine and concluded with the beginning of the Reformation. Catholics and Protestants naturally disagreed about the significance of this chronology. Each blamed the other for loosing Satan from his prison and so putting an end to the thousand years (Rev. 20:7). Even Presbyterians like Richard Baxter looked back to Constantine and the first thousand years of the Holy Roman Empire as a fulfilment of the promised millennium. Milton did not share this view. In *Of Reformation* he refers scathingly to 'the Roman *Antichrist* . . . bred up by *Constantine*' and argues that '*Constantine* marr'd all in the Church'.[28] For Milton, Constantine's reign marked the end, not the beginning, of an age of purity. Insisting that Constantine opened 'a dore to more mischiefe in Christendome', Milton excoriates those who hearken back to his reign as an ideal for the English Church to aspire to:

There is just cause therefore that when the *Prelates* cry out Let the Church be reformed according to *Constantine*, it should sound to a judicious eare no otherwise, then if they should say Make us rich, make us lofty, make us lawlesse, for if any under him were not so, thanks to those ancient remains of integrity, which were not yet quite worne out, and not to his Government.[29]

When Milton in *Animadversions* refers to '*Constantinian* silver', he is not identifying Constantine's empire with the silver breast and arms in Nebuchadnezzar's dream. He is punning on the prelates' love of silver coin. But the sequence 'gold', 'silver', 'iron', 'brasse', and 'clay' (together with the specific mention of 'ages') clearly glances at the controversy as to just *which* ages the dream had prophesied. The prelates believe that the 'great mountaine' is now here and that they are safely perched on its pinnacle. Milton's imagery dislodges them from that lofty station. Far from being the culmination of Daniel's prophecy, the prelates represent a further degeneration in the succession of ages. Unworthy even to be clay feet, they preside over 'those muddy and strawy ages that follow'.

But change is coming. Six pages after evoking the four kingdoms in Daniel, Milton suddenly invokes the last and best of kings. It is here that he uses the phrase 'at the dore':

> Come therefore O thou that hast the seven starres in thy right hand. . . . Every one can say that now certainly thou hast visited this land, and hast not forgotten the utmost corners of the earth, in a time when men had thought that thou wast gone up from us to the farthest end of the Heavens, and hadst left to doe marvellously among the sons of these last Ages. O perfect, and accomplish thy glorious acts; for men may leave their works unfinisht, but thou art a God, and thy nature is perfection . . . seeing the power of thy grace is not past away with the primitive times, as fond and faithless men imagine, but thy Kingdome is now at hand, and thou standing at the dore. Come forth out of thy Royall Chambers, O Prince of all the Kings of the earth, put on the visible roabes of thy imperiall Majesty, take up that unlimited Scepter which thy Almighty Father hath bequeath'd thee; for now the voice of thy Bride calls thee, and all creatures sigh to bee renew'd.[30]

Many Miltonists have read this passage as a prayer imploring Christ to begin his thousand-year reign on earth.[31] Some might feel that the reference to an 'unlimited Scepter' rules out a millennial reading: how can a kingdom that will last a thousand years be 'unlimited'? I admit that this is a problem, but it is not insurmountable. Milton in *De Doctrina Christiana* insists that a millennial interpretation of Daniel and Revelation can be reconciled with scriptural statements that Christ's kingdom will be 'everlasting' (Dan. 7:14) and endure 'for all ages' (Heb. 1:8). 'My reply', Milton writes, 'is that there will be no end to his kingdom *for all ages*, that is, while the ages of the world endure, until *time will be no more*, Rev. x. 6'.[32] Milton may have modified his views between writing *Animadversions* and *De Doctrina*, but 'unlimited' does not preclude a millenarian reading, and the references to 'visible roabes' and 'the Kings of the earth' work better with a millenarian interpretation. We should also remember that in the closing pages of *Of Reformation*, Milton implores Christ to reign on this earth:

> when thou the Eternall and shortly-expected King shalt open the Clouds to judge the severall Kingdomes of the World, and distributing *Nationall Honours* and *Rewards* to Religious and just *Common-wealths*, shalt put an end to all Earthly *Tyrannies*, proclaiming thy universal and milde *Monarchy* through Heaven and Earth.[33]

Most Miltonists agree that these words refer to the millennium. If that is correct, the passage has strong implications for the 'Kingdome . . . at the dore' in *Animadversions*.

The passage from *Animadversions* demands attention not just because it contains the words 'at the dore'. It also mentions a specific object that the returning king and judge will wield: 'that unlimited Scepter'. This sceptre is worth a closer look. So far as I am aware, only one critic has identified 'that two-handed engine' as a sceptre. E. M. W. Tillyard in 1930 directed us to 'the iron sceptre or rod of Christ's anger: "two-handed" for nothing further than its size and weight'. This is suggestive, but Tillyard misses some things. Firstly, he misses the sceptre in *Animadversions* and so misses the fact that Milton mentions a sceptre in the same breath as he uses the phrase 'at the dore'. Like so many other critics, Tillyard identifies 'the door' in 'Lycidas' with a literal door: 'The "door" is the door of the sheepfold, which was well fenced round, since the shepherds have had to climb into it.'[34] The crassness of this statement should not blind us to the possibility that Tillyard just might be on to something with 'the iron sceptre or rod of Christ's anger'. He cites two texts to support his case. The first is *Of Reformation*. Milton there writes that anyone who rejects 'the Pastorly *Rod*, and Sheep-hooke of CHRIST' must 'feare to fall under the iron *Scepter* of his anger that will dash him to peeces like a Potsherd'.[35] As Tillyard notes, Milton is here alluding to Psalms 2:9. The Geneva version reads: 'Thou shalt crush [A. V. "break"] them with a scepter of yron, and break [A. V. "dash"] them in pieces like a potters vessell.' Milton himself would translate this psalm in 1653, when he would use the phrase 'With Iron Scepter bruis'd' (20).

Tillyard's 1930 argument fell on deaf ears and he himself would eventually abandon it. In 1952 he cast his vote for a sword.[36] My purpose in drawing attention to his earlier argument is not to press the claims of the sceptre over those of the sword. It is significant that every time a plausible candidate is proposed, a rival can be seen lurking just behind it. In the case just cited, Tillyard is forced to name 'the Pastorly *Rod*, and Sheep-hooke of CHRIST' in the same breath as 'the iron *Scepter*'. He does so for the good reason that Milton does, but Tillyard has no use for the sheep-hook and so he ignores it—even though he must have known that other critics had identified the 'two-handed engine' as a shepherd's rod and crook. Tillyard is not alone in pressing his own candidate to the exclusion of all others. As we shall see in a moment, Sansone does something similar. My point (which I want to make with some emphasis) is that we do Milton a disservice when we read him in

this way. Milton is inclusive where his critics are exclusive. Consider the phrase
'Pastorly *Rod*, and Sheep-hooke'. '*Rod*' there refers to a shepherd's staff, but the
word also resonates with 'iron *Scepter*', especially since the iron sceptre of Christ's
wrath was sometimes referred to as 'a rod of iron'. Tillyard hears 'iron *Scepter*' as
an allusion to Psalm 2. It is that, but it is also an allusion to the book of
Revelation where the Son of Man speaks of a reward that awaits the faithful
in the last days: 'For he that overcometh and keepeth my words unto the end,
to him will I give power over nations. And he shall rule them with a rod of
yron: and as the vessels of a potter, shall they be broken' (Rev. 2:26–7). The two
biblical passages were traditionally connected (the Geneva Bible note to Ps. 2:9
directs us to Rev. 2:27) and Milton himself connects them in *De Doctrina Christiana*,
where he reads both as prophecies of Christ's thousand-year reign on earth:

There are any number of texts which show that Christ's reign will take place on the
earth; Psal. ii. 8, 9, compared with Rev. ii 25–27: *I will give the Gentiles to you as your property,
and the ends of the earth will be your rightful possession: you will break them with an iron rod, you will
shatter them like a piece of pottery.*[37]

When Milton in *Of Reformation* speaks in a single breath of a 'Pastorly *Rod*' and
'iron *Scepter*', the rod and sceptre are not unrelated. They are different aspects
of the same thing. Tillyard thinks that the sceptre is 'two-handed' solely on
account of its 'size and weight'. I agree that 'two-handed' implies a bulky
object wielded with two hands, but the phrase also suggests an instrument
that has two distinct aspects for two opposed groups.

Christ's sceptre is 'two-handed' in exactly this way. For the just, it is an
emblem of mild kingship; for the wicked, it is an iron rod that shatters.
Beelzebub in *Paradise Lost* equips the King of Kings with *two* sceptres:

> For he, be sure
> In heighth or depth, still first and last will Reign
> Sole King, and of his Kingdom loose no part
> By our revolt, but over Hell extend
> His Empire, and with Iron Scepter rule
> Us here, as with his Golden those in Heav'n. (ii. 323–8)

Abdiel, addressing Satan, expresses the same idea: 'That Golden Scepter
which thou didst reject / Is now an Iron Rod to bruise and breake / Thy
disobedience' (v. 886–8). These passages from *Paradise Lost* reinforce my sense
that Milton uses the terms 'sceptre' and 'rod' interchangeably. If this is right,
there is no need to see pastorly rod and kingly sceptre as rival candidates for

the privileged status of 'two-handed engine'. Milton's phrase can include both. Both can be wielded with two hands, and both can be wielded in two ways. The two ends of a shepherd's staff serve separate functions. The crook draws back those who stray, while the base (often pointed) can goad the lazy or punish the recalcitrant. The sceptre is golden to the faithful and iron to the wicked. Both kinds of rod can smite, smashing the wicked 'to peeces like a Potsherd'.

What, then, of the other plausible candidates—axe, sword, threshing flail, and winnowing fan? I noted a moment ago that every time a critic advances his or her favoured candidate for the 'two-handed engine', a rival object appears in the background. Critics usually respond in either of two ways. They either ignore the intruder (as Tillyard ignores the shepherd's rod and crook) or they go out of their way to suppress it. I suggest that this is the wrong response. If a rival engine appears, and is genuinely plausible, we should ask ourselves whether it might not help rather than threaten the claims of the engine we want. Take as an example the prayer in *Animadversions* that I quoted a moment ago. I seized upon the phrase 'that unlimited Scepter'. But at the outset of the prayer Milton makes a glancing allusion to another object. When he addresses Christ as 'thou that hast the seven starres in thy right hand', he clearly alludes to Revelation 1:16. Readers who know their Bible will supply (though Milton does not) the whole verse to which he alludes: 'And he had in his Right hand seven starres: and out of his mouth went a sharpe two edged sword.' The two-edged sword of Revelation 1:16 has long been a leading candidate for the two-handed engine. The temptation for someone who wants to press the claims of Christ's sceptre would be to ignore or suppress the sword. But might they not work together? Might there not be precedents for conflating them into a single instrument of divine judgement?

Such precedents do exist and they have biblical support in Revelation 19:15 where Christ returns to crush his foes and bind Satan for a thousand years: 'And out of his mouth went out a sharpe sword, that with it he should smite the heathen: for he shall rule them with a rod of yron.' Jan van der Noodt in *A Theatre for Worldlings* (1569) offers a detailed comment on this sword:

and out of his mouth went a sharp sword, which is that wonderful iudgement of his word. Through this sharpe sword are the faithful and belevers saved to life everlasting, and the wicked infidels iudged to everlasting death and damnation.

For it is unto some a savior of life unto life, and to others a savior of death, unto death. With this sword shall be cut of the dead braunches which in him beare no fruicts and the rotted members from the body. In like manner shalbe the good from the bad, and the Goates from the sheepe, with this sword devided and separated: Oh how terrible, fearefull, and sharpe shalbe the iudgement of the Lord, the rod and scepter of his dominion against the wicked in those dayes.[38]

Like the iron-golden sceptre, Christ's 'sharpe sword' has a double function. It brings 'life everlasting' to 'some', and 'everlasting death' to 'others'. Jan van Noodt conflates sword with sceptre when he exclaims how 'sharpe shalbe the iudgement of the Lord, the rod and scepter'. 'Rod' there is obviously Christ's 'rod of yron' (Rev. 19:15), but coming so soon after the reference to sheep and goats, it also suggests a pastorly sheep-hook. In cutting away 'dead braunches' from fruitless trees, Christ's sword also serves the office of the axe in Matthew 3:10 and Luke 3:9 (I shall return to this axe in a moment).

A Theatre for Worldlings is by no means the only early modern text to conflate biblical images in this way. Calvin in his Institutes quotes one of Cyprian's letters in which the church father conflates Christ's iron rod with a threshing flail and winnowing fan:

Cyprian, then, has put it well: 'Even though there seem to be tares or unclean vessels in the church, there is no reason why we ourselves should withdraw from the church; rather, we must toil to become wheat; we must strive as much as we can to be vessels of gold and silver. But the breaking of earthen vessels belongs solely to the Lord, to whom has also been entrusted an iron rod [Ps. 2:9; Rev. 2:27]. And let no one so claim for himself what is the Son's alone, that it is enough to winnow the chaff and thresh the straw [cf. Matt. 3:12; Luke 3:17] and by human judgment to separate out all the tares [cf. Matt. 13:38-41]. Proud, indeed, is this stubbornness and impious presumption, which wicked madness takes upon itself.'[39]

Calvin and Cyprian write with a more pacific tone than Milton exhibits in St Peter's climactic couplet. Their aim (in this instance) is to heal wounds within the church and warn against excessive zeal; Milton is zealous against the wicked. But Milton might agree that retribution is 'the Son's alone'. If I am right to read 'that two-handed engine at the door' as a reference to the millennium, it is the Son's judgement that Milton zealously implores. The crucial point is that Calvin and Cyprian feel no need to choose between biblical images of divine judgement. Like Jan van der Noodt, they combine them freely. Where van der Noodt moves from sword to axe to sheep-hook to sceptre, Cyprian moves from iron rod to winnowing fan to threshing flail. This kind of conflation also has Jewish precedents. Midrashic exegesis equated the 'iron sceptre' of Psalms 2:9 with a sword.[40]

With these precedents in mind, I should now like to return to Sansone's argument that the two-handed engine is the winnowing-fan of Matthew 3:12. Sansone has made a major contribution, but he paradoxically weakens his argument when he tries to strengthen it by excluding rival engines. In particular, he is too dismissive of the axe that John the Baptist mentions just two verses before the fan. John says: 'And now also is the axe put to the root of the trees: therefore every tree which bringeth not foorth good fruit, is hewen downe, and cast into the fire' (Matt. 3:10). Many early critics, beginning with Newton, identified the two-handed engine with this axe. Later critics would detect a prophecy of Archbishop Laud's execution. Still later critics would discount the axe on the grounds that Milton in 1637 could not have foreseen Laud's bloody end. But Newton did not say that the two-handed engine is an *executioner's* axe; he saw it as a symbol of Reformation. Milton in *Of Reformation* speaks of 'the Axe of Gods reformation hewing at the old and hollow trunk of Papacie'.[41] Newton identified the two-handed engine with *this* axe. The idea is not absurd. On 11 December 1640, 15,000 Londoners petitioned Parliament to abolish episcopacy 'with all its dependencies, roots and branches'. The phrase 'Root and Branch' likely does allude to Matthew 3:10 ('the axe put to the root'). The Geneva Bible reads 'put to', but the King James Version changes this to 'laid unto'. Sansone, eager to press the claims of the winnowing fan, seizes on 'laid unto' as a stroke against the axe. He infers that the axe is lying down, inertly, at the trees' roots: 'the axe is simply lying (κεῖται) on the ground at the foot of the trees, while the winnowing fan is in the hand, ready for use' (333–4). This rings false. To my ears, 'laid unto' works like the modern colloquialism 'lay into', meaning 'hit violently'. The *OED* gives instances of 'lay' meaning 'strike' from as early as 1530 (*OED* 34). Interestingly, this ambiguity exists in the Greek too. Sansone tells us that κεῖται means 'lie down', and Liddell and Scott do give that sense; but their very next sense is 'cleave'. The Geneva version ('put to the root') implies a cleaving axe. My point is not to press the axe's claim before the fan's. There is a precedent for conflating them and Sansone himself provides it. He tells us that John Knox had combined axe and fan 'into one image', 'regarding both as instruments of divine doom' (340). Knox does this in his 1558 pamphlet, *The Appellation of John Knoxe*. Addressing England and Scotland, he writes, 'When I do behold both your two realmes, I see the fanne, I see the axe . . . God shall hew you downe by them therefore, as he hath done other nations by like means and causes, and they shall fanne you furthe of your own huskes and homes, to make you vagaboundes and beggars' (sig. 73v). Sansone rightly insists that this helps his case for the fan, but it helps the axe too, and it supports the idea that the 'two-handed engine' can be more than one thing.

But it is not an infinite number of things. We should draw the line somewhere. I have argued that we should draw it at the Second Coming and the millennium. Critics routinely use the word 'vague' to describe Milton's image, but we should not confuse vagueness with multiplicity. 'That two-handed engine at the door' draws upon multiple biblical images, but all are precise and all point to a single end. Even the word 'engine' is not so much 'vague' as inclusive. The beauty of the word is that it can accommodate precise images (the sheer number of specific engines that have been proposed proves this to be so) and still retain a unifying abstract sense. Here it is useful to compare George Herbert's use of the same word:

> Prayer, the Church's banquet, angels' age,
> God's breath in man returning to his birth,
> The soul in paraphrase, heart in pilgrimage,
> The Christian plummet sounding heav'n and earth,
> Engine against th' Almighty, sinners' tower,
> Reversed thunder, Christ-side-piercing spear.
>
> ('Prayer (I)', 1–6)

'Engine' here includes 'siege engine', and so invites the image of a large battering-ram or siege tower, and the latter image is reinforced by the very next words until we realize that 'sinners' tower' is an allusion to the Tower of Babel. The allusion does not cancel the idea of siege warfare, since Babel itself (in Milton's memorable words) threatened 'Siege and defiance' to heaven;[42] but Herbert now figures prayer as a feat of architectural rather than military engineering. The thunder and spear of the next line are also variations on the theme of 'Engine', and it is possible that the sequence 'Engine', 'Almighty', 'tower', and 'thunder' inspired Milton to put these same words in the mouth of Moloch when he voices a genuine wish to reverse God's thunder:

> let us rather choose
> Arm'd with Hell flames and fury all at once
> O're Heav'ns high Towrs to force resistless way,

Turning our Tortures into horrid Arms
Against the Torturer; when to meet the noise
Of his Almighty Engin he shall hear
Infernal Thunder, and for Lightning see
Black fire and horror shot with equal rage
Among his Angels. (ii. 60–8)

Here too 'Engin' is all the more suggestive for including a variety of possibilities (it has been variously glossed as 'thunder', 'lightning', and 'chariot') while retaining the general (not the same as 'vague') sense as defined in the first English dictionary, Robert Cawdrey's *A Table Alphabetical* (1604): 'ingine, engine} an instrument to doo any thing with'. The two-handed engine of 'Lycidas' has much 'to doo'. It does the work of a winnowing fan, but it also does the work of an axe, a sword, a rod, a sceptre, a sheep-hook, and a threshing flail. Yet all these separate activities amount to just one act: divine judgement. Like the stone in Nebuchadnezzar's dream, 'that two-handed engine at the door' smites, threshes, and winnows all at once in a single climactic act that brings about a final, decisive division: wheat from chaff, fruit from dead wood, sheep from goats, right hand from left. That, it seems to me, is the crucial point that needs to be made, and it divides plausible from implausible interpretations as wheat from chaff.

Notes

1. 'Lycidas' 130–1. Unless otherwise stated, all citations of Milton's poetry are from *The Riverside Milton*, ed. Roy Flannagan (Boston, Mass., 1998).
2. *Areopagitica*, in *CPW*, ii. 514.
3. David Sansone, 'How Milton Reads: Scripture, the Classics, and That Two-Handed Engine', *Modern Philology*, 103 (2006), 332–57.
4. Stanley Fish, *How Milton Works* (Cambridge, Mass., 2001), 273.
5. Christopher Hill, *Milton and the English Revolution* (New York, 1977), 51.
6. Annabel Patterson, 'That Old Man Eloquent', in Diana Treviño Benet and Michael Lieb (eds.), *Literary Milton: Text, Pretext, Context* (Pittsburgh, Pa., 1994), 22–44 at 38.
7. 'An Epitaph on the Marchioness of Winchester', 63; 'Il Penseroso', 19; Sonnet 10, 8.
8. *Paradise Lost* vii. 1–2 and iv. 273–4.
9. William Empson, *Some Versions of Pastoral* (1935), 173–4.
10. Patrick Hume, *Annotations on Milton's 'Paradise Lost'* (1695), 142.
11. Jonathan Richardson, Jr. and Sr., *Explanatory Notes and Remarks on Milton's 'Paradise Lost'* (1734), 151.

12. John Ruskin, *Sesame and Lilies: Two Lectures Delivered at Manchester in 1864* (New York, 1866), 29–30.

13. David Masson, *The Poetical Works of John Milton*, 3 vols. (1874), iii. 455. It is odd that Masson should fall prey to such banal literalism, for he goes on to cite one of the biblical verses that tell against it: 'Behold I stand at the door and knock' (Rev. 3:20). Ignoring the apocalyptic implications of his own evidence, Masson argues that the two-handed engine is '*the English Parliament with its two Houses* . . . A "two-handed engine" at the door of the English Church' (iii. 456).

14. Jonathan Sawday, *Engines of the Imagination: Renaissance Culture and the Rise of the Machine* (2007), 266.

15. Hyde Clarke, *Athenaeum*, 2746 (12 June 1880), 760–1. Campbell and Corns inform us that the document that Clarke cites 'can no longer be identified' (404n1).

16. James Kelly and Catherine Bray, 'The Keys to Milton's "Two-Handed Engine" in *Lycidas* (1637)', *Milton Quarterly*, 44 (2010), 122–42 (see 125).

17. Joseph Moxon, *Mechanick Exercises on the Whole Art of Printing* [1683–4], ed. Herbert Davis and Harry Carter (Oxford, 1962), 49; Kelly and Bray, 'The Keys to Milton's "Two-Handed Engine"', 124.

18. Kelly and Bray, 'The Keys to Milton's "Two-Handed Engine"', 133 and 138 (note 40).

19. Thomas Newton, ed., *Paradise Regain'd . . . And Poems upon Several Occasions* (1752), 493–4.

20. Harry F. Robins, 'Milton's "Two-Handed Engine at the Door" and St Matthew's Gospel', *Review of English Studies*, 5 (1954), 25–36 (see 29).

21. Marjorie Nicolson, 'Milton's "Old Damaetas"', *Modern Language Notes*, 61 (1926), 293–300.

22. Campbell and Corns, 28–9.

23. John P. Rumrich, *Milton Unbound: Controversy and Reinterpretation* (Cambridge, 1996), 39.

24. Joseph Mede, 'Epistle LXVI: *Mr Mede's Answer to Dr. Twisse's 7 Quaere's, viz. about the . . . Meaning of Some Difficult Passages of Scripture, viz. . . .* Matth. 25.31 *&c*', in *The Works of the Pious and Profoundly-Learned Joseph Mede, B. D.* (1664), 1031.

25. Stella Revard, 'Milton and Millenarianism: from the Nativity Ode to *Paradise Regained*', in Juliet Cummins (ed.), *Milton and the Ends of Time* (Cambridge, 2003), 42–81.

26. Revard, 'Milton and Millenarianism', 68.

27. *CPW*, i. 699–701.

28. *CPW*, i. 558–9.

29. *CPW*, i. 560.

30. *CPW*, i. 706–7.

31. Recent critics who have taken this view include Revard, 'Milton and Millenarianism' (see 54) and Barbara Lewalski, 'Milton and the Millennium', also in Cummins, *Milton and the Ends of Time*, 13–28 (see 17–18).

32. *CPW*, vi. 627.

33. *CPW*, i. 616.

34. E. M. W. Tillyard, *Milton* (1930, rev. edn., 1966), 387.

35. *CPW*, i. 605.

36. E. M. W. Tillyard and Phyllis B. Tillyard (eds.), *'Comus' and Some Shorter Poems of Milton* (1952), note to 'Lycidas', 130–1.

37. *CPW*, vi. 624.

38. Jan van der Noodt, *A Theatre Wherein be Represented ... the Voluptous Worldlings* (1569), 66ᵛ–67. See further A. M. Gibbs, 'That Two-handed Engine and Some Renaissance Emblems', *Review of English Studies*, 31 (1980), 178–83 (see 181).

39. John Calvin, *The Institutes of the Christian Religion* [4.1.19], ed. John T. McNeill, trans. Ford Lewis Battles, 2 vols. (Philadelphia, Pa., 1960), ii. 1033. Calvin is citing Cyprian's letter 54, a call for tempered moderation in dealing with sinners within the church. I am grateful to Jason Kerr for drawing Calvin and Cyprian to my attention.

40. See Golda Werman, *Milton and Midrash* (Washington, D.C., 1995), 173.

41. *CPW*, i. 582.

42. *Paradise Lost*, xii.74.

12

Early Poems and Prose: Some Hidden Continuities

Christopher Tilmouth

I

Critical opinion has long been divided as to the politics of early Milton's poetry. The rebelliousness of the anti-prelatical tracts being self-evident, the question has always been, when did such radicalism begin: in 1641, in 1637, or at some earlier date? For Christopher Hill the answer lay in the 1620s, and since Hill's time, Leah Marcus, Michael Wilding, Barbara Lewalski, and David Norbrook have all asserted the radicalism of Milton's earliest poetry, Norbrook most pervasively by reading works ranging from 'At a Vacation Exercise' through to 'Lycidas' in the light of Spenserian tradition and its emphasis on prophetic, apocalyptic, even anti-episcopal themes.[1] On the other hand, John Spencer Hill, Thomas Corns, and Gordon Campbell have cast young Milton as, variously, a reclusive figure, untouched by political events, or a quasi-Laudian, committed to ceremonial Arminianism through-out Charles's personal rule.[2] In practice, these two positions have not always been as diametrically opposed as may at first appear. Norbrook and Campbell and Corns, at least, tread common ground in their respective treatments of the year 1637: Norbrook acknowledges that 'Lycidas' constitutes not a full-frontal attack on episcopacy but only the 'emotional preparation' for such a commitment, whilst the two biographers concede, reciprocally, that Milton's gradual 'process of disengagement' from Laudianism probably began in the year of 'Lycidas', in response to an ecclesiastical visitation to Horton which criticized the Milton family.[3] Even so, such coincidences of critical opinion have not yielded a synthesis. Rather, the third stance on how to interpret early Milton—the position of Annabel Patterson and David Loewenstein[4]— contests the very assumptions about aesthetic unity on which the whole Hill/ Spencer Hill argument rests. Patterson objects that it is a characteristically New Critical error to construe young Milton's works within a single coherent narrative. She seeks, instead, to celebrate the contradictory, Janus-faced relationship with radicalism and reactionary elitism evident in different parts of the early oeuvre.

Differences aside, what unites these three approaches is their tendency to concentrate on questions of explicit belief, arguments about Milton's opinions with respect to class consciousness, prophetic politics, church ceremonialism, the Book of Sports controversy, and the politics of genre. The present essay aims to redefine the coordinates in terms of which relations between early poetry and early prose should be understood—by examining not the judgements about specific historical issues implicit in the works, but the imaginative preoccupations which underpin Milton's writing. Arguably, every human agent adopts the various political or theological beliefs he does over time *because* he is able to map those opinions on to his more basic attitudinal perspectives, particular ways of seeing human nature and the world which are crystallized in that person's habitual figurative language (the *leitmotifs* of his imagination). Whatever the possible discontinuities separating Milton's pre-1637 poetry from his prose of 1641–2, both sets of works reveal hidden continuities of this latter sort, a shared lexicon of images and perspectives on top of which poetry and prose alike are built. The Nativity Ode, 'At a Solemn Music', 'On Time', and the Ludlow *Maske* all, in their different ways, turn upon images of orbing, encircling, and enclosure, and on the centripetal forces which such encircling imposes. In each of these instances, this globing imagery is one of the principal lexicons via which Milton expresses a sense of contentment: contentment, in the *Maske*'s case, with the autonomy and integrity of the individual virtuous soul (a circle unto itself); contentment, in the case of the other three works, with ideas of corporate communion (typically, the individual's immersion within a heavenly choir). 'Lycidas' speaks to this same, latter preoccupation, but its subject is broken communions. It, too, ends with a vision of a chorus, but the elegy's structural properties render that vision faltering and uncertain. Another of Milton's imaginative fixations, his fascination with the dynamics of time, also works negatively in 'Lycidas', fostering scepticism, whereas the same temporal dynamics are positive and confident in the earlier Nativity Ode. Not the least of the traumas in 'Lycidas', then, is that it dramatizes a crisis of confidence in the imaginative register of the early poems. By contrast, the radicalism of *Of Reformation* and *The Reason of Church-Government*—the most visionary of the anti-prelatical pamphlets—apparently provided Milton with a new framework within which he could once again give positive expression to his early verse's figurative concerns (concerns disrupted in 'Lycidas').

Campbell and Corns excepted, none of the critics I have already cited comments in detail on the content of the anti-prelatical tracts. These pamphlets, the assumed end-point of discussions which weigh the radicalism of Milton's Caroline poetry, are typically taken as read. Addressing that lacuna, the second half of this essay examines *Of Reformation* and *The Reason of Church-Government* in depth precisely because both tracts revivify Milton's earlier imaginative attachments. *Of Reformation* recovers the positive vision of time's forward-leaning dynamism, so much a feature of the ode, and it reiterates, too, the poetry's ideals of choral and circular communion. *The Reason of Church-Government* posits a theological rationale for the same temporal dynamic. It also develops an account of congregationalism in which centripetal pressures are central and which once again celebrates the notion of corporate englobing. Paradoxically, though, the pamphlet then uses its globing imagery to idealize the autonomy and spiritual independence of the individual soul, thereby recovering the *Maske*'s ethical emphasis. Importantly, *The Reason of Church-Government* unites in one work the divergent communal and individualist tendencies of the Nativity Ode and *A Maske*, a tension of long-term significance for Milton's career. While illustrating how that comes about is this essay's final concern, its larger purpose is to underline the continuity of the figurative suppositions linking verse and prose, a continuity founded on anti-prelaticism's ability to give revitalized expression to the preoccupations of Milton's moral imagination. Put differently, one might say that Milton gravitated towards anti-prelaticism in 1641 *because* it satisfied the needs of a sensibility he had developed long before 1637, a sensibility which, at the moment of 'Lycidas', had faltered.

I begin, then, with the Nativity Ode, the work which first expressed Milton's confidently commanding attitude towards time and his propensity for deriving reassurance from images of orbing and enclosure—images here expressive of the poet's keen sense of incorporation within a wider elect community.

II

The ode opens by rapidly focussing in on the present moment ('This is the month, and this the happy morn', 1),[5] a process then recapitulated in the shift of tense from narrative past to dramatic present between the proem's second and third stanzas. The latter announces the lyric's intention to 'welcome' Christ '*Now*' to 'his new abode' (18–19), as if he were being born for the first time this very instant, in which respect this birthday ode punningly 'Afford[s] a *present* to the infant God' (16). The same strategy is then pursued throughout the hymn. Milton keeps on pulling away from the past-tense constructions of his narration—the story of the nativity—by deploying present-tense verbs which lend immediate reality to that historical event. We are told, for example, that ahead of his incarnation Christ 'Sent down ... Peace'; that she 'came softly sliding / Down' (46–7). A moment later peace is 'waving' her wand in the present tense; 'She strikes a universal peace through sea and land' (31–2). Immediately thereafter past-tense narration is resumed ('No war ... / Was heard the world around', 53–4), only to revert to the present again a dozen lines later. Lowry Nelson has brilliantly characterized these temporal dynamics as Milton's effort to bring into 'paradoxical contemporaneity' his two 'chief' time planes: the historic past, when Christ was born, and the immediate present of Christmas day, 1629, when the ode would have us witness that birth anew, as if happening now. Nelson shows that Milton then further expands his work's 'time scope' to encompass both the creation and those events leading from an apocalyptic Second Coming to Last Judgement to New Jerusalem.[6] Viewed *sub specie aeternitatis*, all these moments are eternally co-present, and the effect of Milton's dynamic manipulation of tenses is to encourage precisely that perspective: to afford a sense of immediate presentness to the events in Christian eschatology which the ode invokes.

From the outset, Milton involves himself in his narrative. First-person pronouns appear from line 4 onward, and in line 24 the plurality of 'us' gives way to singularity as Milton momentarily pictures himself alone joining the 'angel quire' (27) at Christ's manger-side.[7] This tendency to project himself as incorporate within God's angelic chorus and the community of the elect becomes central as the ode develops. To prepare for it, Milton first lends present-tense immediacy to the instant when heaven's choir descends upon the shepherds to herald the incarnation. The harmonies sung at this juncture make the air 'With thousand echoes still prolongs each heavenly close' (100). The verb 'prolongs' here is potent because it forces a lurch into the present tense after twenty-four lines of past-tense narration. That contemporaneousness is, however, felt the more because one sense of the pre-modifier, 'still', is its adverbial meaning, 'always', implying that the prolongation is eternal, audible not merely in the historic past of the nativity year but even now, in 1629. To this nuance, one source of imaginative intensity, Milton adds another. He visualizes the angels in 'glittering ranks', forming 'A globe of circular light' that '*surrounds* their [the shepherds'] sight' (114, 109–10). The idea of encirclement evoked here is comfortingly encompassing. Crucially, though, such wording also begins, once again, to involve Milton in the incorporating experience. The pronoun in the phrase 'their sight' seems to restrict the communing experience to the shepherds (only they see the angels), but the anonymity of the subsequent passive construction (these singers 'Are seen', 114) suggests otherwise: it hints that Milton and his readers might share in the communion too. The poet pursues such possibilities further in stanza XIII. There, Milton invokes the music of the spheres, commanding the planets to 'Ring out', 'Make up full consort to the angelic symphony', and 'Once bless *our* human ears' (125, 132, 126). *This* consort, clearly, *is* to have man—or at least Milton—at its centre.

The experience which Milton is striving to involve himself in here—divine music's capacity to draw the listener into a communion of souls—is recurrent within his oeuvre. The final ecstasy into which the protagonist of 'Il Penseroso' 'Dissolve[s]' is just such a rapture, engendered by a 'full-voiced choir' which 'bring[s] all heaven' before one's eyes (161–6). 'At a Solemn Music' likewise articulates Milton's longing to be reunited with God's 'celestial consort', to sing again that 'song of pure concent' with which Edenic man used to 'answer' the angelic choir (27, 6, 17–18). That prelapsarian harmony had expressed an ideal circularity, 'all creatures' offering 'fair music' to their Lord whilst he (reciprocally) 'their motion swayed / In perfect diapason' (21–3). Such an ideal, Milton's madrigal implies, will only be realized again in the New Jerusalem, but the Nativity Ode looks forward to just that moment. When Milton demands his own 'full consort' to emulate the shepherds' musical experience, he is really urging on the apocalypse—as becomes clear from what follows his imperative, 'Ring out, ye crystal spheres':

> For if such holy song
> Enwrap our fancy long,
> Time will run back, and fetch the age of gold,
> And speckled vanity
> Will sicken soon and die,
> And lep'rous sin will melt from earthly mould,
> And hell itself will pass away. (133–9)

The 'if' with which this stanza opens puts into question not whether the 'holy song' which Milton craves will be sung, but only how 'long' it will last. In shifting attention on to this doubt about duration, the poet tacitly assumes that his imperative ('Ring out') will be answered in some degree at least: he will be 'enwrapped within / Made incorporate' with a musical communion. The verb 'Enwrap' tucked into the conditional clause of lines 133–4 underlines how far, in assuming this, Milton is imagining for himself the same kind of circular embrace which had already 'surrounded' and englobed the shepherds. This element of wish-fulfilment is the greater because even the doubt about enduringness towards which the conjunction 'if' points is a merely formal conditional. In practice, the polysyndeton of the clauses that follow (135–9) gives those clauses an overwhelming weight. Pummelled by the word 'and', the reader concentrates on the triumphs that will accompany the apocalyptic restoration of the golden age and forgets—as Milton surely does too—the conditional clause on which that vision is, formally speaking, premised. In effect, poet and reader assume that holy song *will* 'Enwrap our fancy long'; that hell *will* pass away. Milton, in placing himself at the heart of heaven's 'full consort', thus effectively projects himself as one incorporate amongst the elect, those who will survive Judgement Day. In so casting himself, he manifests what Fallon calls his sense of his own peculiar grace (see note 7).

As is often noted,[8] Milton is quick to suspend this vision of ecstasy: 'But wisest fate says no, / This must not yet be so' (149–50). It is a mistake, though, to overemphasize this point. Contrary to Fish's claim that the poem's perlocutionary force is to make us stand and wait, the Nativity Ode seems rather to keep leaning into the future, pushing towards the moment of Milton's incorporation amongst the chorus of the elect. Christ may yet be an infant, but he will eventually be crucified 'So both himself and us to glorify' (154). This mention of glorification pushes us forward from crucifixion to New Jerusalem, and although the hymn then immediately retreats from that end-point, it retreats only as far as another future point, the Last Judgement's first trumpet (155–6). An evocation of that moment follows, culminating in the lines—yet another dynamic present-tense construction—'And then at last our bliss / Full and perfect is' (165–6). Again Milton instantly retreats from this, but only as far as the initiating action of the long judgemental process—hence still maintaining a future-oriented perspective:

> But now begins; for from this happy day
> The old dragon under ground
> In straiter limits bound,
> Not half so far casts his usurped sway. (167–70)

The poem's momentum, then, carries on pulling the reader's thoughts forward, even amidst comments which threaten to arrest it. There is a constant movement towards Revelation's defeat of Antichrist.[9] Furthermore, Milton, by including himself in 'our bliss', the 'us' who are glorified, and the subsequent reference to 'Our babe' who shows 'his Godhead true' (227), keeps in play the gratifying assumption that he will number amongst that communion of saints intoning solemn music at the end of time. He also anticipates such music now, insofar as the very process of singing this ode, his own hymn, already brings Milton's voice into harmony with heaven's consort.

This vision of incorporation which Milton conjures for himself is evoked again in 'On Time'. There, too, the poet places himself amongst the elect who 'ever shine / About the supreme throne / Of [God]' (16–8). The pattern of thought is once more orbing, circular, centripetal. God is pictured as the centre-point around which all good things congregate. In fact, young Milton's imagination is repeatedly drawn to such ideas of inclusion within a corporate body, figured either as a harmonious choir, a globe, or a sphere.

The Ludlow *Maske*, though, tells a different story, setting up a tension in the early poet's outlook. In that work, notions of corporate communion are supplanted by ideals of individual self-enclosure and of virtue's private autonomy. Consider, for example, the Elder Brother's comment that his sister's accomplishments include a grasp of 'the sweet peace that goodness bosoms ever' (367). The verb 'bosoms' here means 'carries enclosed in its bosom'; but whether 'goodness' is subject or object of that verb is instructively ambiguous. Is goodness the quality which embosoms—enfolds within itself—the Lady's sweet peace, or is the point rather that, because sweet peace is one of her attributes, she is *able* to bosom goodness within herself? The fact that we tread an endless circle trying to read this line underlines the self-enclosing quality of this Lady's soul. Her capacity for meditation reinforces that attribute. A forerunner of the bird that 'whets and combs' its wings in Marvell's garden, *A Maske*'s contemplative Lady uses her wisdom to 'plume her feathers, and let grow her wings / That in the various bustle of resort / Were all to-ruffled' (377–9). Through her own resources, in other words, she restores her autonomy whenever the world intrudes upon it. Milton's heroine is, besides (and in a tellingly self-inwoven image), 'her own radiant light' (373); and 'He', the brother notes, 'that has light within his . . . breast / May sit i' the centre, and enjoy bright day' (380–1). Carey glosses 'centre' here as the earth's dark centre, but 'centre' also suggests 'centre of oneself', the point being that the Lady is at peace sitting (self-inwovenly) within herself, autonomous and self-encircling.

The character-type epitomized by Comus is introverted too, but in a self-corrupting way. Its body (as it were, facing in on itself) seeps inward, until it 'clots' and 'embodies' the soul within (466–8). The 'sacred rays of chastity' (424) that radiate from the Lady's centre portend the opposite effect. The Elder Brother predicts that his sister's soul (possessing, as it does, a perfect, centripetal tendency) will eventually transform her body into an ethereal substance, drawing it inwards and incorporating it within her 'soul's essence' (458–62). An ideal of incorporation is, therefore, operative in *A Maske*, but it is not one of immersion within a wider community; rather, it entails the chaste individual's ever-increasing withdrawal into herself. The imaginative pull of this ideal is particularly apparent in the poetry which recounts the impact on others of the Lady's singing voice. The Attendant Spirit, on hearing the heroine's song, likens it to an intangible 'steam of rich distilled perfumes' which steals upon the air (555). Comus further emphasizes that intangibility by locating the voice itself not in the Lady but in the air which surrounds her. 'Something holy' within her, he speculates, exudes—suffuses outwards—her inner rapture, and it is then the 'vocal air' which gives material (that is, audible) form to this ecstasy (245–6). Nothing about the Lady herself, it seems, is material, and that impression of incorporeality is enhanced through repeated contrasts, by casting even abstract properties as personified and concrete when in her presence. Silence and Darkness become embodied as birds as the Lady's more ethereal voice floats 'upon the wings' of the former and 'At every fall smooth[es] the raven down' of the latter (248–51). Again, Silence, in discovering that she has been 'took'—penetrated— 'ere she was aware' by the voice of Milton's heroine (556–7), is thereby personified as a more corporeal, more vulnerable virgin than the Lady herself.

A *Maske*'s device of making everything around the Lady seem more bodily than her highlights her status as an isolated, autonomous individual. Thus empowered, Comus cannot touch her 'mind' (662). However, her body, which he does capture, is another matter, and in that regard Cedric Brown is right to argue that A *Maske*'s idealism is pointedly circumscribed.[10] Ultimately, Milton's heroine needs the help of grace and of other people to regain her physical liberty, and insofar as that is so, A *Maske* qualifies its lauding of the self-enclosed individual, emphasizing also (as in the Nativity Ode) the importance of God's community. Grace's importance is apparent the moment the Spirit announces that he has been despatched by Jove to help a 'favoured' one (41, 78). His then appearing dressed as a shepherd looking for lost sheep (496–8) allegorizes him as a pastor. In bestowing haemony on the brothers, he further mediates God's favour, just as Sabrina plays another 'faithful guide' who channels 'grace' (943, 937). Community and sociability are crucial to these same processes. Haemony is introduced as a gift bestowed on the Spirit by a 'shepherd' who 'loved' him, 'in requital' for his singing (618, 622, 625), a gift, therefore, expressive of sociability. Equally, the Spirit learns of Sabrina whilst conversing with Meliboeus who tells how 'the shepherds at their festivals / Carol her goodness' (847–8). Sabrina, then, is the object of communal song, and the lore surrounding her is transmitted in the context of group festivities. Clearly, then, the Lady relies for her release on the actions of others; and once released, she is immediately assimilated into a provincial court busy celebrating its festive cohesiveness.

It is important, though, not to overestimate this qualification to A *Maske*'s celebration of autonomy. It remains a work which, as Leah Marcus and Martin Butler demonstrate,[11] eschews the norms of royal masquing (especially that genre's collectivist emphasis). Granted, it presents the *defence* of virtue as a communal act, but the same is not true of its depiction of virtue's original achievement and expression: these remain the province of the autonomous individual. The Lady does describe her virtuous mind as 'attended', but attended only by abstractions which the imagination objectifies as personified beings: 'a strong siding champion Conscience', 'pure-eyed Faith, white-handed Hope' (210–12). In more typical masques these figures might appear on stage, fleshing out the definition of her spiritual state in a collective display in which multiple actors participate. Not so here. Furthermore, at the height of the confrontation between the Lady and Comus, when one might expect to hear a public articulation of the nature of chastity, there is instead only silence. Milton's heroine tells her adversary, 'Thou hast nor ear, nor soul to apprehend'

> . . . the sage
> And serious doctrine of virginity,
> And thou art worthy that thou shouldst not know
> More happiness than this thy present lot. (783–8)

Again, any communal act of witnessing is denied. The assumption is, rather, that those initiate individuals who are regenerate will already understand this doctrine through their own inner resources, and it suits such people's sense of self-definition not to soil that understanding by sharing it with reprobates. Milton leaves audience members to decide for themselves how far they really grasp the Lady's values—whereas the norm in masques would be to make a virtue of *displaying* the court's shared appreciation of whatever virtue was in play.

If *A Maske*, though, equivocates over the corporate ideal embraced in the Nativity Ode, 'Lycidas' is different again in that it laments broken communions. The idea of a community of poets is implicit immediately in the work's opening verses. Milton presents his elegy as an obligation owed to a fellow artist, one who 'knew / Himself to sing' and so 'must not' go unwept (10–12). Fraternal professionalism aside though, Milton and Lycidas are bound in community in another sense too: as fellow shepherds who used to tend the same flock (23–4). That sometime bond is warmly evoked, Milton emphasizing the whole days spent together, the pair's conscientious care of their charges, and the festive pastoral world created through their music

(25–36, 42–4). In a work peppered with emotive repetitions, the circular two-ness and togetherness of these swains is stressed: they are 'Together both . . . both together' (25–7). The same cannot be said of the shepherds later attacked by Peter. Ignorant of the herdsman's art, they sing 'lean and flashy songs' and abandon their flocks to starvation (114–29). Allusions to John 10 and Ezekiel 34 underline that these false shepherds are clerics who leave their parishioners 'Swoll'n with wind, and the rank mist they draw' (126)—hence, literally hollowed out. Clearly, in inviting us to interpret these figures as one church, the poem simultaneously casts its young swains as another, better kind of communion founded upon good pastoral discipline. The confining of this other church to a circle of two is no impediment to that reading. Milton would later write in *De Doctrina Christiana* that responsibility for discipline is 'not committed only to Peter . . . but to every particular church as a totality, however few its members', for, in Christ's words, where just *'two or three are gathered together in my name, there I am'* (*CPW*, vi. 609). Two communities, then—one of poets, one of pastors—are in play as the poem opens. Both are fractured by Lycidas's drowning. Responding to that event, Milton evinces, on the one hand, a loss of faith in the poet's vocation and its 'thankless muse' (66)—witness his dwelling on Orpheus's fate, torn to shreds by the Thracians (58–63).[12] On the other hand, though, 'the homely slighted shepherd's trade' (65) is also cast as pointless now that one of its exemplars is gone and the profession grown corrupt.

In an effort to allay such desolation 'Lycidas' posits successive consolations for the broken communion, each appealing to the same eschatological perspective that had previously informed the Nativity Ode. However, whilst temporal dynamics functioned positively in that earlier poem, supporting its confident vision, here time is imagined more equivocally. The Nativity Ode took a past-tense narrative—the story of Christ's birth—and repeatedly reset it in the present. 'Lycidas' reverses this dynamic. It begins in the present tense, as the live utterance of a first-person voice; yet multiple touches of narrative framing then intercede, recasting the poem's consolations in particular as past-tense judgements, as if the lyric were receding backwards in time as it is sung. This process begins at line 77, amidst the first-person speaker's reflections on the fruitlessness of any quest for poetic fame:

But the fair guerdon when we hope to find,

...

Comes the blind Fury with th'abhorred shears,
And slits the thin-spun life. But not the praise,
Phoebus replied, and touched my trembling ears; (77)
Fame is no plant that grows on mortal soil,

...

As [all-judging Jove] pronounces lastly on each deed,
Of so much fame in heaven expect thy meed. (73–84)

With the introduction of the past-tense actions attributed to Apollo, Milton's whole preceding speech is suddenly recast within a narrative context. We are asked to make sense of loss by judging worth from Jove's perspective of eternity. Yet Milton's subsequent line, 'But now my oat proceeds' (88), immediately accords an air of provisionality to that Apolline reassurance. As the monologue resumes and we shift back into the present, Apollo's utterance becomes simply a point of view, a perspective which is localized to its narrative moment by Milton's brisk, businesslike 'proceeds' rather than being allowed to linger as a consoling ideal.

Triton—or is it Hippotades's reported speech?—offers the next perspective on Lycidas's fate: 'It was that fatal and perfidious bark / Built in the eclipse, and rigged with curses dark' that did it for him (100–1). This judgement, like Apollo's, transcends everyday time, interpreting the shipwreck as simply another consequence of the Fall and its legacy of corporeal vulnerability. Yet, as before, narrative framing positions this opinion as a past-tense utterance, articulated by a third person at least once and perhaps twice removed in time and voice from the poet-speaker himself. The perspective is thus localized as a point of view specific to a past-moment utterance. The same is equally true of Peter's verdict. This, too, is bracketed within a retrospective frame: the apostle's entry is signalled by the past-tense report, he 'Last came, and last did go' (108); and his exit is marked by a return to present-moment actuality ('the dread voice is past', 132). Peter's litany of priestly corruptions ends, notoriously, with the reflection that wolves scavenging amongst the flock go unchecked, 'and nothing said, / But that two-handed engine at the door, / Stands ready to smite once, and smite no more' (129–31). The use of the biblical metaphor 'standing at the door', signifying imminent judgement, points to an eschatological consolation. Peter's

promise is that false clerics will get their comeuppance; the spiritual communion, broken with Lycidas's death, will one day be mended. Two nuances,
though, compromise this sentiment. First, Peter's final line is shadowed by a
troubling echo of 1 Samuel 26: 8–10. In that text, Abishai implores David, 'let
me smite [Saul] . . . to the earth at once, and I will not smite him'—that is,
will not need to smite him—'the second time'. David declines this request on
the grounds that it is for the Lord alone to smite. Whilst it *is* God who will do
the smiting in the case of Peter's prophecy, the decision to echo Abishai's
boastful language in phrasing that promise is oddly destabilizing. Likewise,
Peter's two-line consolation is uncomfortably perfunctory—rushed even—
after such a long diatribe (seventeen lines) on church corruption. The
punctuation underlines this fact. The introduction of a new thought with
'But' ought to be preceded by a semicolon at least, and yet young Milton
(normally so scrupulously meaningful in his punctuating) closes line 129
with a mere comma, thereby inviting the confusion that 'that' might be a
relative pronoun rather than a demonstrative adjective. These points,
together with the whole speech's positioning, again, as a past-tense occur-
rence, make Peter's prophecy seem as provisional as the other, previous
consolations.[13]

The elegy's final consolation, a vision of Lycidas's apotheosis, is cast in an
emphatic present-tense voice which might seem to override previous anxieties.[14] Witness the lines, 'Weep no more, woeful shepherds', '[Lycidas] hears
the unexpressive nuptial song', and 'There entertain him all the saints above'
(165, 176, 178). By giving present immediacy to this future event, Milton
signals the redemption of both poetic and pastoral vocations. As the reference to angelic 'nuptial' songs indicates, Lycidas is placed specifically amongst
Revelation 19's angels celebrating the marriage of the lamb to the church.
We are thus restored to that encircling communion exulted in the Nativity
Ode and 'At a Solemn Music', one of 'sweet societies / That sing, and singing
in their glory move' ('Lycidas', 179–80). And yet the instant this has been
achieved Milton recasts either this last sequence or, potentially, his entire
elegy as the past-tense utterance of an anonymous shepherd: 'Thus sang the
uncouth swain', the poem concludes (186). What began as a first-person,
present-moment lament, something overheard, ends as some third party's
'lay', apparently to be casually overwritten by a new song tomorrow
('Tomorrow to fresh woods, and pastures new', 193). By such means a

detached Milton again doubles the distance between himself and what has been sung.

This quality in 'Lycidas' has been much discussed, brilliantly by Richard Hooker who sees in such framing actions devices for ecphractically situating the elegy as an artefact, something beautifully crafted yet aware of its contingent obsolescence.[15] However, insightful though this description is, the tail should not wag the dog. I have argued that the intrusions of narrative structuring counteract moments in the poem when attempts are made to divine eschatological significance in Lycidas's fate. Such moments are rendered perspectival, bracketed off as the sometime points of view of particular speakers; but they are not thereby negated. Rather, Milton's elegy achieves a poise, a suspension: the grief in face of broken communions is heartfelt, but whether the successive reassurances offered to combat it are variously compelling or trivial remains indeterminable. The consolations have an air of provisionality about them, so that the poem, in effect, dramatizes an *aporia*. To apply this to the closing gesture of withdrawal in particular, it is ultimately equivocal how far the poet who once imagined his *own* absorption within angelic choric song can now take comfort from another's—Lycidas's—incorporation into the same. The displacement of the act of describing that apotheosis on to an anonymous 'swain' evidences a degree of estrangement from the Nativity Ode's fantasy; but how much is unclear.

III

Milton's early poetry is built, then, upon a substratum of imaginative presuppositions. The Nativity Ode, 'At a Solemn Music', and 'On Time' revolve—literally: the imagery is persistently centripetal—around an ideal of encircling, corporate communion. Typically, that communion is figured as rapturous involvement within a choir. Where such confidence prevails, time is imagined reaching ever-forward, inclining towards the apocalypse. *A Maske*, though, reveals a contrary fascination with singularity, that is, with the autonomous individual's power to be his own, self-enclosing circle. Incorporation within a larger community still features here, but as a secondary concern. 'Lycidas' then expresses complete disillusionment with the idea of communion, in which context Milton's way of imagining time also changes—from a dynamic straining toward the future to an outlook that keeps slipping into retrospection. Musical communion is, eventually, figured anew in Lycidas's apotheosis, but as something provisional, made faltering by the elegy's last, potentially dismissive narrative frame. The imaginative contours of these poems track, therefore—more tellingly than their more overt historical concerns—Milton's fluctuating spiritual confidence. If we turn, now, to the prose, it quickly becomes apparent how and why Milton was nonetheless able to find in anti-prelatical radicalism an outlook that would satisfy the imaginative needs left hanging in the early verse.

Of Reformation clearly indicates that by 1641 Milton had discovered in bishops real-life embodiments of the Comus type. His pamphlet depicts England's prelates as patrons of 'sensuall Idolatry' whose habit is to conceive what should be 'inward acts of the *Spirit*' through, instead, the 'customary ey-Service of the body' (*CPW*, i. 520). Their drift, in contrast to *A Maske*'s Lady, is towards a gradual 'over-bodying' of the self, a tendency which culminates in the soul's powers 'run[ning] out lavishly to the upper skin, and there harden [ing] into a crust' (i. 522). An essential loss of interiority is involved here: the prelates are hollowed-out figures—'a sort of formal outside men', in the words of *The Reason of Church-Government* (i. 854)—like the wind-swollen sheep of 'Lycidas'. That is why in *Of Reformation* the images that compare them to wens, 'harden'd excrements' with no intrinsic function, are so apt (i. 583–4). With the loss of interiority goes also an abandonment of autonomy and personal responsibility. Prelatical religion demands from its laity only 'outward conformity' with church rituals; implicitly, such conformity is sufficient to procure salvation. However, to accept this is to 'give over the earnest study of vertue, and godlinesse as a thing of greater purity then [one] need[s]' (i. 548). For parishioners, it amounts to devolving the 'managing of [their] salvation' on to another (i. 548), which for Milton is a negation of Christianity's essence: the imperative (exhibited by the Lady) to exercise personal 'choice and purpose' (*Reason of Church-Government*, i. 746).

If *Of Reformation* picks up on *A Maske*'s moral imagery, its argument (as Joan Webber realized[16]) also brings renewed point to the early poetry's explorations of temporal dynamics. The contrasting impulses of the Nativity Ode's leap into an apocalyptic future and the faltering, backwards-leaning narrations of 'Lycidas' which induce suspension, are replayed here through the ur-narrative of reformation. That reformation story recalls a glorious, precocious spell of Protestantism under the Tudors; posits a recent collapse which has left Britain poised between pushing time into reverse and pressing on towards futurity; and finally looks forward to Armageddon, imminently available if only the church will precipitate its millennial destiny. Milton depicts the prelates as acutely aware of the turning point before them, 'presaging their time to be but short: and now like those that are sinking... catch[ing] round at that...likeliest to hold them up' (i. 582). Under their influence, time is repeatedly figured in the pamphlet as stagnating or being forcibly put into reverse (the characteristic imaginative movement in 'Lycidas'). Hence, those advancing through the church hierarchy are pictured as seething pots which, on being set to cool, immediately 'exhale the...Gifts... in them, settling in a skinny congealment of...sloth' (i. 536)—just like the clotted Comus-souls of *A Maske*. Equally, 'a dangerous earnest of sliding back to *Rome*' is said to be detectable everywhere (i. 527–8). It is for this cause that the bishops proclaim, at the very moment when the Reformation might seem to be nearing completion, 'Let the Church be reform'd according to *Constantine*' (i. 560), as if to revert now to his 'Tyranny' (i. 551) would be a good thing. Likewise, the attempt to impose the Book of Sports is, for Milton, another sign of regressive tendencies ('Thus did...*Balaam* seeke to subdue the Israelites,' [i. 589]). So is the stirring up of war within the kingdoms (i. 596). Above all, though, the bishops are accused of putting time into reverse by backsliding 'into the Jewish beggary of old cast rudiments' and 'overdated Ceremonies' (i. 519–20). Their Laudianism revives priestly old law practices of the sort that the Gospel's new covenant had overwritten. Milton notes, for instance (with reference to the tuppence extracted from communicants on Easter Sunday), that clerics still make it a parishioner's duty to 'appear before them once a year in *Jerusalem* like good circumciz'd *males*...to be taxt' (i. 612). Such reversals of time's march, a returning to 'the old rode' (i. 522), constitute, for Milton, an unexpected development after Britain's early reformation flourishing, as if we should 'freeze at noone after [an] early thaw' (*Animadversions*, i. 705). They provoke the question, will 'the Sunne'—a millenarian pun—'for ever hide himselfe'? Will time stop?

The very structure of *Of Reformation* dramatizes this threat. Keith Stavely has noted the circular momentum in the pamphlet's individual *sentences*, the inevitability that 'All levels of syntax' descend 'into patterns of worldliness and tyranny'[17]—an observation which implies that we stagnate rather than progress as we read. A sense of eternal recurrence is apparent on a larger scale too. Even across the work's first several pages, as Milton laments the resurgence of a carnal approach to piety and church practice, it is left purposefully unclear whether the degradations he is describing are historical (those of the pre-Reformation church) or contemporary (those of the backsliding church now). The unclarity is deliberate because it serves to underline history's repetitiousness: everything before the apocalyptic moment is a perpetual reiteration of the same old carnality, time circling back on itself rather than moving forward. Much later, in Book 2 (when discussing tyranny's habit of fostering public immorality to justify the need for its own authoritarianism), Milton characterizes the people as laying down 'their necks for some wily Tyrant to get up and ride'; but this image is a flat repetition of one some seventeen pages earlier (i. 588; cf. 571). Likewise, Book 2 recounts the story of how Pope Zacharias conspired to make Pepin king of France and then, with Pepin's aid, captured for himself the 'exarchat of *Ravenna*' (i. 578–81). Seventeen pages later the Ravenna exarchate is invoked again, this time as an analogy to gloss Laud's empire-building (i. 594–5). At both points in the text first Chaucer and then Paolo Sarpi is invoked to warn against clerical ambition, again emphasizing time (and this argument's) repetitiousness.

Of Reformation's retrograde structure is countered, and Milton resurrects the temporal mode of the Nativity Ode, late on in the pamphlet. Taking heart from the failure to impose the Prayer-Book on Scotland, he switches into a sustained prophetic vein, urging his countrymen to resume their role as proponents of pan-European reformation (i. 597). What really fires him, though, to abandon the backward-turning dynamics of 'Lycidas' is his ambition to defeat opponents of Root and Branch reform. Provoked by them, Milton makes an impassioned case not for gradual but precipitate reformation, hence imagining time, once again, as hurtling forward into its own future:

the greater extremity of *Vertue* and superlative *Truth* we run into, the more *virtuous*, and...*wise*, wee become; and hee that flying from degenerate...corruption, feares to shoot himselfe too far into the meeting imbraces of a Divinely-warranted *Reformation*, had better not have run at all...Speedy and vehement were the *Reformations* of all the good Kings of *Juda*. (i. 601–2)

Other familiar idioms then follow. Milton calls to Christ to 'unite us intirely, and appropriate us to thy selfe' (i. 615), that is, to realize the ideal of communion previously broached in the Nativity Ode. This takes the form of a return to the conceit of incorporation within God's choir, although now Milton's presence within that choir is oblique ('some one'): 'Then amidst the *Hymns*, and *Halleluiahs* of *Saints* some one may perhaps bee heard offering at high *strains* in new and lofty *Measures* to sing and celebrate' (i. 616). (Such choral incorporation informs *Animadversions* too, where Milton imagines the saints addressing their voices to God whilst, again, an oblique poet sings 'an elaborate Song of Generations' [i. 706].) Given the whole tract's apocalyptic framework, *Of Reformation*'s song, like the one heard in 'Lycidas', necessarily recalls the marriage of the lamb (and in fact this connection is explicit in *Animadversions* [i. 707]). Beyond that association, though, *Of Reformation* also recuperates the idea of encirclement so prominent in the Nativity Ode. The sequel to the song here is a vision of that moment when all God's saints will 'clasp inseparable Hands' and 'progresse' through the '*datelesse . . . irrevoluble* Circle of *Eternity*' (i. 616). Milton finds his way back, then, to those circular images which had originally expressed his spiritual contentment.

What one might call the recovery of faith in time evident by the end of *Of Reformation* is apparent also in *The Reason of Church-Government*. Here again, as prelates once more threaten to turn the 'Angell of the Gospell . . . out of his rode' (i. 850), Milton thinks of providential history in dynamic terms: 'The doore of grace turnes upon smooth hinges wide opening to send out, but soon shutting to recall the precious offers of mercy . . . which unlesse . . . Zeale . . . be there . . . to receave, we loose: and still the ofter we loose, the straiter the doore opens, and the lesse is offer'd' (i. 797). Now, though, Milton attends more fully to that Jewish–Christian distinction adumbrated in *Of Reformation* because it lends the assurance of theological justification to his forward-reaching image of time. The inspiration here is Calvin's *Institutes* and their glossing of Galatians 4:1.[18] According to Calvin, Jews and Christians constitute the same one church, but the former are as children, 'not yet able to governe [themselves]' and so dependent on the tutelage of the old law (*Institvtion*, 209). The Mosaic law's ceremonial requirements convey spiritual promises obliquely, 'shadowed' in 'earthly' terms, training the Jews by 'outward observations' so as to prepare them for Christ's incarnation (*Institvtion*, 211). Hence, ceremonies such as animal sacrifice are valuable not in themselves but because they prefigure the idea of ultimate sacrifice (*Institvtion*, 156–7). With the coming of Christ these practices must be abrogated. Otherwise their continued observance would obscure their meaning as mere symbolic anticipations of the crucifixion, distracting attention from that greater event's transcendent significance. 'At the death of Christ', writes Calvin, alluding to 2 Corinthians 3:14, 'the veile of the Temple . . . was torne in two', the 'true' image of heavenly things being brought to 'light' (*Institvtion*, 164). The old law's ceremonies are (as per Eph. 2:14) that 'middle wall of partition' between man and Christ which the incarnation and passion, in necessitating the abrogation of such laws, demolish. For the Christian, to be under the Gospel is to understand precisely this, and thus to move forward with the natural flow of spiritual time.

Calvin's interpretation of the Jewish–Christian distinction was important to Puritan reformers. John Field and Thomas Wilcox had it in mind when, in their *Admonition to the Parliament* (1572), they criticized those who took Moses's law 'for a rule' in ordaining the modern church's ceremonies. Bishops of this mindset, they said, defied the message of Hebrews 10:1 that religion should 'nomore [be] darkened with . . . figures or shadows'; implicitly, such prelates made the church Judaic instead of Christian.[19] The anti-prelates of 1641 took up this theme. Henry Burton insisted, in the face of Caroline episcopal practice, that the 'worship of God . . . must not be in shadowes and types, in imitation of the Jewes in their Leviticall services, but . . . in spirit and truth'.[20] Katherine Chidley and Lord Brooke struck similar notes.[21] None of these reformers, though—least of all Smectymnuus in the original answer to the *Humble Remonstrance*—emphasized Calvin's distinction as much as did Milton. *The Reason of Church-Government* treats the tendency of Bishop Hall[22] and of the authors of the *Certain Briefe Treatises*[23] to validate Laudian liturgy and the episcopal hierarchy by comparing both to Jewish practices as amongst their most egregious errors, proofs of the wish of the bishops to turn back time.

The preface of *The Reason of Church-Government* differentiates immediately between 'the obscurity of Ceremoniall rites' and a new-found knowledge 'under the Gospell' (*CPW*, i. 751), and subsequent chapters then embed this theme. For example, Milton goes on to insist that the Old Testament's models of Solomon's temple are descriptions appropriate to 'the apprehension of [their] times, typicall and shadowie', but were never intended to be realized 'literally'. On the contrary, their ultimate purpose was 'to weane the hearts of the Jewes from their old law to expect a . . . reformation under Christ' (i. 757). Hence Solomon's temple is no precedent to justify material structures, though England's prelates imagine it is when they cite it as offering literal patterns of episcopacy. Rather, it is simply a prototype of that interior, 'rationall temple', the properly governed soul, which the Gospel enjoins us to cultivate 'the sooner to...accomplish that immortall stature of Christs body...his Church' (i. 758). On Milton's reading, our task is to recreate the 'elegant...symmetry' of Ezekiel's temple *typologically*, as 'inward beauty', in order to transform our Christian souls (collected together as a single church) into the bride of Christ. The imperative to do this 'sooner' rather than later reflects Milton's recurrent interest in hurrying towards the end-time of Revelation's nuptial ceremony. In ignoring that interpretation and reading the temple, instead, 'under a vaile'—Milton's phrase here recalls Calvin and Corinthians—the bishops 'mean to annihilat the Gospel' (i. 757). Their purpose is to frustrate that flow of time which Milton would accelerate. This point is underlined repeatedly. Milton follows Calvin again, for instance, in describing the Jewish law as a child, not a tutor; yet the prelates, he then says, would have 'the ripe age of the Gospell...put to schoole againe' to learn 'from the infancy of the Law' (i. 762–3). Worse, they would make religion 'runne back...to the old pompe...of the flesh' (i. 766)—reversing, therefore, time and the natural order of maturation. Conversely, still another chapter looks forward to the moment when, with Christ's triumph, 'law and Priesthood' together will both 'fade away...and passe into aire like a transitory vision', just as Prospero's dubious magic (half-remembered here) did (i. 771). The dynamics of time, then, and history's apocalyptic trajectory are as central to this pamphlet as to other works but are now played out through a specific understanding of what it means for the Gospel to supersede the old law.

For Milton as for Calvin that triumph of the Gospel over Judaism guaranteed so-called Christian liberty. The Gospel recasts the law as something inward, interpreted according to the spirit within one, and so the question of how to observe that law ceases to be an issue on which an authoritarian priestly class can dictate. It becomes, instead, a matter of personal responsibility. Laudian prelates may try to encourage 'an unactive blindnesse of minde' amongst the laity, pursuant to their aim of 'inthraul-[ing]' men's liberties (i. 784, 851). However, it is the duty of Christians to liberate themselves from such Judaic recidivism and from 'the bondage of the [old] Law' (i. 763), becoming, rather, legislators unto themselves, their own priesthood of all believers. Here again Milton turns to the Pauline / Calvinist language of veils to epitomize the point. No longer should any parishioner be separated off 'by vails and partitions as laicks and unclean' (i. 838). Instead, each should be 'admitted to wait upon the tabernacle as the rightfull Clergy of Christ'. To exclude the people from this role would be to 'sow up that Jewish vail which Christ . . . rent in sunder' (i. 839). Accordingly, *The Reason of Church-Government* develops a detailed account of how congregations should discipline themselves,[24] without resort to higher clerical authorities. At the same time, this is also an account of how to realize the ideal of community explored in the earlier poems, but now in a more prosaically practical sense.

Milton's notion of congregational community starts from an idea of divine 'fellowship' (i. 837). God is said to foster 'familiar' relations with every worshipper. Gone is his Judaic role of 'judge' and 'schoolmaister'; now he is only an 'indulgent father' to sons who have attained the age of discretion. The bonds uniting a congregation should be of this same 'familiar' order. The wider brethren should join their local minister in forming 'a Saintly communion' simply as a matter of 'mutuall honour and love' (i. 838, 844). Where this happens, every communicant will willingly involve himself in the processes of disciplining on which church unity depends; and Milton dwells upon this process because its cooperative nature best expresses the congregation's sense of communion. Miltonic disciplining, then, begins with the pastor making private, gentle representations to a given sinner. 'This not succeeding after once or twice or oftner', the communitarian circle is widened such that 'in the presence of two or three his faithfull brethren appointed thereto' the minister advises the transgressor to repent (i. 846). 'If this obtaine not, . . . the counsel of more assistants' is invoked to 'lay nearer siege', and 'friends' more generally 'intreat, exhort, adjure' (i. 846–7). If that fails, admonition then gives way to reproof, the minister now exercising two 'engines of terror' assigned to his 'hand' (not another 'two-handed engine', surely?). 'One while he shakes [the sinner's] stubbornnesse with racking convulsions': this, the work of violent criticism; 'other whiles with deadly corrosives . . . to bring him to life through . . . death': this, the action of excommunication, led by the priest but performed by the whole congregation (i. 847). The emphasis throughout this process is clear. Numerous, escalating efforts are made to reform each lost sheep, and the agency behind that collective, participatory exercise in which 'some tend, some watch, some visit' (i. 838) is an ever-widening circle of congregants. Furthermore, that the individual feels such a circle bearing in upon him is evident from Milton's talk of shame. For all the focus on Christian eschatology, the tract's allusions to Plato's *Laws* (646e ff., 671a–d), Seneca's 11th and 25th epistles, and perhaps

Montaigne's 'On Solitude'—its admiring reference, too, to 'the wisdom of the Romans' and their institution, the Censor (i. 831–3)—underline how far a republican tradition of shame-culturing reinforces Milton's concept of disciplining.[25] Shame, the painful thought of being made 'outcast' by those one has grown up revering (i. 841), manifests itself to the mind as the image of one's being observed by others doing something demeaning. Shame's mode of being is distinctively visual and self-objectifying: it imagines the self at the centre of a circle of scrutinizers all bearing witness to the transgressor's self-degradation. This is the emotion that Milton makes central to the operation of disciplining—the thought that we each 'reverence the opinion' and pressuring 'countenance' of some 'good man', an eternal looker-on, and 'fear most in his sight to offend' (i. 842).[26]

The idea of a shaming gaze pressing in from without, and of widening circles of congregants working a similar effect, points back to the circling and centripetal tendencies of Milton's previous works, just as this tract's treatment of time also recalls that poetry. There are, though, other ways besides in which the radicalism of *The Reason of Church-Government* provided renewed fulfilment for the earlier Milton's figurative preoccupations. For one thing, discipline, in the tract, is imagined from the outset as functioning exactly as did the music of the spheres in the Nativity Ode. It is supposedly another version of that set of harmonizing chords which holds all things together (i. 751). Secondly, the fact that discipline's prescriptive reach extends even to the blessed in paradise indicates that its effect is not constricting. On the contrary, Milton writes that discipline enables our happiness to 'orb it selfe into a thousand vagancies of glory and delight', just as the planets, though ordered, chart numerous different orbits (i. 752). Orbing, then, the ode's imaginative idiom, is here reintroduced, but now as a conceit of delightful freedom. Furthermore, this same recurs when Milton describes, geometrically, the distinction between prelacy and his own, nominally Presbyterian[27] vision. The prelatical chain of command is imaged as 'ascending' in a seemingly 'continuall pyramid', sharpening towards a lethal point; but every mathematician apparently knows that the triangle is 'the most dividing, . . . schismaticall' of forms (i. 790). Perfection and unity are to be found, rather, amongst the presbyters who 'incube' or—more revealingly—'inglobe' themselves. Here especially, then, Milton identifies his tract's antiprelatical ideal of corporate communion with an earlier image of imaginative pleasure, the angels' englobing of the shepherds.

It would be a mistake, though, solely to think of *The Reason of Church-Government* as promoting a group ideal, and thus to associate it more with the Nativity Ode and with a healing of the scepticism found in 'Lycidas' than with *A Maske*'s ideally autonomous Lady. The liberation wrought by the Gospel's new dispensation lent itself not only to congregational independency but also to individual freedom since it put a premium on the individual's own spiritual understanding of the law. *The Reason of Church-Government*, in developing this emphasis, paved the way for Milton's antinomianism.[28] Indeed, the 1642 tract reaches its logical outcome in *De Doctrina Christiana*'s account of Christian liberty. *De Doctrina* frames the new covenant's abolition of Judaic law as so absolute that under its influence Christians have ceased to be bound even by the decalogue, at least in any 'letter of the law' sense (*CPW*, vi. 532). 'The *substance* of the [old] law' is not, on this perspective, abrogated; on the contrary, 'its purpose is attained' insofar as 'love of God and...neighbour' continues to condition the true Christian's every action (vi. 531). However, under the Gospel each parishioner is now liberated to judge for himself how best to realize this purpose, according to the light of his spirit and his own rational intuition. Furthermore, *De Doctrina* emphasizes the special worth of such personal judgement:

> We have...under the gospel, a double scripture. There is the external scripture of the written word, and the internal scripture of the Holy Spirit...engraved upon the hearts of believers.... [Of these,] the pre-eminent...authority...is...the Spirit,... the individual possession of each man. (vi. 587)

This is the essence, then, of Milton's version of Christian liberty, the antinomian end-point towards which *The Reason of Church-Government*'s Jewish–Christian distinction tends; and, crucially, it supports an ideal of independent autonomy akin to that heroized in the Lady in *A Maske*.

The fact that Milton continued to sense the appeal of that autonomy even as he theorized on the nature of congregationalism is apparent at the heart of *The Reason of Church-Government*'s argument. The tract's account of shame extends to more than just a fear of public infamy. The parishioner who understands that he (like every man) has been 'ordain'd' as one of God's ministers, thereby arrives at a 'true valuation of himselfe' (i. 843–4). He discovers 'an inward reverence' for his own person, a 'pious and just honouring' of the self, that for Milton lies at the heart of Christian liberty and Gospel (as opposed to Judaic) consciousness (i. 841). In this context, shame becomes something inwardly (rather than outwardly) generated—a matter of self-respect. The man of 'self-pious regard' holds himself in 'due esteem...for the dignity of Gods image upon him, and for the price of his redemption' (Christ having died for his sake), and these considerations, more than any anxiety about public vilification, push him to demand of himself the very 'noblest...deeds', and to recoil from anything self-defiling (i. 842). Hence, this more inward kind of shame—the sort of self-esteem that Raphael will later demand of Adam—promotes strenuous self-discipline. It guarantees the moral integrity of the spiritual man by preventing his antinomianism from degenerating into self-indulgent libertinism. Psychologically, such higher shame works by making the agent his own observer, concerned less with picturing how others see him and more with asking what he looks like to himself. Milton's Christian 'dreads...the reflection of his own severe...eye upon himselfe, if it should see him doing or imagining that which is sinfull' (i. 842). The optics here are hard to conceptualize, the eye somehow going outside itself in order to turn back and reflect on the agent that stands behind it; but the idea, clearly, is of a self-generated power pushing in on the soul as if from without, exercising a shaming gaze which forces that soul to maintain its proper character, to be centripetal.

This is the sense, then, in which *The Reason of Church-Government* idealizes the morally autonomous individual even as it also celebrates congregationalism. What is striking, though, is the conceit to which Milton turns to epitomize his individualist, centripetal soul. Again the image is of a globe; again *The Reason of Church-Government* reinvigorates that long-established imaginative fixation. Milton, having figured 'pious and just honouring' of oneself as 'the radical moisture' of virtue, continues this self-esteem's description thus:

although I have giv'n it the name of a liquid thing, yet it is not incontinent to bound it self, as humid things are, but hath in it a most restraining and powerfull abstinence to start back, and glob it self upward from the mixture of any... unbeseeming motion, or any soile wherewith it may peril to stain it self. (i. 841–2)

The emphasis in this orbing soul, clearly, is on individual autonomy and introversion. This globe is as self-inwoven as that Marvellian dewdrop which it anticipates, which 'round in itself encloses'. It recoils fastidiously from all trace of the carnal world, valuing itself by what it excludes and abstains from (rather than what it embraces) and straining 'upward' towards heaven—in both respects precisely *not* englobing itself in this tract's other sense, that of joining in a common phalanx with other men.

At the heart of Milton's exposition of his congregational ideal there lies, then, a metaphor expressive of personal independence. Just as disciplinary shame, as found in Milton's tract, exploits both a communal and a self-reflexive perspective in passing its judgements, so too the tract's globing imagery is simultaneously corporate and yet also individualist. The ethical argument here is thus quintessentially Janus-faced: a principle of autonomy and downright singularity exists in stark tension with *The Reason of Church-Government*'s collectivist vision. That impulse towards singularity signals an alternative ideal that stands ready to detach itself from the pamphlet's congregationalism at a moment's notice—as indeed would happen in Milton's later career. Yet, as the continuities in the language of orbing, circling, and centripetal pressure indicate, that same unresolved tension was a feature even in the poet's earliest works. It is apparent in the gap which separates that urge for assimilation into a 'full consort' or 'song of pure concent' seen in the Nativity Ode and other poems, from *A Maske*'s fascination with rigid autonomy. It is apparent, too, in the disparity between the Lady's impulse to preserve herself from the soiling touch of others, and her absorption, nonetheless, within communal festivities. *The Reason of Church-Government* thus marks not a radical departure from, but a continuation of, those contours evident in the early poetry—contours which define Milton's moral imagination.

Notes

1. Christopher Hill, *Milton and the English Revolution* (New York, 1977), 22–92; Leah Marcus, *The Politics of Mirth: Jonson, Herrick, Milton, Marvell, and the Defense of Old Holiday Pastimes* (Chicago, Ill., 1986), 169–212; Michael Wilding, *Dragons Teeth: Literature in the English Revolution* (Oxford, 1987), 7–88; Barbara K. Lewalski, 'How Radical was the Young Milton?' in Stephen B. Dobranski and John P. Rumrich (eds.), *Milton and Heresy* (Cambridge, 1998), 49–72; David Norbrook, *Poetry and Politics in the English Renaissance* (rev. edn., 2002), 224–69.

2. John Spencer Hill, *John Milton, Poet, Priest and Prophet: A Study of Divine Vocation in Milton's Poetry and Prose* (Toronto 1979), 27–50; Thomas N. Corns, 'Milton before "Lycidas"', in Graham Parry and Joad Raymond (eds.), *Milton and the Terms of Liberty* (Cambridge, 2002), 23–36; Campbell and Corns, 7–151. For another, related argument which reads early Milton as retrospectively positioned amongst reactionary post-Caroline literature, see James Dougal Fleming, 'Composing 1629', *Milton Quarterly*, 36 (2002), 20–33.

3. Norbrook, *Poetry and Politics*, 265–6; Campbell and Corns, 92–6.

4. Annabel Patterson, "'Forc'd Fingers": Milton's Early Poems and Ideological Constraint', in Claude J. Summers and Ted-Larry Pebworth (eds.), 'The Muses Common-Weale': Poetry and Politics in the Seventeenth Century (Columbia, Mo., 1988), 9–22; David Loewenstein, '"Fair Offspring Nurs't in Princely Lore": On the Question of Milton's Early Radicalism', Milton Studies, 28 (1992), 37–48.

5. All references to Milton's poetry and prose are respectively to the Complete Shorter Poems, ed. John Carey, 2nd edn. (1997) and the Complete Prose Works of John Milton, ed. Don M. Wolfe et al., 8 vols. in 10 (New Haven, Conn., 1953–82). Numbers in parentheses for the poetry refer to line numbers; those for the prose refer to the volume and page numbers.

6. Lowry Nelson Jr., Baroque Lyric Poetry (New Haven, Conn., 1961), 42–51.

7. Stephen Fallon traces the interplay that ensues between gestures of self-assertion and self-effacement in Milton's Peculiar Grace: Self-Representation and Authority (Ithaca, N.Y., 2007), 55–60.

8. See Stella Revard, Milton and the Tangles of Neaera's Hair: The Making of the 1645 Poems (Columbia, Mo., 1997), 82–3; Stanley Fish, How Milton Works (Cambridge, Mass., 2001), 313–19.

9. On the ode's millenarianism see Juliet Cummins (ed.), Milton and the Ends of Time (Cambridge, 2003), 55–6, 96–7.

10. Cedric C. Brown, John Milton's Aristocratic Entertainments (Cambridge, 1985), 95–101.

11. Marcus, Politics of Mirth, 187–9, 192–4; Martin Butler, The Stuart Court Masque and Political Culture (Cambridge, 2008), 355–7.

12. See J. Martin Evans, 'Lycidas', in Dennis Danielson (ed.), 2nd edn. The Cambridge Companion to Milton (Cambridge, 1999), 40–2.

13. For additional discussion of this crux, see John Leonard's essay in this volume.

14. Although they disagree about whose voice speaks at this juncture, Joseph Wittreich (Visionary Poetics: Milton's Tradition and His Legacy (San Marino, Calif., 1979), 139–41), G. W. Pigman (Grief and English Renaissance Elegy (Cambridge, 1985), 109–24), and Fish (How Milton Works, 275–9) all agree about its triumphant quality.

15. Richard Hooker, 'Lycidas and the Ecphrasis of Poetry', Milton Studies, 27 (1991), 59–77.

16. Joan Webber, The Eloquent 'I': Style and Self in Seventeenth-Century Prose (Madison, Wis., 1968), 190–3.

17. Keith Stavely, The Politics of Milton's Prose Style (New Haven, Conn., 1975), 33–4.

18. References are to John Calvin, The Institvtion of Christian Religion (1634), trans. Thomas Norton.

19. John Field and Thomas Wilcox, Admonition (1572), sig. c7r.

20. Henry Burton, Englands Bondage and Hope of Deliverance (1641), 27.

21. Katherine Chidley, The Ivstification of the Independent Chvrches of Christ (1641), 28–9; Lord Brooke, A Discovrse Opening the Natvre of that Episcopacie, which is Exercised in England (1641), 7–8, 121–3.

22. Joseph Hall, An Humble Remonstrance to the High Covrt of Parliament (1640), 10–11.

23. Lancelot Andrewes's Summary View of the Government Both of the Old and New Testament and James Ussher's Originall of Bishops and Metropolitans (both included in this 1641

collection) present arguments establishing the parity between Jewish priestly hierarchies and the hierarchy of the early Christian church (which Laudian prelates, in turn, styled themselves as emulating).

24. Revealingly, Milton's account is more detailed than those offered by other anti-prelates of 1641–2. Earlier puritans had commented on the processes of admonition, suspension, and excommunication essential to congregational disciplining—witness, for example, Field and Wilcox, *Admonition*, sig. a6r–v; Thomas Cartwright, *A Second Admonition to the Parliament* (1572), 45–9; Walter Travers, *A Full and Plaine Declaration of Ecclesiasticall Discipline* (Heidelberg, 1574), 163–4, 168–72; or John Robinson, *Of Religious Commvnion Private, & Publique* (Antwerp, 1614), 24–5. Field and Wilcox (*Admonition*, sigs. a5r–v), and Travers (*Ecclesiasticall Discipline*, 177–83), wrote, too, about the disciplinary role to be played by communities of elders. However, Milton aside, propagandists of the 1640s tended not to reiterate these points. In their various attacks on episcopacy, Henry Burton, Katherine Chidley, and Sir Henry Vane, for instance, all avoid prescribing any specific alternative church structure or expatiating on the models of self-governance that might sustain such a thing. *The Reason of Church-Government* is unusual in recovering and deepening the early puritan discussions of discipline, imagining in lingering, particular detail how a disciplinary community should function in order to embody Protestantism's priesthood of all believers.

25. See Christopher Tilmouth, 'Shakespeare's Open Consciences', *Renaissance Studies*, 23 (2009), 501–6.

26. As Webber (*Eloquent 'I'*, 184–5, 194–7) and Fallon (*Peculiar Grace*, e.g., 81–91) note, in all the anti-prelatical pamphlets Milton presents even himself as if from without, as one objectified under the public gaze. (The very grammar of the tracts promotes this impression.) The tendency surfaces particularly strongly in Milton's characterization of himself as 'a true Poem' in the *Apology* ('he who would ... write well ... ought him selfe to bee a true Poem' [*CPW*, i. 890]), in the similarly self-distancing image that he is one 'incorporate' with truth (i. 871), and in the claim (implicit in his offer to 'turn' his very 'inside outwards' [i. 888–9]) that nothing about him is unavailable for scrutiny.

27. In 1641–2 Milton was still courting Presbyterian opinion. Consequently, *The Reason of Church-Government* is framed, throughout, as opposing 'Presbyteriall' to 'Prelaticall' government, always favouring the former (i. 748; cf. i. 750, 761, 781, 790). The tract even purports to demonstrate that Presbyterianism is 'the only true Church-government' (i. 835). Nevertheless, the logic of Milton's actual argument is, as Campbell and Corns have suggested (149–50), congregationalist and independent. Milton's evocation of the individual congregation's disciplinary powers accords an autonomy to each such community which exceeds what the actual Presbyterian hierarchy permitted. Furthermore, his idealization of Presbyterian governance manifestly departs from the reality. Where the latter actually apportioned authority on a vertical scale split into congregations, presbyteries, synods, and the general assembly, Milton acknowledges only three levels: the individual congregations

(each dubbed a 'parochiall Consistory'); regional councils of the same; and one general assembly (i. 789). He then describes every parochial consistory as 'a right homogeneous and constituting part' of the broader council, 'being in it selfe ... a little Synod', and figures each such congregation as moving towards the general assembly 'upon her own basis in a ... firme progression, as those smaller squares in battell unite in one great ... phalanx'. The implication of this language is that the particular church community never compromises the primacy of its own autonomy (its integrity as a 'constituting part' and a distinct 'square'), even when it consults with the larger corporate whole. There is no subservience here, as there was in the actual Presbyterian hierarchy.

28. See the discussions in Joan S. Bennett, *Reviving Liberty: Radical Christian Humanism in Milton's Great Poems* (Cambridge, Mass., 1989), 96–110, and Fish, *How Milton Works*, 1–107, 323–4, 353–4, 367–8, 501–3.

BIBLIOGRAPHY

1. MILTON EDITIONS AND REFERENCE WORKS

Bush, Douglas (ed.), *The Portable Milton* (New York: Viking, 1960).

Campbell, Gordon, *A Milton Chronology* (Harlow: Macmillan, 1997).

—— (ed.), *John Milton: The Complete English Poems, 'Of Education', 'Areopagitica'* (London: Dent, 1990).

Carey, John (ed.), *Milton: Complete Shorter Poems* (1968. 2nd edn., Harlow: Longman, 1997).

Darbishire, Helen (ed.), *The Early Lives of Milton* (London: Constable, 1932).

—— *The Poetical Works of John Milton* (2 vols., Oxford: Clarendon Press, 1952–5).

Flannagan, Roy (ed.), *The Riverside Milton* (Boston, Mass.: Houghton Mifflin, 1998).

Fletcher, Harris Francis (ed.), *John Milton's Complete Poetical Works Reproduced in Facsimile* (4 vols., Urbana: University of Illinois Press, 1943–8).

Fowler, Alastair (ed.), *Paradise Lost* (2nd edn., Harlow: Longman, 1998).

French, J. Milton, *The Life Records of John Milton* (5 vols., New Brunswick, N.J.: Rutgers University Press, 1949–58).

Huckabay, Calvin, and David V. Urban (comps.), Urban, David V., and Paul J. Klemp, *John Milton: An Annotated Bibliography, 1989–1999* (Pittsburgh, Pa.: Duquesne University Press, 2011).

Hughes, Merritt Y. (ed.), *John Milton: Complete Poems and Major Prose* (New York: Odyssey, 1957).

—— (gen. ed.), *A Variorum Commentary on the Poems of John Milton* (6 vols., New York: Columbia University Press, 1970–).

Hume, Patrick, *Annotations on Milton's 'Paradise Lost'* (London, 1695).

Kerrigan, William, John Rumrich, and Stephen M. Fallon (eds.), *The Complete Poetry and Essential Prose of John Milton* (New York: Modern Library, 2007).

Klemp, P. J., *The Essential Milton: An Annotated Bibliography of Major Modern Studies* (Boston, Mass.: G. K. Hall, 1989).

Leonard, John (ed.), *John Milton: The Complete Poems* (London and New York: Penguin, 1998).

Masson, David (ed.), *The Poetical Works of John Milton* (3 vols., London: Macmillan, 1874).

Milton, John, *Accedence Commenc't Grammar* (London, 1669).

—— *A Maske Presented at Ludlow Castle, 1634* (London, 1637/8).

—— *Epistolarum Familiarium* (London, 1674).

—— *Paradise Lost. A Poem Written in Ten Books* (London, 1667).

—— *Paradise Regain'd, A Poem in IV Books. To Which is added Samson Agonistes* (London, 1671).

—— *Poems, &c* (London, 1673)

—— *Poems of Mr John Milton, Both English and Latin, Compos'd at Several Times* (London, 1645).

—— *Poems, Reproduced in Facsimile from the Manuscript in Trinity College, Cambridge, with a Transcript* (Menston: Scolar Press, 1970).

—— *Poems upon Several Occasions* (London, 1695).

Newton, Thomas (ed.), *Paradise Regain'd . . . and Poems upon Several Occasions* (London, 1752).

Nicolson, Marjorie Hope (ed.), *Poems and Selected Prose* (New York: Bantam, 1962).

Orgel, Stephen, and Jonathan Goldberg (eds.), *John Milton* (Oxford: Oxford University Press, 1990).

Patterson, Frank A. (ed.), *The Student's Milton* (rev. edn., New York: Crofts, 1933).

—— (gen. ed.), *The Works of John Milton* (18 vols. in 21, New York: Columbia University Press, 1931–8).

Pickering, William (ed.), *The Poetical Works of John Milton* (3 vols., London, 1885).

Revard, Stella P. (ed.), *John Milton: Complete Shorter Poems* (Oxford: Wiley, 2009).

Richardson, Jonathan, Jr. and Sr. (eds.), *Explanatory Notes and Remarks on Milton's 'Paradise Lost'* (London, 1734).

Shawcross, John T. (ed.), *The Complete Poetry of John Milton* (rev. edn., New York: Doubleday, 1971).

Sumner, Charles R. (ed. and trans.), *A Treatise of Christian Doctrine* (2 vols., Braunschweig, 1827).

Tillyard, E. M. W., and Phyllis B. Tillyard (eds.), *'Comus' and Some Shorter Poems of Milton* (London: Harrup, 1952).

Warton, Thomas (ed.), *Poems upon Several Occasions: English, Italian, Latin* (London, 1785).

Wolfe, Don M. (gen. ed.), *Complete Prose Works of John Milton* (8 vols. in 10, New Haven, Conn.: Yale University Press, 1953–82).

Wright, B. A. (ed.), *Poems* (London and New York: Dent and Dutton, 1956).

Wright, William Aldus (ed.), *The Poetical Works of John Milton* (Cambridge: Cambridge University Press, 1903).

2. MANUSCRIPTS AND BOOKS WITH MANUSCRIPT ANNOTATIONS

Austin, Texas, Harry Ransom Humanities Research Center

Pre-1700 MS 127 (a page of Latin juvenilia attributed to Milton).

Aylesbury, Centre for Buckinghamshire Studies

D/A/V 1-15 (Archidiaconal Visitation Books).
PR 107/1/1 (Parish Register, St Michael, Horton).

Cambridge, Christ's College

Admissions Book.
MS 8 ('Milton's Autographs').

Cambridge, Jesus College

G.16.130 (Thomas Cranmer, *Reformatio Legum Ecclesiasticarum* [London, 1640], with Latin
inscription 'Ex dono D Jo. Milton hunc librum possidet T.Y. D.D').

Cambridge, Trinity College

MS R.3.4 (Milton's notebook, commonly designated the Trinity MS).

Cambridge, Cambridge University Library

Manuscript 154 (Milton's annotated copy of *Justa Edouardo King*).
Ely. A.272 (Milton's annotated copy of Chrysostom's *Orationes LXXX*).

Cambridge, Cambridge University Archives (in Cambridge University Library)

Grace Book Zeta.
Matriculation Book.
Subscription Book.
Supplicats 1627, 1628, 1629.
Supplicats 1630, 1631, 1632.

Dublin, Trinity College

R.dd.39 (ten of Milton's prose tracts sent with his inscription to Patrick Young).

Edinburgh, Advocates' Library, National Library of Scotland

Adv. Ms. 19.3.40 f. 8r (Malatesti's sonnet sequence *La Tina*, dedicated to Milton).

Edinburgh, University Library

Dc.6.45 (1–7) (Melville's unpublished manuscript on educational reform).

Eton, College Library

Eton College Records 62/55 (Audit Book, 1621).
Eton's earliest surviving catalogue, an interleaved copy of the Bodleian 1674 Hyde.

London, Bridgewater House

Bridgewater Manuscript (*A Maske*, 1634).

London, British Library

Add MS 5016* (Diodati's letters to Milton in Greek).
Add MS 32,310 (Milton's family Bible).
Add MS 36, 354 (Milton's Commonplace Book).
C60.1.7 (Milton's annotated copy of Aratus's *Phenomena*, 1559).
MS Egerton 2877 (notes on the sermons of Richard Stock in the commonplace book of Gilbert Frevile).

London, City of Westminster Archives Centre

Parish Register, St Clement Danes.
E 166–173 (St Margaret's, Overseer Accounts, 1652-60).
E 1595–1603 (St Margaret's, Army and Navy Assessments, 1651–54).
Parish Register, St Martin in the Fields.
F3 (St Martin-in-the-Fields, Churchwarden Accounts, 1625–31).
F4 (St Martin-in-the-Fields, Churchwarden Accounts, 1631–35).
F350–59 (St Martin-in-the-Fields, Overseer Accounts, 1623–32/33).
F1011 (St Martin-in-the-Fields, Poor Relief Register, 1632).
F3346 (St Martin-in-the-Fields, Collection for the Repair of Knightsbridge, Chelsea, and Brentford Bridge, 1632).
F3355 (St Martin-in-the-Fields, Plague Relief Ledger, 1630).

London, Guildhall Library

MS 5031 (Parish Register, All Hallows, Bread Street).
MS 6668/1 (Marriage Register, St Andrew Holborn 1559–1698).
MS 6673/2 (Burial Register, St Andrew Holborn 1623–42).
MS 8319 (Parish Register, St Stephen Walbrook).

London, Hammersmith and Fulham Archives and Local History Centre

DD/818/56 (Papers regarding the creation of the Hammersmith Chapel).
PAF/1/21 (Rate Books of the Vestry of Fulham).

London, Inner Temple Archive

Admissions Book 1571–1640.

London, Lambeth Palace Library

MS 770 (*Notitia Academiæ Cantabrigiensis*).
Arc L 40.2/E 29 (Sion College Manuscripts, 1632, 1640–66, 1671–93).

London, National Archives (formerly Public Record Office)

C24 Chancery Town Depositions (supporting evidence for Hammersmith residency).
C54 Chancery Close Rolls (records of Milton family buying property in St-Martin-in-the-Fields).
C152 Chancery Certificates and Recognizances of Statute Staple, Rolls Chapel Office.
LC4 Lord Chamberlain's Department, Recognizance Rolls.
PROB 11 PCC Registered Copy Wills.
Req 1 Court of Requests, Miscellaneous Books.
Req 2 Court of Requests, Proceedings.

New York, The Morgan Library and Museum

MS MA 953 (marriage settlement of Anne Milton and Edward Phillips, witnessed by Milton).

New York, New York Public Library

*KB 1529 (Milton's annotated copy of a volume containing Della Casa's *Rime e Prose*, Dante's *Convivio*, and Varchi's *Sonetti*).
MS 2011 (letter from Carlo Dati to Milton).

Oxford, Bodleian Library

Don.d.2728 (Milton's annotated copy of Euripides' *Tragoediae*).
Lib. Recs. B36 (Library records, Bills to 1763).
MS Aubrey 8 ('Minutes of the Life of John Milton').
MS Ballard 1 (autograph evidence of John Hales).
MS Savile 47 (autograph evidence of John Hales).
MS Tanner 71 (correspondence between Gataker and Ward).
MS Wood D4 (Skinner's 'Anonymous' Life of Milton).

Sheffield, Sheffield University Library

The Hartlib Papers (2nd edn., Sheffield, 2002).
28/2/23B, 29/3/63B, 29/2/1A-65B (*Ephemerides*).

Urbana, Rare Book and Manuscript Division of the University of Illinois Library

IUA 01704 (copy of the Venice 1608 edition of Boiardo's *Orlando Innamorato* sent to Milton by Daniel Oxenbridge).

X 881 H2151544 (Milton's copy of the Basel 1544 edition of Heraclitus of Pontus's *Allegoriae in Homerii Fibula de Diis*).

881 L71601 (Milton's annotated copy of the 1601 Geneva edition of Lycophron's *Alexandra*).

3. PRIMARY SOURCES

Abbot, George, *A Treatise of the Perpetuall Visibilitie and Succession of the True Church in All Ages* (London, 1624).

Aligheri, Dante, *L'Amoroso Convivio* (Venice, 1529).

Ames, William, *A Fresh Suit against Human Ceremonies in God's Worship* (Amsterdam, 1633).

Andrewes, Lancelot, *A Morall Law Expounded* [including] *Seven Sermons on the Wonderfull Combate (for Gods Glory, and Mans Salvation) betweene Christ and Sathane* (London, 1642).

—— *XCVI Sermons . . . Published by His* Majesties *Speciall Command*, ed. William Laud and John Buckeridge (London, 1629).

—— *Responsio ad Apologia Cardinalis Bellarmini* (London, 1610).

—— *A Summarie View of the Government Both of the Old and New Testament* (Oxford, 1641).

—— *Tortvra Torti: Sive, Ad Matthaei Torti Librvm Responsio . . .* (London, 1609).

Aratus, *Phenomena* (Paris, 1559).

Aristotle, *Metaphysics*, ed. Hugh Tredennick and G. Cyril Armstrong (2 vols., Cambridge, Mass.: Harvard University Press, 1933–5).

—— *The Nicomachean Ethics*, trans. David Ross (rev. edn., Oxford: Oxford University Press, 1998).

The Articles and Charge Proved in Parliament Against Doctor Walton, Minister of St Martins Orgars in Cannonstreet (London, 1641).

Articuli de quibus convenit inter archiepiscopos, et episcopos utriusque provinciae, et clerum universum in Synodo, Londini. An. 1562 (Oxford, 1636).

Ascham, Roger, *The Scholemaster*, in *The Works of Roger Ascham*, ed. William Aldis Wright (Cambridge: Cambridge University Press, 1904).

Ausonius, *Ausonius*, ed. Hugh G. Evelyn White (2 vols., Cambridge, Mass.: Harvard University Press, 1921).

Babington, Gervase, *Certaine Plaine, Briefe, and Comfortable Notes upon Everie Chapter of Genesis* (London, 1592).

Baillie, Robert, *Letters and Journals*, ed. David Laing (3 vols., Edinburgh, 1841–2).

Bartholomaeus, Anglicus, *Batman vppon Bartholome, His Booke 'De Proprietatibus Rerum'*, trans. Stephen Bateman (2 vols., London, 1582).

Baxter, Richard, *A Saint or a Brute* (London, 1662).

Baynes, Paul, *The Diocesans Tryall*, ed. William Ames (Amsterdam, 1621).

Bede, *Bedae Anglosaxonis Historiae Ecclesiasticae Gentis Anglorum Libri V*, in Commelin, *Rerum Britannicarum* (Heidelberg, 1587).

—— *Ecclesiastical History*, ed. J. E. King (2 vols., Cambridge, Mass.: Harvard University Press, 1930).

The Bible and Holy Scriptures Conteyned in the Olde and Newe Testament . . . with Most Profitable Annotations (Geneva, 1560).

Birch, Thomas, and Robert Folkestone Williams (eds.), *The Court and Times of James the First* (2 vols., London, 1848).

Blundeville, Thomas, *The True Order and Methode of Wryting and Reading Hystories* (London, 1574).

Boys, John, *An Exposition of the Dominical Epistles and Gospels . . . the Winter Part from the First Adventuall Sunday to Lent* (London, 1610).

—— *An Exposition of the Festivall Epistles and Gospels Used in Our English Liturgie Together with a Reason Why the Church Did Chuse the Same. The Third Part* (London, 1615).

Bracton, Henry de, *De Legibus et Consuetudinibus Angliae*, ed. Samuel E. Thorne (4 vols., Cambridge, Mass.: Harvard University Press 1968).

Bradshaw, William, *A Triall of Subscription* (Middleburg, 1599).

Brooke, Lord (Robert Greville), *A Discovrse Opening the Natvre of that Episcopacie, Which is Exercised in England* (London, 1641).

Burges, Cornelius, *Sion College, What It Is, and Doeth* (London, 1648).

Burmann, Pieter (ed.), *Sylloges Epistolarum* (3 vols., Leiden, 1727).

Burton, Henry, *Englands Bondage and Hope of Deliverance* (London, 1641).

Buxtorf, Johann, *Doctor Perplexorum* (Basel, 1629).

Calvin, John, *The Institutes of the Christian Religion*, ed. John T. McNeil, trans. Ford Lewis Battles (2 vols., Philadelphia, Pa.: Westminster John Knox Press, 1960).

—— *Institutio Christianae Religionis* (Geneva, 1576).

—— *The Institvtion of Christian Religion*, trans. Thomas Norton (London, 1634).

Carew, Thomas, *Coelum Britannicum* (London, 1634).

Cartwright, Thomas, *A Second Admonition to the Parliament* (London, 1572).

Chidley, Katherine, *The Ivstification of the Independent Chvrches of Christ* (London, 1641).

Chrysostom, *Orationes LXXX* (Paris, 1604).

Cicero, *De Oratore*, ed. H. Rackham and E. W. Sutton (2 vols., Cambridge, Mass.: Harvard University Press, 1942).

Clarke, Samuel (ed.), *The Lives of Thirty-Two English Divines, Famous in Their Generations for Learning and Piety, and Most of Them Sufferers in the Cause of Christ* (3rd edn., London, 1677).

Clement of Alexandria, *Opera* (Paris, 1629).

Commelin, Jerome, *Rerum Britannicarum* (Heidelberg, 1587).

Cowell, John, *The Interpreter: Or Booke Containing the Signification of Words* (Cambridge, 1607).

Cranmer, Thomas, *Reformatio Legum Ecclesiasticarum*, ed. John Foxe (London, 1571).

Cuffe, Henry, *The Differences of the Ages of Mans Life* (London, 1633).

Cyprian, Caecilius, *Opera*, ed. J. Golartius (Paris, 1593).

Della Casa Giovanni, *Rime e Prose di Giovanni della Casa* (Venice, 1563).

Downame, George, *A Defence of the Sermon Preached at the Consecration of the L. Bishop of Bath and Welles* (London, 1611).

———— *Two Sermons, the One Commending the Ministerie in Generall: The Other Defending the Office of Bishops in Particular* (London, 1608).

Downe, John, *Not the Consent of Fathers but Scripture the Ground of Faith*, in *A Treatise of the True Nature and Definition of Justifying Faith* (Oxford, 1635).

De Episcopus et Presbyteris, contra D. Petavium Loiolitam Dissertatio Prima (Leiden, 1641).

Erasmus, Desiderius, *De Pueris*, in *Opera Omnia* (1703), ed. Jean le Clerc (Hildesheim: Olms Verlag, 1961).

Euripides, *Euripidis Tragoediae Quae Extant* (2 vols., Geneva, 1602).

Eusebius, *Historia Ecclesiastica Autores* (Paris, 1544).

———— *De Præparatione Evangelii* in *Historiae Ecclesiasticae Scriptores Graeci* (Geneva, 1612).

Field, John, and Thomas Wilcox, *Admonition to Parliament* (London, 1572).

Fletcher, Giles, *Christs Victorie, and Triumph in Heauen and Earth, ouer, and after Death* (Cambridge, 1610).

Fletcher, John, *The Faithful Shepherdess*, in *The Dramatic Works in the Beaumont and Fletcher Canon*, gen. ed. Fredson Bowers (10 vols., Cambridge: Cambridge University Press, 1966–96).

Gataker, Thomas, *Abrahams Decease . . . Delivered at the Funerall of that Worthy Servant of Christ, Mr Richard Stock, Late Pastor of All-Hallowes Bread-street* (London, 1627).

Gil, Alexander, *Alexander Gil's 'Logonomia Anglica'* (1619), ed. and trans. B. Danielsson and A. Gabrielson (Stockholm: Almqvist and Wiksell, 1972).

———— *Parerga, sive Poetici Conatus Alexandri Gil* (London, 1632).

Guillemeau, Jacques, *Child-birth or, The Happy Deliverie of Women . . . To Which is Added, a Treatise of the Diseases of Infants, and Young Children: with the Cure of Them* (London, 1612).

Hale, Matthew, *Historia Placitorum Coronae*, ed. George Wilson (2 vols., London, 1800).

Hales, John, *Works* (3 vols., Glasgow, 1765).

Hall, Joseph, *Defence of the Humble Remonstrance* (London, 1641).

———— *Episcopacie* (London, 1640).

———— *An Humble Remonstrance to the High Court of Parliament* (London, 1640).

Hammond, Henry, *A Letter of Resolution to Six Quaeres of Present Use in the Church of England* (London, 1653).

Heraclitus of Pontus, *Héraclite: Allégories d'Homère*, ed. and trans. Félix Buffière (Paris: Les Belles Lettres, 1962).

Holinshed, Raphael, *Chronicles of England, Scotland and Ireland* (3 vols., London, 1587).

The Holy Bible, Conteyning the Old Testament, and the New, Newly Translated Out of the Originall Tongues: & . . . Revised, by his Maiesties Speciall Commandement. Appointed to be Read in the Churches (London, 1611).

Horace, *Horace: The Odes*, ed. Kenneth Quinn (London: Duckworth, 1999).

Justa Edouardo King Naufrago (Cambridge, 1638).

Kemke, Johannes (ed.), *Patricius Junius (Patrick Young) Bibliothekar der Könige Jacob I. und Carl I. von England: Mitteilungen aus seinem Briefwechsel* (Leipzig, 1898).

Lavaterus, Ludovicus, *In Libros Paralipomenon sive Chronicorum Commentarius* (2nd edn., Heidelberg, 1600).

Leland, John, *Cygnea Cantio* (London, 1645).

—— *De Viris Illustribus*, ed. and trans. James P. Carley (Toronto: PIMS, 2010).

Lightfoot, J. B., *The Apostolic Fathers* (5 vols., London, 1889–90).

Littleton, Adam, *et al.*, anon. rev. of *Linguæ Romanæ Dictionarium Luculentum Novum: A New Dictionary in Five Alphabets* (Cambridge, 1693).

Locke, John, *Some Thoughts Concerning Education*, ed. John W. Yolton and Jean S. Yolton (Oxford: Oxford University Press, 1989).

Lycophron, *Alexandra* (Geneva, 1601).

Maimonides, Moses, *The Guide of the Perplexed*, trans. Shlomo Pines (2 vols., Chicago, Ill.: University of Chicago Press, 1963).

Malatesti, Antonio, *La Tina, Equivoci Rusticali* (London, 1757).

Mede, Joseph, 'Epistle LXVI: *Mr Mede's Answer to Dr. Twisse's 7 Quaere's, viz. about the . . . Meaning of Some Difficult Places of Scripture, viz. . . . Matth. 25.31 &C.,*', in *The Works of the Pious and Profoundly-Learned Joseph Mede, B. D.* (London, 1664).

Mersenne, Marin, *Correspondance*, gen. ed. Cornelis de Waard (17 vols., Paris: Editions du Centre de la Recherche Scientifique, 1932–88).

Metzger, Bruce, and Roland Murphy (eds.), *New Oxford Annotated Bible* (Oxford, 1991).

Montagu, James, 'The Preface to the Reader', in James I, *The Workes of the Most High and Mightie Prince, Iames by the Grace of God, King of Great Britaine, France and Ireland, Defender of the Faith, &c.*, ed. James Montagu (London, 1616).

Montagu, Richard, *Appello Caesarem* (London, 1625).

Montaigne, Michel de, *Les Essais*, gen. ed. Jean Balsamo (Paris: Gallimard, Bibliothèque de la Pleiade, 2007).

Moxon, Joseph, *Mechanick Exercises on the Whole Art of Printing*, ed. Herbert Davis and Harry Carter (Oxford: Oxford University Press, 1962).

Origen, *Homilia IV in Ezechielem 1* in *Patrologiae Cursus Completus, Series Graeca* (Paris, 1857–1912).

Ovid, *Metamorphoses*, ed. and trans. Frank Justus Miller (3rd edn., 2 vols., Cambridge, Mass.: Harvard University Press, 1997).

—— *P. Ovidi Nasonis: 'Amores', Medicamina Faciei Femineae, 'Ars Amatoria', 'Remedia Amoris'*, ed. E. J. Kenney (Oxford: Oxford University Press, 1961).

Parker, Matthew, *De Antiquitate Britannicae Ecclesiae* (London, 1572).

Parr, Richard (ed.), *The Life of the Most Reverend Father in God, James Usher* [sic] . . . *with a Collection of Three Hundred Letters between the said Lord Primate and Most of the Eminentest Persons for Piety and Learning in his Time, both in England and beyond the Seas* (London, 1686).

Phillips, Edward, *Letters of State, Written by John Milton . . . to which is added, An Account of his Life* (London, 1694).

The Pilgrimage to Parnassus, in *The Three Parnassus Plays*, ed. J. B. Leishman (London: Nicholson and Watson, 1949).

Plato, *Parmenides*, trans. H. N. Fowler (Cambridge, Mass.: Harvard University Press, 1926).

Prynne, William, *Healthes: Sicknesse* (London, 1628).

Puttenham, George, *The Arte of English Poesie* (London, 1589).

Quintilian, *Institutio Oratoria*, trans. H. E. Butler (4 vols., Cambridge, Mass.: Harvard University Press, 1953).

Randolph, Thomas, *The Jealous Lovers* (Cambridge, 1632).

—— *Poems With the Muses Looking Glasse: With Amyntas* (Oxford, 1638).

The Registers of All Hallows, Bread Street, and of St. John the Evangelist, Friday Street, London, ed. W. Bruce Bannerman, *Harleian Society* 43 (London, 1913).

Rerum Anglicarum Scriptores (London, 1596).

Robinson, John, *Of Religious Commvnion Private, & Publique* (Antwerp, 1614).

Rogers, Richard, *Seven Treatises* (London, 1603).

Ruskin, John, *Sesame and Lilies: Two Lectures Delivered at Manchester in 1864* (New York, 1866).

Sandys, George, *Ovid's Metamorphosis Englished* (London, 1628).

Selden, John, *Mare Clausum, seu de Dominio Maris* (London, 1636).

—— *Mare Clausum*, trans. Marchamont Nedham (London, 1654).

—— *Uxor Hebraica* (London, 1646).

Shakespeare, William, *Complete Sonnets and Poems*, ed. Colin Burrow (Oxford: Oxford University Press, 2002).

Sophocles, *Oedipus Tyrannus*, ed. R. C. Jebb (Cambridge, 1893).

Speed, John, *The History of Great Britaine* (London, 1611).

Spelman, Henry, 'Concilia, Decreta, Leges, Constitutiones', in *Re Ecclesiarum Orbis Britannici* (London, 1639).

Spencer, John, *Catalogus Universalis . . . Collegii Sionii* (London, 1650).

Spenser, Edmund, *The Faerie Queene*, ed. A. C. Hamilton (Harlow: Longman, 2001).

Statutes at Large, from the First Year of King Edward the Fourth to the End of the Reign of Queen Elizabeth (London, 1786).

Stock, Richard, *A Learned and Very Usefull Commentary upon the Whole Prophesie of Malachy* (London, 1641).

—— *A Stock of Divine Knowledge* (London, 1641).

Tacitus, *Agricola. Germania. Dialogue on Oratory*, ed. M. Hutton and W. Peterson (Cambridge, Mass.: Harvard University Press, 1914).

Tertullian, *Aduersos Iudaeos*, 7.4., in *Corpus Christianorum. Series Latina* (Turnhout, Brepols, 1953–).

—— *Opera*, ed. Nicholas Rigault (Paris, 1634).

Thomas, William, *A Preservative of Piety* (London, 1662).

Travers, Walter, *A Full and Plaine Declaration of Ecclesiasticall Discipline* (Heidelberg, 1574).

Ussher, James, *Originall of Bishops and Metropolitans* in *Certain Briefe Treatises, Written by Diverse Learned Men* (Oxford, 1641).

—— *The Reduction of Episcopacy unto the Form of Synodical Government Received in the Ancient Church* (London, 1656).

van der Noodt, Jan, *A Theatre wherein be represented . . . the voluptuous Worldlings* (London, 1569).

Varchi, Benedetto, *Sonetti* (Venice, 1555).

Virgil, *P. Vergili Maronis Opera*, ed. R. A. B. Mynors (Oxford: Oxford University Press, 1969).

Watson, Thomas, 'Epigraph: Exodus 20.12, Honor thy Father and thy Mother', in *A Body of Practical Divinity* (London, 1692).

Wheare, Degory (ed.), *Camdeni Insignia* (Oxford, 1624).

—— *The Method and Order of Reading both Civil and Ecclesiastical Histories*, trans. Edmund Bohun (London, 1685).

—— *De Ratione et Methodo Legendi Historias Dissertatio* (London, 1625, 1637).

Whitaker, William, *An Answere to the Ten Reasons of Edmund Campian*, trans. Richard Stock (London, 1606).

—— *Ad rationes decem Edmundi Campiani . . . responsio* (2nd edn., London, 1581).

—— *Responsionis ad decem illas rationes . . . defensio contra confutationem Joannis Duraei Scoti, Presbyteri, Iesuitae* (London, 1583).

William of Malmesbury, *Willielmi Monachi Malmesburiensis de Gestis Regum Anglorum Libri Quinque* in *Rerum Anglicarum Scriptores*, ed. Henry Saville (London, 1596).

Wood, Anthony, *Athenæ Oxonienses/Fasti Oxonienses*, ed. Phillip W. Bliss (2 vols., Oxford, 1691–2).

Young, Thomas, *Dies Dominica* (London, 1639).

—— *Dies Dominica, or The Lords Day*, trans. Richard Baxter (Oxford, 1672).

—— *The Lords-Day*, trans. Anon., ed. Richard Baxter (Oxford, 1672).

4. SECONDARY SOURCES

Allen, D. C., 'Milton's '*Comus*' as a Failure in Artistic Compromise', *ELH*, 16 (1949), 104–19.

Ayris, Paul, 'Canon Law Studies', in Paul Ayris and David Selwyn (eds.), *Thomas Cranmer: Churchman and Scholar* (Woodbridge: Boydell, 1993), 316–22.

Backus, Irena, *Historical Method and Confessional Identity in the Era of the Reformation (1378–1615)* (Leiden: Brill, 2003).

—— *Lectures Humanistes de Basile de Césarée: Traductions Latines, 1439–1618* (Paris: Institut d'études Augustiniennes, 1990).

—— *Reformation Readings of the Apocalypse: Geneva, Zurich and Wittenberg* (Oxford: Oxford University Press, 2000).

Baker, David Weil, '"Dealt with at his Owne Weapon": Anti-Antiquarianism in Milton's Prelacy Tracts', *Studies in Philology*, 106 (2009), 207–34.

Barker, Arthur, 'Milton's Schoolmasters', *Modern Language Review*, 32 (1937), 517–36.

Beal, Peter, 'Milton', in *Index of English Literary Manuscripts, 1625–1700*, vol. 2, part 2 (London: Mansell, 1987–93), 69–104.

—— 'Notions in Garrison: The Seventeenth-Century Commonplace Book', in W. Speed Hill (ed.), *New Ways of Looking at Old Texts* (Binghamton, N.Y.: MRTS, 1993), 131–47.

Beer, Anna, *Milton: Poet, Pamphleteer, and Patriot* (London: Bloomsbury, 2008).

Bennett, Joan S., *Reviving Liberty: Radical Christian Humanism in Milton's Great Poems* (Cambridge, Mass.: Harvard University Press, 1989).

Biberman, Matthew, 'Milton, Marriage, and a Woman's Right to Divorce', *Studies in English Literature 1500–1900*, 39 (1999), 131–53.

Birley, Robert, *The History of Eton College Library* (Eton, 1970).

—— 'Robert Boyle's Head Master at Eton', *Notes and Records of the Royal Society of London*, 13 (1958), 104–14.

Blair, Ann, 'Note Taking as an Art of Transmission', *Critical Inquiry*, 31 (2004), 85–107.

Blatchly, John M., 'Francis Bacon', *ODNB*.

—— (ed.), *The Town Library of Ipswich* (Woodbridge: Boydell, 1989).

Booty, John E., *John Jewel as Apologist of the Church of England* (London: Society for the Promotion of Christian Knowledge, 1963).

Brain, Robert, *Friends and Lovers* (London: Basic Books, 1976).

Bray, Alan, *The Friend* (Chicago, Ill. and London: University of Chicago Press, 2003).

Bredvold, Louis I., 'Milton and Bodin's *Heptaplomeres*', *Studies in Philology*, 21 (1924), 399–402.

Bremer, Francis J., *Puritanism: A Very Short Introduction* (Oxford: Oxford University Press, 2009).

Brooks, Cleanth, and John Edward Hardy, 'The Progress and Form of the Early Career', in *'Poems of Mr. John Milton', The 1645 Edition with Essays in Analysis* (New York: Harcourt, Brace and Co., 1951), 238–49.

Brooks, Douglas A., 'Introduction: Milton and the Jews: "A Project Never So Seasonable, and Necessary, As Now"', in Douglas A. Brooks (ed.), *Milton and the Jews* (Cambridge: Cambridge University Press, 2008), 1–12.

Brown, Cedric C., *John Milton's Aristocratic Entertainments* (Cambridge: Cambridge University Press, 1985).

—— 'The Legacy of the Late Jacobean Period', in Thomas N. Corns (ed.), *A Companion to Milton* (Oxford: Blackwell, 2003), 109–23.

—— 'The Letters, Verse Letters and Gift Texts', in Stephen B. Dobranski (ed.), *Milton in Context* (Cambridge: Cambridge University Press, 2010), 35–45.

Butler, Martin, *The Stuart Court Masque and Political Culture* (Cambridge: Cambridge University Press, 2008).

Cameron, Euan, 'Medieval Heretics as Protestant Martyrs', in Diane Wood (ed.), *Martyrs and Martyrologies* (Oxford: Ecclesiastical History Society, 1997), 185–207.

Campbell, Gordon, 'The Life Records', in Thomas N. Corns (ed.), *A Companion to Milton* (Oxford: Blackwell, 2001), 483–98.

—— 'Milton's *Index Theologicus* and Bellarmine's *Disputationes de Controversiis Christianae Fidei Adversus Huius Temporis Haereticos*', *Milton Quarterly*, 11 (1977), 12–16.

Campbell, Gordon, and Thomas N. Corns, *John Milton: Life, Work, and Thought* (Oxford: Oxford University Press, 2008).

Campbell, Gordon, Thomas N. Corns, John K. Hale, and Fiona J. Tweedie, *Milton and the Manuscript of 'De Doctrina Christiana'* (Oxford: Oxford University Press, 2007).

Capern, Amanda L., 'The Caroline Church: James Ussher and the Irish Dimension', *Historical Journal*, 39 (1996), 57–85.

Carey, John, 'The Date of Milton's Italian Poems', *Review of English Studies*, 14 (1963): 383–6.

—— *Milton* (New York: Arco, 1970).

Chambers, David S., 'The Earlier "Academies" in Italy', in David S. Chambers and F. Quiviger (eds.), *Italian Academies of the Sixteenth Century* (London: Warburg Institute, 1995), 1–14.

Chaplin, Gregory Ronald, '"One Flesh, One Heart, One Soul",' *Modern Philology*, 99 (2001), 266–92.

Clark, David Lemen, *John Milton at St Paul's School* (New York: Columbia University Press, 1948).

Clarke, Hyde, *Athenaeum*, 2746 (12 June 1880), 760–1.

Clavering, Rose, and John T. Shawcross, 'Anne Milton and the Milton Residencies', *Journal of English and Germanic Philology*, 59 (1960), 680–90.

Coffey, John, *John Goodwin and the Puritan Revolution: Religion and Intellectual Change in Seventeenth-Century England* (Woodbridge: Boydell, 2006).

Coiro, Ann Baynes, 'Anonymous Milton, or *A Maske* Masked', *ELH*, 71 (2004), 609–29.

Collinson, Patrick, *Godly People: Essays on Protestantism and Puritanism* (London: Continuum, 1983).

—— *The Religion of Protestants: The Church in English Society, 1559–1625* (Oxford: Oxford University Press, 1982).

Como, David R., *Blown by the Spirit: Puritanism and the Emergence of an Antinomian Underground in Pre-Civil-War England* (Palo Alto, Calif.: Stanford University Press, 2004).

Condee, Ralph W., 'The Structure of Milton's *Epitaphium Damonis*', *Studies in Philology*, 62 (1965), 577–92.

Corns, Thomas N., 'Milton Before "Lycidas"', in Graham Parry and Joad Raymond (eds.), *Milton and the Terms of Liberty* (Cambridge: D. S. Brewer, 2002), 23–36.

Corthell, Ronald, '"Go Ask Alice": Daughter, Patron, and Poet in *A Maske Presented at Ludlow Castle*', *Milton Studies*, 44 (2005), 111–28.

Costello, William T., *The Scholastic Curriculum at Seventeenth-Century Cambridge* (Cambridge, Mass.: Harvard University Press, 1958).

Crawford, Michael H. (ed.), *Antonio Augustin Between Renaissance and Counter-Reform* (London: Warburg Institute, 1993).

Creaser, John, '"The Present aid of this occasion": The Setting of *Comus*', in David Lindley (ed.), *The Court Masque* (Manchester: Manchester University Press, 1984), 111–34.

Cressy, David, *Birth, Marriage, and Death: Ritual, Religion, and the Life-Cycle in Tudor and Stuart England* (Oxford: Oxford University Press, 1997).

Cummins, Juliet (ed.), *Milton and the Ends of Time* (Cambridge: Cambridge University Press, 2003).

Curtis, Mark H., 'The Alienated Intellectuals of Early Stuart England', *Past and Present*, 23 (1962), 25–43.

—— *Oxford and Cambridge in Transition, 1558–1642* (Oxford: Clarendon Press, 1959).

Dale, T. C. (ed.), *The Inhabitants of London in 1638* (London: Society of Genealogists, 1931).

Darbishire, Helen, 'The Chronology of Milton's Handwriting', *The Library*, 14 (1934), 229–35.

Davis, Natalie Zemon, *The Gift in Sixteenth-Century France* (Oxford and New York: Oxford University Press, 2000).

De Filippis, Michele, 'Milton and Manso: Cups or Books', *PMLA*, 51 (1936), 745–56.

Derrida, Jacques, *The Politics of Friendship*, trans. George Collins (1997; London and New York: Verso, 2005).

Diekhoff, John S., 'Critical Activity of the Poetic Mind: John Milton', *PMLA*, 55 (1940), 748–72.

—— 'The Text of *Comus*, 1634 to 1645', *PMLA*, 52 (1937), 705–27.

Dobranski, Stephen, *Milton, Authorship, and the Book Trade* (Cambridge: Cambridge University Press, 1999).

Dockery, John Berchmans, *Christopher Davenport: Friar and Diplomat* (London: Burns and Oates, 1960).

Dorian, David C., *The English Diodatis* (New Brunswick, N.J.: Rutgers University Press, 1950).

Dubrow, Heather, 'The Masquing of Genre in *Comus*', *Milton Studies*, 44 (2005), 62–83.

Edwards, Karen L., 'Raphael, Diodati', in Donald R. Dickson and Holly Faith Nelson (eds.), *Of Paradise and Light: Essays on Henry Vaughan and John Milton in Honor of Alan Rudrum* (Newark, Del.: University of Delaware Press, 2004), 123–41.

Elson, James, *John Hales of Eton* (New York: King's Crown Press, 1948).

Empson, William, 'Milton and Bentley', in *Some Versions of Pastoral* (London: Chatto and Windus, 1935), 149–94.

Evans, J. Martin, '*Lycidas*', in Dennis Danielson (ed.), *The Cambridge Companion to Milton* (2nd edn., Cambridge: Cambridge University Press, 1999), 39–53.

—— *The Miltonic Moment* (Lexington Ky.: University Press of Kentucky, 1998).

Fallon, Robert T., *Milton in Government* (Philadelphia, Pa.: Pennsylvania State University Press, 1993).

Fallon, Stephen M., *Milton among the Philosophers: Poetry and Materialism in Seventeenth-Century England* (Ithaca, N.Y.: Cornell University Press, 1991).

—— *Milton's Peculiar Grace: Self-Representation and Authority* (Ithaca, N.Y.: Cornell University Press, 2007).

Feingold, Mordechai, 'The Humanities', in Nicholas Tyacke (ed.), *The History of the University of Oxford IV: The Seventeenth Century* (Oxford: Oxford University Press, 1997), 211–359.

Fincham, Kenneth, 'Clerical Conformity from Whitgift to Laud', in Peter Lake and Michael Questier (eds.), *Conformity and Orthodoxy* (Woodbridge: Boydell, 2000), 125–58.

Fish, Stanley, *How Milton Works* (Cambridge, Mass.: Harvard University Press, 2001).

Fleming, James Dougal, 'Composing 1629', *Milton Quarterly*, 36 (2002), 20–33.

Fletcher, Angus, *The Transcendental Masque: An Essay on Milton's 'Comus'* (Ithaca, N.Y.: Cornell University Press, 1972).

Fletcher, Harris Fletcher, *The Intellectual Development of John Milton* (2 vols., Urbana, Ill.: University of Illinois Press, 1956–61).

—— 'The Seventeenth-Century Separate Printing of Milton's *Epitaphium Damonis*', *Journal of English and Germanic Philology*, 61 (1962), 788–96.

Ford, Alan, *James Ussher: Theology, History and Politics in Early-Modern Ireland and England* (Oxford: Oxford University Press, 2007).

Fordyce, C. J., *Catullus: A Commentary* (Oxford: Oxford University Press, 1961).

Forsyth, Neil, *John Milton: A Biography* (London: Lions Gate, 2008).

—— '"Lycidas": A Wolf in Saint's Clothing', *Critical Inquiry*, 35 (2009), 684–702.

Francis, Jane, 'The Kedermister Library: An Account of its Origins and a Reconstruction of its Contents and Arrangement', *Records of Buckinghamshire*, 36 (1994), 62–85.

Fransen, J. Karl, 'The Diodatis in Chester', *Notes and Queries*, 234 (1989), 435.

French, J. Milton, *Milton in Chancery: New Chapters in the Lives of the Poet and His Father* (New York: Modern Language Association of America, 1939).

French, J. Milton, and Maurice Kelley, 'That Late Villain Milton', *PMLA*, 55 (1940), 102–18.

Frye, Northrop, 'Introduction to *"Paradise Lost" and Selected Poetry and Prose*', in Angela Esterhammer (ed.), *Northrop Frye on Milton and Blake* (Toronto, Buffalo, and London: University of Toronto Press, 2005), 3–23.

Fulton, Thomas, *Historical Milton: Manuscript, Print, and Political Culture in Revolutionary England* (Amherst, Mass.: University of Massachusetts Press, 2010).

Gibbs, A. M., 'That Two-handed Engine and Some Renaissance Emblems', *Review of English Studies*, 31 (1980), 178–83.

Gibson, Kenneth, 'George Downham', *ODNB*.

Greenberg, Janelle, 'Nathaniel Bacon', *ODNB*.

Gregory, Victoria, 'William Bradshaw', *ODNB*.

Greteman, Blaine, '"Perplex't Paths": Youth and Authority in Milton's *Maske*', *Renaissance Quarterly*, 62 (2009), 410–43.

Grogan, Jane, *Exemplary Spenser: Visual and Poetic Pedagogy in 'The Faerie Queene'* (Burlington, Vt.: Ashgate, 2009).

Gyll, G. W. J., *History of the Parish of Wraysbury, Ankerwycke Priory, and Magna Carta Island; with the History of Horton, and the Town of Colnbrook, Bucks* (London, 1862).

Haan, Estelle, '"Both English and Latin": Milton's Bilingual Muse', *Renaissance Studies*, 21 (2007), 679–700.

—— *From Academia to Amicitia: Milton's Latin Writings and the Italian Academies* (Philadelphia, Pa.: American Philosophical Society, 1998).

—— 'Milton and Two Italian Humanists: Some Hitherto Unnoticed Neo-Latin Echoes in *In Obitum Procancellarii Medici* and *In Obitum Praesulis Eliensis*', *Notes and Queries*, 44 (1997), 176–81.

Hale, John K., 'The Audiences of Milton's Italian Verses', *Renaissance Studies*, 8 (1994), 76–88.

—— 'Milton Playing with Ovid', *Milton Studies*, 25 (1989), 3–19.

—— *Milton's Cambridge Latin: Performing the Genres, 1625–1632* (Tempe, Ariz.: Medieval and Renaissance Texts and Studies, 2005).

—— *Milton's Languages: The Impact of Multilingualism on Style* (Cambridge: Cambridge University Press, 1997).

—— 'Sion's Bacchanalia: An Inquiry into Milton's Latin in the *Epitaphium Damonis*', *Milton Studies*, 16 (1982), 115–30.

Hamilton, Donna, 'Catholic Use of Anglo-Saxon Precedents, 1565–1625', *Recusant History*, 26 (2003), 537–55.

Hanford, James H., 'The Chronology of Milton's Private Studies', *PMLA*, 36 (1921), 251–314.

—— 'The Pastoral Elegy and Milton's "Lycidas"', *PMLA*, 25 (1910), 403–47.

Hankins, James, 'The Myth of the Platonic Academy of Florence', *Renaissance Quarterly*, 44 (1991), 429–75.

Heal, Felicity, 'Appropriating History: Catholic and Protestant Polemics and the National Past', *Huntington Library Quarterly*, 68 (2005), 109–32.

—— 'What Can King Lucius Do for You? The Reformation and the Early British Church', *English Historical Review*, 120 (2005), 593–614.

Hetherington, W. M., *A History of the Westminster Assembly of Divines* (Philadelphia, Pa., 1841).

Hill, Christopher, *Economic Problems of the Church: From Archbishop Whitgift to the Long Parliament* (Oxford: Clarendon Press, 1956).

Hill, Christopher, *Intellectual Origins of the English Revolution Revisited* (rev. edn., Oxford: Oxford University Press, 1997).

—— *Milton and the English Revolution* (New York: Viking, 1977).

Hill, John Spencer, *John Milton, Poet, Priest and Prophet: A Study of Divine Vocation in Milton's Poetry and Prose* (London: Macmillan, 1979).

—— 'Poet-priest: Vocational Tension in Milton's Early Development', *Milton Studies*, 8 (1975), 40–69.

Hooker, Richard, '*Lycidas* and the Ecphrasis of Poetry', *Milton Studies*, 27 (1991), 59–77.

Hoover, David L., and Thomas N. Corns, 'The Authorship of the Postscript to *An Answer to a Booke Entituled, An Humble Remonstrance*', *Milton Quarterly*, 38 (2004), 59–75.

Hunter, William B., 'A Bibliographical Excursus into Milton's Trinity Manuscript', *Milton Quarterly*, 19 (1985), 61–71.

—— *Milton's 'Comus': Family Piece* (Troy, N.Y.: Whitson, 1983).

Hutton, Ronald, *Blood and Mistletoe: the History of the Druids in Britain* (New Haven, Conn.: Yale University Press, 2009).

Jones, Edward, '"Church-outed by the Prelats": Milton and the 1637 Inspection of the Horton Parish Church', *Journal of English and Germanic Philology*, 102 (2003), 42–58.

—— '"Ere Half My Days": Milton's Life, 1608–1640', in Nicholas McDowell and Nigel Smith (eds.), *The Oxford Handbook of Milton* (Oxford: Oxford University Press, 2009), 3–25.

—— '"Filling in a Blank in the Canvas": Milton, Horton, and the Kedermister Library', *Review of English Studies*, 53 (2002), 31–60.

—— 'Select Chronology: "Speak of things at hand/Useful"', in Angelica Duran (ed.), *A Concise Companion to Milton* (Oxford: Blackwell, 2006), 217–34.

—— 'Thomas Young', *ODNB*.

—— 'The Wills of Edward Goodall and Thomas Young and the Life of John Milton', in Kristin A. Pruitt and Charles W. Durham (eds.), *John Milton: 'Reasoning Words'* (Selinsgrove, Pa.: Susquehanna University Press, 2008), 60–76.

Kahn, Victoria, *Machiavellian Rhetoric: From the Counter-Reformation to Milton* (Princeton, N.J.: Princeton University Press, 1994).

Keene, Nicholas, 'Brian Walton', *ODNB*.

Kellett, Katherine, 'The Lady's Voice: Poetic Collaboration in Milton's *Maske*', *Milton Studies*, 50 (2009), 1–19.

Kelley, Maurice, 'Additional Texts of Milton's State Papers', *Modern Language Notes*, 67 (1952), 18–19.

—— 'Grammar School Latin and John Milton', *The Classical World*, 52 (1959), 133–8.

—— 'Milton's Dante—Della Casa—Varchi Volume', *Bulletin of the New York Public Library*, 66 (1962), 499–504.

Kelly, James, and Catherine Bray, 'The Keys to Milton's "Two-Handed Engine" in *Lycidas* (1637)', *Milton Quarterly*, 44 (2010), 122–42.

Kerrigan, William, *The Prophetic Milton* (Charlottesville, Va.: University of Virginia Press, 1974).

—— *The Sacred Complex: On the Psychogenesis of 'Paradise Lost'* (Cambridge, Mass. and London: Harvard University Press, 1983).

Kess, Alexandra, *Johann Sleidan and the Protestant Vision of History* (Aldershot: Ashgate, 2008).

Kirk, James, 'Andrew Melville', *ODNB*.

—— '"Melvillian" Reform in the Scottish Universities', in A. A. MacDonald, Michael Lynch, and Ian B. Cowan (eds.), *The Renaissance in Scotland: Studies in Literature, Religion, History and Culture Offered to John Durkan* (Leiden: Brill, 1994), 276–300.

Knafla, Louis A., 'Sir Henry Yelverton', *ODNB*.

Knight, Sarah, 'Flat Dichotomists and Learned Men: Ramism in Elizabethan Drama and Satire', in Steven Reid and Emma Wilson (eds.), *Ramus, Pedagogy and the Liberal Arts* (Aldershot: Ashgate, 2011), 47-67.

—— 'Milton's Forced Themes', *Milton Quarterly*, 45 (2011), 145–60.

—— 'Milton's Student Verses of 1629', *Notes and Queries*, 255 (2010), 37–9.

—— 'Royal Milton', *Times Literary Supplement* (5 February 2010), 15.

Knighton, C. S., 'William Whitaker', *ODNB*.

Kraye, Jill, 'Moral Philosophy', in Charles B. Schmitt, Quentin Skinner, Eckhard Kessler, and Jill Kraye (eds.), *The Cambridge History of Renaissance Philosophy* (Cambridge: Cambridge University Press, 1988), 171–97.

—— 'The Transformation of Platonic Love in the Italian Renaissance', in Anna Baldwin and Sarah Hutton (eds.), *Platonism and the English Imagination* (Cambridge: Cambridge University Press, 1994), 76–85.

Laing, David, *Biographical Notices of Thomas Young* (Edinburgh, 1870).

Lake, Peter, *The Boxmaker's Revenge: 'Orthodoxy', 'Heterodoxy' and the Politics of the Parish in Early Stuart London* (Manchester: Manchester University Press, 2001).

—— 'Defining Puritanism – Again?' in Francis J. Bremer (ed.), *Puritanism: Trans-Atlantic Perspectives on a Seventeenth-Century Anglo-American Faith* (Boston, Mass.: Massachusetts Historical Society, 1993), 3–29.

—— 'The Historiography of Puritanism', in John Coffey and Paul C. H. Lim (eds.), *The Cambridge Companion to Puritanism* (Cambridge: Cambridge University Press, 2008), 346–71.

—— *Moderate Puritans and the Elizabethan Church* (Cambridge: Cambridge University Press, 1982).

—— 'Moving the Goal Posts? Modified Subscription and the Construction of Conformity in the Early Stuart Church', in Peter Lake and Michael Questier (eds.), *Conformity and Orthodoxy in the English Church c. 1560–1660* (Woodbridge: Boydell, 2000), 179–205.

Lake, Peter, 'Reading Clarke's *Lives* in Political and Polemical Context', in Kevin Sharpe and Steven N. Zwicker (eds.), *Writing Lives: Biography and Textuality, Identity and Representation in Early Modern England* (Oxford: Oxford University Press, 2008), 293–318.

Le Comte, Edward S., 'Sly Milton: The Meaning Lurking in the Context of His Quotations', *Greyfriar*, 19 (1978), 3–28, rpt. in Edward S. Le Comte, *Milton Re-Viewed: Ten Essays* (New York: Routledge, 1991), 51–82.

Leedham-Green, Elisabeth S., *Books in Cambridge Inventories: Book Lists from Vice-Chancellor's Court Probate Inventories in the Tudor and Stuart Periods* (Cambridge: Cambridge University Press, 1986).

Lewalski, Barbara K., 'How Radical was the Young Milton?' in Stephen B. Dobranski and John P. Rumrich (eds.), *Milton and Heresy* (Cambridge: Cambridge University Press, 1998), 49–72.

—— *The Life of John Milton: A Critical Biography* (rev. edn., Oxford: Blackwell, 2003).

—— 'Milton and the Millennium', in Juliet Cummins (ed.), *Milton and the Ends of Time* (Cambridge: Cambridge University Press, 2003), 13–28.

—— 'Milton's *Comus* and the Politics of Masquing', in David Bevington and Peter Holbrook (eds.), *The Politics of the Stuart Court Masque* (Cambridge: Cambridge University Press 1998), 296–320.

Lingelbach, William E., 'The Merchant Adventurers at Hamburg', *The American Historical Review*, 9 (1904), 265–87.

Loeffelholz, Mary, 'Two Masques of Ceres and Proserpine: *Comus* and *The Tempest*', in Mary Nyquist and Margaret W. Ferguson (eds.), *Re-membering Milton: New Essays on the Texts and Traditions* (New York: Methuen, 1987), 25–42.

Loewenstein, David, '"Fair Offspring Nurs't in Princely Lore": On the Question of Milton's Early Radicalism', *Milton Studies*, 28 (1992), 37–48.

——— *Milton and the Drama of History: Historical Vision, Iconoclasm and the Literary Imagination* (Cambridge: Cambridge University Press, 1990).

MacCulloch, Diarmaid, 'Thomas Cranmer', *ODNB*.

——— *Thomas Cranmer: A Life* (New Haven, Conn.: Yale University Press, 1996).

MacLure, Millar, *The Paul's Cross Sermons, 1534–1642* (Toronto: University of Toronto Press, 1958).

Malcolm, Noel, 'Jean Bodin and the Authorship of the *Colloquium Heptaplomeres*', *Journal of the Warburg and Courtauld Institutes*, 69 (2006), 95–150.

Maltzahn, Nicholas von, 'Making Use of the Jews: Milton and Philo-Semitism', in Douglas A. Brooks (ed.), *Milton and the Jews* (Cambridge: Cambridge University Press, 2008), 57–82.

Marcus, Leah, *The Politics of Mirth: Jonson, Herrick, Milton, Marvell, and the Defense of Old Holiday Pastimes* (Chicago, Ill.: University of Chicago Press, 1986).

Martin, Catherine Gimelli, 'The Non-Puritan Ethics, Metaphysics, and Aesthetics of Milton's Spenserian Masque', *Milton Quarterly*, 37 (2003), 215–44.

Masson, David, *The Life of John Milton: Narrated in Connexion with the Political, Ecclesiastical, and Literary History of His Time* (7 vols., London: Macmillan, 1859–94).

——— 'Local Memories of Milton', *Good Words*, 34 (1893), 41–4.

McCabe, Richard, 'The Form and Methods of Milton's *Animadversions upon the Remonstrant's Defence against Smectymnuus*', *English Language Notes*, 18 (1981), 266–72.

McCullough, Peter, 'James Montagu', *ODNB*.

——— 'Making Dead Men Speak: Laudianism, Print, and the Works of Lancelot Andrewes, 1626–1642', *The Historical Journal*, 41 (1998), 401–24.

McDowell, Nicholas, 'The Caroline Court', in Stephen B. Dobranski (ed.), *Milton in Context* (Cambridge: Cambridge University Press, 2010), 237–47.

Melton, Frank, *Sir Robert Clayton and the Origins of English Deposit Banking, 1658–1685* (Cambridge: Cambridge University Press, 1986).

Messina, Davide, '*La Tina* Regained', *Milton Quarterly*, 45 (2011), 118–22.

Miller, Jeffrey Alan, 'Reconstructing Milton's Lost *Index Theologicus*: The Genesis and Usage of an Anti-Bellarmine, Theological Commonplace Book', *Milton Studies*, 52 (2011), 187–219.

Miller, Leo, 'The Italian Imprimaturs in Milton's *Areopagitica*', *Papers of the Bibliographical Society of America*, 65 (1971), 345–55.

—— *John Milton and The Oldenburg Safeguard* (New York: Loewenthal Press, 1985).

—— *John Milton's Writings in the Anglo-Dutch Negotiations* (Pittsburgh, Pa.: Duquesne University Press, 1992).

—— 'Milton's Clash with Chappell: A Suggested Reconstruction', *Milton Quarterly*, 14 (1980), 77–87.

Milton, Anthony, *Catholic and Reformed: The Roman and Protestant Churches in English Protestant Thought, 1600–1640* (Cambridge: Cambridge University Press, 1995).

Momigliano, Arnaldo, 'Ancient History and the Antiquarian' (1950), in *Studies in Historiography*, 13 (1966/69), 1–39.

—— 'The Origins of Ecclesiastical Historiography', in *The Classical Foundations of Modern Historiography* (Berkeley: University of California Press, 1992), 132–52.

Morgan, Victor, 'Volume 2: 1546–1750' in Christopher N. L. Brooke (ed.), *A History of the University of Cambridge* (4 vols., Cambridge: Cambridge University Press, 1988–2004).

Moseley, C. W. R. D., *The Poetic Birth: Milton's Poems of 1645* (Aldershot: Scolar Press, 1991).

Moss, Ann, *Printed Commonplace-Books and the Structuring of Renaissance Thought* (Oxford: Oxford University Press, 1996).

Nardo, Anna K., 'Academic Interludes in *Paradise Lost*', *Milton Studies*, 27 (1991), 209–41.

Neill, Kerby, 'Spenser's Shamefastnesse, *Faerie Queene*, II.ix.40–44', *Modern Language Notes*, 49 (1934), 387–91.

Nelles, Paul, 'The Uses of Orthodoxy and Jacobean Erudition: Thomas James and the Bodleian Library', *History of Universities*, 22 (2007), 21–70.

Nelson, Alan H., 'Women in the Audience of Cambridge Plays', *Shakespeare Quarterly*, 41 (1990), 333–6.

Nelson, Lowry, Jr., *Baroque Lyric Poetry* (New Haven, Conn.: Yale University Press, 1961).

Neveu, Bruno, 'L'érudition Ecclésiastique du XVIIe Siècle et la Nostalgie de l'antiquité Chrétienne', in Keith Robbins (ed.), *Religion and Humanism* (Oxford: Blackwell, 1981), 195–223.

Nichols, Fred J., '"Lycidas", *Epitaphium Damonis*, the Empty Dream, and the Failed Song', in J. Ijsewijn and E. Kessler (eds.), *Acta Conventus Neo-Latini Lovaniensis* (Leuven: Wilhelm Fink Verlag München, 1973), 445–52.

Nicolson, Marjorie, 'Milton's "Old Damaetas"', *Modern Language Notes*, 61 (1926), 293–300.

Norbrook, David, 'Euripides, Milton, and *Christian Doctrine*', *Milton Quarterly*, 29 (1995), 37–41.

—— *Poetry and Politics in the English Renaissance* (rev. edn., Oxford: Oxford University Press, 2002).

—— 'The Reformation of the Masque', in David Lindley (ed.), *The Court Masque* (Manchester: Manchester University Press, 1984), 94–110.

Orgel, Stephen, 'The Case for Comus', *Representations*, 81 (2003), 40–1.

Oxford Dictionary of National Biography (Oxford and London: British Academy and Oxford University Press, 2004–) [online edition].

Oxford English Dictionary, ed. J. A. Simpson and E. S. C. Weiner (2nd edn., 20 vols., Oxford: Oxford University Press, 1989).

Packer, John W., *The Transformation of Anglicanism, 1643–1660, with Special Reference to Henry Hammond* (Manchester: Manchester University Press, 1969).

Palmer, A. N., 'The Broughtons of Marchwiel: A Contribution to the History of the Parish of Marchwiel', *Y Cymmrodor*, 14 (1901), 45–8.

Parker, Patricia, 'Preposterous Reversals: *Love's Labour's Lost*', *Modern Language Quarterly*, 54 (1993), 435–82.

Parker, William R., *Milton: A Biography*, ed. Gordon Campbell (2nd edn., 2 vols., Oxford: Clarendon Press, 1996).

—— 'Milton and Thomas Young, 1620–1628', *Modern Language Notes*, 53 (1938), 399–407.

—— *Milton's Debt to Greek Tragedy in 'Samson Agonistes'* (Baltimore, Md.: Johns Hopkins University Press, 1937).

—— 'Wood's Life of Milton: Its Sources and Significance', *Papers of the Bibliographical Society of America*, 52 (1958), 1–22.

Parry, Graham, *The Arts of the Counter-Reformation: Glory, Laud and Honour* (Woodbridge: Boydell, 2006).

—— *The Trophies of Time: English Antiquarians of the Seventeenth Century* (Oxford: Oxford University Press, 1995).

Patrides, C. A. (ed.), *Milton's 'Lycidas': The Tradition and the Poem* (1961; 2nd edn., Columbia, Mo.: University of Missouri Press, 1983).

Patterson, Annabel, '"Forc'd Fingers": Milton's Early Poems and Ideological Constraint', in Claude J. Summers and Ted-Larry Pebworth (eds.), *'The Muses Commonweale': Poetry and Politics in the Seventeenth Century* (Columbia, Mo.: University of Missouri Press, 1988), 9–22.

—— 'That Old Man Eloquent', in Diana Treviño Benet and Michael Lieb (eds.), *Literary Milton: Text, Pretext, Context* (Pittsburgh, Pa.: Duquesne University Press, 1994), 22–44.

Pattison, Mark, *Milton* (London, 1909 [1879]).

Pigman, G. W., *Grief and English Renaissance Elegy* (Cambridge: Cambridge University Press, 1985).

Platt, Anthony, and Bernard L. Diamond, 'The Origins of the "Right and Wrong" Test of Criminal Responsibility and Its Subsequent Development in the United States: An Historical Survey', *California Law Review*, 54 (1966), 1227–60.

Pocock, J. G. A., *Barbarism and Religion: Volume 2: Narratives of Civil Government* (Cambridge: Cambridge University Press, 1999).

Poole, William, 'The Genres of Milton's Commonplace Book', in Nicholas McDowell and Nigel Smith (eds.), *The Oxford Handbook of Milton* (Oxford: Oxford University Press, 2009), 367–81.

Popkin, R. H., 'The Dispersion of Bodin's *Dialogues* in England, Holland, and Germany', *Journal of the History of Ideas*, 49 (1988), 157–60.

Quantin, Jean-Louis, *Le Catholicisme Classique et Les Pères de l'Eglise: Un Retour aux Sources (1669–1713)* (Paris: Brepols, 1999).

—— *The Church of England and Christian Antiquity: The Construction of a Confessional Identity in the 17th Century* (Oxford: Oxford University Press, 2009).

—— 'Du Chrysostome Latin au Chrysostome Grec. Une Histoire Européenne (1588–1613)', in Martin Wallraff and Rudolf Brändle (eds.), *Chrysostomosbilder in 1600 Jahren: Facetten der Wirkungsgeschichte eines Kirchenvaters* (Berlin: Walter de Gruyter, 2008), 267–346.

—— 'The Fathers in Seventeenth-Century Catholic Theology' and 'The Fathers in Seventeenth-Century Anglican Theology', in Irena Backus (ed.), *The Reception of the Church Fathers in the West: From the Carolingians to the Maurists* (2 vols., Leiden: Brill, 1997), ii. 842–65.

—— 'L'Orthodoxie, La Censure et La Gloire: La Difficle Édition Princeps de L'Épître de Barnabé, de Rome à Amsterdam (1549–1646)', in Mariarosa Cortesi, *'Editiones Principes' Delle Opere Dei Padri Greci e Latini* (Firenze: SISMEL, 2006), 103–62.

Quehen, Hugh de, 'Politics and Scholarship in the Ignatian Controversy', *The Seventeenth Century*, 13 (1998), 69–84.

Quentin, Henri, *Jean-Dominique Mansi et les Grandes Collections Conciliaires* (Paris, 1900; Whitefish, Mont.: Kessinger Publishing, 2010).

Raylor, Timothy, 'Milton, the Hartlib Circle, and the Education of the Aristocracy', in Nicholas McDowell and Nigel Smith (eds.), *The Oxford Handbook of Milton* (Oxford: Oxford University Press, 2009), 382–406.

—— 'New Light on Milton and Hartlib', *Milton Quarterly*, 27 (1993), 19–31.

Raymond, Joad, 'The Literature of Controversy', in Thomas N. Corns (ed.), *A Companion to Milton* (Oxford: Blackwell, 2001), 191–210.

Revard, Stella P., 'Apollo and Christ in the Seventeenth-Century Religious Lyric', in John Roberts (ed.), *New Perspectives on the Seventeenth-Century English Religious Lyric* (Columbia, Mo.: University of Missouri Press, 1994), 143–67.

—— '"L'Allegro" and "Il Penseroso": Classical Tradition and Renaissance Mythography', *PMLA*, 101 (1986), 338–50.

—— 'Milton and Millenarianism: From the Nativity Ode to *Paradise Regained*', in Juliet Cummins (ed.), *Milton and the Ends of Time* (Cambridge: Cambridge University Press, 2003), 42–81.

—— *Milton and the Tangles of Neaera's Hair: The Making of the 1645 'Poems'* (Columbia, Mo.: University of Missouri Press, 1997).

Robins, Harry F., 'Milton's "Two-Handed Engine at the Door" and St Matthew's Gospel', *Review of English Studies*, 5 (1954), 25–36.

Rosenblatt, Jason, *Renaissance England's Chief Rabbi: John Selden* (Oxford: Oxford University Press, 2006).

Rumrich, John P., 'The Erotic Milton', *Texas Studies in Language and Literature*, 41 (1999), 128–41, rpt. in J. Martin Evans (ed.), *John Milton: Twentieth-Century Perspectives* (London: Routledge, 2002), 32–45.

—— *Milton Unbound: Controversy and Reinterpretation* (Cambridge: Cambridge University Press, 1996).

Samuel, Irene, *Plato and Milton* (Ithaca, N.Y.: Cornell University Press, 1947).

Sansone, David, 'How Milton Reads: Scripture, the Classics, and That Two-Handed Engine', *Modern Philology*, 103 (2006), 332–57.

Sawday, Jonathan, *Engines of the Imagination: Renaissance Culture and the Rise of the Machine* (London and New York: Routledge, 2007).

Schwartz, Regina, *Remembering and Repeating: On Milton's Theology and Poetics* (Chicago, Ill.: University of Chicago Press, 1993).

Seaver, Paul S., *The Puritan Lectureships: The Politics of Religious Dissent, 1560–1662* (Palo Alto, Calif.: Stanford University Press, 1970).

Sharp, Ronald, *Friendship and Literature: Spirit and Form* (Durham, N.C.: Duke University Press, 1986).

Shawcross, John T., *'The Arms of the Family': The Significance of John Milton's Relatives and Associates* (Lexington, Ky.: University Press of Kentucky, 2004).

—— 'Certain Relationships of the Manuscripts of *Comus*', *Papers of the Bibliographical Society of America*, 54 (1960), 38–58.

—— 'The Date of the Separate Edition of Milton's *Epitaphium Damonis*', *Studies in Bibliography*, 18 (1965), 262–5.

—— *The Development of Milton's Thought: Law, Government, and Religion* (Pittsburgh, Pa.: Duquesne University Press, 2008).

—— *John Milton: The Self and the World* (Lexington, Ky.: University Press of Kentucky, 1993).

—— 'Milton and Diodati: An Essay in Psychodynamic Meaning', *Milton Studies*, 7 (1975), 127–64, rev. in *John Milton: The Self and the World*, 43–59.

—— 'Speculations on the Dating of the Trinity MS. of Milton's Poems', *Modern Language Notes*, 75 (1960), 11–17.

—— 'A Survey of Milton's Prose Works', in Michael Lieb and John T. Shawcross (eds.), *Achievements of the Left Hand: Essays on the Prose of John Milton* (Amherst, Mass.: University of Massachusetts Press, 1974), 291–391.

Shullenberger, William, '"Imprimatur": The Fate of Davanzati', in Mario Di Cesare (ed.), *Milton in Italy: Contexts, Images, Contradictions* (Binghamton, N.Y.: MRTS, 1991), 175–96.

—— *Lady in the Labyrinth: Milton's 'Comus' as Initiation* (Madison, N.J.: Fairleigh Dickenson University Press, 2008).

Simons, Louise, '"And Heaven Gates Ore My head": Death as Threshold in Milton's *Mask*', *Milton Studies*, 23 (1987), 153–96.

Sir John Kederminster's Library (Langley, 1999).

Smet, Ingrid de, 'Nicolas Rigault', in *Centuriae Latinae II: Cent une Figures Humanistes de la Renaissance aux Lumières* (Geneva: Droz, 2006), 727–33.

Smith, A. Hassell, 'Edward Bacon', *ODNB*.

Sprott, S. E., (ed.), *'A Maske': The Earlier Versions* (Toronto: University of Toronto Press, 1973).

Staveley, Keith, *The Politics of Milton's Prose Style* (New Haven, Conn.: Yale University Press, 1975).

Stenhouse, William, *Reading Inscriptions and Writing Ancient History: Historical Scholarship in the Late Renaissance* (London: University of London Institute of Classical Studies, 2005).

Sterry, Wasey (ed.), *The Eton College Register, 1441–1698* (Eton: Spottiswode and Ballantyne, 1943).

Stone, C. F., III, 'Milton's Self-Concerns and Manuscript Revisions in *Lycidas*', *Modern Language Notes*, 83 (1968), 867–81.

Stone, Lawrence, 'The Educational Revolution in England, 1560–1640', *Past and Present*, 28 (1964), 41–80.

Stoye, John, *English Travellers Abroad, 1604–1667* (rev. edn., New Haven, Conn.: Yale University Press, 1989).

Swanson, Donald, and John Mulryan, 'The Son's Presumed Contempt for Learning in *Paradise Regained*', *Milton Studies*, 27 (1991), 243–61.

Teskey, Gordon, *Allegory and Violence* (Ithaca, N.Y.: Cornell University Press, 1996).

Thomas, Keith, *The Ends of Life: Roads to Fulfillment in Early Modern England* (Oxford and New York: Oxford University Press, 2009).

Tillyard, E. M. W., *Milton* (rev. edn., London: Chatto and Windus 1966).

Tilmouth, Christopher, 'Shakespeare's Open Consciences', *Renaissance Studies*, 23 (2009), 501–6.

Timberlake, P. W., 'Milton and Euripides', in Hardin Craig (ed.), *Essays in Dramatic Literature: The Parrott Presentation Volume* (Princeton, N.J.: Princeton University Press, 1935).

Todd, Margo, 'Samuel Ward', *ODNB*.

Toomer, G. J., *John Selden: A Life in Scholarship* (2 vols., Oxford: Oxford University Press, 2009).

Trevor-Roper, Hugh, 'The Church of England and the Greek Church in the Time of Charles I', in *From Counter-Reformation to Glorious Revolution* (Chicago, Ill.: University of Chicago Press, 1992), 83–111.

—— 'The Great Tew Circle', in *Catholics, Anglicans, Puritans: Seventeenth Century Essays* (Chicago, Ill.: University of Chicago Press, 1987), 166–230.

—— 'James Ussher', in *Catholics, Anglicans, and Puritans: Seventeenth Century Essays* (Chicago, Ill.: University of Chicago Press, 1987), 120–65.

Tyacke, Nicholas, *Anti-Calvinists: The Rise of English Arminianism, c.1580–1640* (Oxford: Oxford University Press, 1987).

—— 'Lancelot Andrewes and the Myth of Anglicanism', in Peter Lake and Michael Questier (eds.), *Conformity and Orthodoxy in the English Church, c. 1560–1660* (Woodbridge: Boydell, 2000), 5–33.

Usher, Brett, 'Richard Stock', *ODNB*.

Villani, Stefano, 'The Italian Protestant Church of London in the 17th Century', in Barbara Schaff (ed.), *Exiles, Emigres and Intermediaries: Anglo-Italian Cultural Mediations* (Amsterdam and New York: Rodopi, 2010), 217–36.

Watson, Thomas, *A Body of Practical Divinity* (London, 1692).

Webber, Joan, *The Eloquent 'I': Style and Self in Seventeenth-Century Prose* (Madison, Wis.: University of Wisconsin Press, 1968).

Webster, Tom, *Godly Clergy in Early Stuart England: The Caroline Puritan Movement, c.1620–1643* (Cambridge: Cambridge University Press, 1997).

Weiss, Roberto, *The Renaissance Discovery of Classical Antiquity* (Oxford: Humanities Press, 1969).

Welch, Anthony, 'Milton's Forsaken Proserpine', *English Literary Renaissance*, 39 (2009), 527–56.

Werman, Golda, *Milton and Midrash* (Washington, D.C.: Catholic University Press of America, 1995).

West, Michael, 'The Consolatio in Milton's Funeral Elegies', *Huntington Library Quarterly*, 34 (1971), 233–49.

Wilding, Michael, *Dragons Teeth: Literature in the English Revolution* (Oxford: Oxford University Press 1987).

Willen, Diane, 'Thomas Gataker and the Use of Print in the English Godly Community', *Huntington Library Quarterly*, 70 (2007), 343–64.

Wilson, Emma Annette, 'The Art of Reasoning Well: Ramist Logic at Work in *Paradise Lost*', *Review of English Studies*, 61 (2010), 55–71.

Wittreich, Joseph, *Interpreting 'Samson Agonistes'* (Princeton, N.J.: Princeton University Press, 1986).

—— *Visionary Poetics: Milton's Tradition and His Legacy* (San Marino, Calif.: Huntington Library Press, 1979).

Yates, Frances A., 'The Italian Academies', in *Renaissance and Reform: The Italian Contribution* (London: Routledge and Kegan Paul, 1983), 6–29.

INDEX